Khrushchev and Brezhnev as Leaders:
Building Authority in Soviet Politics

To my parents,
Marianne and Henry Breslauer
And to my wife,
Yvette

Khrushchev and Brezhnev as Leaders: Building Authority in Soviet Politics

GEORGE W. BRESLAUER
Department of Political Science,
University of California, Berkeley

London
GEORGE ALLEN & UNWIN
Boston   Sydney

George Allen & Unwin (Publishers) Ltd,
40 Museum Street, London WC1A 1LU, UK

George Allen & Unwin (Publishers) Ltd,
Park Lane, Hemel Hempstead, Herts HP2 4TE, UK

Allen & Unwin, Inc.,
9 Winchester Terrace, Winchester, Mass. 01890, USA

George Allen & Unwin Australia Pty Ltd,
8 Napier Street, North Sydney, NSW 2060, Australia

First published in 1982

British Library Cataloguing in Publication Data

Breslauer, George W.
  Khrushchev and Brezhnev as leaders.
1. Soviet Union – Politics and government – 1953–
I. Title
320.947   JN6581
ISBN 0–04–329040–X   **92489**
ISBN 0–04–329041–8 Pbk

Library of Congress Cataloging in Publication Data

Breslauer, George W.
  Khrushchev and Brezhnev as leaders.
Bibliography: p.
Includes index.
1. Soviet Union – Politics and government – 1953–
2. Elite (Social sciences) – Soviet Union. 3. Khrushchev,
Nikita Sergeevich, 1894–1971. 4. Brezhnev, Leonid
Il'ich, 1906–   . I. Title.
JN6581.B73 1982   947.085   82–8835
ISBN 0–04–329040–X   AACR2
ISBN 0–04–329041–8 (pbk.)

Set in 10 on 11 point Plantin by Grove Graphics, Tring
and printed in Great Britain
by Biddles Ltd, Guildford, Surrey

Contents

Preface

Two men—Nikita Khrushchev and Leonid Brezhnev—have served as First Secretary (or "General Secretary") of the Communist Party of the Soviet Union for almost the entire period since Stalin's death in March 1953. Each in his own time, and in his own way, consolidated his power and advanced comprehensive policy programs. Each saw his program frustrated by a variety of factors beyond his control. Each responded to that frustration by searching for new ways to make his policies more effective and his political position more secure. Thus, each grappled continuously with the challenge of building up his authority as leader, even though he occupied by far the most powerful position in the Soviet political system.

This book is a study of the means by which Khrushchev and Brezhnev attempted to build up their authority as leaders. It explores similarities and differences in the ways these two leaders fashioned their policy appeals and personal images so as (hopefully) to increase elite confidence in, or dependence upon, their stewardship. More specifically, it explores their policy programs and political strategies in dealing with some of the central issues of Soviet domestic politics: investment priorities, incentive policy, administrative reform, and political participation. The purposes of the investigation are several-fold: (1) to develop a persuasive portrait of the positions these men adopted on the issues in question; (2) to examine the evolution of their positions and approaches over time; (3) to explore the interaction between their evolving political programs and their strategies for augmenting their authority within the political elite; (4) to compare and contrast the evolution of Khrushchev's approaches with the evolution of Brezhnev's, in order to separate the common from the distinctive features of their behaviour; and (5) to draw from these comparisons some lessons about factors that shape the behavior of the Party leader.

There was a time when studies of elite politics and policy preferences were in abundance in the field of Soviet studies. Throughout the 1960s and into the 1970s, important (and often provocative) studies of the Khrushchev administration were published, examining the ways in which Khrushchev dealt with many of the issues noted above. Some of those books included the first years of the Brezhnev administration as well, in order to highlight the contrast in policy preferences and political style with Brezhnev's predecessor. A few books focused comparatively on the last years of the Khrushchev administration and the first years of Brezhnev's. But no research monograph on Soviet elite politics has taken a long view of both administrations.[1] Hence, we have no complete base of evidence for drawing lessons about the behavior of the Party leader in the post-Stalin era.

One obvious explanation for this gap is that Brezhnev did not match Khrushchev in political longevity as Party leader until the mid-1970s. This matter of simple timing may have influenced the choice of research topics, but it is a partial explanation at best, for listings of dissertation topics in Soviet studies during the late 1970s do not indicate a change.[2] I believe there have been a number of more fundamental factors at work. First, the abuses of kremlinology by some of its practitioners have discredited the methodology *per se* in the eyes of many scholars. Second, the inability to study policy-making processes on the grand issues of Soviet politics, without employing some variant of the kremlinological method, has led scholars to study decision-making on less politicized issues (such as housing, urban planning, ecology, crime control) that do not occupy much of the attention of the Politburo.[3] Third, a lack of new ideas about the nature of Soviet elite values, and the lack of an accepted methodology for tapping them, has led scholars simply to stop debating key historical issues about the nature of Khrushchev's policies and the extent of his power, or about the relative balance of conflict and consensus in the Soviet Politburo under both Khrushchev and Brezhnev.

On the issue of investment priorities, for example, the image of Khrushchev as an embattled consumer advocate has been incorporated

[1] See Carl Linden, *Khrushchev and the Soviet Leadership 1957–1964* (Baltimore, Md: Johns Hopkins University Press, 1966); Sidney Ploss, *Conflict and Decision-Making in Soviet Russia: A Case Study of Agricultural Policy, 1953–1963* (Princeton, NJ: Princeton University Press, 1965); Mark Frankland, *Khrushchev* (New York: Stein & Day, 1967); Edward Crankshaw, *Khrushchev: A Career* (New York: Viking Press, 1966); Michel Tatu, *Power in the Kremlin: From Khrushchev to Kosygin* (New York: Viking Press, 1969); Roy Medvedev and Zhores Medvedev, *Khrushchev: The Years in Power* (New York: Norton, 1977); Abraham Katz, *The Politics of Economic Reform in the Soviet Union* (London: Pall Mall Press, 1973); Werner Hahn, *The Politics of Soviet Agriculture, 1960–1970* (Baltimore, Md: Johns Hopkins University Press, 1972); Martin McCauley, *Khrushchev and the Development of Soviet Agriculture* (London: Macmillan, 1976).

[2] See the listings of annual dissertations in Soviet studies in the December issues of the journal, *Slavic Review*. An exception may be the work of Bruce Parrott.

[3] See, for example, William Taubman, *Governing Soviet Cities* (New York: Praeger, 1973); Peter Solomon, Jr, *Soviet Criminologists and Criminal Policy: Specialists in Policy-Making* (New York: Columbia University Press, 1978).

into the conventional wisdom of the field among American political scientists. A few individuals have indicated their skepticism of the image by marshaling *ad hoc* bits of evidence against it.[4] But no one, to my knowledge, has systematically analyzed the evidence for the image and offered an alternative interpretation of Khrushchev's behaviour during 1953–64. Similarly, the literature on Khrushchev's major doctrinal innovation in the field of political participation—the state and party "Of All the People"—presents at least a half-dozen contrasting explanations of the intent behind the innovation.[5] But no one has attempted to resolve these contradictions in the course of a broader reinterpretation of Khrushchev's approach to political participation. Furthermore, the sparse literature on Brezhnev's leadership generally portrays it as either dull, continuous, or both. No one, how-

[4] This image of Khrushchev is the main theme in Linden, *Khrushchev and the Soviet Leadership* and in Ploss, *Conflict and Decision-Making*. Those who have made passing references to bits of evidence that contradict the image include Jerry Hough, "Enter N. S. Khrushchev," *Problems of Communism* (July–August 1964), p. 31; and Katz, *Politics of Economic Reform*, p. 95.

[5] Michel Tatu, for example, wrote that "needless to say, the new terminology had no effect whatever on the actual state and party structure. Obviously, the changes in wording were prompted by the needs of foreign propaganda rather than by actual developments at home." He then quotes an aside in the speech by O. Kuusinen, and concludes that the changes were prompted by the "embarrassing fact that the Soviet regime officially acknowledged itself to be a dictatorship" (*Power in the Kremlin*, p. 165). Similarly, Merle Fainsod concluded that the changes were "designed to provide a more attractive gloss on party rule," and that they "risk dismissal as rather clumsy exercises in semantic manipulation" ("Khrushchevism," in Milorad M. Drachkovitch [ed.], *Marxism in the Modern World* [Stanford, Calif.: Stanford University Press, 1965], p. 130).

Sidney Ploss, saw the "State of All the People" as a change directed specifically at the anti-rural bias in the system (*Conflict and Decision-Making*, p. 230); Roger Kanet was less certain, but saw it as a means of inspiring the entire population to participation in societal affairs, in addition to being "related to the process of de-Stalinization" ("The rise and fall of the 'All-People's State': recent changes in the Soviet theory of the State," *Soviet Studies* [July 1968], pp. 87–8); George Brinkley examined "the theory of Soviet statehood" entirely in terms of its implications for mass participation at the local level ("Khrushchev remembered: on the theory of Soviet statehood," *Soviet Studies* [January 1973], pp. 387–401); Richard Lowenthal interpreted the changes as a pledge that violent revolution from above had come to an end in the USSR, and that the withering of the state would begin ("Development versus Utopia in communist policy," in Chalmers Johnson [ed.], *Change in Communist Systems* [Stanford, Calif.: Stanford University Press, 1970], p. 97). More recently, I have offered my own interpretation that attempts to synthesize many of the above ("Khrushchev reconsidered," *Problems of Communism* [September–October 1976]). For the most recent statement on the subject, see Theodore Friedgut, *Political Participation in the USSR* (Princeton, NJ: Princeton University Press, 1979), ch. 2.

ever, has carefully analyzed how Brezhnev's leadership strategies evolved and changed over time.[6]

Selected passages in this book have appeared in articles previously published: "Khrushchev reconsidered," *Problems of Communism* (September–October 1976); "The Twenty-Fifth Party Congress: domestic issues," in Alexander Dallin (ed.), *The Twenty-Fifth Congress of the CPSU* (Stanford, Calif.: Hoover Institution Press, 1977); "On the adaptability of Soviet welfare-state authoritarianism," in Karl Ryavec (ed.), *Soviet Society and the Communist Party* (Amherst, Mass.: University of Massachusetts Press, 1978); "Reformism, conservatism, and leadership authority at the Twenty-Sixth Party Congress," in Seweryn Bialer and Thane Gustafson (eds), *Russia at the Crossroads: The 26th Party Congress of the CPSU* (London: Allen & Unwin, 1982); "Political succession and the Soviet policy agenda," *Problems of Communism* (May–June 1980).

A number of institutions have been generous in providing me with fellowships over the years. The National Academy of Sciences' Arms Control and Disarmament Agency supported me during the academic year 1970–1, which gave me the opportunity to begin my doctoral dissertation. The International Research and Exchanges Board (IREX) sponsored my research in the Soviet Union during 1974. The Hoover Institution gave me a National Fellowship during 1975–6, which made possible a "great leap forward" in my research. The Regents of the University of California were kind enough to award me a Regents Summer Fellowship during Summer 1977. In addition, several organizations have been generous in allotting funds for xeroxing, research assistance, and travel: the Institute of International Studies, the Center for Slavic and East European Studies, and the Committee on Research, all of the University of California at Berkeley. I hope the final product justifies their trust; either way, I am more than grateful.

Several individuals have contributed greatly to my intellectual development. It is a pleasure to have the opportunity to say "thank you!". Wolfgang Leonhard, in a seminar at the University of Michigan in 1967, transmitted to me his extraordinary enthusiasm for the study of Soviet elite politics. Throughout my graduate studies at the University of Michigan, William Zimmerman and Alfred G.

---

[6] Portraits of Brezhnev's leadership that picture it as either dull, continuous, or both can be found in: John Dornberg, *Brezhnev: The Masks of Power* (New York: Basic Books, 1974); Adam B. Ulam, *A History of Soviet Russia* (New York: Praeger, 1976), ch. 9; Vladimir Solovyov and Elena Klepikova, "Inside the Kremlin," *Partisan Review*, vol. 48, no. 2 (1981); Dennis Ross, "Coalition maintenance in the Soviet Union," *World Politics* (January 1980). An exception is Alexander Yanov, *Detente after Brezhnev* (Berkeley, Calif.: University of California, Institute of International Studies, 1977).

Meyer broadened my understanding of the Soviet political system. They also made available to me every opportunity to expand my horizons and advance my career. My colleague, Kenneth T. Jowitt, through written work and conversations, communicated to me his unusual sensitivity to the ways in which communist leaders conceive of their identity. This allowed me to see beyond considerations of political power and economic development alone, and to explore the socio-political implications of policy-decisions. Finally, Alexander Yanov sensitized me to the possibility that Brezhnev was doing something truly innovative at the Twenty-Fourth Party Congress in 1971. Moreover, Yanov schooled me in the reformist implications of such administrative changes as the Shchekino experiment and the production associations.

Other individuals have contributed to improving the quality of successive drafts of the manuscript. Peter Hauslohner supplied a brilliant critique of the earliest version of the book. In addition, I received extended comments on later drafts from Paul Marantz, Ted Friedgut, Valerie Bunce, Don Van Atta, and Steven Walt. To all of you I am most grateful. It goes without saying that I alone am responsible for the final product.

My deepest debts are neither financial nor intellectual, but emotional. My parents, Marianne and Henry Breslauer, have never ceased to provide encouragement, motivation, and opportunities for me to develop. My wife, Yvette, has been the perfect companion and emotional support-system. Without my intellectual creditors, this would have been a very different book. Without my emotional creditors, this book would never have been written. I therefore dedicate the book to my parents and my wife, with love and profound gratitude.

Khrushchev and Brezhnev as Leaders: Building Authority in Soviet Politics

Part One
Introduction

1 Building Authority since Stalin

Building authority is not the same as consolidating power. Most Western literature on Soviet elite politics has been concerned with power consolidation: with the ability of Party leaders to strengthen their grip on office, and to parry challenges to their right to rule. That literature has focused largely on the formal institutional mechanisms manipulated by the General Secretary to protect and aggrandize power: patronage allocation, patron–client obligations, and purge. Beyond patronage, analyses have focused on the ability of Party leaders to buttress their power by fashioning policies that appeal primarily to one or two of the main institutional pillars of the Soviet establishment: the party apparatus, the state bureaucracy, the military, the police, and the military–industrial complex. Thus, through a combination of patronage and payoff, power consolidation allows the General Secretary to outflank rivals and rise within the leadership.[1]

Building authority refers to another dimension of elite politics that has generally been neglected in the study of Soviet politics. Authority is legitimized power.[2] Building authority is the process by which Soviet leaders seek to legitimize their policy programs and demonstrate their competence or indispensability as leaders. A concern with building authority assumes that "pulling rank" may not always be effective in mobilizing political support if a leader is perceived to be incompetent or dispensable. And it assumes that, in the post-Stalin era, when regime goals are more diversified and trade-offs more complex, coalitions must be built across institutions, with policies that appeal to a diverse set of cadre orientations. A leader may consolidate his power through patronage and through priority emphasis on currying support in one or two institutions, but his

---

[1] In this book, I shall use the term, "national leadership," to refer to the highest levels of the policy-making arena, that is, Politburo-members and candidate members, and their immediate subordinates within the party and state hierarchies. In contrast, I shall use the terms, "political elite" or "political establishment," to refer to policy influentials at all levels of the party and state hierarchies.

[2] For a perceptive discussion of authority after Stalin and Mao, see Jeremy T. Paltiel, "DeStalinization and DeMaoization," paper presented at the Annual Meeting of the Canadian Political Science Association, Université du Québec à Montréal, June 2–4, 1980.

authority as leader cannot be increased beyond a certain point on these bases alone. As T. H. Rigby has observed:

> Formal positions have, of course, been vital as means to and channels of personal authority, but there is none in the Soviet Union that suffices to impart it: except for Lenin, leaders have had to work and fight for it *after* appointment to high office.[3] (Italics in original)

There are two roles the post-Stalin Party leader plays in seeking to build his authority: problem-solver and politician. As problem-solver he attempts to forge policy programs that promise to further the goals of the post-Stalin era. As politician he attempts to create a sense of national élan, so as to increase the political establishment's confidence in his leadership ability.

Political conflict since Stalin has rarely revolved around whether or not to pursue new goals. Rather, it has centered on the costs to be borne in traditional values in pursuing the new tasks on the political agenda. As problem-solver, the General Secretary has sought to demonstrate his political skill and intellectual vision in forging programs that will implement the new, post-Stalin consensus without foresaking traditional values. His coalition-building strategy has typically centered on efforts to build support in various institutional constituencies for his distinctive synthesis of conflicting values.

The Khruschchev and Brezhnev administrations shared a broad regime consensus[4] on behalf of breaking with the extremes of Stalinism and tackling new tasks: increased consumer satisfaction; greater material incentives for the masses; deconcentration of public administration;[5] expanded political participation by social activists and

[3] T. H. Rigby, "A conceptual approach to authority, power, and policy in the Soviet Union," in T. H. Rigby, Archie Brown, and Peter Reddaway (eds), *Authority, Power, and Policy in the USSR* (New York: St Martin's Press, 1980), p. 16.

[4] Throughout this book, I shall document the policy consensus that emerged after Stalin and after Khrushchev. Use of the terms, "agreement," "majority consensus," "broad consensus," and the like does not refer to unanimity. But it does mean something considerably greater than a narrow majority, and it includes both the Party First Secretary (or General Secretary, as Brezhnev came to be called in 1966), and the Chairman of the Council of Ministers.

[5] The post-Stalin effort to deburden higher levels of administration of excessively detailed planning is not decentralization, but deconcentration. Decentralization, or "marketization," would require the extension to local executives of genuine autonomy from party or ministerial intervention, and the establishment of markets as coordinating devices. Neither Khrushchev nor Brezhnev stood for this. For further discussion of this distinction, see Donald V. Schwartz, "Decisionmaking, administrative decentralization, and feedback mechanisms: comparison of Soviet and Western models," *Studies in Comparative Communism* (Spring–Summer 1974).

specialists; a narrower definition of political crime; an end to mass terror; and greater collective leadership. All of which pointed in the direction of greater political, social, and economic equality than existed under Stalin.

Efforts to cope with these new tasks, however, have been shaped by constant tension and competition with ongoing elitist features of the Soviet tradition: heavy-industrial and military priorities; party activism and pressure as spurs to labor productivity, and political intervention as a spur to managerial initiative; the leading role of party apparatchiki in political, economic, and social life; a strong commitment to social discipline, political obedience, and the work ethic ("he who does not work, neither shall he eat"); a tendency to look to a strong leader to provide both leadership and a symbol of unity around which to rally the nation; and a preference for big projects to generate national unity, élan, and fervor.

In building his authority in post-Stalin politics, the Party leader has rarely chosen between traditional values and new goals. Rather, in his role as problem-solver, he has sought to demonstrate his ability to synthesize the two—or to put together packages that borrow from each.

Both the egalitarian and elitist orientations find substantial legitimation in Marxist–Leninist and Stalinist theory and practice. For the Soviet political tradition is multifaceted and contradictory.[6] Yet there are limits to the degree of diversity easily legitimized by that tradition. Neither the elitist nor the egalitarian strand sanctions the dominance of political or economic *markets*: private ownership of the means of production on a large scale; consumer sovereignty; multiparty competition; autonomous concentrations of political or economic power; or a conception of the public arena as a "marketplace of ideas." Hence, the challenge facing the Soviet Party leader since Stalin has been to propose innovative policies that would move beyond Stalinism without creating an economic or political order based on autonomous markets. His challenge has been to move in a more egalitarian direction without overly compromising traditional elitist values. Conceptualization of the character and limits of "Post-Stalinism" in the USSR appears in Table 1.1.

But politics is more than just coalition-building for the advancement of concrete material and institutional interests. It is also a process of generating and manipulating more diffuse appeals. In his role as politician, the General Secretary has sought to build his authority by propagandizing appeals that will (hopefully) create a sense of national

---

[6] For the argument that Soviet history has been marked by a "dual political culture," see Stephen F. Cohen, "The friends and foes of change: reformism and conservatism in the Soviet Union," *Slavic Review* (June 1979).

Table 1.1   *Stalinism and Beyond*

Policy Realm	Regime-Type		
	Stalinist	*Post-Stalinist*	*Liberal-Democratic Polity; Affluent Society*
Investment Priorities	Military/Heavy-Industrial monopoly	Selective reallocation	Consumerism
Incentive Policy	Mass exhortation and coercion	Increased material incentives	Consumerism
Administration	Terroristic; super-centralized	Reduced pressure; deconcentration	Decentralization; marketization
Social and Individual Autonomy	Little social autonomy; broad definition of political crime	Increased social autonomy; narrower definition of political crime	Social pluralism; very narrow definition of political crime
Political Participation: officials vis-à-vis masses and specialists	Autocratic/ highly exclusionary	Expanded participation	Political marketization
Authority-building: Party leader vis-à-vis political elite	Autocratic	Increased collective leadership	Constitutional

purpose, élan, or fervor, and by manipulating the language and arenas of politics in ways that will increase the political elite's sense of dependence upon him for leadership, direction, or protection. There are many ways to do this, the effectiveness of which will depend upon the climate of opinion prevailing within the political establishment at the time. Thus, he may create or exploit an atmosphere of crisis or threat, in order to parry criticism or present himself as a national "hero."[7] He may generate ideological or nationalistic appeals, or launch economic campaigns, for purposes of creating a sense of dynamism, progress, and solidarity that transcends narrow political interests or material concerns. He may make common cause with the masses in order to intimidate organized political interests. Toward

[7] On heroic leadership, see James MacGregor Burns, *Leadership* (New York: Harper & Row, 1978), ch. 9.

this same end, he may expand the scope and visibility of political conflict, activating previously passive groups on his behalf.[8] Alternatively, he may eschew strategies of intimidation, presenting himself as the political leader best able to protect the elite, both from the masses and from the threat of purge.

An ineffective authority-building strategy would be one that failed to persuade influentials within the political establishment of his problem-solving competence and political indispensability. This state of affairs would not necessarily lead to his dismissal from office, for the General Secretary might still be able to fend off challenges to his rule by "pulling rank" and mobilizing his political clients. His power would be less broadly legitimate, but he could still be powerful enough to coerce opponents. This seems to have been the state of Brezhnev's authority in the late 1970s. At some point, however, the perception that a leader is incompetent and dispensable—indeed, threatening—can become so widespread that it can undermine his hold on office. This is what happened to Khrushchev in 1964.

Strategies for authority-building have become more important to Soviet leaders since Stalin's death. Stalin, in his last years, was able to terrorize members of the leadership through his independent control of a vast police empire. Stalin's successors reined in the secret police and put an end to terror as a means of ordering relationships among individuals and groups within the political establishment.

This change had momentous implications for the relationship between power and authority in Soviet elite politics. The key to power consolidation was still the accumulation of patronage and cultivation of the party apparatus and military–industrial complex as bases of support. The General Secretary still had plentiful political resources with which to pull rank (as Krushchev demonstrated in 1957). But the change after Stalin meant that political support became more contingent as the stakes in political conflict were reduced. The abandonment of terror, and the rise in collective restraints on the leader, fostered a reduction in the reliability of patronage as a source of support.[9] Clients of the leader would be less likely than in the past to ignore their personal policy preferences, the interests of their nominal constituents, or the interests of the bureaucracies in which they worked in order to support the program of their patron. As a result, Party leaders have had to worry more since Stalin about how to increase their authority in order to maintain their grip on office,

---

[8] Expanding the scope of political conflict as a basic technique of political struggle is the theme of E. E. Schattschneider's *The Semi-Sovereign People* (New York: Holt, Rinehart & Winston, 1960).

[9] On this point, see Grey Hodnett, "The pattern of leadership politics," in Seweryn Bialer (ed.), *The Domestic Context of Soviet Foreign Policy* (Boulder, Colo.: Westview Press, 1980).

and in order to maintain control over the policy agenda and parry challenges to their policy programs.

It is puzzling that so little attention to authority-building can be found in the literature on Soviet elite politics.[10] The primary reason for this neglect, I suspect, has been the tendency among Soviet specialists to debate a false dichotomy; power versus principle as the primary motivations for elite behavior in the USSR.

Authority-Building and Kremlinology

The study of Soviet elite politics is often referred to as "kremlinology." Two types of kremlinological analysis have dominated the field. One variant looked upon the game of politics in the Kremlin as an entirely opportunistic, Byzantine power struggle.[11] Policies were embraced or abandoned in order to outflank or discredit rivals. The task of the observer was to search through protocol evidence and reports of personnel changes for subtle clues as to who was winning or losing the power struggle. Nor surprisingly, this variant of kremlinology was

---

[10] An exception is Myron Rush, *Political Succession in the USSR*, 2nd edn (New York: Columbia University Press, 1968), although many of our interpretations differ. A recent book, Rigby, Brown, and Reddaway (eds), *Authority, Power, and Policy*, is an advance, but deals very little with the post-Stalin era in discussions of elite politics. Rigby's important introductory chapter ("A conceptual approach") deals largely with the relationship between state and society, while Archie Brown's chapter, "The power of the General Secretary," makes no formal distinction between power and authority, and deals only with a restricted range of questions about the leverage of the General Secretary and the means available to increase it. Alfred G. Meyer's stimulating essay, "Authority in communist political systems," in Lewis J. Edinger (ed.), *Political Leadership in Industrialized Societies* (New York: Wiley, 1967), also deals largely with the relationship between party and society, rather than with the relationship between the General Secretary and the political elite. An article that does not deal with the distinction between power and authority, but which is an exemplary discussion of the diffuse appeals Stalin sought to generate in order to increase his authority in the 1920s is Robert Daniels, "Stalin's rise to dictatorship, 1922–29," in Alexander Dallin and Alan F. Westin (eds), *Politics in the Soviet Union: Seven Cases* (New York: Harcourt, Brace & World, 1966). In a similar vein, see Robert C. Tucker, *Stalin as Revolutionary 1879–1929* (New York: Norton, 1973), ch. 10.

[11] See, for examples of this genre, Robert Conquest, *Power and Policy in the USSR* (New York: Harper & Row, 1961); Boris Nicolaevsky, *Power and the Soviet Elite* (New York: Praeger, 1965); and Myron Rush, *The Rise of Khrushchev* (Washington, DC; Public Affairs Press, 1958). The practitioners of this variant did not explicitly deny that leaders fought over policy preferences. However, the methodologies with which they worked were uniquely suited to tapping or imputing power considerations alone.

developed and applied in efforts to fathom the Byzantine world of high politics under Stalin.

The second variant of kremlinology gained legitimacy and widespread use in the 1960s, and postulated that power struggle is only one component (though a very important one) of Kremlin politics, and that leaders struggle as well over their personal definitions of what ought to be done to deal with economic, social, and broader political problems.[12] In addition to examining protocol evidence and personnel changes, this variant identified the policy preferences of the leader by studying his statements and patterns of behavior, and by comparing these with the statements and apparent policy preferences of other members of the Politburo. Disparities then became the basis for alleging the existence of conflict over policy preferences.

Yet, while formally acknowledging the role of power as a motivation, these studies employed methodologies that were uniquely suited to tapping policy preferences. What they sought to demonstrate was that the earlier variant of kremlinology was wrong. What they actually demonstrated was that they themselves had embraced methodological and analytic assumptions about Soviet politics that led them to paint historically inaccurate portraits of the Khrushchev administration. For one thing, they oversimplified the choices facing Soviet leaders in each issue-area. For another, they sought to document conflict without first documenting the policy consensus within which that conflict was taking place. The result of these tendencies was that the books in question exaggerated the level of polarization in the Soviet leadership. Khrushchev, for example, was portrayed as a leader who fought against overwhelming odds to impose his radical policy preferences on the Soviet elite.[13] The reader was left to wonder just why a shrewd politician would undertake such a thankless struggle— why he would so frontally challenge his power bases for the sake of his preferences.

But the terms of the debate between the two variants of kremlinology were set. The focus was on elite motivations, with the alternatives effectively defined as "pure power" motives versus "policy preferences." Such a definition of the issue was a prescription for an endless debate that could never be resolved. First, the pursuit of

---

[12] For examples of this genre, see Linden, *Khrushchev and the Soviet Leadership*; Ploss, *Conflict and Decision-Making*; Tatu, *Power in the Kremlin*; Hahn, *Politics of Soviet Agriculture*; and Wolfgang Leonhard, *The Kremlin since Stalin* (New York: Praeger, 1962).

[13] This is the dominant theme of Linden, *Khrushchev and the Soviet Leadership* and of Ploss, *Conflict and Decision-Making*, both of which have had a profound impact on accepted images of the Khrushchev administration among many US political scientists.

power is a political imperative in most political systems. Few leaders consciously undermine their power, and most leaders view (or come to view) the further consolidation of their power as a requisite for the implementation of their preferred programs. Second, it is usually impossible to discern the true policy preferences of leaders in the absence of memoirs, interviews, or participant observation. We can observe their behaviour in public, and decipher their policy commitments through close study of their speeches. But we cannot, in most cases, know whether they embraced those commitments due to intense personal preferences or due to political calculation.

My definition of authority-building seeks to reconcile and combine these two approaches, rather than choosing between them. I take power consolidation to be a given. But I assume that, in the absence of terror, authority-building is necessary to protect and expand one's base of political support. Authority-building requires both problem-solving capacities and political skills. The speeches of Khrushchev and Brezhnev allow us to discern their respective strategies for demonstrating to the political elite their problem-solving competence and political indispensability. Just why they embraced their respective strategies, rather than others, is a matter for further research and conjecture (about which more in the Conclusion), and would take us into the realm of personal motivation and purpose. First we must determine what those strategies were, and how they evolved over time.

Khrushchev and Brezhnev as Authority-Builders

The literature on executive leadership typically distinguishes two strategies of authority-building: the consensual and the confrontational. The consensual approach is the province of the "political broker or artful synthesizer," whose authority derives in large part from his skill in building consensus for policies that will appease the masses without threatening the prerogatives of established, organized interests. The confrontational approach, in contrast, is adopted by the "populist hero," who tries to "stand above politics and particular interests." The populist is by definition anti-Establishment, in that he confronts established interests by making common cause with the masses.[14]

The Soviet political tradition can legitimize either of these

[14] The quoted distinctions in this paragraph are from Lester Seligman, "Leadership: political aspects," in David L. Sills (ed.), *International Encyclopedia of the Social Sciences* (New York: The Free Press, 1968), Vol. 9, p. 107.

approaches—or a mix of them—for that tradition is dualistic on matters of leadership. On the one hand, the tenets of democratic centralism, the stress on voluntarism in Leninist theory, and the tradition of reverting to strong leadership to guide the "construction of socialism and communism" support personalistic rule. On the other hand, the Leninist rejection of the *Fuehrerprinzip*, the emphasis on collective leadership, the leading role of the party, and the notion that social forces, not individual leaders, make history, support oligarchic rule.

Khrushchev and Brezhnev differed significantly in the types of authority-building strategies they employed, first to rise within the collective leadership, then to consolidate their authority and push their comprehensive programs, and finally to defend their policy effectiveness after those programs had faltered. This observation should come as no surprise to students of Soviet politics for, broadly speaking, Westerners have thought of Khrushchev as a populist leader and of Brezhnev as a political broker and consensus-builder. What is missing from the literature, however, is an exposition of how Khrushchev and Brezhnev manipulated their personal and policy appeals in order to build authority, and of how these strategies evolved over time. This book attempts to fill that gap.

For example, in his role as problem-solver, Khrushchev sought to demonstrate that increased consumer satisfaction could be realized without massive reallocations of funds out of the military and heavy-industrial sectors, and he also sought to demonstrate that a reduction in bureaucratic centralism could be effected without a loss of political control. The key to synthesizing these conflicting priorities was political and social transformation, accompanied by large-scale economic campaigns to overtake and surpass the advanced capitalist states in per capita production and in standard of living. Restructuring authority relationships and generating nationwide campaignist fervor, he argued, would release the initiative of managers, specialists, and social activists alike, achieving gains in both labor productivity and political cohesion that no amount of budgetary reallocation or formal political indoctrination could otherwise attain. Restructuring authority relationships, however, required a confrontation with very powerful political interests.

In contrast to Khrushchev, Brezhnev defined his role as problem-solver in ways that substituted nationalistic appeals ("Soviet patriotism") and budgetary redistributions for political and social transformation. Rejecting any fundamental restructuring of authority relationships, Brezhnev proposed to advance the cause of increased consumer satisfaction by pouring enormous sums into agriculture, rural development, and material incentives, and by greater largesse for private economic activity. And he sought to reconcile political control with "socialist legality" by squelching the anti-Stalin campaign and cracking down on dissenters, but simultaneously creating a more predictable and less pressured environment for the politically conformist. Thus, in both his economic and participatory policies, Brezhnev defined his role as a consensus-builder who would not confront, or radically deprive, major institutional interests.

In their roles as politicians, Khrushchev and Brezhnev differed in ways that paralleled the differences in their approaches to problem-solving: Khrushchev was confrontational, while Brezhnev was consensual.

Khrushchev's strategy was to exploit the atmosphere of crisis after Stalin to make common cause with the masses against intransigent forces within the establishment. He played upon elite fears of the masses by intentionally raising popular expectations, or prematurely publicizing policy proposals, and then argued within the political elite that mass pressure made the acceptance of these proposals a necessity. He would openly encourage the masses to be more demanding toward their hierarchical superiors, and then present himself to the political elite as the man most able to provide the leadership required to meet mass demands. In like manner, Khrushchev would make big promises in public, coupled with allusions to the threatening mass mood when speaking to the political elite, in hopes of increasing the sense of elite dependence upon him for direction.

Brezhnev's rejection of radical political transformation, and his greater emphasis on budgetary redistribution and material incentives, were consistent with his embracing a posture as political broker. He eschewed appeals to the masses over the heads of his colleagues, avoided playing too heavily upon elite fears of the masses, and avoided raising consumer expectations for personal political gain. Instead, Brezhnev tried to create a sense of elite dependence upon him by presenting himself as the leader best qualified to build coalitions that would induce the most powerful institutional interests to reorient their operations and make the system work more effectively without a purge, a populist leader, or mass disorder. Thus, whereas Khrushchev's strategy fostered and built upon an elite atmosphere of urgency, fear, and yearning for revitalization, Brezhnev's strategy fostered and built upon elite yearning for stabilization and steady, measured progress, based on growing confidence that problems could be managed, and tensions contained, without a *vozhd'* to show them the way.

These thumbnail sketches capture broad differences between Khrushchev and Brezhnev, but they can be misleading. For each of these leaders' strategies evolved over time. Indeed, both administrations went through roughly analogous stages of development. A period of political succession was followed in both cases by a period during which the Party leader rose to an ascendant position in the Politburo, outflanking or purging his rivals, and forging a comprehensive program that bore his stamp. In both administrations, that program was frustrated rather soon after its promulgation, leading the General Secretary to redefine once again his authority-building strategy.

Moreover, a single word, such as "confrontational" or "consensual," can only capture the dominant features of each leader's strategy. For these strategies not only evolved over time; they also varied among issue-areas. Khrushchev's investment priorities during 1953–60, for example, were accommodative of entrenched elite interests; his participatory policies were not. Thus, because the two administrations went through analogous stages of development, and because the leaders' positions varied by issue-area, I have organized the book, first, by administration, then, by stages within the administration, and, finally, by issue-area within each stage. The concluding chapter will draw out some lessons to be learned from closer comparison and contrast of the evolution of Khrushchev's and Brezhnev's strategies.

Finally, concepts that highlight differences between Khrushchev and Brezhnev run the risk of obscuring the similarities. One fundamental similarity deserves mention at this point, because it informs a theme that runs through the entire book: both Khrushchev and Brezhnev were "party men," who defended the primacy of political-mobilizational approaches to public administration, incentive policy, and participation. Both of them forged programs that relied heavily on party activism and political intervention for their realization. Both men sought to create a sense of campaignist fervor on behalf of their programs. The turn away from utopian values after Khrushchev did not mean a turn away from party-mobilizational fervor *per se;* it meant rather a redefinition of the content and purpose of that fervor.[15]

Yet the change was consistent with the distinction between Khrushchev's confrontational, and Brezhnev's consensual, strategies. For Khrushchev sought to redefine the character of party mobilization in an anti-elitist direction, thereby challenging the prerogatives of the party apparatchiki. He advocated new methods of mobilization, with active party members and specialists taking the lead. In contrast, Brezhnev advocated methods of mobilization that would further

---

[15] The terms, "party activism," "party intervention," and "political mobilization" will be used interchangeably in this book. Jowitt provides a useful definition of "political mobilization": "Political mobilization is marked by controlled or elite-directed *disruption* . . . of established routines—social, personal, institutional, and psychological . . ." (Kenneth Jowitt, "Inclusion and mobilization in European Leninist regimes," *World Politics* [October 1975], p. 95).

post-Stalin goals without challenging the prerogatives of party apparatchiki. Political mobilization under Brezhnev has been elitist in character—though not as elitist as was the case under Stalin.

Sources and Standards of Evidence

My methodology for documenting authority-building strategies is to conduct an informal content analysis of the entirety of Khrushchev's and Brezhnev's statements on the issues in question. Four objections might be raised against such an approach to the study of politics.

One objection would be that Soviet leaders rarely, if ever, write their own speeches. Therefore, how can we use those speeches as indicators of their political strategies? My response is simple and direct: leaders of large countries rarely write their own speeches, but they hire and train staffs of speechwriters whose job it is to know their boss's interests or commitments, and to reflect these in his speeches. There is no reason to believe that it is any different in the Soviet Union; if anything, Soviet leaders are more careful to ensure that their speeches reflect their interests as they currently wish to project them, given the secretive nature of policy-making in that system, and the importance placed on political communication between patrons and clients. Indeed, an empirical test of this objection revealed that provincial party secretaries in the RSFSR (Russian Republic) are highly attentive to the content of articles published under their name.[16]

A second objection would be that Soviet leaders' speeches are filled with meaningless rhetoric and lies; hence, we must judge their strategies, not by what they say, but by what they do. This objection strikes me as particularly misplaced, for the following reasons: (1) the study of Soviet leaders' speeches has long been a standard methodology for studying Soviet elite politics, even among those analysts who believe Soviet leaders utter mostly lies;[17] (2) those speeches are certainly filled with rhetoric and with manipulative statements, but not entirely; the trick is to locate the operative statements that reflect perspectives on what needs to be done to deal with problems facing the regime; (3) if those speeches contained no operative statements, we could not explain why Soviet leaders' speeches change so much over time; (4) an examination of policy

---

[16] George Breslauer, "Research note," *Soviet Studies* (July 1981). The study was based upon interviews with Soviet émigrés who had participated in the process of writing local politicians' speeches in the USSR.

[17] See, for example, the chapters by Boris Nicolaevsky and Robert Conquest, in Sidney Ploss (ed.), *The Soviet Political Process* (Waltham, Mass.: Ginn, 1970).

or personnel changes does not tell us how these came about; we cannot know what Soviet leaders are advocating behind the scenes without searching for clues in their public statements; (5) we are not seeking to tap feelings or preferences, but strategies; we are not concerned whether the leader truly believes in what he is advocating; hence, there is even a place for "lies" that reflect the image the leader is trying to project and the policies he has decided to push, if only for political reasons; (6) Soviet leaders' speeches are political acts in and of themselves; they affect lower-level political struggles by lending top-level legitimation to one or the other position. Khrushchev's anti-Stalin speeches, or his speeches on behalf of overtaking the USA economically, for example, reflected both his problem-solving and political strategies. So did Brezhnev's speeches on behalf of agricultural development or the opening of Siberia; (7) in Chapters 7 and 15, I shall systematically compare the evolution of regime policy with the evolution of Khrushchev's and Brezhnev's public statements, and will demonstrate a very high correlation between "what they say" and "what they do."

Much kremlinology has been discredited, however, because analysts were not careful or persuasive in using leaders' speeches. With that in mind, I make a continuous effort to separate empty rhetoric from operative statements by going beyond slogans and individual phrases to discern, on the basis of their many speeches in a given period, what Khrushchev and Brezhnev meant by "material incentives," "consumer goods," "political involvement," and so on, and how their positions on a variety of issues intermeshed. I have offered representa-- tive quotations in the body of the text, while including in the notes numerous citations to similar statements before a variety of audiences, thereby controlling for a leader's efforts to deceive individual audiences. On those occasions that I seek to document political conflict and polemics between leaders (Brezhnev and Kosygin; Khrushchev and Malenkov), I have employed the standard kremlinological technique of focusing on the conflicting thrusts of selected statements at roughly the same point in time, but have sought multiple instances of such conflict for the sake of credibility.

A third objection to my methodology would be that, in seeking to document strategies, one runs the risk of imposing too much coherence and calculation on the thinking of political leaders. Soviet leaders, like their counterparts elsewhere in large, complex, industrial societies, must make choices in conditions that are filled with uncertainty. They are frequently forced to make choices on an *ad hoc* basis, and rarely have the time to reflect on how their specific commitments hang together. Moreover, the political demands they face often lead them to make compromises that, willy-nilly, may sacrifice the coherence of their program in a particular issue-area.

This objection is a powerful one, but may not be relevant to this study. It emerges from a body of literature that is grounded in American politics, that focuses largely on technical issues (or, at least, lower-order issues) rather than grand priorities and directions, and that examines decision-making over a very short period of time.[18] Given the structure and ideology of US politics, the level of uncertainty and type of bargaining on lower-order issues, and the short time-span studied, an emphasis on uncertainty, ambivalence, compromise, and incoherence is entirely justified. This study, in contrast, examines leadership in the more centralized and concentrated Soviet political arena, within an ideological and economic planning context that encourages the search for coherence and purposiveness. Moreover, I deal with the grand issues of Soviet politics—All-Union budgetary priorities, incentive policy, administrative reform policy, and approaches to political participation. These issues receive constant attention by the Politburo, which makes considered choices about the basic direction of policy within each realm. Finally, I study leadership strategies for dealing with these issues over a long period of time: eleven years in the case of Khrushchev; seventeen years in the case of Brezhnev. This allows me to identify the points in each administration when Soviet leaders embraced or abandoned given strategies, and the nature of those strategies during the years they were being used. Khrushchev and Brezhnev were neither omniscient nor omnipotent; they operated in conditions of uncertainty and political constraint. That much I take for granted. But they also struggled to impose a certain measure of coherence on their problem-solving and political strategies in order to perform their functions as leaders.

A fourth objection to my methodology would be that Soviet leaders' speeches are made up, in large part, of reportage of decisions made by the collective leadership, with or without the consent of the Party leader. Hence, it is not possible to study these speeches in search of the leader's personal authority-building strategy. At best, one can use them to discern the collective leadership's strategy for building the authority of the regime in the eyes of the population at large, or in the eyes of lower-ranking officials within the political establishment.

---

[18] Some landmarks in the evolution of this body of literature are: Chester Barnard, *The Functions of the Executive* (Cambridge, Mass: Harvard University Press, 1945); James G. March and Herbert A. Simon, *Organizations* (New York: Wiley, 1958); and Charles E. Lindblom, "The science of 'muddling through,'" *Public Administration Review*, no. 19 (1959). In contrast, literature on decision-making that examines the definition and redefinition of basic policy directions over time emphasizes coherence and purpose (though, of course, not omniscience): Philip Selznick, *Leadership in Administration* (New York: Harper & Row, 1957); Geoffrey Vickers, *The Art of Judgment* (London: Chapman & Hall, 1965); Amitai Etzioni, *The Active Society* (New York: The Free Press, 1968).

This objection reflects a basic split between students of Soviet elite politics. Some observers of Soviet leadership behavior interpret initiatives through an oligarchic perspective. This assumes a relatively balanced collective leadership, in which speeches by the Party leader report decisions of the collective and legitimize efforts of the collective to govern the country. Other observers interpret behaviour by Soviet leaders through a more conflictual lens. They emphasize the power of the General Secretary to pack key institutions with his clients, and to consolidate political leverage vis-à-vis associates or rivals within the Politburo. Hence, they view actions or speeches of the General Secretary as political acts that largely reflect his interests.

I take an intermediate position on this issue. Following Grey Hodnett's pioneering work,[19] I see Soviet elite politics since Stalin as shaped by a shifting mix of collective and personal leadership. Khrushchev came to be less constrained by the collective than Brezhnev, but within his administration, Brezhnev was more constrained at some points than at others. In the early years (late 1960s), collective restraints appear to have been stronger than in the later years (late 1970s). It is unwise, in my opinion, to adopt a methodology for the study of Soviet leaders' speeches that assumes a pure form of either the oligarchic or the conflictual view. It is misleading to assume overwhelming consensus, or "political peace," within the Politburo, and to interpret the Party leaders' speeches as simply reportage of a collective strategy. It is also misleading to assume such a high level of dissensus and conflict that Party leaders' speeches are interpreted as little more than efforts to undercut rivals within the leadership.

For these reasons, I trace the regime consensus within each collective leadership period (immediately after Stalin and after Khrushchev), in order to appreciate the consensual context within which political conflict is taking place. I then explore similarities and differences between the positions taken by the Party leader and head of government, in order to establish the extent and nature of political conflict. Later, when dealing largely with speeches by the General Secretary (after the stage of political succession), I tap his distinctive priorities and political strategies by looking for those issues that are accompanied by the *language of insistence, accusation, urgency, and/ or defensiveness.* I assume that such is the language of struggle in Soviet politics. When a leader seeks to push his priorities, or defend his shaken authority in the face of policy reversals, he reverts to this language, as we shall see throughout this book.

My focus on both consensus and conflict allows me to treat Party leaders' speeches as, in part, reportage, but, in large measure, as personal advocacy. But rather than viewing that advocacy as neces-

[19] See note 9 above.

sarily part of a zero-sum power struggle against top-level challengers, I view it as part of an ongoing effort on the part of the General Secretary to build or maintain his authority as leader. Speeches are a major channel through which the General Secretary manipulates the climate of opinion within the political establishment, and seeks to shape the policy agenda, in ways that will project for him an image as effective problem-solver and indispensable politician. The post-Stalin consensus on behalf of increasing consumer satisfaction and political participation without terror or despotism ensures that building or maintaining the authority of the regime is a constant concern of post-Stalin politics and policy-making. The General Secretary, though, is on center stage, for it is his job to take the lead—to devise programs and appeals that inspire confidence about his ability to meet that post-Stalin consensus effectively, and without too high a cost in traditional values. His speeches reflect efforts to convince the political establishment that he has done precisely that. His speeches, in other words, contain the clues to his authority-building strategy.

I have used many sources in analyzing Khrushchev's statements. The most useful is the eight-volume collection of Khrushchev's speeches and memoranda on agricultural affairs, which cover his statements between September 1953 and March 1964. The volumes are entitled *Stroitel'stvo kommunizma v SSSR i razvitie sel'skogo khoziaistva* [The construction of communism in the USSR and the development of agriculture] and were published during 1962–4.[20] Some speeches and memoranda appear in these volumes only; they were never published in the open press. Yet most of the speeches appearing in these volumes were published in the press. When possible, I have checked the *Pravda* version with that in the volumes, and have occasionally turned up discrepancies. For the most part these reflected earlier specific policy commitments that Khrushchev had disowned by the time the volumes were published. For example, Khrushchev's defense of the private sector in agriculture in his September 1953 speech to the Central Committee Plenum does not appear in the speech as published in the collected volumes in 1962. Similarly, Khrushchev's boast of 1957 that Soviet farmers would exceed US levels of meat and milk production by 1960 is altered in the speech as published in 1962. Accordingly, when speeches or memoranda appear in these volumes that also appeared in *Pravda* at the time they were delivered or written, I have relied upon the *Pravda* version as the historical record.[21]

[20] Moscow: Gospolitizdat. Hereafter, these volumes will be cited as *Stroitel'stvo kommunizma I–VIII*.
[21] However, for ease of reference, I shall cite passages in ibid., when these correspond to the *Pravda* rendition.

Speeches by Khrushchev that do not appear in the volumes, or that appear there in abbreviated form, have been examined in the following sources: (1) *Pravda;* (2) *Current Digest of the Soviet Press* (hereafter, *CDSP*); and (3) *Current Soviet Policies*, a digest of major speeches at each of the party congresses since 1952.[22]

For Brezhnev's speeches I have employed: (1) a seven-volume set of Brezhnev's collected speeches, entitled *Leninskim kursom* [On Lenin's path];[23] (2) other speeches by Brezhnev during 1964–81, as published in *Pravda, CDSP, Current Soviet Policies,* and the Russian-language stenographic reports of the party congresses during Brezhnev's years in power;[24] and (3) abbreviated versions of previously unpublished speeches by Brezhnev at end-of-year Central Committee plenary sessions, as these appeared in the two-volume set, *Ob osnovnykh voprosakh ekonomicheskoi politiki KPSS na sovremennom etape* [On basic questions of the CPSU's economic policy at the

[22] Leo Gruliow (ed.), *Current Soviet Policies: The Documentary Record of the Nineteenth Communist Party Congress and the Reorganization after Stalin's Death* (New York: Praeger, 1953); Leo Gruliow (ed.), *Current Soviet Policies II: The Documentary Record of the 20th Communist Party Congress and Its Aftermath* (New York: Praeger, 1957); Leo Gruliow (ed.), *Current Soviet Policies III: The Documentary Record of the Extraordinary 21st Congress of the Communist Party of the Soviet Union* (New York: Columbia University Press, 1960); Leo Gruliow and Charlotte Saikowski (eds), *Current Soviet Policies IV: The Documentary Record of the 22nd Party Congress of the Communist Party of the Soviet Union* (New York: Columbia University Press, 1962); Leo Gruliow, *et al.* (eds), *Current Soviet Policies V: The Documentary Record of the 23rd Congress of the Communist Party of the Soviet Union* (Columbus, Ohio: American Association for the Advancement of Slavic Studies, 1973); Leo Gruliow, *et al.* (eds), *Current Soviet Policies VI: The Documentary Record of the 24th Congress of the Communist Party of the Soviet Union* (Columbus, Ohio: American Association for the Advancement of Slavic Studies, 1973); Leo Gruliow, *et al.* (eds), *Current Soviet Policies VII: The Documentary Record of the 25th Congress of the Communist Party of the Soviet Union* (Columbus, Ohio: American Association for the Advancement of Slavic Studies, 1976). The entire editorial staff of the *Current Digest of the Soviet Press* deserves credit for these invaluable volumes and excellent translations. However, for economy of reference, they will hereafter be cited as Gruliow, *Current Soviet Policies I-VII.*

[23] Moscow: Politizdat, 1970–9. Hereafter, these will be cited as Brezhnev, *Leninskim kursom I-VII.*

[24] *XXIII s"ezd Kommunisticheskoi Partii Sovetskogo Soiuza, 29 marta–8 aprelia 1966 g.: Stenograficheskii otchet,* 2 vols (Moscow: Politizdat, 1966); *XXIV s"ezd Kommunisticheskoi Partii Sovetskogo Soiuza, 30 marta–9 aprelia 1971 g.: Stenograficheskii otchet,* 2 vols (Moscow: Politizdat, 1971); *XXV s"ezd Kommunistichekoi Partii Sovetskogo Soiuza, 24 fevralia–5 marta 1976 g.: Stenograficheskii otchet,* 3 vols (Moscow: Politizdat, 1976). Hereafter, these will be referred to, respectively, as *XXIII s"ezd I-II; XXIV s"ezd I-II;* and *XXV s"ezd I-III.*

current stage].[25] When possible, care has been taken to rely on those versions of speeches which were least likely to have been doctored by the publishers.

Speeches by Alexei Kosygin appear in *Pravda, CDSP, Planovoe khoziaistvo*, and a volume of Kosygin's selected speeches and articles, entitled *A. N. Kosygin: izbrannye rechi i stat'i* [A. N. Kosygin: selected speeches and articles].[26] In addition, his speeches at three party congresses appear in *Current Soviet Policies V–VII*. Kosygin's speeches have been analyzed, and compared to Brezhnev's, only at the three party congresses and during the stage of political succession. For the most part, this book does not investigate political conflict among Politburo-members after the ascendancy of the Party leader within the leadership.

Other bodies of evidence on the policies and politics of Khrushchev and Brezhnev have been consciously excluded from this study: literature by Soviet dissidents, Soviet émigrés, and the Soviet regime itself (including Brezhnev's "memoirs"), all of which is proliferating at a rapid rate. All of these sources will at some point be useful to historians of the post-Stalin era. At the moment, however, they present special methodological problems that raise crucial difficulties of interpretation. *Ad hoc* inclusion of evidence from these sources would undermine the systematic quality of this study, encumber the text, and confuse matters.

The memoirs of Nikita Khrushchev, however, are an important source—the direct and lengthy testimony of one of the main protagonists in this book, smuggled out of the Soviet Union.[27] They deserve careful analysis and comparison with the statements of Khrushchev when in power. Hence, in the notes I shall include corroborating or disconfirming evidence from Khrushchev's memoirs, juxtapose them to the portrait drawn from our main sources, and offer explanations of similarities and differences.

[25] Moscow: Politizdat, 1975.
[26] Moscow, Politizdat, 1974.
[27] *Khrushchev Remembers*, Vol. 1, translated and edited by Strobe Talbott (Boston, Mass.: Little, Brown, 1970); *Khrushchev Remembers: The Last Testament*, Vol 2, translated and edited by Strobe Talbott (Boston, Mass.: Little, Brown, 1974).

Part Two
The Khrushchev Years

2 Political Succession and Consumer Satisfaction, 1953-7

The budgetary priorities of 1952 were those of a war economy. Military and heavy-industrial production held a near-monopoly over access to scarce resources. Neither agriculture, light industry, housing, nor consumer services received sufficient attention to relieve the poverty of the masses. Instead, the doctrine of the times identified military and heavy-industrial advance with progress, power, and national security, while encouraging the masses to avoid "consumerism" and to sacrifice for the sake of future generations.[1]

The authority crisis following Stalin's death led his successors quickly to reopen the whole question of budgetary priorities. Perhaps because of fear, perhaps for other reasons, a rather broad consensus emerged within the national leadership on the need to break with the past, and to offer a new deal to the urban and rural consumer. Malenkov, Khrushchev, even Kaganovich endorsed such a program, while Molotov grudgingly accepted it as something of a regrettable necessity.[2]

[1] For the official justification of late-Stalinist investment priorities, see the speeches of Khrushchev, Malenkov, and Saburov at the Nineteenth Party Congress (Gruliow, *Current Soviet Policies I*), as well as the following: "On the means for the gradual transition from socialism to communism," *Voprosy ekonomiki* (October 1950), pp. 99–108 (*CDSP*, vol. 3, n. 2, pp. 3–9); P. Khromov, "On opportunities for raising labor productivity in socialist industry," *Bolshevik* (February 1951), pp 22–31 (*CDSP*, vol. 3, no. 19, pp. 9–11); V. Kuznetsov, "For further advance in socialist competition," *Pravda*, 3 October, 1951 (*CDSP*, vol. 3, no. 40, pp. 11–13); 3 Ts. Stepanyan, "From socialism to communism," *Komsomol'skaya Pravda*, 16 October, 1951 (*CDSP*, vol. 3, no. 42, p. 9); I. Kuzminov, "Increased labor productivity is major condition for triumph of communism," *Pravda*, 16 October, 1951 (*CDSP*, vol. 3, no. 42, pp. 9–10).

[2] These themes are common to the following speeches: Malenkov's Supreme Soviet address (*Pravda*, 9 August, 1953); Khrushchev's Central Committee Plenum address (ibid., 15 September, 1953); election speeches by Khrushchev (ibid., 7 March, 1954), Malenkov (ibid., 13 March, 1954), Shvernik (ibid., 8 March, 1954), Voroshilov (ibid., 11 March, 1954), Bulganin (ibid., 11 March, 1954), Pervukhin (ibid., 12 March, 1954), Saburov (ibid., 13 March, 1954), Suslov (ibid., 10 March, 1954); Malenkov's Supreme Soviet address (ibid., 27 April, 1954), the election and Supreme Soviet addresses of Kaganovich (ibid., 13 March, 1954, and 27 April, 1954), and the Supreme Soviet address of Khrushchev (ibid., 27 April, 1954).

The speeches of V. Molotov are not included in this consensus, because the Soviet Foreign Minister adopted an obstructionist position on many issues. Although he may have begrudgingly accepted certain specific changes

But the consensus was ill-defined and unspecified. Stalin's successors could largely agree on the need to increase consumer satisfaction, but they could not agree so easily on the way to achieve this. They disagreed over how to deal with the dilemmas of reallocating resources in the Soviet war economy: (1) how extensively to redistribute resources; (2) which heavy-industrial or military programs to cut back for the sake of reallocation; (3) which consumer-oriented sectors to give preference: food, soft goods, consumer durables, housing, or services; (4) how much emphasis to place on increasing consumption in the short term, as opposed to investing in future consumption; and (5) the relative balance of material incentives versus party exhortation and mobilization as spurs to labor initiative.

Answers to these questions had momentous political implications. They became the objects of intense political conflict, for they revolved around the costs to be borne in meeting the new commitment to the consumer—costs that involved treading on the prerogatives of the military–industrial complex, redefining the role of party activism in Soviet economic affairs, making choices between the relative priority of the urban and rural consumers, and making estimates of the implications for political stability of the whole consumption issue.

Khrushchev seized the initiative on this issue by offering a program that promised to improve the grain situation in both town and countryside on short order, and at relatively restricted cost to the military–industrial complex, or to the CPSU's mobilizational role. In this respect, his budgetary priorities were in sharp contrast to those of Malenkov, who was willing to pay a much greater short-term cost for the sake of promised long-term gains.

Malenkov's Abortive "Consumerism"

As outlined in several major speeches during August 1953–April 1954,[3] Malenkov's program called for an immediate increase in current consumption of soft goods and consumer durables by the urban middle class, a long-term, sharp increase in food consumption

in policy, he dissented continuously from the majority consensus in favor of a decisive break with Stalinism. For the evidence on this score, see Leonhard, _Kremlin since Stalin_, pp. 102–3, 106–8; also, an earlier version of this manuscript, George Breslauer, "Dilemmas of leadership in the Soviet Union since Stalin 1953–1976" (unpublished, 1978), pp. 7–26 to 7–28.

See also the documentation of the reform consensus at the July 1953 Plenum, in R. J. Service, "The road to the Twentieth Party Congress: an analysis of the events surrounding the Central Committee Plenum of July 1953," _Soviet Studies_ (April 1981), pp. 232–45.

[3] _Pravda_, 9 August, 1953, 13 March, 1954, and 27 April, 1954.

by all classes, deep cuts in the military and heavy-industrial budgets to finance simultaneous agricultural and light-industrial development, and a sharp increase in the amount of money in the hands of the population. To buttress these demands, Malenkov introduced far-reaching doctrinal innovations, rejecting the Stalinist notion that heavy industry should always grow faster than light industry, and arguing that war would now destroy both capitalism and socialism (thereby implying that costly new programs for expansion of the defense establishment were no longer needed). Malenkov's solution to Soviet rural backwardness was a long-term program of intensive agricultural development in the western regions of the country, raising yields through higher material incentives, increased electrification, and large-scale inputs of mineral fertilizer, irrigation equipment, and agricultural machinery. In the short run, Malenkov proposed emergency measures (importation of foreign consumer goods, release of state grain reserves, and conversion of a number of heavy-industrial and military establishments to consumer-goods production) to increase the food and light-industrial products available in Soviet cities.

Malenkov's program constituted a bold new departure, but it was vulnerable to criticism on many counts. Some of those vulnerabilities were purely power-political: the fact that Malenkov was the first among Soviet leaders to put himself out on a limb with a comprehensive new program made him vulnerable to opportunistic criticism; and the fact that Malenkov justified his proposals with major doctrinal revisions made him vulnerable to the charge of being an extremist.

But there were economic and socio-political vulnerabilities as well. First, although long-term benefits to the rural and urban consumer were implicit in the commitment to intensive agricultural development, the short-term payoffs were far more restricted. Advances in current consumption would be enjoyed primarily by the urban population, and perhaps only by the professional and administrative classes within that population. Thus, Malenkov's program frontally challenged military and heavy-industrial interests without promising an immediate, compensatory increase in mass consumer satisfaction. Hence, to the extent that short-term mass consumer satisfaction could be defined as the main issue, the Soviet premier would be on the defensive. Second, in its emphasis on increasing the incomes of the urban and rural consumer, but deferring sharp increases in mass consumption, Malenkov's program threatened to aggravate inflation and to reinforce elite fears of mass disorder.[4] Third, in downplaying

---

[4] These fears were undoubtedly distributed unevenly throughout the political elite, and may have coexisted even in the same individual with genuine enthusiasm for the task of upgrading consumer satisfaction. But the existence of such fears in both the national and territorial elite can be assumed from several sources: (1) the message from the Presidium to the

the role of party activism (as opposed to material incentives) in stimulating labor initiative, the program constituted still another sharp break with Soviet tradition, and was largely devoid of mobilizational fervor.

In sum, Malenkov's program was vulnerable to criticism because it was couched in extremist terms, was contradictory, and lacked a mythology with broad roots in the Stalinist tradition.[5] It was only a

population after Stalin's death that they should avoid "confusion and panic" (Leonhard, *Kremlin since Stalin*, p. 33); (2) testimony of insiders to the effect that the agricultural crisis, in particular, stirred trepidation among members of the Central Committee (Medvedev and Medvedev, *Khrushchev*, pp. 5–6); (3) elite conflict (documented below) over authority-building strategies and over the wisdom of adopting policies that would aggravate repressed inflation.

[5] The interpretation of Malenkov's light-industrial program is rather uniform in the Western literature. But Malenkov's policy preferences regarding the rural sector are a source of differences among historians of the period. Most observers take little note of Malenkov's agricultural program, skipping quickly to Khrushchev's program in that realm. Some observers, in contrast, argue that Malenkov's agricultural program reflected his *conservative* inclinations. Thus, Ploss (*Conflict and Decision-Making*, p. 68) concludes that Malenkov was one of those "uninterested in short-term improvement of the welfare of the broadest circles of the population" and one for whom "austerity and regimentation for the multitude . . . were the nostalgic values." The problems with this interpretation are: (1) It draws a conclusion about Malenkov's *preferences* on the basis of a program that may well have been based on a positive attitude toward mass consumption but a belief that there was no alternative to a long-term costly program of agricultural development, the payoffs from which would necessarily be delayed. (2) It ignores the political bind in which Malenkov found himself: even if he believed a crash program for grain production was necessary to augment current consumption, to have sponsored such a program would have required self-criticism on his part, since only a year earlier, at the Nineteenth Party Congress, he had been the one to announce that the grain problem had been solved. (3) It obscures the fact that Malenkov's far-reaching doctrinal innovations would hardly have been necessary to justify only a very limited program.

More recently, still another interpretation of Malenkov's commitment to agriculture paints the picture of a conservative (McCauley, *Khrushchev and the Development of Soviet Agriculture*, pp. 46–7, 72, 194, 195, 216–17, 219). McCauley's interpretation of Malenkov's policy preferences is nuanced, but difficult to pin down. In some places he emphasizes the limits of Malenkov's commitment (ibid., pp. 46, 72, 194) by pointing, for example, to the fact that, in his August 1953 speech, Malenkov failed to enumerate the size of the capital investments required by his agricultural program. In other places, McCauley (ibid., pp. 195, 216–17) stresses the political constraints that Malenkov would have encountered had he been First Secretary of the CPSU and tried to implement a costly program. In the end, the reader is unclear as to what Malenkov's actual policy preferences were in McCauley's eyes, regardless of whether his program was politically acceptable. Moreover, it does not strike me as unusual that, in the politically opportunistic atmosphere of the times (a point McCauley *does* stress, see ibid., p. 44),

month before Nikita Khrushchev began to seize upon the vulnerabilities in Malenkov's program and offered programs based upon
a different set of appeals.

The Khrushchevian Alternative[6]

Unlike Malenkov, Khrushchev defined the consumer situation as
dangerous and urgent (or so he said), but came forth with an
approach that would not require deep cuts in the heavy-industrial
and military budgets. He presented himself as the man uniquely
suited to combining material security with national security, policy
innovation with policy continuity, leadership with moderation,
political mobilization with economic betterment. He proposed to
accomplish this by concentrating all attention on the grain situation,
by launching a massive, nationwide campaign (the Virgin Lands
Program) for bringing millions of square acres of unused land under
grain cultivation, and by depending heavily on party activism as a
substitute for sharp increases in material incentives. Thus, the Khrushchevian synthesis called for emphasizing immediate mass consumption
of grain, campaignist fervor, and resistance to deep cuts in the defense
budget.

These were the very terms in which Khrushchev presented the
Virgin Lands Program to his Presidium colleagues: a relatively low-
cost program, promising big payoffs in the near-term. Emphasizing
the equal importance of cost and time, Khrushchev pointed to the
"inexhaustible reserves" available for the development of Central
Asia, and dubbed his program a "vital task of great national significance" in light of the "dangerous" situation that had arisen on the
consumer front: "As much bread as possible without large capital

Malenkov would demur from enumerating the investments required for the
agricultural program. Indeed, Malenkov's doctrinal innovations geared toward
sharp reductions in the defense budget may be interpreted as an effort to
foster an international atmosphere that would legitimize the diversion of funds
to agriculture required by his program. Until that revision had been accepted
by a majority of the political elite, however, there was little point in specifying investment totals.

   6 *Stroitel'stvo kommunizma I* covers the speeches by Khrushchev on
agriculture from the September 1953 Plenum through the January 1955
Plenum. The volume includes many previously unpublished memoranda he
wrote to the Presidium in the course of his national barnstorming. Some
passages in the plenary speeches have been altered by the publishers, however. They can be found, as originally reported, in *Pravda*, 15 September,
1953, 21 March, 1954, and 3 February, 1955. Khrushchev's speech to the
Plenum of June 1954 was not published in the Soviet press. It appears in
Stroitel'stvo kommunizma I, pp. 306–36, though I cannot say whether it was
altered before this appearance eight years later.

expenditures. There is no other course of equal value. It would be criminal of us not to exploit the huge possibilities we now have."[7]

However cheap in relative terms, the Virgin Lands Program would still require expanded production of agricultural machinery, a significant infusion of funds, and a national commitment to solve the grain crisis. In justifying the program, Khrushchev was careful to avoid Malenkov's doctrinal heresies, but still felt the need to revise Stalinist doctrine. Toward these ends, the Party leader sought terminology that would maintain the priority status of heavy industry, while upgrading the relative status of agriculture-oriented tasks within the industrial complex. Thus, at the September 1953 Plenum, Khrushchev denounced those who "do not understand the simple truth that without an advance in agriculture, the tasks of communist construction cannot be solved successfully."[8] Later, he dubbed agriculture a "cause of all the people"[9] and advised workers and managerial personnel in heavy industry that agricultural machine-building was an "honorable task."[10] When speaking at industrial conferences, he incorporated discussions of agricultural affairs into the very beginning of his speeches.[11] And when addressing matters of doctrine, he would explain that the need for agricultural mechanization proved the leading role of heavy industry in the economy.[12]

Khrushchev was not as generous when it came to the relative prestige of light industry and consumer soft goods. In seeking to forge a relatively inexpensive alliance of heavy industry and agriculture for the immediate satisfaction of mass desires for basic foodstuffs, he spoke often of the need to subordinate attention to light industry to the prior development of agriculture.[13]

[7] *Stroitel'stvo kommunizma I*, pp. 88–91, 85–8, 331–2.

[8] *Pravda*, 15 September, 1953.

[9] *Stroitel'stvo kommunizma I*, p. 238 (February 1954 Plenum); also, ibid., p. 438 (January 1955 Plenum).

[10] *Pravda*, 15 September, 1953.

[11] ibid., 28 December, 1954, and 19 May, 1955.

[12] *Stroitel'stvo kommunizma II*, pp. 21–2. For analogous statements of Khrushchev's view of the agricultural investment situation, see *Stroitel'stvo kommunizma I*, pp. 344, 364–5, 377–8; *Pravda*, 28 December, 1954; *Stroitel'stvo kommunizma II*, pp. 11, 27–9, 103, 123; *Pravda*, 19 May, 1955; and corroborating testimony in Khrushchev, *Khrushchev Remembers*, Vol. 2, pp. 106–39. For rare statements indicating Khrushchev's awareness of the need eventually to build up the fertilizer industry, see *Stroitel'stvo kommunizma I*, p. 246; *Stroitel'stvo kommunizma II*, p. 46; *Pravda*, 22 January, 1956.

[13] *Stroitel'stvo kommunizma I*, pp. 221–2, 330, 368; *Stroitel'stvo kommunizma II*, p. 21. For cases in which the same point is made by omission (that is, by the failure to include light industry in a listing of regime investment priorities), see ibid., p. 154; Khrushchev, *Khrushchev Remembers*, Vol. 2, p. 12. And for a case in which Khrushchev argued that construction materials for housing qualified as much as textiles as a "consumer good," see *Pravda*, 28 December, 1954.

If agricultural expenditures were to be contained, and light-industrial investments to be sharply curtailed, on what did Khrushchev propose to spend the billions of rubles that distinguished his budgetary priorities from those of Malenkov? Khrushchev's answer was the modernization of the defense establishment for use in the nuclear age. Although the Party Secretary did not speak much at the time on matters relating to the defense budget, his position can be persuasively inferred from four mutually reinforcing sources: (1) Khrushchev's denunciation of the doctrinal revisions through which Malenkov had hoped to legitimize cuts in the defense budget; (2) esoteric polemics on the issue of defense expenditures in speeches by Khrushchev and Malenkov in April 1954 (about which more below); (3) the fact that defense expenditures were raised sharply, and weapons development decisions made, in the months surrounding Khrushchev's disgrace of Malenkov in January 1955; and (4) a flood of admissions by Khrushchev in his memoirs that he was long a strong supporter of defense modernization.[14]

Khrushchev also made good use of the other vulnerabilities in Malenkov's program, namely, the inflationary stress on material incentives, and the failure to accord a central role to party activism in spurring economic achievement. Here the coherence in Khrushchev's program became manifest. Holding down the scope of reallocation, he could hardly afford to overemphasize material incentives without becoming vulnerable to the charge that he was both fostering inflation and excessively straining the national budget. And by laying emphasis instead on party activism, exhortation, and pressure as substitutes for continuing increases in procurement prices, material incentives, and state funding of rural development, he could appeal to constituencies that Malenkov had ignored or defied.

Thus, at the September 1953 Plenum, Khrushchev echoed Malenkov's call for increasing procurement and purchase prices for agricultural produce, and for strengthening the material incentive of the collective farmer. In this respect, Khrushchev reflected the post-Stalin, "new deal" consensus. But that was as far as he went, for in the very next paragraph Khrushchev qualified the endorsement:

[14] On the first and third of these points, see H. S. Dinerstein, *War and the Soviet Union*, rev. edn. (New York: Praeger, 1962), pp. 71–7; and Lincoln P. Bloomfield, Walter C. Clemens, Jr, and Franklyn Griffiths, *Khrushchev and the Arms Race* (Cambridge, Mass.: MIT, 1966), pp. 50–8; on the fourth point, see Khrushchev, *Khrushchev Remembers*, Vol. 1, pp. 516–17, and Vol. 2, pp. 11–12, 30–3, 43–4, 51–2, 55, 60, 194, 220, 270, 535. There are other places in the memoirs in which Khrushchev speaks of cutting military spending, but these reflect either his early efforts to reduce military manpower while building up the rocket forces, his later, 1963–4, efforts to trim military spending over all, his general cost consciousness in all areas of public spending, or conclusions reached while in retirement.

Increasing the procurement and purchase prices and reducing the norms for obligatory deliveries are highly important in strengthening the material interest of the collective farms and farmers in further advancing agriculture. However, these measures must be properly evaluated. Their importance and necessity at the present time is obvious, but they do not determine the main path for developing collective farming.

And later on in his address, Khrushchev made clear that the national budget could not absorb further increases in procurement prices; if such increases took place nonetheless, they would have to be paid for by increasing urban retail prices.[15] No such opposition to procurement price increases, and no such linkage between procurement prices and urban retail prices, appears in the speeches of Georgi Malenkov.

A comparison of Khrushchev's and Malenkov's electoral and Supreme Soviet speeches of March/April 1954 indicates quite baldly that the differences between their respective approaches had crystallized across a broad range of issues, and that the two Soviet leaders were ready to polemicize in public.[16] Thus, on the issue of defense modernization, Malenkov argued that the Soviet armed forces were now fully equipped to perform their duties, whereas Khrushchev demanded further strengthening of the armed forces. Regarding agricultural machine-building (read: the Virgin Lands Program), Khrushchev spelled out the need for expanded production, and defined the task in socio-political terms that would underscore the proposed elevation of agricultural status ("the working class . . . must continue to render greater and greater assistance to the collective farmer"). Malenkov never even mentioned agricultural machine-building, let alone justified the solution in these terms. Further, Khrushchev, in his speech to the Supreme Soviet, said nothing about the established policy of reducing urban retail prices; Malenkov, in contrast, endorsed the policy and insisted that it continue. Finally, in his election speech, Krushchev said nothing about material incentives, collective farmers' incomes, or procurement prices, whereas Malenkov took note of the measures for augmenting material incentives, and pointed out approvingly that "collective farmers' incomes have increased." The following month, Khrushchev remained silent again on the issue of material incentives, while Malenkov spoke of raising "the material interest and economic incentive of the farm workers." While it is often hazardous to use silence as an indicator of dissent, the differences mapped here are striking, precisely because there are so many of them.

15 *Pravda*, 15 September 1953.
16 ibid., 7 March, 1954 (Khrushchev); 13 March, 1954 (Malenkov); 27 April, 1954 (Khrushchev and Malenkov).

This polemic was subtle; it was also rather true to the policies each leader had advocated. It did not entail mutual accusations or opportunistic exaggeration of each others' positions. In contrast, at the January 1955 Central Committee Plenum, Khrushchev had outflanked Malenkov politically, and forced him to resign his post as Chairman of the Council of Ministers. In the process, Khrushchev seized the initiative by accusing Malenkov of a "right-wing deviation" reminiscent of Bukharin. He made every effort to pin the extremist label on his rival, to exaggerate their differences, and to play down the post-Stalin consensus in which both of their programs were embedded.[17]

Although Khrushchev's accusations were exaggerated, there was a kernel of truth in them. For Malenkov had presented himself as a leader who would usher in a sharp break with the past, whereas Khrushchev was presenting himself as a leader who would effectively synthesize traditional values with new tasks. In proposing an alliance between heavy industry and agriculture, in seeking to augment the status of rural development in the budgetary process, and in defining immediate mass consumption of grain products as a major issue, Khrushchev cultivated the image of a leader who was willing and able to meet the regime's new commitment to the consumer. In reaffirming the privileged status of heavy industry, in proposing a measured, nondisruptive pace of reallocation, in backing modernization of defense forces, in avoiding far-reaching doctrinal revisions, in suggesting low-cost, high-pressure solutions to the agricultural problem, and in launching a huge project that required great fervor and effort, Khrushchev projected the image of a leader who was sensitive to the fears and stakes of those who were potentially threatened by the new consensus.

But could such a synthesis work? Was it realistic to assume that Khrushchev's program could yield the benefits it promised? It was one thing to buttress one's authority by presenting a program that preempted the centrist position on the policy spectrum. It was another thing to demonstrate one's policy effectiveness. The Virgin Lands Program might yield short-run benefits from the standpoint of grain production. But what about other agricultural regions and other agricultural products? How would these fare in the absence of large new investments? Ostensibly, Khrushchev would feel the need to demonstrate that he was not oblivious to the complexities, and that he had a strategy for dealing with this problem as well. Indeed, his speeches reveal that he spent a great deal of time and energy during these years seeking to demonstrate that he had such a plan.

[17] *Pravda*, 3 February, 1955.

Developmental Perspectives: Khrushchev as Problem-Solver

According to Khrushchev, there was immense, untapped capacity for growth in the rural sector. The point was not to pour money into an inefficient administrative funnel, but to concentrate on the more rational organization of production, tapping of reserves, and cutting of costs at the local level. In his speech to the September 1953 Plenum of the Central Committee, Khrushchev sought to show just how this might be brought about. He launched into a detailed demonstration that any collective farm could be brought up to the level of the advanced farms within its region, given skilled and energetic personnel capable of mobilizing reserves through improvements in the organization of production. He followed these generalizations by detailed discussions of agronomic techniques (the square-cluster method of planting; the use of corn as fodder; planting of seedlings in peat humus pots; and so on) that could radically improve the productivity of agriculture without large expenditures.[18]

If we look beyond this single speech, we find that such an approach was implicit in much of what Khrushchev had to say about agriculture during these years. Thus, Khrushchev would constantly criticize local officials for what he called *izhdivenie*, a term that I shall translate as "dependency," but which has the stronger connotation conveyed by the notion of "parasitism." He attributed this both to personal laziness and to an incentive system that allowed local officials to avoid the hard work required to mobilize latent resources. It followed, therefore, that if they were cut off from the governmental dole, they would be forced to mobilize those untapped human and material resources. There was no question that the resources were there: "In many provinces they don't take this question seriously. Everyone counts only on central supplies and they don't make use of their rich local potential."[19] At times Khrushchev made such comments in response to local demands for credits or technology; at other times, as part of his efforts to rationalize the material incentive system and ensure that lagging farms should not be subsidized indefinitely; at still other times his ire was raised by a perception of massive inefficiency at the local level.[20]

Since the untapped resources were assumed to be there, it was Khrushchev's contention that, given skilled leadership and proper organization of production, most farms and regions could be raised

[18] ibid., 15 September, 1953.
[19] *Stroitel'stvo kommunizma I*, p. 392.
[20] For examples of Khrushchev's denunciations of dependency, see ibid., pp. 169–70, 202, 302, 313, 315, 324, 385, 397, 472; *Stroitel'stvo kommunizma II*, pp. 90, 104, 116, 144, 225–7, 386; *Pravda*, 15 September, 1953.

to the highest levels of productivity. True, he at times acknowledged the existence of variations in resource endowment, climatic conditions, and location, but he refused to accept the notion that these were the decisive factors in determining differences in level of production among farms. Local leadership was: "I repeat. Give me the most difficult district . . . Before all honest people I declare that we will send people— I'll go myself, if the CC sends me—and I will make a signed statement at this meeting that we will not only fulfill, we will overfulfill, the task posed by the January Plenum."[21]

It would be easy to fault Khrushchev for simplistic logic. One could argue, for example, that his assertion that all farms could shortly be raised to the level of the most advanced was not capable of being disproved, for whenever a farm failed to make progress, he could blame the leaders for incompetence or bad faith in failing to mobilize "incalculable" resources. Moreover, one could point out that generalizing from a single case relieved Khrushchev of the responsibility of proving that the case was actually representative of the material and human endowment of all farms. Such objections, however, would miss the point for, to Khrushchev, the issue was not really whether each and every farm could attain a specific level of production, but whether each and every farm-worker and farm official would at least aspire to attain that level. The issue was one of potential and commitment; those who would not aspire to greatness would never mobilize the resources available to them, and would never attain the unprecedented results Khrushchev was seeking and promising. Indeed, when occasionally challenged for his method of calculating capacity, Khrushchev could be quite candid as to his real intentions: "I want . . . to raise your ire against shortcomings in the work of state farms, to make you want to raise the state farms more quickly to the necessary level."[22]

Khrushchev's effort to stimulate local initiative was consistent with his stated commitments regarding price policy; it was also consistent with his stated vision of the path through which collective farms would attain abundance. The principal feature of that vision was self-reliance. As Khrushchev envisaged it, the remedial measures of 1953 would lead to higher earnings for the collective farmers, who would plow back these extra earnings into the development of the rural

[21] *Stroitel'stvo kommunizma II*, p. 75; for other examples of Khrushchev's belief in the decisive importance of leadership and organization, see ibid., pp. 152, 161–2, 179; *Stroitel'stvo kommunizma I*, pp. 115–16. For some examples of Khrushchev's tendency to hold up model farms or regions as the norm for all farms and regions, see ibid., pp. 211, 245, 329, 445; *Stroitel'stvo kommunizma II*, pp. 17, 171, 396; *Pravda*, 15 September, 1953, and 3 February, 1955.

[22] *Stroitel'stvo kommunizma I*, p. 168; see also ibid., p. 188.

economy, rather than merely accumulating higher earnings for themselves. He rejected calls for still further rises in procurement prices. Indeed, the First Secretary spoke often of the day when an abundance of farm products would make it possible for the state to lower prices once again, thereby forcing the collective farmers to sell their surpluses at those lower prices.[23]

In this light we can also better understand Khrushchev's polemics with Malenkov on the issue of material incentive. Beyond the remedial measures of 1953–4, Khrushchev's use of the term, "strengthening material incentives," was entirely consistent with his position on procurement price policy. For the First Secretary was campaigning for rationalization of the structure of material incentives at current price levels in order to make the on-farm incentive structure more capable of eliciting initiative from the most active and competent farmers.[24] Khrushchev also campaigned for a promise of early abundance (an intangible material reward) that would itself inspire the masses to higher levels of activism.

But Khrushchev's positions on resource allocation were not solely a product of his efforts to build an intra-elite coalition capable of outflanking Malenkov, or of his efforts to demonstrate his effectiveness as a problem-solver. They were also a product of the strategy he embraced for manipulating the climate of opinion within the elite in ways that would increase the sense of dependence upon him for leadership.

Khrushchev as Politician

In striking contrast to the centrist position Khrushchev adopted as problem-solver on issues of investment priorities and incentive policy, the First Secretary's public posture as a politician was distinctly confrontational. He attempted to steal the initiative from his colleagues

---

[23] For Khrushchev's collective-farm development strategy, see *Pravda*, 15 September, 1953; *Stroitel'stvo kommunizma I*, pp. 99, 116–18, 298–302, 324–5, 332, 334, 368, 385, 389–90, 400, 404, 461–2; *Stroitel'stvo kommunizma II*, pp. 60, 64, 84, 157–8, 160–1, 233–4, 249, 262, 289; *Pravda*, 3 February, 1955.

[24] See *Stroitel'stvo kommunizma I*, pp. 118, 195, 297, 309, 316–18, 351, 388, 391–2; *Stroitel'stvo kommunizma II*, pp. 88, 146; *Pravda*, 3 February, 1955, and 22 January, 1956; Gruliow, *Current Soviet Policies II*, p. 45. For analogous examples of Khrushchev's concern for the structure of material incentives in the industrial sector, see *Pravda*, 28 December, 1954, and Gruliow, *Current Soviet Policies II*, p. 48. And for the mix of elitist and egalitarian components in Khrushchev's approach to incentive policy, as reported in his memoirs, see Khrushchev, *Khrushchev Remembers*, Vol. 2, pp. 114–15, 117, 119–20, 123, 128, 144, 147.

in the leadership by creating a climate of campaignist fervor on behalf of far-reaching developmental goals. And he then sought to intimidate potential skeptics within the political elite by reinterpreting that climate as one of crisis. He played upon elite fears of the masses by encouraging an atmosphere of urgency about the consumer situation, and then used this atmosphere as justification for his programs and his personal leadership.

Consider, for example, Khrushchev's behavior in expanding the scope of the Virgin Lands Program. The First Secretary repeatedly violated the norms of secrecy in Presidium policy-making by making public commitments before wider audiences that would then constrain the leadership to follow him and his programs. Six days after his memorandum of 22 January, 1954, in which Khrushchev proposed a goal of 13 million hectares, the First Secretary announced to a convocation of Machine Tractor Station officials a decision to assimilate 13 million hectares of idle land by the end of 1955. Eight days later, the Soviet leader spoke to a gathering of state-farm officials, and indicated his preference that these lands be assimilated by the end of 1954. On 15 February, he suggested to a meeting of RSFSR officials that the total be increased to 15 million hectares. On 22 February, in a speech to members of the Communist Youth League, Khrushchev reiterated the goal of 15 million hectares, but called this a minimum, suggesting that the regime aim for an additional 10 million hectares. And all this took place before the February Plenum met to approve the Virgin Lands Program! Nor did Khrushchev's momentum stop at that point. By 5 June, 1954, he was ready to propose to his colleagues in the Presidium a total goal of 30 million hectares, to be assimilated by the end of 1956, and he also broached the topic of turning the Virgin Lands into a permanent breadbasket for the nation, rather than just an emergency, short-term project.[25]

During the second half of 1954 and into 1955, Khrushchev explicitly defended his investment priorities, and took the offensive against Malenkov in order to destroy him politically. This coincided with a further augmentation of the promises and targets to which he sought to commit the political elite. Thus, at the June 1954 Plenum, he defended as realistic the new goal of 30 million hectares.[26] At the January 1955 Plenum, he demanded that agricultural workers aim for a harvest of 10 billion poods of grain per year from the Virgin Lands.[27] In January 1956, the First Secretary proclaimed that the problem of turning the Virgin Lands into a breadbasket had been

[25] For this sequence, see *Stroitel'stvo kommunizma I*, pp. 89, 133, 153, 197, 222; *Pravda*, 21 March, 1954; *Stroitel'stvo kommunizma I*, p. 303.

[26] *Stroitel'stvo kommunizma I*, pp. 329–32.

[27] *Pravda*, 3 February, 1955.

solved, but demanded that attention to the area should not be relaxed, that new, higher sights be set (a demand that was not included in the reprint of the speech published six years later).[28] In the meantime, a new theme along these lines was entering Khrushchev's speeches— the need to extend the scope of development still further eastward, into Siberia. Extolling the "endless expanses" and "incalculable reserves" of Siberia, Khrushchev proposed this as the new frontier for agricultural and industrial development.[29] Indeed, in a speech after the Twentieth Party Congress, the Soviet leader suggested that the Young Communist League recruit 300,000 to 500,000 young people for great construction projects in Siberia, a task he subsequently referred to as the "quickest possible assimilation of the inexhaustible riches of Siberia, the Far East, Kazakhstan and the regions of the North."[30]

Nor did Khrushchev confine this strategy to the issues of grain production and Siberian development. He urged officials to give meat, milk, and trousers—not just ideological phrases—to the public.[31] He expressed his sense of shame that Denmark and Holland, mere specks on the map compared to the Soviet Union, were outstripping his country in total production of dairy products.[32] He demanded that official criteria for the evaluation of progress be changed from the self-congratulatory practice of demonstrating how far things had progressed since 1913, to a self-critical posture of comparison with the levels of advanced capitalist countries.[33] Already in July 1954, Khrushchev announced that, by the 1970s, the USSR would supply its population with a range of consumer goods at a level higher than that of the USA.[34] This foreshadowed a steady stream of demands

---

[28] Compare *Pravda*, 22 January, 1956 with *Stroitel'stvo kommunizma II*, p. 181.

[29] *Stroitel'stvo kommunizma I*, pp. 337–8; see also his discussion of the matter at the Twentieth Party Congress (Gruliow, *Current Soviet Policies II*, pp. 41–2).

[30] *Pravda*, 13 April, 1956; *Komsomol'skaia Pravda*, 7 June, 1956 (*CDSP*, vol. 8, no. 23, p. 9). Moreover, Khrushchev continued to use public forums in calling for higher targets for assimilating new lands (*Stroitel'stvo kommunizma II*, pp. 253, 273–6).

[31] *Stroitel'stvo kommunizma II*, pp. 126–7.

[32] *Stroitel'stvo kommunizma I*, p. 343; *Stroitel'stvo kommunizma II*, p. 26.

[33] "Our people must live better than working people in the most developed capitalist countries. Of course, it is important to remember the point at which we started. Tsarist Russia did not leave us a rich inheritance. But, comrades, we are already in the thirty-eighth year of Soviet power. This is no small time span. This means it is shameful for us to cite Nicholas II at this time, for he is long since dead" (*Stroitel'stvo kommunizma II*, p. 27). For additional emphasis on cross-national standards of comparison, see *ibid.*, pp. 145–6; and *Stroitel'stvo kommunizma I*, pp. 99–100, 219.

[34] *Stroitel'stvo kommunizma I*, p. 358.

during 1955–6, as Khrushchev announced and pressed a campaign for Soviet agriculture to compete with the USA in the production of meat, milk, and butter.[35] Undoubtedly, Khrushchev's penchant for steadily raising targets and launching bold new ventures enabled him to seize the initiative from his colleagues, to generate enthusiasm among those sharing his optimistic perspectives, and to project himself as a national hero, capable of leading the nation out of the agricultural crisis. But the behaviour of the First Secretary also raised serious apprehensions and objections within the political elite. Khrushchev's response was consistent with his confrontational inclinations: he humiliated and chided doubting colleagues in public.[36]

A final component of Khrushchev's authority-building strategy was an attempt to increase official sense of dependence upon him for leadership by playing upon elite fears of the masses. Malenkov, too, had sought to exploit these fears for personal political gain, for in his August 1953 Supreme Soviet address outlining his consumer goods and agricultural programs, he noted that the people had a "right to demand consumer goods of high quality."[37] Khrushchev did not try to advance a similar argument in his September 1953 speech outlining his agricultural program. But once the very poor harvest of 1953 had gone on record, Khrushchev stole this issue from Malenkov as well, arguing in a memorandum to the Presidium that the existing gap between supply and demand for agricultural products was large and serious.[38] He then took this line of argumentation to the Central Committee Plenum which met to discuss the Virgin Lands Program:

> Thus, where Soviet citizens in many cases formerly had to be satisfied with ordinary bread, *they are now asking more and more* for higher grades. The *demand* for sugar, fruit, berries, and grapes *is growing*. Where the working people formerly had to limit consumption of animal products, *they now can and want* to consume more meat, butter, milk, and eggs. . . . Can we cope with the task of putting 13,000,000 hectares of land under cultivation in such a short time? Yes, we can and *we must*.[39] (Italics added)

Nor was this simply a message for the Central Committee. At numerous forums during these years in front of a variety of mass and

35 *Stroitel'stvo kommunizma II*, pp. 58, 69, 118, 222–89 *passim*; Gruliow, *Current Soviet Policies II*, p. 45; *Pravda*, 19 May, 1955, 13 April, 1956, and 1 August, 1956; *CDSP*, vol. 8, no. 23 (June 1956), pp. 8–10.
36 For Khrushchev's public humiliation of Anastas Mikoyan, see *Stroitel'stvo kommunizma II*, pp. 272–3; for his public chiding of Madame Furtseva, see *CDSP*, vol. 8, no 23 (June 1956), p. 9.
37 *Pravda*, 9 August, 1953.
38 *Stroitel'stvo kommunizma I*, pp. 85–8.
39 *Pravda*, 21 March, 1954 (*CDSP*, vol. 6, no. 12).

official constituencies, Khrushchev encouraged the elevation of mass consumer expectations (for example, "these are legitimate demands"),[40] and warned officials of the dangers inherent in failing to meet those demands.[41]

Once Khrushchev had seized the initiative on behalf of an emergency program, further invocation of the spectre of the mass mood would logically work to his political benefit. That this was the conclusion drawn by rival Soviet leaders became clear in March 1954, when each addressed his electoral constituents and, as we have seen, polemicized over the tasks of the regime with respect to consumer satisfaction. Khrushchev continued to define the task as one of meeting *subjective* requirements, demanding that the party "abundantly satisfy the public's demand." In contrast, Malenkov avoided such terminology, opting for *objective* indicators of progress by demanding "first a sufficiency and then an abundance of all food products . . . [and] a sharp increase in consumer goods production."[42]

But Khrushchev could not escape the entanglements of the web he was weaving. The very process of augmenting elite dependence upon the leader was simultaneously increasing the leader's dependence upon the workers, peasants, and local officials. For without their cooperation, Khrushchev's development strategy could not work and his credibility as an indispensable leader could not be maintained. His efforts to stimulate mass expectations therefore served the dual purpose of pressuring the elite and attempting to inspire mass labor contributions through a promise of imminent abundance as a payoff for hard work. Hence, throughout the period in question, Khrushchev traveled around the country, exhorting the masses, cajoling local officials, and turning up the pressure for extraordinary results. He exploited this atmosphere by constantly giving detailed agronomic advice on how to achieve those results without heavy funding from the center. And this was surely part of his effort to demonstrate his indispensability. But he also felt the need to impose such agronomic schemes at this point, given the logic of interaction between his image as problem-solver and his image as politician. Khrushchev's intense, personal involvement in agricultural affairs is usually explained as a product of his personality, but the explanation is incomplete. For Khrushchev was now dependent upon the masses and local officials to produce the results required to maintain his credibility within the political elite.

[40] *Stroitel'stvo kommunizma I*, p. 135.

[41] *ibid.*, pp. 154, 220–1, 330–1, 342–3, 357; *Pravda*, 24 December, 1954, 28 December, 1954 and 3 February, 1955; *Stroitel'stvo kommunizma II*, pp. 38, 118, 137; Khrushchev, *Khrushchev Remembers*, Vol. 2, pp. 100–2, 118–19, 139, 146.

[42] *Pravda*, 7 March, 1954, and 13 March, 1954.

3 Political Succession and Administrative Reform, 1953-7

The command economy established during the Stalin era was geared toward controlling, industrializing, transforming, and (after World War II) reconstructing the country in the shortest time possible.[1] The system was highly centralized and based on extraordinary pressure. Local officials' tasks were prescribed in detail from the center, while the penalty for failure could range as high as death.

Such a system of administrative control worked reasonably well in advancing the goals of the 1930s and 1940s. However, once mass consumer satisfaction, product quality, and advanced technological innovation became operative goals of the Soviet leadership during the post-Stalin era, the authorities felt the need to search for new approaches to administrative organization and control. And once terror was abandoned as a system of rule, Soviet leaders had to redefine their political relationship with the party and state officials who administered the Soviet economy.

What type of administrative reform might be enacted, however, was an open question. A comparison of speeches by Khrushchev, Malenkov, Kaganovich, and Bulganin during 1953-5 reveals a consensus on the need to rationalize the supercentralized command economy inherited from Stalin.[2] They all regularly endorsed the need for greater devolution of responsibility for day-to-day decision-making, rationalization of the administration of planning and supply, and a reduction in the size of the bloated administrative apparatus. They all railed against red tape and assorted bureaucratic maladies. But beyond this highly generalized consensus on behalf of streamlining public administration, the leadership was split over how to deal with the dilemmas of administrative reform: (1) What kinds of reform are most likely to increase efficiency without undercutting the primacy of central planning? (2) What should be the balance of party inter-

---

[1] The term, "command economy," is from Gregory Grossman, "Notes for a theory of the command economy," *Soviet Studies* (October 1963), pp. 101–23, and refers to an economic order in which the firm is charged with executing detailed directives passed down from above.

[2] Khrushchev's speeches will be be cited more fully below. The other speeches in question are by Malenkov (*Pravda*, 9 August, 1953, 13 March, 1954, and 27 April, 1954); Kaganovich (ibid., 13 March, 1954, 27 April, 1954, 24 May, 1954, and 7 November, 1955); and Bulganin (ibid., 11 March, 1954, 17 May, 1955, and 17 July, 1955).

vention versus material incentives as spurs to managerial initiative? (3) What level of pressure on managerial and ministerial personnel is required to elicit plan fulfillment and technological innovation?[3]

Georgi Malenkov and his supporters opted for an approach to these dilemmas that stood in sharp contrast to Khrushchev's. Beyond endorsing the consensus on behalf of limited devolution and rationalization of the ministerial structure, they called for a reduction of pressure on managers, a posture of regime accommodation with officialdom, and restraints on party intervention in managerial affairs.

Khrushchev seized the initiative on administrative reform, proposing an alternative that would protect the "leading role of the party." Khrushchev sought to demonstrate that significant devolution of decision-making to the locales could be combined with increased local party activism, with high pressure for results, and with high penalties for failure. He rejected any blanket accommodation with officialdom, arguing that such an approach would maintain administrative stagnation. And he sought to mold the issue in ways that would highlight his personal indispensability as a leader who could solve the problem of administrative efficiency without paying too high a price in party values.

The "Technocratic" Impulse

Georgi Malenkov and his associates had relatively little of note to say about administrative reform beyond the consensus on behalf of streamlining and rationalizing the ministerial and planning bureaucracies. But this in itself was significant, for the problem-solving perspectives they advocated were vulnerable to the charge of being "technocratic." They emphasized streamlining the state bureaucracy, rather than augmenting the interventionist role of party organs. They implied that rationalization of the managerial apparatus would proceed through measures to improve the quality of central planning, reduce irrational pressures on managerial personnel, and improve existing bureaucratic monitoring devices. They did acknowledge the need for a certain measure of devolution of decision-making responsibility within the state bureaucracy (indeed, this was a component of the post-Stalin consensus on administrative affairs). And N. Bulganin did advocate expanded rights for enterprise managers vis-à-vis their

[3] The level of pressure is distinct from the level of centralism in an administrative hierarchy. See Herbert Levine, "Pressure and planning in the Soviet economy," in Henry Rosovsky (ed.), *Industrialization in Two Systems: Essays in Honor of Alexander Gerschenkron* (New York: Wiley, 1966). The level of pressure is a product of the relationship between demands placed on executives and the resources available to meet those demands, as well as the severity of the punishment for failure to fulfill the plan.

ministerial superiors. But the scope of such rights was not spelled out; nor were the implications for limited marketization of the economy. The result was that those leaders responsible for industrial administration during the political succession struggle lacked a problem-solving strategy that was either sufficiently far-reaching to markedly increase administrative efficiency or, failing this, sufficiently in tune with the Soviet tradition of political intervention.

The political strategy embraced by these leaders was accommodative and consensual. They advocated a new era of reconciliation with Soviet officialdom. In contrast to the ethos of the Nineteenth Party Congress (October 1952), at which accusations against officials of "anti-state" behavior and "crimes against the people" had been legion,[4] neither Malenkov, Kaganovich, nor Bulganin, during March 1953–Spring 1957, ever publicly accused Soviet officials of anti-state behavior in the course of criticizing bureaucratic problems. Moreover, none of them called for the "criticism from below" that had been so heavily emphasized in 1952. None called for widespread purging of incompetent or dishonest officials. And none went so far in the criticism of defects as to imply that bureaucracy was an entrenched phenomenon requiring unusual methods for its eradication. Rather, by what they failed to say, they were implying that rationalization of the managerial apparatus would proceed through measures to ensure the political and personal security of state and party officials. Thus, Kaganovich assured the Supreme Soviet that "we are struggling legally against bureaucratism"[5] (that is, through the strengthening of administrative law, rather than through purge mechanisms); and he stressed "self-criticism" over criticism from below in his speech to a conference of railwaymen.[6] Similarly, Malenkov and Bulganin praised managerial personnel as "commanders of production."[7] Their chosen political constituency clearly lay within the state apparatus, as many scholars have noted, but they were also implicitly offering security to party officials as well—perhaps to compensate for a reduction in those officials' interventionist prerogatives. This political strategy of "no more purging" must have had its appeals, but it must also have raised doubts about just how effective it would be in overcoming the stultification of public administration bequeathed by Stalin. Khrushchev seized on these doubts, exploiting the vulnerabilities, and seizing the initiative with a program that placed political intervention and administrative transformation at the center of attention.

---

[4] For such accusations at the Nineteenth Party Congress, see Gruliow, *Current Soviet Policies I*, pp. 108, 113, 117–19, 135–6.

[5] *Pravda*, 27 April, 1954.

[6] ibid., 24 May, 1954.

[7] ibid., 27 April, 1954 (Malenkov); 17 July, 1955 (Bulganin).

The Khrushchevian Alternative

The bulk of Khrushchev's statements on administrative reform during this period dwelled on the area for which he had assumed personal responsibility: agriculture. His problem-solving strategy in that sector called for a combination of limited regionalization and intensified political pressure on managers.

According to Khrushchev, the most troubling consequence of administrative rigidification in the rural sector had been the extreme stifling of local initiative among party and state officials. His speeches during these years were filled with exhortations and threats, demanding that officials exercise initiative and accept responsibility for ambitious tasks, involving themselves in concrete production and mobilization activities, rather than exercising "leadership from the desk," based on "administrative fiat," "general formulae," and "superficial instructions."[8] He called upon local officials to broaden their horizons, adopting an inter-branch, regional focus that had been discouraged by the vertical, compartmentalized system of ministerial rule. He constantly urged local party officials to travel to model farms in the district, region, or republic, learn the details of the most up-to-date production techniques, and diffuse those innovations to backward farms in their districts.[9] This was the way to tap the nation's "inexhaustible reserves," and to bring closer the era of abundance.

To be sure, these officials were expected to attend first of all to governmental priorities, as expressed in directives and plans sent down from Moscow. But Khrushchev made efforts to diminish the flow of detailed, short-term directives from the State Planning Committee and the Ministry of Agriculture, and to induce local officials to combine short-term considerations with sustained attention to the long-term development of economic units for which they were responsible. Thus, he was attempting to restructure the vertical link between local and central officials of the state bureaucracy, in order to induce authentic local initiative. As he once declared in apparent exasperation, "does there have to be a government order even on this?"[10]

Yet Khrushchev did not claim that managerial autonomy was a prerequisite for local initiative—quite the contrary. To the extent that he was seeking to reduce vertical forms of centralization, he was

[8] For Khrushchev's critique of dependency at this time, see the sources cited in Chapter 2, note 20. The other themes run persistently through his speeches in this period. For example, see his major plenary session addresses (*Pravda*, 15 September, 1953, 21 March, 1954, and 3 February, 1955); see also *Stroitel'stvo kommunizma I*, pp. 111–12, 170–2, 204, 310, 387–8; *Stroitel'stvo kommunizma II*, pp. 36, 57–8, 74–5, 78, 88, 163–4.

[9] *Pravda*, 15 September, 1953; *Stroitel'stvo kommunizma I*, pp. 183, 216, 271, 278–9; *Stroitel'stvo kommunizma II*, pp. 87, 96–7.

[10] *Pravda*, 21 March, 1954.

also seeking to increase horizontal centralization at the local level. Khrushchev demanded that local party officials "penetrate deeply into collective farm affairs," that they give "concrete and comprehensive guidance" to farm officials, and that they get "closer to production":

> We should forbid district [party] workers to write directives or compose general instructions; we should see to it that they spend time in the collective farms and organize people at *real* work [*na zhivoe delo*]. Then they will know well the state of affairs in each economic unit, and will be able to adopt measures rapidly and on the spot.[11]

Strengthening the horizontal link at the expense of the vertical also informed the type of administrative reform toward which Khrushchev was leaning during these years.[12] In contrast to his colleagues' more centralist approach, the First Secretary was speaking in regional terms. His constant references to getting "closer to production" meant more than just party activism at the local levels. They also referred to the transfer of personnel from upper to lower levels of the bureaucracy, the transfer of chief administrations and trusts from Moscow to the provinces and regions they were charged with supervising, the transfer of scientific research institutes to the countryside or to the provinces, and the shifting of regional coordinative personnel to the primary economic units for the sake of closer supervision of day-to-day affairs.[13]

Moreover, Khrushchev spoke often of the need for regions to become self-sufficient in the production of certain agricultural products or implements, so as to cut down on transportation costs and on interbranch coordination problems.[14] All of which was entirely consistent with a strategy of agricultural development that called for the farms to become richer until they could finance their own further development. "Local initiative" complemented the need for party officials to "penetrate" the economy, get "closer to production," and offer "concrete guidance," thereby fostering agricultural self-reliance based upon the exploitation of "inexhaustible reserves."

[11] *Stroitel'stvo kommunizma I*, pp. 192–3. For analogous demands for administrative "penetration," "concrete guidance," etc., see ibid., pp. 189, 216, 271, 277–80, 321–2, 398–9, 480, 487–8; *Pravda*, 15 September, 1953, and 21 March 1954; *Stroitel'stvo kommunizma II*, pp. 74–5, 87, 94, 117–18.

[12] The image of Soviet managers being subject to both "vertical" and "horizontal" sources of control is borrowed from Yanov, *Detente after Brezhnev*.

[13] See *Pravda*, 15 September, 1953, and 21 March, 1954; *Stroitel'stvo kommunizma I*, pp. 124, 192–4, 277.

[14] See *Stroitel'stvo kommunizma I*, pp. 397–408; *Stroitel'stvo kommunizma II*, pp. 151–2, 166, 249.

The exploitation of those reserves implied a continuing commitment to ambitious plans and high pressure for results, even though that pressure would now be channeled from the center through the local party organs. Given this commitment, recruitment of able, energetic officials was only the first step toward ensuring administrative responsibility. What came next was the establishment of a system of administrative monitoring that would ensure against malfeasance on the part of local state and party officials. On this score, Khrushchev echoed the Stalinist distrust of bureaucrats, while his advocacy of regionalization without genuine decentralization increased the need for new methods to monitor the behavior of local officialdom.[15]

Khrushchev's solution was to pinpoint the specific responsibilities of all local officials, increase their visibility, and hold them strictly accountable for meeting their responsibilities. Such a goal was a constant source of frustration for Khrushchev in trying to disentangle the morass of conflicting and overlapping jurisdictions inherited from Stalin.[16] In contrast to his colleagues, though, Khrushchev's prescription for ensuring such responsibility involved not only clarification of jurisdictions and improvement of bureaucratic monitoring techniques, but also mobilization of the masses against officials of both the party and the state.

While his colleagues spoke of the need for expanded "criticism" and "self-criticism," Khrushchev continued the Stalinist call for criticism "from below."[17] This demand was backed up by speeches to more restricted audiences, at which Khrushchev often called upon the masses to criticize their hierarchical superiors, promising them political support if they did so: "If your leaders are bad, it is your own fault. You pester your leaders very little; you don't demand that they work well."[18] Or in reference to leaders of Machine Tractor Stations (MTS): "It is necessary to struggle against such evil, and at the forefront of the struggle must stand the chief agronomist of the MTS with the entire army of collective farm agronomists, brigade leaders, and collective farm chairmen. We shall always be on their side . . ."[19]

Indeed, Khrushchev almost always was on their side. The Soviet leader's innumerable trips into the countryside were consistent with

[15] Thus, Khrushchev was advocating a regional *deconcentration* of public administration. See Chapter 1, note 5.

[16] *Pravda*, 15 September, 1953. See also *Stroitel'stvo kommunizma I*, pp. 106–7, 122–3, 311–12, 387–8, 391–2, 400, 481–2; *Stroitel'stvo kommunizma II*, pp. 9, 36, 100; *Pravda*, 21 March, 1954.

[17] In his March 1954 election speech (*Pravda*, 7 March, 1954).

[18] *Stroitel'stvo kommunizma I*, p. 203.

[19] ibid., pp. 110–11. See also *Stroitel'stvo kommunizma II*, pp. 112, 235; *Pravda*, 22 January, 1956.

his energetic personality. But they were also consistent with his claim that criticism from below would have to be combined with constant pressure from above in order to root out "that great evil—bureaucratism."[20] Given his rivals' posture of reconciliation with officialdom, Khrushchev was distinguishing himself with a more confrontational approach that required the authoritative interventions from above that he proposed to supply.

Thus, his speeches during this period were filled with personal accusations against individual officials, and he made frequent use of the words, "guilt," "guilty," and "guilty ones" in searching for the causes of specific failures.[21] Only rarely did he acknowledge that some failures might be in the nature of the task or a result of contradictory pressures. This would have been a concession to those who found excuses in "objective conditions,"[22] and would have reduced his personal indispensability as an "inspector general," while also reducing the legitimacy of local party intervention in managerial affairs. The main task was now to pressure officials into a sense of personal responsibility and a position of visibility, and thereby to foster the initiative required for the great goals envisaged: "Once we shake-up the officials—and we must do this—then you will see what the land of this vast district is capable of."[23] The assumption was that this would be sufficient to prevent Soviet cadres from experiencing the fate of Comrade I. A. Benediktov who, Khrushchev argued, had lost his capacity for initiative and innovation once he became Minister of Agriculture, despite the fact that he had been trained as an agronomist. How had this happened? Khrushchev supplied the answer: "Evidently bureaucracy sucked him in."[24]

In sum, Khrushchev refused to play the politics of accommodation and reconciliation with officials of the state bureaucracy. Instead, the First Secretary continued the Stalinist equation of deviance with sabotage. Thus, in his reports to the September 1953 and February 1954 Plenums, he characterized bureaucratic deviance as "anti-state" behavior.[25] And in the vast majority of the times that he spoke of

---

[20] *Pravda*, 21 March, 1954.
[21] For personalized explanations of bottlenecks, see *Stroitel'stvo kommunizma I*, pp. 146–7, 157, 163, 167, 170, 312–13, 327, 400; *Stroitel'stvo kommunizma II*, pp. 6, 63, 189. For specific examples of his use of the terms, "guilt" and "punishment," see ibid., pp. 63, 189; *Stroitel'stvo kommunizma I*, pp. 312–13, 322, 483.
[22] For a rare case of such a concession, see *Stroitel'stvo kommunizma I*, pp. 351–6.
[23] ibid., p. 204.
[24] *Pravda*, 21 March, 1954.
[25] *Pravda*, 15 September, 1953, and 21 March, 1954.

the options during this period, Khrushchev demanded that incompetent or dishonest officials be fired rather than retrained.[26]

This was not a full-scale continuation of the line of the Nineteenth Party Congress, however, for Khrushchev did not direct any accusations of anti-state behavior at the party apparatus—only the ministries associated with agriculture. Nor did he call for large-scale replacement of party officials, or accuse the party apparatus of the degree of corporate protectionism and bureaucratic entrenchment of which he accused the ministerial apparatus. While he had many harsh words to say about party officials who avoided responsibility, lacked initiative, or defended their personal comforts, and while he sought to pressure local party officials from above and below, he did not define the party as an entrenched bureaucracy requiring extraordinary methods for the elimination of defects.

Moreover, Khrushchev had chosen his political constituency. His struggle against the ministries was a component of his effort to weaken his Presidium-level rivals, who were attempting to consolidate a political base within the state bureaucracy. But such an explanation, while illuminating, is also incomplete, for its highlights only the institutional coalition-building features of Khrushchev's strategy. Khrushchev was also arguing on behalf of his effectiveness as a problem-solver. His claims about what was needed to increase consumer satisfaction, release local initiative, and improve administrative efficiency were consistent with his claim that the party apparatus could be used as an instrument for breaking through bureaucratic inertia in the state bureaucracy, making public administration a more flexible instrument of mobilization, and bringing administrators closer to production.

Industrial Administration and the Twentieth Party Congress

Khrushchev did not often speak publicly about industrial administration during 1953–5, but when he did, his statements were in obvious contrast to those of his colleagues, and mirrored the authority-building strategy outlined regarding agricultural affairs. Thus, in his March 1954 election speech, the First Secretary offered generalizations about

---

[26] *Stroitel'stvo kommunizma I*, pp. 102–3, 114, 314, 348; *Stroitel'stvo kommunizma II*, pp. 10, 37, 175, 225; *Pravda*, 7 March, 1954. Khrushchev's memoirs generally support the portrait of Khrushchev's approach to administration outlined in this chapter. On his frustration with overbureaucratization before 1953, see *Khrushchev Remembers*, Vol. 1, pp. 168, 184–6, 191, 193, 196, 232–3; and *Khrushchev Remembers*, Vol. 2, pp. 115–16, 152. On his frustration with overbureaucratization after 1953, see Vol. 2, pp. 124, 131, 133. In addition, see Vol. 1, pp. 32, 117, 182, 242, 250, 390.

bureaucracy which implied that it was a systemic phenomenon.[27] He attacked the "machinery of the state," demanded that criticism of officials be expanded, but "especially criticism from below," and insisted that "such officials must decidedly be got rid of." None of these themes appeared in Malenkov's election speech, for he merely offered a generalized acknowledgment of the need to expose and struggle to eliminate "shortcomings, . . . backwardness and neglect wherever they exist in our socialist construction," noted the need for greater self-criticism, and added one tepid paragraph about the need to perfect the state apparatus which still had "bureaucratic distortions in its work."[28]

Furthermore, in addresses to industrial conferences during December 1954 and May 1955, Khrushchev never used the term "commanders of production" in speaking of enterprise managers (in contrast to Malenkov and Kaganovich).[29] Nor did he endorse Kaganovich's notion that the struggle against bureaucratism was being conducted "legally." And Khrushchev's depiction of the desired type of industrial reform differed conspicuously from that suggested by his colleagues in 1955–6. In contrast to Bulganin's advocacy of expanded rights for enterprise managers vis-à-vis their ministerial superiors,[30] and in contrast to others' advocacy of technocratic rationalization of ministerial planning, Khrushchev called for regional foundries and supply depots, as well as improved regional planning, as the bases for administrative reform[31]—a suggestion that paralleled similar emphases in his discussions of agricultural needs.

But the level of conflict between Khrushchev and his rivals on questions of administrative reform was tempered during 1953–5 by a division of labor within the leadership. Khrushchev was apparently given a relatively free hand in agricultural affairs, in exchange for his deferring to Malenkov, Bulganin, and Kaganovich on matters of industrial administration. This placed limits on Khrushchev's ability to build his authority by seizing the initiative with a program that synthesized new approaches with traditional ones. By 1956, however, Khrushchev felt strong enough to expand his role decisively into the industrial realm, and to seize the initiative there as well. He did this at the Twentieth Party Congress, in February of that year.

At the Party Congress, Khrushchev spoke at length about industrial administration, in terms that echoed his statements of earlier years on agricultural administration.[32] But he also went a step further, now

27 *Pravda*, 7 March, 1954.
28 ibid., 13 March, 1954.
29 ibid., 28 December, 1954, and 19 May, 1955.
30 ibid., 17 May, 1955, and 19 July, 1955 (speeches by Bulganin).
31 ibid., 19 May, 1955.
32 Gruliow, *Current Soviet Policies II*, pp. 39, 54, 56.

incorporating a demand that party officials study and master the economics of industrial and agricultural management.[33] If administrative efficiency was to result from greater party intervention in managerial affairs, the credibility of such a problem-solving strategy would hinge on the technical-economic skills of the interveners. Given the low level of economic literacy among the Stalinist generation of party officials, many managers, specialists, and central leaders could legitimately have wondered how greater authority for that generation of apparatchiki would improve economic performance. Khrushchev preempted the issue—and the criticism—with his demand for sharply upgrading the skills of the apparat.

But this left open a critical political consideration: how would such a change in orientations and competence be brought about—through replacement or retraining? And if it was to occur through replacement, would this take place slowly, by attrition, or rapidly and on a large scale? If by attrition, how would Khrushchev reconcile such largesse with his promises of economic abundance in the near future? Khrushchev did not address these questions directly in his main speech to the congress. Indeed, for all his criticism of party and state administration, he did not publicly accuse anyone of "anti-state behavior." It remained far from clear how he was going to reconcile such a posture with his problem-solving strategy.

The secret speech after the congress provided the answer.[34] That speech, by attacking Stalin's treatment of the party, has been interpreted by some scholars as an assurance to the political elite that Stalinist methods of administrative and political control would no longer be employed.[35] At the same time, the speech has been interpreted by others as an attack on local party secretaries ("little Stalins" within their domains), whose rudimentary economic skills, exclusivist political orientations, and entrenched positions were justified by Stalinist doctrine, and who could only be dislodged by an attack on that doctrine.[36] Finally, the speech has been viewed simply as a power play by Khrushchev, designed to keep his rivals off balance and to discredit them for their roles at the center of the Stalinist system.[37]

We should be suspicious of monocausal explanations. For a recon-

---

[33] ibid., p. 57.

[34] The speech was never published in the USSR, but was leaked to Western sources. A translation of the accepted version is available in ibid., pp. 172–88.

[35] Friedgut, *Political Participation*, p. 298, fn. 14; Arrigo Levi, "The evolution of the Soviet system," in Zbigniew Brzezinski (ed.), *Dilemmas of Change in Soviet Politics* (New York: Columbia University Press, 1969), p. 139.

[36] Leonhard, *Kremlin since Stalin*, pp. 184–92.

ciliation of these interpretations is possible, on the basis of a more complex appreciation of Khrushchev's authority-building strategy. The secret speech implied a new era of *physical security* for Soviet officialdom as a whole, when political demotion would no longer imply physical extermination. But it also implied an era of *political insecurity* for entrenched Stalinist administrators in the party, state, and police apparatuses. Unlike his colleagues in the leadership, Khrushchev claimed to see a fundamental contradiction between the skills, orientations, and entrenched power of Stalinist officials and the new tasks on the policy agenda. He argued the need for a political break-through[38] to overcome the measured and contradictory changes of 1953-5, and was offering himself as the leader with both the vision and the power to combine limited reconciliation, institutional trans-formation, and a sense of national purpose. The secret of Khrushchev's authority-building strategy lay in his simultaneous commitment to reassuring, inspiring, *and* transforming Soviet officialdom.

[37] Jerry Hough and Merle Fainsod, *How the Soviet Union is Governed* (Cambridge, Mass.: Harvard University Press, 1979), p. 214; Conquest, *Power and Policy in the USSR*, pp. 278-87.

[38] The concept of "breakthrough" was first introduced into Soviet studies in Kenneth Jowitt, *Revolutionary Breakthroughs and National Development* (Berkeley, Calif.: University of California Press, 1971).

4 Political Succession and Political Participation, 1953-7

Under Stalin, ultimate political power rested largely in the hands of the dictator himself. However, Soviet officials, within their domains, exercised extensive power over the masses in the implementation of national policy. The regime made a conscious effort to insulate factory and farm officials from excessive "familiarity" with the masses, in order to prevent "liberalism" in their treatment of the working masses.[1] And the secret police, assisted by detailed bureaucratic controls, attempted to minimize the average citizen's independent political initiative.

The views instilled in Soviet officials supported such a posture of avoidance and command. It was taken for granted in Stalinist doctrine that liberalization of controls was a risky proposition, and that many citizens could not be trusted to advance regime goals in the absence of pressure. Fear of the masses was accompanied by distrust of the critical instincts of the cultural intelligentsia, and a similar fear of free inquiry in the social, and many of the natural, sciences.

Stalin's successors were largely in agreement on the need to transform this atmosphere and to redefine the terms of participation in public affairs for politically conformist specialists and masses. Differences among Soviet leaders revolved around their conceptions of how to reconcile expanded political participation with protection of the prerogatives and authority of state and party officials.[2] Specifically: (1) How does one reconcile encouragement of expanded popular initiative with protection of the right of Soviet officials to regulate and channel that initiative? (2) How does one reconcile expanded input, feedback, and criticism with protection of the right of party officials to define the goals and direction of policy? (3) How does one encourage citizens to exercise their new rights vis-à-vis executive authority while simultaneously discouraging an adversarial relationship between citizens and their hierarchical superiors? In sum, the fundamental question was whether the party leadership would allow expanded political participation after Stalin to evolve in an anti-elitist direction, or whether it would strive primarily to keep

[1] See "Against familiarity on the job," *Trud*, 5 August, 1952 (*CDSP*, vol. 4, no. 32).

[2] The concept, "expanding political participation," is from Solomon, *Soviet Criminologists and Criminal Policy*, ch. 3.

expanded participation within bounds that protected the political and bureaucratic authority of officialdom.

Malenkov and his associates opted for the more conservative, elitist approach to the issue. Khrushchev, in contrast, attempted to seize the initiative by encouraging anti-elitist forces, by arguing that such a popular surge was necessary for realizing Soviet economic goals, by claiming that such a surge would not get out of hand and threaten political stability, and by offering himself as the leader with the combination of brains, determination, toughness, and risk-taking ability required to preside over such a balance between expanded participation and the maintenance of control.

The Conservative Impulse

During these years, Malenkov, Kaganovich, and Bulganin broke with the ethos of late-Stalinism.[3] They no longer stressed the need for vigilance against the internal enemy. They called for expanded criticism and feedback. They acknowledged the need for less secrecy in contemporary life and for a reduction of dogma in order to narrow the gap between Soviet and world science. By implication, they conceded that the "class struggle" was over, that society had been reconstructed, and that the regime could come to peace with the populace. They did not, however, go beyond this. They did not see "coming to peace with the populace" as a process that required more far-reaching changes. If we may judge by what they failed to say in public speeches, they did not view a hierarchical, elitist political structure to be in conflict with the advancement of their socio-economic and political goals. Only Bulganin, in Spring/Summer 1955, came even close to suggesting the need to go further. Thus, in his May 1955 speech to an industrial conference, he observed that "the introduction of a new machine demands tremendous pressure, and not every inventor and designer can muster such pressure."[4] And in his July 1955 Central Committee Plenum address, he made a few modest remarks proposing an expanded role for trade unions in defending workers against labor safety violations.[5] But these statements were exceptions, and are more noteworthy for their limits. They were entirely consistent with an approach that saw no fundamental contradiction between calls for expanded initiative or criticism and prevailing authority relationships.

[3] For citation of the speeches in question, see Chapter 3, note 2.
[4] *Pravda*, 17 May, 1955.
[5] ibid., 17 July, 1955; for an interpretation of these remarks, see Blair Aldridge Ruble, "Soviet trade unions: changing balances in their functions" (unpublished PhD dissertion, University of Toronto, 1977), ch. 3, p. 18.

Khrushchev's Populist Alternative

In searching for ways to solve the agricultural problem, Nikita Khrushchev advanced the claim that problems of economic growth could not be solved without eliciting authentic mass initiative—and he searched for new methods of leadership and mobilization that might elicit such initiative. In the process, he confronted the exclusivist, dogmatic, and heavy-handed orientations of Stalinist officialdom. This led him to argue that the stimulation of authentic popular initiative could not be accomplished without a far-reaching redefinition of authority relationships. In contrast to Stalin, Khrushchev was more interested in stimulating the growth of Soviet agriculture than in reinforcing existing political controls. And, in contrast to Malenkov, he felt it necessary publicly to confront issues of political status in order to expand political participation and foster economic progress.

The issue, according to Khrushchev, was one of trust: could the new socialist society be trusted to exercise "creative initiative" without threatening political stability? And if it could, how would political relationships throughout the system be affected by such initiative?

In the case of the peasantry, Khrushchev argued that the regime could no longer afford to base its relationship with the peasant on forced exploitation, confiscation, and neglect. Establishing a national commitment to rural development required a dilution of the Stalinist distrust of peasant initiative which, in turn, required an attack on prevailing notions about the political status of the Soviet peasantry. Thus, in trying to get urban Communists to work in the countryside, Khrushchev criticized the "lordly and bureaucratic attitude toward the village which has arisen among some Communists."[6] In trying to legitimize a reduction of restrictions on the private sector, he chastised those who believed that private peasant livestock "can constitute any sort of danger to the socialist system."[7] In attempting to prevent local officials from confiscating the seed reserves of collective farmers, Khrushchev pointed out that "we have long since been without a kulak class in the countryside."[8] And in trying to reduce detailed central control in order to release local initiative, Khrushchev criticized those who saw this as one step toward "private peasant farming."[9]

Khrushchev also argued that a redefinition of political relationships was necessary for the success of his program of agricultural development. His notion that almost any farm could be brought up to the

---

[6] *Pravda*, 15 September, 1953; for analogous statements, see *Stroitel'stvo kommunizma I*, p. 180; *Stroitel'stvo kommunizma II*, p. 91.

[7] *Pravda*, 15 September, 1953.

[8] *Stroitel'stvo kommunizma I*, p. 319.

[9] *Stroitel'stvo kommunizma II*, p. 106.

level of the most advanced presumed a fundamental change in methods of political leadership in the countryside. Thus, he called upon Soviet officials to abandon "rule by fiat" and "commandism," and to create an enthusiastic, involved citizenry through "individual work with people."[10] In contrast to the Stalinist dictum against excessive "familiarity" with the workers, Khrushchev called upon officials to get closer to the masses, to explain things to them "directly and tactfully," and to emphasize human solidarity rather than avoidance.[11]

Here, then, was the key to synthesizing Khrushchev's continuing commitment to political control with his proposed vision of an active, voluntarily hard-working population: the debureaucratization of local leadership. Khrushchev argued that he could mold Soviet officialdom into a more effective mobilizing agent by purging it of its bureaucratic-statist features, by reducing the social and political distance between leaders and led, and by encouraging the masses to be more critical of their hierarchical superiors. This was certainly consistent with his desire to undermine the political base of his opponents in the Presidium. But Khrushchev's purposes went far beyond purely power considerations. As a problem-solver, he advanced rather clear ideas about what kinds of changes were needed to improve the effectiveness of the political system in inspiring the citizenry and delivering the goods. As he defined it, his program required changes in the terms of political participation of a populist sort. Moreover, Khrushchev's opponents built their political support in the state bureaucracy; yet Khrushchev was not hesitant to attack local party officials as well as state bureaucrats as part of his program for revitalizing the political order.[12]

His efforts to modernize Soviet agriculture led Khrushchev to adopt similar positions regarding the rural intelligentsia. The First Secretary argued that Soviet agriculture could not be radically improved without a greater decision-making role for the rural intelligentsia.[13] But Khrushchev also expressed skepticism about the

---

[10] *Pravda*, 21 March, 1954 (The Virgin Lands Program).

[11] "The collective farmer and the MTS or state farm employee . . . want to share with him their thoughts and concerns, to talk about their needs and to receive necessary help. Inattentiveness to a person is the greatest insult. Where Party leaders forget this, many shortcomings arise" (*Stroitel'stvo kommunizma I*, p. 489). For analogous examples during this period, see ibid., pp. 126, 142, 178–9, 182–3, 192, 205, 279, 394–5, 490–2; *Stroitel'stvo kommunizma II*, p. 65; *Pravda*, 5 September, 1953, and 21 March, 1954.

[12] The characterization of Khrushchev's regime as one of "revitalization" can be found in Hough and Fainsod, *How the Soviet Union Is Governed*, ch. 6.

[13] See *Pravda*, 15 September, 1953; *Stroitel'stvo kommunizma I*, pp. 189–90, 323; *Pravda*, 3 February, 1955.

willingness of rural officials to heed the advice of specialists. Accordingly, he argued that only a redefinition of the relative political status of specialists and officials could advance his economic goals. All of which led Khrushchev to articulate during these years a virtually adversarial conception of the relationship between rural specialists and rural officials.

Thus, at the September 1953 Plenum, Khrushchev advocated removing the chief agronomist of the Machine Tractor Station (MTS) from formal subordination to that symbol of political control, the MTS director.[14] Four months later, he called for the chief agronomist to be given the formal right to supervise the work of the MTS, broadcasting his faith that specialists would be more genuinely interested in production advances.[15] And, in keeping with his distinctive approach to administrative control, Khrushchev went one step further, advocating a popular upsurge, led by rural specialists, that would struggle against inertial tendencies among all local officials—party, state, and MTS leaders alike.[16]

Here, then, was the corollary of Khrushchev's claim that bureaucracy would "suck in" even the most enthusiastic and dedicated party and state officials. The Soviet leader expressed suspicion of information received from local officials, and called upon local party and nonparty activists as his tacit allies. On several occasions he indicated that, in his opinion, local activists were less likely than administrators to conceal capacity and avoid ambitious production targets.[17] This, in turn, reinforced his claim that "inexhaustible reserves" could be tapped through the release of popular initiative.

Khrushchev's ideal conception of decision-making processes at the grass-roots ("closer to production") demanded cooperative problem-solving among talented actors who placed criteria of technical rationality over considerations of official political status. He was publicly impatient with institutional boundaries, ego defense, and other inhibitions to political responsiveness. Thus, listen to him haze Comrade Krivoshein "Why, I ask, don't you go learn from Comrade Filatov? Obviously, Comrade Krivoshein did not want to

---

[14] *Pravda*, 15 September, 1953.

[15] *Stroitel'stvo kommunizma I*, p. 108; see also Khrushchev's follow-up remarks in ibid., pp. 108–10, as well as his comments on the matter in *Pravda*, 3 February, 1955. Thus, in order to expand the *role* of rural specialists, Khrushchev was calling for an increase in their political *status*. This Weberian distinction between role and status has been introduced into communist studies in Jowitt, "Inclusion and mobilization in European Leninist regimes."

[16] *Stoitel'stvo kommunizma I*, pp. 110–11.

[17] *Pravda*, 15 September, 1953, and 21 March, 1954; *Stroitel'stvo kommunizma I*, p. 313; *Stroitel'stvo kommunizma II*, p. 152.

learn. After all, he's a former minister, and he must go to study under a simple agronomist. That would be beneath his dignity."[18]

But such a critique was not limited to state bureaucrats. Khrushchev frequently demanded that local party officials go to the collective farmers and "learn from them," and he denounced the "vanity" of those who considered this a blow to their political status.[19]

Given these demands, and given Khrushchev's simultaneous efforts to improve the structure of material incentives as a spur to production initiative, the First Secretary came to the conclusion that party officials should also be subject to the material-performance principle in evaluations of their work.[20] A party official should be no more exempt from meeting economic performance goals than any other citizen, and his pay should reflect this philosophy. Apparently, there were objections to these proposals by those who felt that party leaders did not need material incentives in light of their higher levels of political consciousness. Khrushchev rejected this argument, declaring: "Party workers are not the only politically conscious [*ideinye*] people among us. Each Soviet person—worker, collective farmer, and member of the intelligentsia—is politically conscious."[21] Thus, evaluating results by the material-performance principle clashed with the corporate exclusiveness of party officials. Elevating the performance principle relative to criteria of political reliability was therefore a leveling process, and a step in the direction of status equalization between apparatchiki, specialists, and social activists.

Populism and Tolerance

Yet even while he argued that Soviet society had been decisively reconstructed, that certain groups' political status had to be raised, and that a new leadership orientation was required, Khrushchev remained committed to central definition of the direction and rate of change, and to party activism as a mechanism for shaping the direction of local initiative. He never publicly idealized the distinctiveness of the peasantry, intelligentsia, or other groups. He would argue for their recognition as citizens who could be trusted to advance regime goals without overt violence and widespread police arrests. But he did not renounce overt coercion as a means of imposing his

[18] *Stroitel'stvo kommunizma I*, p. 178.

[19] *Pravda*, 15 September, 1953; *Stroitel'stvo kommunizma II*, pp. 31, 62, 69, 94, 96–7, 114, 124–5; *Foreign Broadcast Information Service, Daily Report, USSR* (Khrushchev's speech of 30 March, 1955). Curiously, these passages were excised from the version of Khrushchev's 30 March, 1955 speech as published in *Stroitel'stvo kommunizma II*, pp. 47–65, despite the fact that the volume was ultimately published in 1962, at the height of Khrushchev's campaign against political elitism among party officials.

[20] *Stroitel'stvo kommunizma II*, p. 170.

[21] ibid., p. 384.

will on specific issues, or as a means of prosecuting campaigns for social transformation. Stalin had used terror and violence. Khrushchev would sharply reduce the incidence of political arrest, and would rely, to a much greater extent, on moral coercion and social pressure (along with education and material incentives) to realize his goals. The level of autonomy from external intrusions into one's life remained low; what had changed was the type of coercion employed.

Thus, when informed of young people who were resisting the call for "volunteers" for the Virgin Lands, Khrushchev called for the arousal of public opinion against them, such that overwhelming social pressure would make them change their minds.[22] Or when demanding changes in methods of shepherding, he suggested that coercion be used if necessary, since some tasks require it.[23] Indeed, the First Secretary could be quite unabashed about the advocacy of coercion when his personal authority or his ego was involved in an issue. (This was especially the case with resistance to his corn campaign.[24]) And when challenged for being inconsistent, Khrushchev could argue that people's consciousness needed to be rearranged, and that the task had to be approached "boldly."[25] In retrospect, in 1956, he could rationalize that the people of Kalinovka were thanking him for having forced corn upon them.[26]

Khrushchev's inclination to use coercion was reinforced by the authority-building strategy for which he had opted. He had chosen to build his authority in part by promising big results in a short period of time. These commitments made him supremely receptive to agronomic panaceas. Many a scientist recognized the folly of these schemes, but was for long helpless in the face of Khrushchev's personal absolutism in agricultural affairs.[27] Hence, even as Khrushchev was arguing for raising the status of specialists, he was using pressure against those specialists who might frustrate his schemes. He justified this contradiction by expounding a theory of science which viewed it as anything but neutral, and called for expanded input from those scientists "who understand the interests of science, the state, and the people, and who skillfully combine them."[28]

[22] *Stroitel'stvo kommunizma I*, pp. 198–9.

[23] ibid., p. 394.

[24] *Stroitel'stvo kommunizma II*, pp. 113–14, 145; but he could also be inconsistent, as in ibid., p. 239.

[25] ibid., pp. 140–2.

[26] ibid., p. 285.

[27] See David Joravsky, *The Lysenko Affair* (Cambridge, Mass.: Harvard University Press, 1970); and Zhores Medvedev, *The Rise and Fall of T. D. Lysenko* (New York: Columbia University Press, 1969), for details.

[28] *Stroitel'stvo kommunizma I*, p. 139; see also ibid., pp. 162, 382–3; *Stroitel'stvo kommunizma II*, pp. 45, 55–7, 79, 108, 169. Khrushchev's damnation of agronomical tendencies of which he disapproved are too numerous for individual citation.

A superficial interpretation of Khrushchev's posture vis-à-vis the scientific and technical intelligentsia would see a contradiction between his calls for raising the political status of specialists and his attacks on specialists who did not follow his wishes. In fact, no such contradiction existed, for these political goals touched upon discrete sets of relationships within the system. Khrushchev was attempting to maintain his personal absolutism in the resolution of certain developmental problems, and demanded that all groups—officials, specialists, and masses alike—follow his dictates.[29] At the same time, he was trying to redefine the relationship between local officials and local specialists, so as to ensure that specialists responding to his approaches would gain access to, and responsiveness from, local officials. The Khrushchevian ideal was personified by Professor Zubrilin, "a great specialist and a good citizen" (*obshchestvennik*), who recognized the boundaries between technical and political decisions, and knew how to lend support to "correct" decisions from on high.[30]

In sum, during 1953–5 Khrushchev cultivated the image of an innovative problem-solver who would synthesize populist political reforms with assured political cohesion in ways that would service the goals of economic effectiveness and political legitimacy.[31]

Yet Khrushchev's approaches to these problems were not yet generalizable to all issue-areas. During 1953–5, he rarely spoke in public about cultural and industrial affairs and, when he did, he

[29] The term, "personal absolutism," was suggested by Arthur E. Adams, "Educated specialists and change in Soviet agriculture," *Agricultural History* (January 1966), p. 10.

[30] *Stroitel'stvo kommunizma I*, p. 174.

[31] Khrushchev's memoirs support the image of Khrushchev's approach to political participation outlined in this chapter. The main problems in interpreting the memoirs regarding this issue are: (1) that Khrushchev's statements often reflect his current thinking in retirement; and (2) that his statements about political participation during 1953–64 only occasionally specify the precise years within his administration that he advocated given policies or orientations. For Khrushchev's endorsement of the need to "trust" the population, see his *Khrushchev Remembers*, Vol. 1, pp. 8–9, 112, 114, 124, 229, 287, 295 307, 521–2, 524, 525; Vol. 2, pp. 12, 59–60, 83–4, 112, 129. On the need for local officials to be tolerant, humble, concerned about the masses, able to get along with people, and in touch with local conditions, see Vol. 1, pp. 27, 34, 50, 56, 61–3, 76, 108, 133, 160, 170, 237; Vol. 2, p. 121. On the equal need for leaders to be firm, goal-oriented, and determined, see Vol. 1, pp. 34, 37, 50, 61, 78, 108. On the need for public criticism of problems or officials, see ibid. pp. 224, 285, 312–13. On Khrushchev's relations with specialists, see Vol. 2, pp. 22–50, *passim*. For his criticism of the low quality of expertise in the 1950s, see ibid., pp. 116, 117. For his claim that technical questions should be separated from political ones, that experts should judge the work of other experts, and that specialists should be put in charge of local administration, see ibid., pp. 83, 136–8; and Vol. 1, pp. 274, 290, 293.

failed to echo the types of populist perspectives that marked his statements regarding the rural sector.[32] Yet despite this reticence, Khrushchev could not have been insensitive to the welling controversies of the time. The "Thaw" in literature, and regime calls for greater specialist input into policy-making, had been intended to elicit criticism of obsolete policies and dogmas, but instead fostered unexpected criticism of the Stalinist generation of officials, and of cultural controls as a whole. Moreover, the local official reaction to this ferment, as well as the local official response to demands for administrative rationalization, made clear that it would be easier to elicit public criticism than to ensure party and state responsiveness to suggestions for change. The policies of this period in most areas of social, economic, and administrative life were decidedly measured and inconsistent, both reflecting and generating tensions between forces pushing for expanded liberalization, and political interests seeking to keep criticism, initiative, and political reform within strict bounds.[33] Perhaps the Malenkovs in the leadership, less sensitive to the sociopolitical dilemmas involved in trying to realize their economic goals, would have allowed this pattern to continue, without leading either a backlash or a breakthrough. Khrushchev, however, concluded that a breakthrough was required, and that expanded criticism and initiative were more pressing imperatives than close protection of the political authority of Soviet officials.[34] Moreover, there might even be rapid political gains to be had from seizing the initiative, and expanding his role into the industrial and cultural realms.[35]

[32] I have in mind his speech to the conference of builders and architects (*Pravda*, 28 December, 1954), and his speech at the industrial conference (ibid., 19 May, 1955).

[33] For discussion of tensions during this period, see Leonhard, *Kremlin since Stalin*, ch. 3; Abraham Rothberg, *The Heirs of Stalin* (Ithaca, NY: Cornell University Press, 1972), ch. 1; Harold Swayze, *Political Control of Literature in the USSR, 1946–1959* (Cambridge, Mass.: Harvard University Press, 1962), ch. 3; for an interpretation, see Jeremy Azrael, "Varieties of de-Stalinization," in Chalmers Johnson (ed.), *Change in Communist Systems* (Stanford, Calif.: Stanford University Press, 1970), pp. 135–52 also Medvedev and Medvedev, *Khrushchev*, pp. 19–23.

[34] The characterization of Khrushchev's secret speech as an attempt to "break through" accumulating tensions was suggested by Azrael, "Varieties of de-Stalinization."

[35] The sociological concept of "role expansion" was first applied in Soviet studies in Grey Hodnett, "Succession contingencies in the Soviet Union," *Problems of Communism* (March–April 1975).

The Twentieth Party Congress

In his main report to the Twentieth Party Congress, Khrushchev went beyond earlier discussions of political participation in the rural sector to call for new forms of participation in the urban-production and urban-public sectors as well. Greater popular involvement in public affairs, expanded rights, collective leadership, and expanded specialist input were the themes of his speech. Thus, he called for resuscitating the local soviets and making them more accountable to the masses; he decried the bureaucratization and declaratory leadership of the Young Communist League; and he insisted that official organs develop truly collective leadership and increase their "ties with the working people."[36] Going further, he called upon the trade unions to "wrangle really hard" with the managers, increasing their defense of workers' legal rights.[37] Whereas speakers at the Nineteenth Party Congress had called upon all citizens to be "vigilant" against the internal enemy, Khrushchev now called upon all citizens to be "vigilant" against all manifestations of lawlessness and arbitrariness on the part of state organs.[38] And he spoke forcefully on behalf of a reduction of dogma in the social sciences and expanded input from the intelligentsia on ways to solve pressing problems of economic and social development.[39]

Despite Khrushchev's stress on expanded political participation, nothing could have prepared the delegates for what was to follow. In his secret speech, Khrushchev frontally and emotionally attacked Stalin, the "cult of personality," secret police domination of Soviet life, and heavy-handed leadership styles. He declared that the Stalinist "class struggle" thesis justifying continued terror was a concoction from its very inception, thereby reemphasizing that Soviet society was not only decisively reconstructed, but that it had been so since 1934. But even beyond this doctrinal innovation, the terms of Khrushchev's secret speech legitimized a form of systemic criticism. The Party leader made clear that the attack on Stalin was more than a call for reevaluating Soviet history; it had vast implications for the present. The criticism of the "cult of the individual leader" in Khrushchev's speech was linked to "the problem of liquidating its burdensome consequences," which included "bureaucratizing [of] the whole [party and state] apparatus."[40] With this speech, Khrushchev brought together the various strands of his authority-building strategy during

[36] Gruliow, *Current Soviet Policies II*, p. 53.
[37] ibid., p. 59.
[38] ibid., p. 54.
[39] ibid., p. 60.
[40] For the formulations in the secret speech, see ibid., pp. 172–4, 177, 186, 188.

the stage of political succession. Public criticism of local official performance was a central feature of his program for solving economic problems and improving administrative performance. It was also his prescription for revitalizing Soviet political life in ways that would ostensibly create a sense of political community, élan, and fervor. Beyond that, such public criticism would create an atmosphere of controlled tension in which the political elite would feel more dependent on Khrushchev for direction. And it would provide a pool of social activists on whom Khrushchev could draw for purposes of intimidating doubting members of the political establishment. Finally, such an atmosphere of revitalization would allow Khrushchev to keep his elite rivals off balance, as he seized the initiative, expanded his policy role, and preempted or coopted new issues.[41]

But Khrushchev was not prepared for the torrent of criticism and disobedience that swept Eastern Europe during the year following his secret speech. He was thrown onto the defensive, and sought ways to reestablish a balance that would not require either a return to Stalinism or public opposition to the regime. Moreover, he had to find a balance that would neutralize or defeat growing opposition to his leadership within the Presidium. The showdown came in Spring 1957, and resulted in a Khrushchevian victory. That victory ushered in the next stage of the Khrushchev era: the stage of ascendancy.

41 When I use the term, "national leadership," I am referring to the Politburo, which also contained those individuals referred to as Khrushchev's "elite rivals." When I speak of the "political elite" or the "political establishment," I am referring to local, regional, and central officials of the party and state apparatuses. Cultivation of an atmosphere of crisis, or of campaignist fervor, increases the sense of dependence on the leader among members of the political elite, thereby intimidating or outflanking rivals in the national leadership.

5 Khrushchev Ascendant, 1957-60

The period from Winter/Spring 1957 through mid-1960 can be viewed as a distinct stage of the Khrushchev era. It was marked by the Party leader's power consolidation, the extension of his policy role into all realms, and his forging and presentation of a comprehensive program for progress in all areas. During most of 1957–8, Khrushchev led the effort to hammer out such a program. In January 1959 he presented the program for "the full-scale construction of communism" at the Twenty-First Party Congress. During 1959 and the first half of 1960 he monitored and elaborated on the program. And in Summer/Fall 1960 he became aware that the program had proved to be unworkable, and needed to be redefined.

Khrushchev's program envisaged the attainment of levels of abundance, productivity, and political participation associated with the vision of communism outlined in the works of Marx and Lenin. However, Khrushchev's plan for reaching this goal was based on the distinctive approaches to problem-solving that he had been advocating during the political succession struggle. Thus, Khrushchev promised the attainment of consumer abundance without a sharp diversion of funds from defense, heavy industry, or Siberian development. Instead, he came forth with proposals for social, administrative, and political transformations, as well as economic campaigns, that would purportedly release unprecedented levels of popular and managerial initiative.

Budgetary Priorities

In 1959 a new Seven-Year Plan was enacted to replace the Five-Year Plan for 1956–60 that had been scrapped.[1] The new plan constituted a grandiose, almost breathtaking vision of imminent all-round abundance. It called for further rates of increase in both industrial and agricultural production that would equal or surpass the impressive rates attained in 1953–8. It called for the attainment of US levels of

[1] For a translation of the Seven-Year Plan, see Gruliow, *Current Soviet Policies III*, pp. 1–29; for analyses, see Harry Schwartz, *The Soviet Economy since Stalin* (Philadelphia, Pa: Lippincott, 1965), pp. 122–34; and Alec Nove, *An Economic History of the USSR* (London: Allen Lane, 1969), pp. 352–4.

per capita output and consumer affluence no later than 1970. It provided for the large-scale exploitation of Siberian and Central Asian energy and mineral resources, and directed 40 percent of current investment toward that end. It invested huge sums in housing, hospital, and educational construction, in the conversion of Soviet industry to an advanced technological footing (non-ferrous metals, petroleum refining, advanced engineering, and other substitutes for coal and steel), in defense modernization and missile deployment, in the space program, and in foreign aid.

In rhetoric, and in targets, these programs appeared to promise consumer abundance. However, even an uninformed observer would have had to wonder where the capital toward meeting these targets was to come from. Indeed, when we look beyond the goals to the sources of funding to meet those goals, we find that the Seven-Year Plan was not based upon radical budgetary reallocation at all. Most of the sectors deprived of needed investments were those benefiting the urban and rural consumer. Thus, the plan called for deep cuts in state investment in agriculture, and in the delivery of new machinery to the rural sector. In like manner, the plan demanded a sharp increase in agricultural investment on the part of the collective farms themselves, while the regime added to collective farms' financial strain by demanding that they pay in full for the machinery delivered as a result of the abolition of Machine Tractor Stations in 1958.

But how could the vision of overtaking and surpassing the USA in standard of living be realized on the basis of such a plan? And how could agriculture be expected to repeat its phenomenal rates of production increase of 1953–8 in the face of such deprivation? Moreover, how could Nikita Khrushchev, who was foremost in touting the vision of abundance and who had applied himself so industriously to monitoring agricultural affairs, countenance the cuts?

These are among the central puzzles about the Khrushchev era. In recent years, the conventional wisdom in much Western literature about Soviet elite politics resolves the puzzle by viewing Khrushchev as an embattled consumer advocate, who led a "pro-consumer" faction within the Presidium against usually successful obstructionism by representatives of heavy industry and defense. According to this image, the policy trends of these years reflected Khrushchev's political weakness, and concealed his continuing efforts behind the scenes to gain a better deal for the urban and rural consumer.[2]

This study reaches very different conclusions. The evidence here assembled suggests that, at this time, Khrushchev expanded his political commitments beyond the heavy-industry-agricultural alliance

[2] This is the argument advanced in Linden, *Khrushchev and the Soviet Leadership*, and in Ploss, *Conflict and Decision-Making*.

of 1955–6, seeking to develop sectors that would eventually further the causes of technological advance, consumer soft goods, and intensive agricultural development. He was aware of the growing squeeze on available investment capital, yet he opted for developing the growth potential of the Soviet economy, rather than giving in to calls for cuts in investment in heavy industry for the sake of agriculture, light industry, or current consumption. He was continuing efforts to implement and expand the "new deal" consensus of the post-Stalin regime, but he did not claim a fundamental shift in investment priorities to be necessary at the time to advance the goal.

Let us begin with agriculture. An examination of Khrushchev's public statements during this period suggests that he supported the cutbacks in state investment in rural development. He acknowledged that, at some point, a turn toward a more costly approach would be required, but he claimed no urgency about such a change of direction.

Thus, during his campaign for sharply increasing meat and milk production, launched formally in 1957,[3] but with roots already in Khrushchev's exhortations of 1955–6, he almost never referred to the need for increased state funding. On the contrary, he consistently referred to the need for local officials to mobilize "reserves" in order to meet the targets.[4] (Indeed, the concept of mobilizing reserves suddenly returned to the semi-annual slogans of the Central Committee during 1957–60.)[5] Furthermore, when referring back to this campaign in speeches before other audiences the Soviet leader almost always eschewed state responsibility for ensuring its success, indicating that it had begun "on the initiative of leading collective farms," or as a result of the "appeal" (*prizyv*) of those farms to overtake US levels of production.[6]

In like manner, Khrushchev consistently rejected appeals for enlarged investment in the intensive development of agriculture. On numerous occasions, he pointed out that the regime could not spare

[3] Khrushchev's speeches during this campaign are available in *Stroitel'stvo kommunizma II*, pp. 298–475.

[4] Use of the term, "reserves," is incessant. For a few examples, see ibid., pp. 312, 344–5, 508.

[5] Reference was made to "reserves," and the need to mobilize them, during 1952–3. Such reference was dropped in 1954–6. It returned for the entire period, 1957–60. In fairness, though, we should note that the return of this reference was initially couched in terms of exploiting reserves released by the regionalization of industry and construction. See, for example, *Pravda*, 13 October, 1957, slogans 46 and 47.

[6] See *Stroitel'stvo kommunizma II*, p. 437; *Stroitel'stvo kommunizma III*, pp. 484, 490, 494; *Current Soviet Policies III*, p. 48; and *Pravda* for the following dates: 7 November 1957, 1 March 1958, 21 June 1958, 15 December 1958, 20 December 1958, 30 July 1959, 29 December 1959, and 6 May 1960.

funds for drainage, land reclamation, mineral fertilizers, rural construction, and irrigation.[7] Indeed, even after the poor agricultural
results in the Virgin Lands during 1959, when demands from within
the political elite for heavier funding of agricultural development
appear to have grown, Khrushchev held these forces at bay:

> The December Plenum was a plenum for the mobilization of our
> reserves. I should tell you that when we were preparing for this
> plenum, our agricultural organs . . . worked out fairly extensive
> proposals for the development of all branches of agriculture in the
> Soviet Union. We rejected these proposals. The Central Committee
> considers that the basic landmarks for the development of agricul-
> ture are set forth well in the Seven-Year Plan.[8]

Khrushchev did support further expansion of agricultural machine-
building, but he argued that this was a long-term, not an immediate
consideration. After the transfer of technologies from the Machine
Tractor Stations to the collective farms, Khrushchev argued that the
rate of delivery of such machinery could now be cut back while new
models were being developed. Throughout 1957–60 he called continually for the research and development of new models that would
ultimately reduce the cost of agricultural production.[9] In his speech
at the December 1958 Plenum, he explicitly justified the cutback by
pointing out that "the main thing now is not to be carried away by
the job of swelling tractor and combine production, but rather to
organize sufficient production of other machines that agriculture

---

[7] See *Stroitel'stvo kommunizma II*, pp. 363, 374–5, 501, 526; *Stroitel'stvo
kommunizma III*, pp. 190, 512; and *Pravda* for the following dates: 22
February 1958, 28 February 1958, 28 March 1958, 15 December 1958;
20 December 1958, and 29 December 1959.

[8] *Stroitel'stvo kommunizma IV*, p. 109; contrast the interpretation in
Ploss, *Conflict and Decision-Making*, pp. 172–9, which is based in part on
exclusion of the first and last sentences of this quotation.

[9] Statements about the need for new *types* of machinery may be found in
Stroitel'stvo kommunizma II, pp. 354, 374, 395, 525; *Stroitel'stvo kommunizma III*, pp. 309, 319, 521–2; *Stroitel'stvo kommunizma IV*, pp. 44–6,
120–1; Gruliow, *Current Soviet Policies III*, p. 48; and *Pravda* for the
following dates: 18 February 1958; 1 March 1958; 28 March 1958; 15
December 1958; 20 December 1958; 2 July 1959; 8 October 1959; 29
December 1959; 6 May 1960.

[10] *Pravda*, 16 December 1958. Note that this statement was omitted from
the reprint of this speech in *Stroitel'stvo kommunizma III*, p. 396. Apparently, when this volume was published in 1962, Khrushchev was attempting
to dissociate himself from the earlier decision.

greatly needs."[10] That this was the position taken by the First Secretary was confirmed by him on subsequent occasions.[11]

In January 1959 the Twenty-First Party Congress met to ratify the Seven-Year Plan and to usher in the period of the "full-scale construction of communism." Khrushchev's speech to the assembled delegates reflected both his optimism about the nation's ability to realize the new plan, and the crystallization of his approach to reconciling heavy-industrial and military values with expanded consumer satisfaction.[12] The key was technology. In contrast to the Twentieth Party Congress, he avoided calling heavy-industrial development "the general line of our party." But in keeping with his new synthesis, whereby preponderant investment in heavy industry would result in short-term heavy-industrial growth and long-term advances in consumption, he noted that economic growth would proceed "on the basis of the preponderant development of heavy industry."[13] In like manner, he announced that the new task of building the "material-technical base of communism" was now a fundamental component of the docrine, in contrast to the earlier vacillation between the terms, "material-technical base" and "material-production base."[14] He enumerated the prerequisites of the material-

---

[11] Consider, for example, the following revealing exchange at the December 1959 Plenum. The speaker is the director of an enterprise specializing in the construction of agricultural machinery. Khrushchev interrupts his speech, and a spontaneous interchange takes place:

Ivanov: While many of our machines have very real shortcomings and need to be replaced with new ones, nonetheless, comrades, under no circumstances could industry deliver in the next two to three years the quantity of machinery that the Ministry of Agriculture is now asking for and boosting.

Khrushchev: Correct!

Ivanov: But we must overtake the United States in agricultural output and, as the results of recent years have shown, this can be done.

Khrushchev: Comrade Ivanov, new machinery will always be better than old. (See *Plenum tsentral'nogo komiteta Kommunisticheskoi Partii Sovetskogo Soiuza, 22–25 dekabria 1959 g.: Stenograficheskii otchet* [Moscow, 1960], p. 249.)

[12] Gruliow, *Current Soviet Policies III*, pp. 41–72.

[13] ibid., p. 43.

[14] For the ambiguous Stalinist usage, see "On the means for the gradual transition from socialism to communism," *Voprosy ekonomiki* (October 1950), pp. 99–108 (*CDSP*, vol. 3, no. 2, pp. 3–9). Indeed, Khrushchev continued to employ the Stalinist formulations in his speech at the January 1955 Plenum (*Pravda*, 3 February 1955), though the term was changed to "material-technical base" in the reprint of the speech seven years later (*Stroitel'stvo kommunizma I*, p. 423). Khrushchev also used the Stalinist formulation at the Twentieth Party Congress (Gruliow, *Current Soviet Policies II*, p. 60).

technical base of communism almost entirely in terms of the development of advanced technologies.[15] And perhaps in response to pressures from within the political elite for greater attention to current consumption, he explicitly underlined the assumptions behind his investment priorities:

> Our plan does indeed envisage a large capital investment in developing heavy industry. But could it be otherwise? To have a sufficiency of consumer goods, means of production are required, metal must be obtained, machines built, automatic machine lines installed . . . Development of industry, growth of the means of production—this is our powerful steed. If we have the steed, we shall have everything else as well.[16]

But Khrushchev's program was not merely an extension of his earlier budgetary priorities. It also incorporated policies that selectively accommodated positions associated with his defeated rivals. The accommodative features were three-fold: (1) development of the chemicals industry as a means, among other things, of expanding the availability of textiles for clothing; (2) deferral of the serial production of ICBMs until a new generation of missiles had been developed, amidst arms control efforts to slow down US ICBM development and avoid expenditures associated with further spirals in the arms race; (3) an agreement to funnel the savings from eventual overfulfillment of the Seven-Year Plan in heavy industry to the benefit of agriculture and light industry. But, in contrast to Malenkov's budgetary priorities of 1953–4, these accommodative features were secondary components of Khrushchev's programs. He was expanding his commitments, but not forsaking his earlier priorities.

In his anniversary speech of November 1957 Khrushchev gave indications that he was ready to accommodate new commitments.[17] He failed to reiterate the doctrine that heavy industry was the "general line of our party," and he pointed out that a new stage of development had been reached when, "without detriment to the futher development of heavy industry and machine-building, we can develop light industry at a considerably faster pace." But where were the funds to come from? Khrushchev gave few indications in his speech. He ruled out cutbacks in defense expenditures, given the "hostile policy and actions of the ruling groups of imperialist states." Moreover, he projected a substantial increase in the production of steel over the coming fifteen years, as well as a 'substantial increase in the production of metal" by developing iron-ore deposits recently discovered. He boasted of

[15] Gruliow, *Current Soviet Policies III*, pp. 64–5.
[16] ibid., pp. 52–3.
[17] *Pravda*, 7 November 1957.

the immense potential waiting to be tapped in the expanses of Siberia and Central Asia, thereby indicating his intention to channel investment funds in those directions. He gave some attention to the potential for cost-cutting inherent in the development of chemicals and plastics, indicating that the latter could be substituted for metal in machine-building and construction. But, as the speech wore on, the attentive listener might have wondered where the funds for light industry were to come from in light of all these commitments.

Four months later, when speaking to his electoral constituents, Khrushchev addressed the issue again.[18] The way to meet the rising demand for consumer soft goods, he noted, was not simply to wait for agriculture to produce the raw fibers needed for the production of textiles. The latest in industrial technologies could be developed into a foundation for the production of synthetic fibers. And the same industry—chemicals—which he had earlier touted as a source of plastics for machine-building and construction could at once serve multiple purposes.

Two months later, on 6 May 1958, Khrushchev delivered the keynote address at a Central Committee Plenum convened to discuss the development of the chemicals industry.[19] By this time, Khrushchev's public statements on the practical applications of chemicals, as well as the doctrinal issues involved, had crystallized. He now sought to demonstrate that development of the chemicals industry could contribute to a harmonious synthesis of the contending positions on resource allocation articulated during 1953–7. He dwelled at length on the use of chemicals and petrochemicals in heavy-industrial conversion to an advanced technological footing. He further sought to demonstrate that chemicals could simultaneously provide a synthetic fiber base for light industry and a mineral fertilizer base for the eventual intensive development of agriculture.

The critical question for our understanding of Khrushchev's priorities during this period, however, relates not to whether he was expanding his commitments in advancing the chemicals program (for that is self-evident), but to the way in which he defined the trade-offs between growth and consumption, long-term benefits and short-term benefits, industry versus agriculture in distributing resources within the budget for chemicals development, and domestic versus foreign sources of funding of this development. Closer examination of Khrushchev's statements during this period reveals unmistakably that, in advancing the chemicals program, Khrushchev was not advocating budgetary reallocations that would redound to the short-term benefit of the consumer.

Thus, in his Central Committee address, Khrushchev lauded the

18 ibid., 15 March 1958.
19 ibid., 10 May, 1958.

preponderant growth of heavy industry as the general line of the party, in terms not heard since the Twentieth Party Congress two years earlier. He pointed out that the further growth of heavy industry remained the basis of the nation's defense posture. And he rejected the notion that growth ought to be slowed for the sake of current consumption: "To slacken attention to heavy industry would mean to impede economic development, fall into a consumer policy and eat up everything we produce. This, in turn, would lead to a lag and could lose us the positions we have won." These were very strong words indeed, and would hardly have been advanced as eyewash by a leader who was simultaneously calling for a race with the USA in economic progress. Moreover, in outlining the chemicals program, Khrushchev discussed its multiple applications but the fact that his primary (or even secondary) purpose in advancing the program was not agricultural was indicated by the fact that the speech—in whole or even in part—was never published in Khrushchev's collected speeches on agriculture.[20] And to the extent that agricultural applications were a component of Khrushchev's purposes, they were not intended to have a short-term payoff. Khrushchev admitted as much at the Twenty-First Party Congress in January 1959.[21] He further confirmed the point at the plenary session of March 1962 (by which time he had every incentive to disavow the earlier commitment), where he explained that the period 1959–61 had been seen as one of research and development, during which the planning agencies and ministries would work out and implement plans for initiating development of the chemicals industry.[22] Finally, Khrushchev's approach to the funding of chemicals development was not redistributive of assets within the national budget. For, in his May 1958 speech, he explicitly linked funding to the acquisition of credits, investments, equipment, and expertise from East European, West European, and American sources, and then followed this up with just such a search for foreign assistance.[23]

Thus, Khrushchev's behaviour with respect to the chemicals program does not support the image of a leader who demagogically denounced Malenkov's consumer-goods program only to adopt that program once Malenkov had been defeated. Rather, it supports the image of a leader who temporarily exaggerated his own defense of traditional values in order to pin the extremist label on his rival, destroyed that rival politically, and then returned to the post-Stalin

[20] See *Stroitel'stvo kommunizma III*, where the speech would otherwise have been reprinted.

[21] Gruliow, *Current Soviet Policies III*, p. 50.

[22] *Stroitel'stvo kommunizma VI*, pp. 425–6.

[23] *Pravda*, 10 May 1958; *New York Times*, 20 January 1959, 17 May 1959, and 18 September 1959.

task of increasing consumer satisfaction. But this reexpansion of his commitment to the consumer was set within the strict limits defined by his earlier commitments to heavy-industrial growth, defense modernization, Siberian development, and a low-cost approach to increasing agricultural output.

Analysts who claim that Khrushchev was an embattled consumer advocate during his stage of ascendancy sometimes point to his behavior at the January 1960 meeting of the Supreme Soviet to buttress the case. In his speech at that session, Khrushchev announced a further cut in the total troop strength of the Soviet armed forces, which called for the demobilization of 1·2 million men by the end of 1961.[24] And after the U-2 affair of May 1960 exacerbated international tensions, Khrushchev again addressed the Supreme Soviet, defending the troop cuts and calling for their eventual extension.[25] All of which could be cited as evidence of pro-consumer inclinations.

But the linkage would still have to be demonstrated, for even Khrushchev's proposals of January and May 1960 are easily reconciled with the very different portrait painted in this chapter. In 1955 large-scale demobilization of Soviet troops had begun at precisely the time that Khrushchev was advocating (and securing) an expensive crash program of defense modernization and an increase in the total military budget. During the entire period 1955–60 manpower costs in the Soviet defense establishment were being reduced, even as, during 1957–9, there took place a steady, sharp increase in advanced-weapons-systems expenditures, and a steady sharp increase in the total military budget. During the year 1960 the total military budget remained relatively steady, as increases in weapons expenditures were counterbalanced by continuing reductions in manpower costs.[26]

This pattern puts Khrushchev's behavior in an entirely different light. Khrushchev's troop cut proposals of January 1960 were apparently not motivated by a concern for inter-sectoral redistributions, but by an effort to hold down manpower expenditures within the military budget so as to finance increases in other components of the military budget, namely, strategic and tactical weapons development. To be sure, maintaining high troop levels, or pushing the expansion of Soviet conventional forces, while simultaneously advancing the cause of nuclear modernization, would have been still more costly. In this sense, Khrushchev certainly was oriented toward

---

[24] *Pravda*, 15 January 1960.
[25] ibid., 6 May 1960, and 8 May 1960.
[26] On Soviet military expenditures during 1955–60, see Bloomfield, Clemens and Griffiths, *Khrushchev and the Arms Race*, pp. 51–8; and Abraham Becker, *Soviet Military Outlays since 1955* (Santa Monica, Calif.: RAND Corporation, 1964).

cutting costs; indeed, this might even be viewed as a compromise feature of his program. But that is not the issue in the debate over whether or not Khrushchev's behavior during 1957–60 was oriented primarily toward improving the lot of the consumer. Closer inspection of Khrushchev's public statements reveals that, in January 1960, the First Secretary proposed troop cuts primarily as a means of both relieving the labor shortage in the civilian economy and freeing up funds for further defense modernization.[27]

But there was also an apparently new wrinkle in Khrushchev's approach to defense modernization. The Soviet leadership decided at this time (1958–9) to defer serial production of ICBMs until a new generation of strategic missiles came on line. Khrushchev did not address the issue in public, for it was highly sensitive, and would have undermined his efforts to deceive the USA about Soviet strategic capability. But Khrushchev's efforts during 1959 on behalf of US–Soviet détente and arms control would square with a decision to marginally deescalate the arms race in order to improve the prospects of striking a deal with the USA, and thereby avoid a budgetary crunch.[28]

This interpretation must remain speculative, however. For one thing, this study does not delve into foreign affairs in sufficient depth to render a judgment based on evidence systematically drawn. For another thing, the base of evidence is slim and circumstantial, forcing us—in contrast to the methodology generally employed in this book—to infer Khrushchev's strategy not from what he said, but from policies adopted at the time. Those policies, after all, might have been adopted over his objections.

A third, accommodative feature of Khrushchev's program called for channeling above-plan accumulations in heavy industry into the light-industrial and agricultural sectors. At the Twenty-First Party Congress, Khrushchev announced that such a deal had been reached behind the scenes, and his musings about the possibilities inherent in such an approach suggest that he was, at a minimum, not opposed.[29]

---

[27] Khrushchev's memoirs suggest that he was long an advocate of defense modernization and expansion, not just during the period of political succession (see source citations in Chapter 2, note 14).

[28] On these points, see Adam Ulam, *Expansion and Coexistence*, 2nd edn (New York: Praeger, 1974), pp. 621–9; Arnold Horelick and Myron Rush, *Strategic Power and Soviet Foreign Policy* (Chicago: University of Chicago Press, 1966), pp. 50–70.

[29] Gruliow, *Current Soviet Policies III*, p. 51. Implicit evidence that Khrushchev favored such a compromise as a means of meeting the regime commitment to the consumer in the late 1950s may be found in *Stroitel'stvo kommunizma II*, pp. 378, 393, 460–1; and in *Pravda*, 7 November 1957, and 6 May 1960. And later on, when Khrushchev sought to "call in" this deal, he acknowledged its existence: *Stroitel'stvo kommunizma IV*, pp. 180–1, 289.

This was not the same as the original Malenkov approach, which had called for immediate budgetary reallocations and industrial conversion to consumer-goods production. But it was a nod in that direction, for it acknowledged the eventual need to channel more funds away from priority sectors than the Seven-Year Plan had allowed. In the short run, however, Khrushchev presented himself as the leader who could combine priority emphasis on the leading sectors with steady increases in the standard of living, through political mobilization in the countryside.

Incentive Policy

Consistent with his budgetary priorities, Khrushchev proposed to demonstrate that high labor productivity could be achieved without a marked increase in monetary incentives for the rural population. Instead, a combination of administrative pressure, social pressure, intangible material incentives (such as the promise of imminent abundance as the reward for hard work), and a more rational material-incentive structure, he claimed, could do the job. Moreover, Khrushchev added an ideological appeal to his problem-solving strategy, attempting to demonstrate that social transformations in an egalitarian, communitarian direction could contribute to both utopian and developmental goals.

Thus, during these years Khrushchev remained faithful to his earlier promise that price rises would not define the character of his agricultural program. It is true that, in June 1958, the Party leader was enthusiastic about the prospect of doing away with compulsory deliveries and of placing regime procurement of agricultural produce on a cash basis.[30] It is equally true that, in the same speech, he was also willing to acknowledge that prices should be adjusted to make them more uniform, to bring them closer to costs, and to reduce the fiscal burden of collective and state farmers. Indeed, these changes were consistent with the post-Stalin consensus (that united Malenkov's and Khrushchev's perspectives on agricultural development) that regime-peasant relations should be based on exchange, not confiscation.

But the measures just noted were as far as Khrushchev went. In his speech to the Central Committee Plenum, he was decidedly un-enthusiastic about the procurement price increases, characterizing them as little more than regrettable necessities. The price increases themselves were partially offset by reductions in procurement prices for a variety of other crops; and even with respect to livestock products, the price increases still left them far below the level required

[30] *Pravda*, 21 June 1958.

to cover the costs of production. Moreover, Khrushchev was to some extent in a bind. He had warned in 1953 that further price increases would not be absorbed by the state budget, and would result in higher urban retail prices. In 1958 he backed off from this commitment, and no such jump in retail prices was enacted, just as no call for such a rise appeared in his Plenum speech.

But a perceptible change in Khrushchev's behaviour *did* take place in light of the pricing dilemma he had confronted. During the year following the Central Committee Plenum, Khrushchev spoke often to rural officials, warning that the recent price rise was an exceptional event, not a precedent. Whereas in earlier years he had emphasized the obligations of the working class to the peasantry, he was now stressing the opposite message when speaking to the peasantry: "You must think not only of yourself, but also of your older brother— the working class."[31] Evidently, the First Secretary was intent on making his campaignist approach work.

Khrushchev's augmentation of the pressure for extraordinary results also increased the complaints from harried local officials, but the First Secretary stuck to his guns. In the face of complaints about the price structure, he pointed to model farms which were making profits under the same procurement and purchase prices.[32] When faced with skepticism about the realism of the targets, Khrushchev would point to the accomplishments of the USA, Holland, Denmark, and Finland as a means of shaming his audience and defending his authority.[33] When asked to increase central funding, the First Secretary railed against "dependency," the high cost of collective-farm produce compared to products delivered from state farms, the irrational structure of material incentives on collective farms, their poor organization, and their large pools of redundant labor.[34]

In like manner, during the abolition of the Machine Tractor Stations, it was he who argued against allowing some overburdened farms to receive the machinery free of charge. The rationale he provided echoes a persistent refrain in his speeches, and one that was integral to his authority-building strategy: "It could only lead to an increasing tendency toward dependency, and to undermining the collective farmers' material incentive to develop production."[35]

[31] *Stroitel'stvo kommunizma III*, p. 311; for similar declarations at this time, see ibid., pp. 12–13, 402, 499–500; *Stroitel'stvo kommunizma IV*, pp. 12–13.
[32] *Stroitel'stvo kommunizma II*, pp. 308–9, 329.
[33] ibid., pp. 306–8, 316, 449–50.
[34] ibid., pp. 306–8, 310–11, 319–20, 328–9, 331, 336–7, 361, 380–1, 386, 400.
[35] *Stroitel'stvo kommunizma III*, p. 149.

Incentive Policy and Social Transformation

The "full-scale construction of communism" called for rapid progress toward a more egalitarian, consensual, and collectivist society, in which people would contribute to the extent of their abilities, and would receive rewards in accordance with their needs. In addition to the obvious ideological appeals, Khrushchev's proposals for social transformation, and for changes in incentive policy, served his low-cost approach to the furtherance of current consumption.

In both the industrial and agricultural sectors, Khrushchev now suggested that the authorities emphasize collective material rewards ("better housing, better public catering, better services, more children's institutions, improved public education, organizing recreation, improving medical service, building cultural institutions, etc."),[36] rather than wage increases and private accumulation. Since the availability of many collective goods varied by enterprise profitability, workers would partake of these benefits to the extent that their enterprises were productive. And it was up to the enterprise officials to see to it that access to collective goods varied according to the productivity of the individual workers. Hence, it was not at all inconsistent for Khrushchev to call simultaneously for expanding collective material rewards and for the elimination of "leveling" in their distribution.[37] For the First Secretary was combining the egalitarianism inherent in a turn toward need-based social rewards, with the elitism inherent in his approach to structuring material incentives.

In the rural sector, Khrushchev's campaigns for social transformation served a similar mix of goals. Campaigns against the private sector in Soviet agriculture, launched with great intensity in 1958–9, would at once promote the communalization of Soviet agriculture and an increase in labor available to develop the communal sector, while the phenomenal growth of agriculture during 1953–8 would reduce the material dependence of collective farmers on private sources of income.[38] In addition, pressure on collective farms to increase their investments in rural construction as their wealth increased, rather than simply allowing rapid private accumulation, not only provided the basis for a collectivist psychology, but squared fully with the demands of the Seven-Year Plan that a larger proportion of investment in agricultural needs be provided by the collective and state farms themselves. Khrushchev was wary of efforts to cut the

[36] Gruliow, *Current Soviet Policies III*, p. 51.
[37] ibid., p. 66.
[38] For the definitive account of Khrushchev's campaign against the private sector in Soviet agriculture, see Karl-Eugen Waedekin, *The Private Sector in Soviet Agriculture* (Berkeley, Calif.: University of California Press, 1973), chs. 8–9.

personal incomes of collective farmers, for fear that a campaign in this direction might destroy the incentive effect of material rewards.[39] But when faced with evidence of high levels of private accumulation, coupled with low levels of communal investment on the part of given collective farms, his egalitarian advocacy predominated over the elitist. Under these circumstances he would suggest party intervention to ensure greater emphasis on collective material rewards.[40] Collective goods would thus serve as a material reward that would simultaneously foster rural development, urban and rural consumer satisfaction, and social transformation.

Administrative Reform

Khrushchev's program for administrative reform was, like his policy in other spheres, an extension of the approach he had advocated in the agricultural sector during the struggle for political succession. When Khrushchev consolidated his power and expanded his role during 1957–9, he also saw to the extension of his distinctive approach into the industrial realm. The program combined devolution of greater decision-making responsibility to regional levels of public administration with an intensification of pressure on managers from the central party apparatus, regional party organizations, and the masses.

Counterattacking against the technocratic forces which had coalesced in December 1956, Khrushchev demanded and secured the reversal of reforms enacted at that time, and pushed through a reform that called for abolishing most central ministries in favor of regional economic (*sovnarkhozy*). Those councils would ostensibly place great emphasis on regional planning, and thereby overcome the functional biases and blinders built into the ministerial system.[41] Khrushchev explained[42] that such a reform would bring the "center of gravity" of public administration "closer to production." This would make possible the "tapping of reserves that are latent in the socialist economy." The Party leader anticipated, though, that such regional devolution might foster "localist" tendencies, inhibiting inter-regional coordination. His proposed solution followed logically from his rejection of genuine decentralization and his consistent advocacy of outside intervention in managerial affairs: "disclosure and struggle

[39] *Stroitel'stvo kommunizma IV*, pp. 98–9.

[40] *Stroitel'stvo kommunizma II*, pp. 356–7; *Stroitel'stvo kommunizma III*, pp. 125–6, 407–8, 531–2; *Stroitel'stvo kommunizma IV*, pp. 14, 99.

[41] On the administrative logic of the *sovnarkhoz* reform, see Nove, *An Economic History*, pp. 342–4, 358–9; on the political logic, see Leonhard, *Kremlin since Stalin*, pp. 235–41.

[42] *Pravda*, 30 March 1957.

against these harmful tendencies . . . must be constantly the focus of attention of party, soviet, government, economic, and trade union agencies." Or, as he told the delegates to the Twenty-First Party Congress, "it is a matter of organizing a campaign, truly embracing all the people . . ."[43]

Political Participation

In the period 1957–9 Khrushchev also expanded his program for political participation. The measured reconciliation with the masses during 1953–5, whereby cautious moves were made to expand public involvement, initiative, input, and rights, had created unresolved tensions over the extent to which these changes could develop without threatening the political privileges of Soviet officials. Khrushchev's secret speech attempted to break through this stalemate, but fostered greater ferment than either the First Secretary or his colleagues were willing to countenance. Yet Khrushchev was also not willing to sponsor a return to the conservative approach to political participation advocated by Malenkov, Kaganovich, and Bulganin. His economic program required a sharp increase in popular initiative in the production sectors. His ideological program called for such initiative in the public sectors. But each of these, according to Khrushchev, required a critical posture toward the local "bosses" on the part of the masses.

Speaking on the fortieth anniversary of the Bolshevik ascension to power, in November 1957, Khrushchev revealed his intention to push on with de-Stalinization and to sponsor structural changes with populist implications: "the socialist state cannot remain unchanged, stagnant, fixed for all time in the same form."[44]

Within half a year Khrushchev made clear what he had in mind. Speaking to the Congress of the Young Communist League in April 1958, Khrushchev complained that League organizations lacked the capacity genuinely to inspire youth and to elicit initiative.[45] As far as he was concerned, this resulted from the bureaucratization of all tasks, and the pervasive state regulation of social behavior which, in turn, had been based on lack of trust in the population. "Some comrades," he revealed, "fear that the trade unions will be unable to organize physical culture work and that a state inspector is required. If there is such an inspector people will jump, run, and swim, but if there is no inspector everything will go to pieces. This is nonsense

---

[43] Gruliow, *Curent Soviet Policies III*, p. 50.
[44] *Pravda*, 7 November 1957.
[45] *Stroitel'stvo kommunizma III*, p. 170.

. . . It is wrong to reduce matters to channeling everything through state agencies."[46] Popular initiative, then, would be stimulated by depoliticization of many social initiatives, thereby legitimizing their removal from formal subordination to state officials.

Such depoliticization implied greater trust in society, for it assumed that decompression of political controls would not foster political deviance. Moreover, the depoliticization of social initiatives was, in Khrushchev's view, a prerequisite for the stimulation of authentic initiative. As he put it in the speech to the Young Communist League just cited, "what kind of initiative is it when there are guides and nursemaids everywhere in the form of paid instructors, propagandists, physical culture inspectors, and other officials?"[47] Thus, according to Khrushchev, social and political cohesion were not threatened by decompression precisely because of the basic trustworthiness of the population, and the ability of rank-and-file activists to maintain control and exercise leadership without the regime's having to resort to widespread "administrative methods" and police power.

As had been the case during 1953–6, however, Khrushchev's perspectives were dualistic. Whereas Khrushchev was arguing for new arenas of politics and less explicitly administrative control, his emphasis on social control did not sanction liberalization or diversification. Rather, he viewed social control as the most effective means of creating social discipline and attitudinal homogeneity which he, in turn, viewed as prerequisites for the properly self-regulating communist society.[48]

Many of the themes Khrushchev introduced in 1957–8 found expression in his address to the delegates to the Twenty-First Party Congress. There he announced the "final and complete" victory of socialism in the USSR, the end of class-based, oppositional political crime, and the end of capitalist encirclement.[49] It would no longer be possible to use Stalinist doctrine to justify a state of siege against the population. Administrative methods could hardly be justified against a population that was itself the main bulwark against capitalist restoration. Even the continued existence of a hostile capitalist world, Khrushchev argued, could not destabilize Soviet society. Moreover, the abolition of political crime served further to legitimize the depoliticization of social initiatives. Hence, Khrushchev called for a diminished role for formal state agencies, and the transfer of many social functions to public organizations that would have independent

[46] ibid., pp. 171–3.
[47] ibid., p. 173.
[48] Gruliow, *Current Soviet Policies III*, p. 54.
[49] ibid., pp. 67, 68.

jurisdictions, working "alongside and parallel with . . . state agencies."[50]

Much of the political program that Khrushchev was advancing constituted an assault on the bureaucratic prerogatives of state officials. The Party leader came close to articulating an adversarial definition of the relationship between state bureaucrats and their clients. But, except for general doctrinal changes to legitimize coming to terms with a reconstructed socialist society, Khrushchev's program during the stage of ascendancy was not an assault on the political prerogatives of party officials. That would come later.

Ascendancy and Accommodation: Khrushchev as Politician

In his capacity as politician, Khrushchev's authority-building strategy roughly paralleled the pattern of his problem-solving strategy: he first embraced a strategy of confrontation as a means of ensuring his ascendancy, and then reverted to a posture of reconciliation.

The stage of ascendancy was marked by Khrushchev's power consolidation. In June 1957 he succeeded in ousting the Anti-Party Group from the Presidium. In that same year the abolition of most central ministries destroyed a potential power base for erstwhile rivals, while the purge of Marshal G. Zhukov from the Presidium cut short the career of a potential critic. In 1958 Khrushchev replaced N. Bulganin as Chairman of the Council of Ministers, thereby combining in his person the positions of head of government and leader of the party. All of which culminated in 1959, at the Twenty-First Party Congress, in the flowering of a genuine cult of Khrushchev's personality, as indicated by the effusiveness of the praise accorded him by most speakers, and by the failure of most significant speakers even to mention the principle of collective leadership.[51]

Khrushchev also extended further his use of public criticism as a means of gaining political leverage. In December 1958 Khrushchev initiated the practice of expanded plenary sessions of the Central Committee, packing those sessions with outsiders (in some cases, nonparty members) whom Khrushchev could use as leverage against groups within the political elite. And at the same time, he initiated the practice of publishing verbatim transcripts of those Central Committee sessions, increasing the visibility of the political process and ostensibly increasing the intimidation level among those with doubts about Khrushchev's policies.

The extension of Khrushchev's personal rule was striking. In the earlier period, he had demoted rivals; now he purged them from the

---

[50] ibid., p. 67.
[51] Leonhard, *Kremlin since Stalin*, p. 333.

leadership. Earlier he had expanded his policy role; now he went beyond that role expansion to assume formal leadership of the state bureaucracy. Earlier he had sought to destroy politically the leaders of agricultural ministries; now he abolished almost all ministries as a power base. Earlier he had sought to intimidate the Central Committee with allusions to the mass mood; now he invited the masses into the meetings.

Beyond power consolidation, Khrushchev continued to rely on ambitious campaigns and encouragement of public criticism in order to maintain the initiative and keep skeptics or rivals off balance. During 1957–8 he went back on the offensive. Thus, after the record harvest of 1956 had been recorded, the First Secretary lost no time in going out to the provinces to advertise a campaign for further increasing the production of meat and milk. Within months he had committed local officials to pledges to surpass US levels of dairy production by 1961.[52] Similarly, throughout 1958, Khrushchev unilaterally, and in public, escalated targets for agricultural production and rural development. Thus, in 1956 he had boasted of "thousands of farms" with "large incomes."[53] Now listen to him in 1958. In February he claimed that rich farms "could now take upon themselves the task of completely rebuilding their villages."[54] By August he proclaimed that all backward collective farms could reach the level of the advanced "in a short time."[55] In October he predicted that the government would soon be able to bid down the price of bread it purchased from collective farms.[56] And in December he made the startling assertion that, because some farms had achieved a 250 percent increase in meat production and deliveries, it was now possible for the entire country to do this.[57]

These predictions served many purposes. They created an atmosphere of élan and fervor. They kept Khrushchev on the initiative. They raised mass-consumer expectations, and thereby played upon elite fears of the masses, increasing, in turn, an elite sense of dependence on Khrushchev for protection and direction.

And Khrushchev knew it. He spent much time in the countryside, making clear to local officials that dire consequences would ensue

[52] *Pravda*, 24 May 1957; the paragraphs containing these predictions were not reprinted five years later in Khrushchev's collected speeches (*Stroitel'stvo kommunizma II*, p. 449).

[53] Gruliow, *Current Soviet Policies II*, p. 46.

[54] *Stroitel'stvo kommunizma III*, p. 37.

[55] ibid., p. 275.

[56] ibid., p. 297.

[57] ibid., p. 413; see also his claim, made at the December 1958 Central Committee Plenum, that the agricultural problem had been solved (ibid., pp. 351–2).

for those who failed to fulfill their obligations, referring to "crimes," "sins," "punishment," and "guilt."[58] And when addressing the central elite, Khrushchev played upon these fears by averring that opponents would be subject to the test of public criticism. Thus, in his anniversary speech of November 1957, Khrushchev returned to the confrontational language of the Twentieth Party Congress, placing great emphasis on the existence of contradictions in Soviet society. He spoke of the "contradictions between the growing requirements of the members of socialist society and the still insufficient material and technical base for meeting them." He indicated that the further development of Soviet society would proceed through "the disclosure and overcoming of contradictions," which included "the contradictions between the new and the old, the advanced and the backward."[59]

But a spirit of reconciliation with Soviet officialdom became evident in Khrushchev's address to the Twenty-First Party Congress,[60] after he had consolidated his power and ensured acceptance of his program. At the Party Congress, he made no claims (in contrast to 1956) that bureaucratization had become a class phenomenon. He also said nothing about contradictions in Soviet society, or about the "struggle of the new against the old." Nor did he warn of a threatening mass mood, or of his intention to "punish the guilty" for "crimes." And four months later, in a speech to members of the cultural intelligentsia, he encouraged intellectuals to criticize, but then warned them not to "overgeneralize" their criticism.[61]

Khrushchev had encouraged more generalized criticism in his secret speech after the Twentieth Party Congress. He subsequently had tried to prevent the backlash of 1956–7 from crippling both his personal authority and his program. He reverted again to highly generalized criticism in November 1957 in order to push his program and his power consolidation. By 1959, however, he was ready to emphasize harmony and unity between himself and officials—assuming they accepted the content of his program and the fact of his leadership.

---

[58] *Stroitel'stvo kommunizma II*, pp. 332, 341, 346, 367, 386. He also warned local officials that they, not he, would be held responsible by the masses for failure to deliver the goods: *Stroitel'stvo kommunizma III*, p. 492; *Stroitel'stvo kommunizma IV*, p. 79.

[59] *Pravda*, 7 November 1957.

[60] Gruliow, *Current Soviet Policies III*, pp. 41–72.

[61] *Pravda*, 24 May 1959. In contrast to this interpretation, some analysts claim that Khrushchev orchestrated or encouraged threats at the Twenty-First Party Congress to bring members of the "Anti-party Group" to trial (Linden, *Khrushchev and the Soviet Leadership*, pp. 73–7). Note, however, that the evidence is indirect, because Khrushchev never publicly committed himself on the matter. For a rebuttal of Linden's evidence when it first appeared in article form, see T. H. Rigby, "The extent and limits of authority (a rejoinder)," *Problems of Communism* (September–October 1963).

Khrushchev's program incorporated multiple appeals to a variety of constituencies. It held out the promise of consumer satisfaction without attacking the primacy of heavy-industrial and defense interests. It called for social transformation that would simultaneously increase collectivism and economic growth rates. It envisaged new terms of political participation that would prove to some people that expanded initiative and criticism were not synonymous with "anarchy," while demonstrating to others that political control need not be synonymous with bureaucratic commandism and terror. It proposed an administrative reform that would ostensibly release regional initiative without subverting the primacy of central planning. It included both an external ideological appeal (the prospect of overtaking US levels of production and consumer affluence) and an internal appeal (the prospect of socio-political transformation in directions suggested in Lenin's *State and Revolution*). It generated mobilizational fervor, and called for a sharp increase in party activism, but called for new methods of leadership to elicit initiative. And it projected Khrushchev as the national hero who would head the march toward communism without requiring a terror apparatus to back up his accumulation of power and authority.

To be sure, Khrushchev's policies and authority-building strategy must have alienated many people during this period. Specifically, those people would have been disgruntled whose ideals, interests, or practical beliefs led them to favor radical budgetary reallocation at the expense of the military–industrial complex, less intervention by outsiders in managerial affairs, a bureaucratic-centralist pattern of political authority, or an oligarchic pattern of central leadership. In addition, all those who supported a return to Stalinism or, alternatively, a breakthrough into economic or political democracy, would have been disaffected. And all those who were sufficiently perceptive to recognize the contradictions in Khrushchev's program, its unworkability and inconsistency, are likely to have been disgruntled by the bandwagon effect under way during 1957–9.

At the time, however, these individuals and interests had been outflanked. Khrushchev had put himself on record with big promises and public commitments that probably had broad appeal. He had promised much, and now he had to deliver.

6 Frustration and Reaction, 1960-4

The year 1960 was a turning-point in Khrushchev's tenure in office. It ushered in a turn from a mood of high optimism to one of near panic on the part of the First Secretary. In all realms of policy, the tensions and contradictions in Khrushchev's program were coming to the fore.[1] Output in the Virgin Lands continued to plummet after the disastrous delivery performance of 1959. Prices for meat, milk, and butter procurements remained insufficient to cover the cost of production, which deterred the collective farmer from making a serious, voluntary effort to produce and sell these commodities to the state. Overburdened collective farmers frequently had neither the skills nor the financial resources to maintain and operate the farm technology passed on to them as a result of the dissolution of the Machine Tractor Stations. Under these conditions of financial burden, most collective farms also had little hope of expanding communal investments. Then, too, it was becoming increasingly clear that Khrushchevian campaignism was causing local party officials to confiscate both produce and seed supplies, further undermining the incentive structure. And campaignism for the sake of social transformation was leading local party officials to attack the private sector, causing collective and state farmers frequently to slaughter their cattle rather than surrender them, and to withhold their valuable produce from the markets.

In the urban-industrial sector, things were going more according to plan. Many targets of the Seven-Year Plan for heavy industrial output and for consumer durables were being met. But the very successes in these sectors highlighted the growing gap between industry and agriculture, augmenting elite awareness of the dangers of shocks to current consumption. Inflationary pressures mounted; worker riots in Fall 1959 and January 1960 indicated one possible mass response to those pressures. Moreover, disturbing reductions in budgetary slack were appearing at precisely the time when greater capital available for investment might have alleviated the situation. In 1958 investment had increased by 16 percent over the previous year. By 1960

[1] On the emergence of these tensions, see Erich Strauss, *Soviet Agriculture in Perspective* (New York: Praeger, 1969), pp. 166–227; Nove, *An Economic History*, pp. 363–8; Waedekin, *The Private Sector*, pp. 274–304; Tatu, *Power in the Kremlin*, pp. 114–15, 166–70; Lowenthal, "Development versus Utopia in communist policy," pp. 91–8.

investment increased by only 8 percent over the previous year.

All these trends were casting doubt as well on Khrushchev's approach to administration. Credible reports were being amassed in Moscow, demonstrating that Khrushchev's campaignism had led to widespread dissimulation and fraud among local party officials who saw this as the only way to advance their careers in the face of impossible pressures from above.

As in the economic realm, Khrushchev's ambitious programs were also being frustrated in the realm of political participation within a year or two of their announcement. Efforts to expand the role and status of the *aktiv* were resisted by Soviet officials, who tried wherever possible to regulate social initiatives, to give activists menial tasks rather than real influence, and to blunt their ability to penetrate the inner workings of the decision-making process. Behind the scenes political forces were making efforts to dilute the doctrinal innovations articulated at the Twenty-First Party Congress. Those efforts were successful, for the Party Program of 1961 was noteworthy for its vision of again channeling mass initiative through state agencies (thereby reducing the importance of self-regulation), for its repudiation of "revolutions from above" (thereby implicitly criticizing Khrushchev's campaignism in the realm of social transformation), and for its view that socio-political transformation would be a measured outgrowth of long-term economic growth (thereby implicitly rejecting Khrushchev's optimistic claims about the compatibility of his utopian and developmental goals).

It was only in the late Summer and early Fall of 1960 that Khrushchev became visibly aware of the extent to which his program was faltering.[2] His reaction to these multiple setbacks was to redefine his policy program during the period, October 1960–October 1961. One of the first things he did in this connection was to abandon the compromise features of his program of 1959. But he simultaneously intensified and extended campaignist and confrontational approaches to problem-solving and authority-building.

Thus, with respect to investment priorities, Khrushchev jettisoned his commitment to greater investment in light industry and textiles, calling for a return to priority attention to the alliance of heavy industry and agriculture, through increased investment in agricultural machine-building and the Virgin Lands Program. Simultaneously he intensified campaignism in the rural sector, expanding the scope of the Virgin Lands Program and forcing local cadres to adopt a variety of low-cost agronomic panaceas.

The same pattern of contracted commitments and intensified

---

[2] In contrast, Khrushchev's international program faltered in May 1960, with the U-2 incident and the scuttling of the Paris Summit.

pressure appears in other issue-areas. With respect to incentive policy, Khrushchev retreated from his earlier emphasis on collective material rewards, but continued to argue behind the scenes against increasing procurement prices for agricultural produce, even as he raised the pressure on local cadres for large deliveries of unprofitable crops. In the realm of administrative reform, Khrushchev abandoned his posture of reconciliation with officialdom, carried out a purge of the regional party elite, raised the level of administrative centralization, and expanded mass monitoring of administrative behaviour. Finally, with respect to political participation, Khrushchev retreated from his harmony position of 1959 vis-à-vis local party officials, now sponsoring doctrinal and structural changes that would foster an adversarial relationship between those officials and the party and nonparty masses.

But intensified campaignism and confrontation could not solve the problems faced by the Soviet leader. And, as time went on, Khrushchev himself became increasingly aware of this. His statements became contradictory; his behavior, erratic and impulsive. Self-assertion alternated with selective backtracking; self-confidence with self-doubt.

The causes of this inconsistency are not self-evident. In any given case, the behavior of the Party leader might have been a product of his impetuous personality, his befuddlement or ambivalence about how to deal with problem-solving dilemmas, or political opposition to his preferences within the national leadership or broader political elite. Those who analyze this period through the prism of the "conflict model" typically stress factional opposition as the cause of Khrushchev's frustration, but that explanation is surely incomplete. It would take a broader assemblage of evidence than that undertaken in this book to decide the matter. The burden of this chapter is to display the inconsistencies in Khrushchev's behavior and policy advocacy, and the dilemmas of problem-solving and political credibility with which he wrestled.

Whatever the causes of those inconsistencies, their impact was clear. Agriculture continued to stagnate; the rate of growth of light industry slowed to a near halt; the rate of expansion of heavy industry also slowed down markedly, as did the rate of increase of capital investment. Administrative disruption and budgetary bottlenecks became increasingly acute. Almost all major institutional interests were deprived and alienated by Khrushchev's leadership, and the First Secretary did not have a terror apparatus with which to stifle actual and potential opposition. His authority as a problem-solver and as politician eroded precipitously as bottlenecks accumulated in the economy and in foreign policy. The result was that, in October 1964, a bitter and confused Nikita Khrushchev was unceremoniously removed from office and exiled to his summer cottage.

Budgetary Priorities and Incentive Policy

The conventional wisdom in Western literature on Soviet elite politics during 1960–4 is that Khrushchev was fighting hard to advance the cause of the consumer on all fronts. Specifically, Khrushchev is portrayed as going public with a Malenkovian approach that demanded heavy investment in light industry and agriculture at the expense of heavy industry and defense.[3] The conventional wisdom is wrong. Khrushchev was not consistent in his policy advocacy, was apparently ambivalent about policy trade-offs, actually advocated attention to agriculture at the expense of light industry, consistently argued against procurement price rises for agricultural products, and rarely argued for cutting the defense budget. Even in 1964, when Khrushchev went furthest in finally facing up to the budgetary implications of consumer needs, he did not embrace Malenkov's program. The First Secretary was consistent in one respect: in his effort to reconcile the post-Stalin commitment to the consumer with his earlier promises that this commitment could be met on the cheap.

Until the second half of 1960, Khrushchev displayed no sense of urgency about the ominous economic trends beginning to converge. He was able to rationalize the poor harvest of 1959 with reference to his theory that in Soviet agriculture "good years alternate with bad ones."[4] His May 1960 speech to the Supreme Soviet, which called for the more rapid development of light industry in order to reduce inflationary pressures, and which announced the abolition of income taxes and a shortened work week as well, may have been a response to the worker riots of earlier months. But it was not inconsistent with the First Secretary's modestly expanded commitment to investment in light industry during 1958–9. Moreover, in light of subsequent events, it appears to have been a measure of Khrushchev's confidence that no crisis existed on the agricultural front, and that the broad-based political coalition of 1957–9 could be held together.[5]

---

[3] Ploss, *Conflict and Decision-Making*; Linden, *Khrushchev and the Soviet Leadership*; Hahn, *Politics of Soviet Agriculture*; Tatu, *Power in the Kremlin*.

[4] He made this statement at the December 1958 Plenum (*Pravda*, 15 December 1958), after a record harvest. Thus, it was not a manipulative excuse at the time, but a belief that Khrushchev would be able to tap a year later. I have no evidence, however, that he explicitly referred back to the belief at the end of 1959. The existence of the belief in Khrushchev's mind, though, would lend support to my contention that he was not advocating a change in investment priorities or agricultural strategy at the December 1959 Plenum.

[5] *Pravda*, 6 May 1960. Moreover, Khrushchev expressed little sense of urgency about the problem. He pointed out that plans for consumer-goods production were only in the planning stages, which implied that their impact would not be immediate.

In August 1960, however, after the mid-year results of the harvest had come in from the provinces, Khrushchev expressed doubts, and started to move in the direction of accepting the budgetary and political implications of the agricultural slowdown.[6] He acknowledged the need for new expenditures on irrigation and land reclamation, but was still ambivalent about the extent of reallocation needed.[7] By October, however, such ambivalence was no longer in evidence. The third-quarter results were in, coupled with indications of widespread fraud by local party officials in pretending to meet their targets. In an angry and panicky memorandum to his colleagues in the Presidium, Khrushchev demanded that the deal worked out at the Twenty-First Party Congress now be applied to agriculture's need for mechanization, fertilizers, irrigation, chemicals, and herbicides.[8] This memorandum constituted the opening salvo in a hectic four-year period which ended with Khrushchev's dismissal. At several points during these years, Khrushchev shifted his economic perspectives and political strategies. Hence, I have sub-periodized the larger time period in order to highlight these shifts and, later, to show how they interacted with shifts in other realms. In a sense, then, the final stage of the Khrushchev era was one of multiple frustrations and reactions.

Frustration and Reaction: October 1960–Spring 1961

Khrushchev's response to his perception of crisis was to abandon the expanded coalition of 1957–60 and to reforge the alliance of agriculture and heavy industry. However, as he now defined the problem, his demands on heavy industry were more far-reaching than they had been during 1953–6. Thus, at the January 1961 Plenum, he demanded "serious adjustments in the appropriations for the needs of agriculture," insisted that such appropriations would have to come from a reduction in the growth rate of heavy industry and the size of the defense budget, criticized those who "have now developed an appetite for giving the country as much metal as possible," and pointed out that heavy industry and agriculture would henceforth have to develop at the same rate.[9]

Moreover, Khrushchev made it clear that under these conditions further expansion of investment in light industry had become an

[6] See his memorandum to the Presidium, in *Stroitel'stvo kommunizma IV*, pp. 137–50.

[7] "At one time we considered the question of reclaiming the Akhtubinskii flood plain, but decided to postpone the matter since it would require large capital investments. I think that we ought to return to this question . . . But we should resolve it, not, as some suggested, by reclaiming the entire flood plain in a short period of time. We should approach this task more modestly, reclaiming the plain in stages" (ibid., p. 146).

[8] ibid., pp. 180–1.

unaffordable luxury. Thus, in his October 1960 memorandum to the Presidium, he pointed out that the demand for consumer goods had risen, but especially the demand for food products rather than consumer soft goods.[10] At the January 1961 Plenum, he mentioned light industry only in passing, and spoke at length only about agricultural needs.[11] Two weeks later, on a barnstorming tour to propagandize the results of the Plenum, Khrushchev told a gathering in Tbilisi that above-plan accumulations were going to fabrics, clothing, and other such commodities, but that food was of greater priority than textiles—an observation that served as a prelude to a pitch for agricultural investments.[12]

Khrushchev also made clear what he wanted done with the new

[9] ibid., pp. 286–7, 289, 291.

[10] ibid., p. 165.

[11] See ibid., pp. 281–378.

[12] ibid., p. 452 ("It is important to have good clothing and good footwear, but it is still more important to have a tasty dinner, breakfast, and lunch . . ."). Thus, it would appear that, far from being a long-embattled advocate of the needs of light industry, Khrushchev turned his attention to this sector only when all appeared to be well in the agricultural sector. His polemic with Malenkov had in fact been couched in these terms. In addition, his 1957 advocacy of expanded attention to light industry came on the heels of the record harvest of 1956. His mid-1959 suggestions that production of textiles be expanded came after the record harvest of 1958. And his modest program for urban consumer welfare at the May 1960 Supreme Soviet session came before his recognition of the urgency of the agricultural situation.

Hence, when in May 1961 Khrushchev was quoted as telling foreign journalists that light industry would henceforth develop at rates equal to those of heavy industry (*New York Times*, 21 May 1961), one suspects that the statement was not an indication of Khrushchev's behind-the-scenes struggle for augmenting light-industrial investment, but one or more of the following: (1) an effort to bluff the West into thinking that Soviet defense expenditures would be cut; (2) a symbolic affirmation of Khrushchev's commitment to cut heavy-industrial expenditures and reduce the status of the "citadel" of heavy industry in the Soviet budgetary process; or (3) to the extent that he intended those funds to be channeled to Group B industries, he did not specify which sectors of Group B. From his statements of earlier months, he might well have had in mind the food-processing industry, rather than textiles. Moreover, the fact that Khrushchev's remarks were never published in the Soviet press—usually interpreted as a sign of factional opposition ascendant—might well reinforce the first of our three alternative explanations: that the statement was made for foreign consumption. It would not have been the only time when Khrushchev had sought to distinguish between foreign and domestic audiences when delivering messages (see *New York Times*, 2 March 1959). And if this was part of a more general pattern or strategy on his part, we would have to discount some of his other calls for defense budget cuts made at private audiences with foreigners (compare the following contradictory statements before such audiences: *Stroitel'stvo kommunizma VII*, pp. 100–1 [13 July 1962]; *Stroitel'stvo kommunizma VIII*, p. 51 [30 July 1963]; and *Pravda*, 25 October 1963).

investments in agriculture. In his speeches and memoranda during this sub-period, he stressed the need to increase production and delivery of advanced farm technology, and to build up the Virgin Lands into a major center for animal husbandry.[13] In his memoranda of August and October 1960, he had noted a broad range of agricultural needs, but the operative emphasis in subsequent speeches was almost always on farm technology and infrastructural development of the Virgin Lands.

These were programs that would not increase consumption in the immediate future. They required time. But Khrushchev was not of a mind to be patient. He was advocating programs that would build up the ability of the rural sector to increase consumption in the long run. But he simultaneously intensified pressure on rural cadres in order to meet the needs of short-term consumption. Indeed, at the January 1961 Plenum, Khrushchev acknowledged the duality of his position. After discussing at length the budgetary reallocations required for intensive development of Soviet agriculture, he added: "Comrades! I have been discussing long-term questions. But the main thing now is to use existing possibilities for a sharp increase in production of grain, technical cultures, meat, milk, and other products already in the present year and in the immediate future."[14]

After the Plenum, Khrushchev traveled far and wide throughout the federation, pressuring local officials to increase their targets and pledges, demanding reductions in fallow lands and the planting of high-yield crops. He railed against dependency.[15] And lest we interpret

Finally, Linden (*Khrushchev and the Soviet Leadership*, p. 108) cites a passage from Khrushchev's speech in Alma-Ata on 24 June 1961, in which the First Secretary spoke on behalf of light industry. That passage, however, amounts to little more than a rhetorical flourish, and inspection of the speech in question (*Pravda*, 25 June 1961) reveals that it was tucked away toward the end of the speech with no further elaboration.

[13] For Khrushchev's advocacy of advanced technology, see his memoranda to the Presidium of 31 March 1961 (*Stroitel'stvo kommunizma V*, pp. 313–52) and of 20 July 1961 (ibid., pp. 418–41); see also his statements to this effect at the January 1961 Plenum (*Stroitel'stvo kommunizma IV*, pp. 289–93, 308). For his advocacy of expanded Virgin Lands development, see ibid., pp. 169–75, 339–50; *Stroitel'stvo kommunizma V*, pp. 196–352, *passim* (NB: "This is a new, second stage of the assimilation of virgin lands," ibid., p. 317.)

[14] *Stroitel'stvo kommunizma IV*, pp. 297–8.

[15] Evidence for these assertions is too voluminous for individual citation. It can be found in almost any speech by Khrushchev during 1961, and in most speeches during 1962–3. The skeptical reader may wish to read some speeches at random, beginning with *Stroitel'stvo kommunizma IV*, p. 162. For evidence along these lines from a source not yet cited, see Khrushchev's heckling of speakers at the January 1961 Plenum, as condensed and translated in *CDSP*, vol. 13, no. 5, pp. 11–15; vol. 13, no. 6, pp 12–17, 45; vol. 13, no. 7, pp. 11–14.

such pressure as merely symbolic rhetoric, we should note that Khrushchev incorporated the demands for extraordinary targets into his memoranda to the Presidium.[16]

Nor did the agricultural crisis cause Khrushchev to back down from his commitments on price policy. At the Ukranian Central Committee Plenum of January 1961, he was vehement in his opposition to further price rises, calling upon rural officials instead to cut costs and make a profit within the current price structure.[17] Moreover, in that same speech, he explicitly linked further procurement price rises to a prospective rise in urban retail prices ("And isn't it important to the worker that agricultural produce—meat, milk, butter—be cheaper?"). There is little point in arguing that Khrushchev was dissimulating, advocating one thing in public and the opposite behind the scenes. He made this speech in the same month as his speech to the January 1961 Plenum, where he pulled out all stops in attacking the defense budget and calling for a purge of regional cadres (about which more below). This was a month during which Khrushchev candidly went public with a new program in response to his perception of crisis. But that new program did not include reconsideration of the position on price policy that was basic to his low-cost approach to rural development and central to his authority-building strategy.

One way to cut costs without raising prices, and before the delivery of new technology, Khrushchev argued, was to rationalize the organization of labor and to increase social inequality. Hence, during this period, we no longer find in Khrushchev's speeches a concern for channeling collective farm surpluses into the indivisible (that is, reinvestment) funds; and we no longer encounter complaints about excessive private accumulation—quite the contrary. Now aware that the agricultural problem was far from solved, Khrushchev fell back upon a stronger emphasis on private material reward as a means of spurring productivity. During 1961 his demands focused on the need to develop an adequate system of supplementary pay on collective farms, on the need to expand piecework pay on state farms, and on those delinquent officials who were denying supplementary allocations-in-kind to collective farmers who had overfulfilied their plans.[18]

Yet there were limits to the extent to which Khrushchev was willing to retreat from collectivist ideals for the sake of economic growth. Given the renewed emphasis on private material reward as a spur to productivity, some officials suggested that restrictions on the private sector in agriculture should also be lifted. Khrushchev had earlier

[16] See *Stroitel'stvo kommunizma IV*, pp. 162–86; *Stroitel'stvo kommunizma V*, pp. 313–52, 418–41.

[17] *Stroitel'stvo kommunizma IV*, pp. 390–1. See also *Stroitel'stvo kommunizma V*, pp. 129ff.

[18] *Stroitel'stvo kommunizma V*, pp. 17, 86–7, 169, 298, 346, 421–2.

called a halt to the vigorous campaign against that sector, but had not lifted the formal restrictions enacted in the late 1950s. Nor was he willing to do so in 1961.[19] Whether he believed that the private sector could not relieve the economic crisis; or whether he felt it would damage his political credibility to retreat that far; or whether he was simply wedded to the social values involved is unclear. But the result was clear enough. Khrushchev, during October 1960–Spring 1961, was trying to solve the agricultural problem through limited budgetary redistributions, and intensification of pressure on local cadres, while still maintaining his restrictions on the private sector and abandoning his earlier efforts to combine collectivist egalitarianism with rapid economic achievement.

Tortured Search: Summer 1961–Spring 1963

For the next two years there appeared a notable change in Khrushchev's public position on resource allocation. He raised his demands for redistributing funds to the benefit of agriculture, and called for the funding of a broader array of rural needs. But he no longer called for cutting the defense budget to accomplish these ends.

During Summer/Fall 1961, ostensibly in response to President Kennedy's augmented military budget, and then in response to the Berlin crisis of August 1961 (which he precipitated), Khrushchev announced the cancellation of Soviet plans to cut troop levels further, indicated that the defense budget would be raised by one-third, and announced unilateral resumption of nuclear testing by the Soviet Union.[20] The final version of the Party Program published in October 1961, and Khrushchev's speeches at the Twenty-Second Party Congress in October 1961, reflected the regime's, and Khrushchev's, retreat to a more explicit defense of military interests in the budgetary process.[21]

Nor was this a temporary phenomenon. At no time during the two-year period, July 1961–Spring 1963, when addressing a domestic audience, did Khrushchev make the kind of linkage between consumer needs and defense expenditures that he had made at the January 1961 Plenum. His speeches at the Twenty-Second Party Congress gave roughly equal weight to increasing consumer satisfaction and

---

[19] *Stroitel'stvo kommunizma IV*, p. 434.

[20] *Pravda*, 9 July 1961, and 31 August 1961.

[21] The draft version of the Party Program conceded more to the consumer than the final document (compare *Pravda*, 30 July 1961 with ibid., 2 November 1961). For Khrushchev's balanced remarks on resource allocation at the Twenty-Second Party Congress, see Gruliow, *Current Soviet Policies IV*, pp. 53, 55, 63, 67, 75, 89–90, 91, 98, 106.

maintaining traditional budgetary priorities. His main report to the March 1962 Plenum, where he spoke forcefully in favor of increasing agricultural investments, differed sharply from his analogous speech at the January 1961 Plenum, in that he never mentioned the defense budget as the source of expanded capital investment in agriculture.[22] His concluding speech to that Plenum explicitly rejected the idea that such investments might come from the defense budget, adding the forceful caveat that "the strengthening of the might of the Soviet Union, of its defenses, is our most important task, and we shall perform it unswervingly. This is the foundation of foundations [*osnova osnov*] of the existence of our socialist state, of its development and successes."[23] Similarly, after the Cuban missile crisis (October 1962), Khrushchev again augmented his rhetorical association with defense interests. Thus, in his election speech of February 1963, Khrushchev chose exceptionally strong terminology to defend the priority of defense expenditures:

> The voters . . . would rightly judge it a crime if, out of a desire to make a display of extraordinary successes in satisfying people's everyday needs, an underestimation of the country's defenses were permitted. Our people know from experience that this cannot be allowed.
> The Soviet people experienced the second world war . . .
> If we stop paying attention to our defense capabilities, then the balance of forces can change to our disadvantage. . . . Such economy would have to be paid for in the people's blood . . .[24]

It is difficult to say whether Khrushchev's retreat to a "defense of defense" was forced upon him by others in the national leadership, or was a product of his personal choice. At a minimum, we can say that those who unambiguously defend the political explanation are probably overstating the case.[25] For one thing, the international atmosphere had sharply worsened during 1961; the change in Khrushchev's position on the defense budget, therefore, could have reflected his personal reaction to the worsening international situation. For another thing, Khrushchev's behavior during 1961–3 contained numerous impetuous and irreverent elements: willingness to appeal

22 See *Pravda*, 6 March 1962.
23 ibid., 11 March 1962.
24 ibid., 28 February 1963 (*CDSP*, vol. 15, no. 9).
25 This is the pattern of explanation suggested in Linden, *Khrushchev and the Soviet Leadership*, pp. 140, 164–5; Ploss, *Conflict and Decision-Making*, pp. 251–2 (commenting on the March 1962 Plenum); Tatu, *Power in the Kremlin*, pp. 214–19, 331–2; also, Robert M. Slusser, *The Berlin Crisis of 1961* (Baltimore: John Hopkins University Press, 1973), *passim*. In fairness, we should note that Tatu dates Khrushchev's open struggle against the military – heavy-industrial complex only back to 1960.

above the heads of his colleagues in public, to demand and secure far-reaching changes in authority relationships, and to force through wild schemes for administrative reform on short notice. It is possible to argue that Khrushchev was able to secure these kinds of changes, but not to secure changes in the defense budget. But, if this had been the case, it seems unlikely that he would have kept his mouth shut. Had Khrushchev not believed the statements he was making with respect to defense expenditures, it is unlikely that he would have chosen such forceful terminology in defending the military budget, or that he would never have made contrary public statements in front of domestic Soviet audiences during the two-year period under discussion.

Let us be clear as to what such an alternative interpretation would imply, however. Khrushchev was certainly in favor of holding down costs in the defense sector, and this was reflected most openly in his running debates with military leaders over the relative value of rockets versus land armies, strategic forces versus conventional armaments in the nuclear age.[26] However, this did not distinguish Khrushchev's attitude toward the defense sector from his attitude toward any other sectors. He was a vociferous supporter of cost-cutting in heavy industry, agriculture, and light industry as well. Indeed, such an orientation was fundamental to his claim that he could address simultaneously the manifold developmental needs of industry, agriculture, and defense. Moreover, the pattern of Khrushchev's statements indicates that he hoped eventually to cut the defense budget in favor of consumer-oriented expenditures, but that the international configuration of forces would first have to be appropriate to such a step. His foreign-policy behavior during this period is beyond the scope of this volume, and may have reflected a willingness to sacrifice certain foreign policy goals in pursuit of a détente that would allow him to cut the defense budget.[27] But his behavior on the domestic scene

---

[26] For a vivid and persuasive account of these debates, see Thomas Wolfe, *Soviet Strategy at the Crossroads* (Cambridge, Mass.: Harvard University Press, 1965).

[27] This is a major theme of Linden's *Khrushchev and the Soviet Leadership*, and is not one with which I am attempting to quarrel in this book, if only because the present study largely ignored the foreign-policy dimension. In addition to confirming that Khrushchev was long an advocate of defense modernization, his memoirs also indicate that he bemoaned the drain on scarce funds resulting from military needs (*Khrushchev Remembers*, Vol. 1, pp. 508, 518–19, 520; Vol. 2, p. 34), and that he was highly conscious of costs and the efficient use of allocated funds (ibid., pp. 32, 100, 399). But the memoirs also convey the impression of a leader who when the budget had to be set, ultimately gave in to the advice of his military advisors on what constituted a national security threat (ibid., pp. 411–12, 540). Khrushchev does reveal for the historical record that, toward the end of his years in office, he sought to reduce the rate of increase of military spending:

suggests an individual whose main priorities were national security and agriculture in the context of the changed international environment that followed the Berlin crisis.

Within these new budgetary limits, Khrushchev expanded the range of agricultural needs he considered critical, and was as forceful as ever in demanding reductions in the heavy-industrial budget—or redirection of expenditures within that budget—for the sake of agriculture. At the March 1962 Plenum, he complained that agricultural machine-building was being slighted, dwelled at length on agriculture's need for advanced technology, fertilizers, herbicides, and electrification, and averred that, "in the interests of the further development of agriculture, we must undertake these capital investments."[28] He continued to press the causes of agricultural machine-building and mineral fertilizer production at the November 1962 Plenum.[29] All along, however, his demands concentrated on the development of new technologies that would raise productivity and economize on metal, while his solutions to the problems of current consumption focused on plowing up millions more hectares of fallow and virgin lands. Investment in light industry received little attention in his speeches.

But we also find during this period the introduction of a measure of doubt, befuddlement, or self-protection into the statements of the First Secretary regarding the needs of agriculture. Thus, with respect to land reclamation: on 12 January 1962 and 27 March 1962, he indicated grave reservations about the wisdom of investing scarce funds in this area.[30] On the other hand, in statements of 5 September 1962 and 1 October 1962 he indicated no such ambivalence.[31] In the interim, there was a note of chagrin and sincerity in Khrushchev's observation of 20 April 1962 that "the more deeply we delve into agricultural problems, the more attention and resources we need to devote to their resolution."[32] Whether this inconsistency and befuddle-

---

"The modernization of our army took years of work and cost billions. However, once we had equipped ourselves with the missiles, airplanes, submarine fleet, and nuclear warheads needed for our defense, we were able to reconsider our military budget" (ibid., p. 220). He also reveals that he initiated an economizing trend in military expenditure, which was reversed after his dismissal (ibid., pp. 535–6; Vol. 1, p. 520). Unfortunately, Khrushchev's testimony does not reveal whether his decision to "reconsider our military budget" came in 1961 (the January Plenum?), 1961–3, or still later.

[28] *Pravda*, 6 March, 1962.

[29] ibid., 20 November 1962.

[30] *Stroitel'stvo kommunizma VI*, pp. 328–9; *Stroitel'stvo kommunizma VII*, p. 14.

[31] *Stroitel'stvo kommunizma VII*, pp. 144, 222–3.

[32] ibid., p. 27.

ment was more a product of political than economic dilemmas is difficult to say.

Yet Khrushchev remained committed to a low-cost approach in the rural sector when the issue was one of price policy. Thus, at the March 1962 Plenum, where he spoke so forcefully on behalf of agricultural investments, he reiterated his long-standing insistence that price adjustments are not "the decisive factor" in agricultural development.[33] Later that month he expressed dismay that his model village —Kalinovka—was unable to meet the costs of production on eggs, pork, and poultry, an expression of dismay that presaged the price increases of June 1962.[34] It would appear that these price increases were either forced upon Khrushchev by political opposition, or represented his concession to economic reality. For after justifying these measures in rather defensive tones in two speeches during June 1962,[35] the First Secretary returned to his traditional theme: that prices were now high enough to ensure "large accumulations," and that the operative goal of regime policy remained to reduce prices once again as soon as possible.[36] And well he might argue in these terms, for the procurement price increases were absorbed, in part, by a sharp increase in urban retail prices, sparking riots in several large cities. Khrushchev's long-standing commitment to demonstrating that he could reconcile urban–rural terms of trade by holding down prices and cutting costs in the agricultural sector had met its severest test— and had failed.

To compensate for the crisis in current consumption, and to avert further price increases, Khrushchev intensified his efforts to pressure local cadres to rationalize the organization of production, cut costs, and raise private material rewards for productive workers. During the period under review he became increasingly explicit about the need to manipulate material rewards to the advantage of the best workers, and to deny rewards to the "laggards."[37] He extolled the motives of farm-workers who dreamed of accumulating large sums in order to purchase private motorcycles. And in the same breath he encouraged farms to accumulate "large earnings for their workers."[38] This from the Party Secretary who, some two years earlier, had been criticizing just such a trend!

A similar backlash became evident in the industrial sector. From 1962 onward leading figures in the Khrushchev administration (A. P.

---

[33] *Pravda*, 6 March 1962.
[34] *Stroitel'stvo kommunizma VII*, p. 10.
[35] ibid., pp. 33f., 48f.
[36] ibid., pp. 123, 154–5, 222, 307; the quotation about "large accumulations" is from ibid., p. 155.
[37] *Stroitel'stvo kommunizma VI*, pp. 112–13, 156–7, 248–9, 288, 332.
[38] *Stroitel'stvo kommunizma VII*, p. 14.

Volkov, Chairman of the State Labor and Wages Committee; V. V. Grishin, Chairman of the Central Trade Union Council; and L. F. Ilyichev, Head of the Central Committee Department for Agitation and Propaganda) engaged in sustained critiques of leveling tendencies within brigades receiving collective premiums, and called for bonuses to increase relative to wages as a proportion of total earnings.[39] Private material rewards were increased from this period forward, but were accompanied by campaigns to mobilize workers to uncover production reserves and to overcome inertia or resistance in revealing the true capacity of the enterprise. Anti-parasite campaigns added to the atmosphere of pressure, as the authorities sought to induce contributions from productive workers, and to punish the unproductive.

Khrushchev did not speak often of the role of wages in the industrial sector, but when he did his positions supported the combination of private material rewards and augmented pressure for results. He criticized a situation in which expenditures on wages were outpacing the rate of growth of labor productivity. He called for higher output norms; and he was a leading figure in threatening the "undisciplined."[40]

The partial retreat of these years was already foreshadowed at the Twenty-Second Party Congress in October 1961. Khrushchev's statements in that forum continued to stress the expanding role of social consumption funds in the course of "building communism." But his definition of the relative weight of wages as incentives for labor appears to have shifted slightly since the Twenty-First Party Congress. Although the shift was not as decisive as that which would follow Khrushchev's dismissal, it was real nonetheless, and mirrored the First Secretary's reemphasis on private material rewards as a spur to initiative:

Khrushchev: Twenty-First Party Congress[41]	*Khrushchev: Twenty-Second Party Congress*[42]
Should we raise the living standard solely by increasing wages and reducing prices? *It goes without saying that the Party and the government will consistently pursue the standing policy in regard to increasing*	Ought we to pursue the task of further improving the material living standards of the working people solely through direct wage increases and price reductions? *To be sure, the wage will for a long time continue to be the*

[39] See Volkov, in *Pravda*, 4 April 1962; Ilyichev, in ibid., 23 April 1962; Grishin, in ibid., 22 November 1962, 27 April 1963, 22 June 1963, 29–30 October 1963, and 12 December 1963.

[40] See, for example, Gruliow, *Current Soviet Policies IV*, pp. 65, 98, 101, 111–12; *Stroitel'stvo kommunizma VII*, pp. 374–83; *Pravda*, 26 April 1963.

[41] Gruliow, *Current Soviet Policies III*, pp. 51–2.

[42] Gruliow, *Current Soviet Policies IV*, pp. 63–4.

wages and reducing prices. But this is only one way . . . Satisfaction of the individual requirements of each person . . . must proceed not only through raising wages, but also through social funds, the role and significance of which will increase more and more. (Italics added)

principal form of material incentive for workers, and will depend on their labor contribution to social production. But at the same time the Soviet people are deriving an ever greater portion of their material and cultural benefits from public sources. (Italics added)

But just as there were limits in the agricultural sector to Khrushchev's willingness to sacrifice social values to immediate economic needs, so in the industrial sector Khrushchev led a campaign against private housing construction, and he vetoed demands for mass automobile production. Repressed inflation may have been a problem, but the First Secretary was not prepared to absorb excess purchasing power and spur labor initiative by encouraging such individualistic activities. In the case of automobile production, he may have seen the main constraint as budgetary. But in the case of private housing construction, he was apparently motivated by collectivist ideals.

Reallocation and Panaceas: Spring 1963–Fall 1964

During Spring/Summer 1963 Khrushchev's search for an effective problem-solving strategy took another turn. He was now ready once again to call for cuts in the defense budget to finance programs geared toward raising consumption. Perhaps this is to be explained by the sudden incapacitation of Politburo-member Frol Kozlov in April 1963. Such a political explanation, however, seems far from complete, for several other factors coincided to reshape the intellectual, economic, and international context within which Khrushchev was acting. Internationally, a thaw in Soviet–US relations had already begun in March, with the signing of the first of four limited-arms-control agreements that would culminate during the summer in the Nuclear Test-Ban Treaty. Economically, the first- and second-quarter results indicated that the year's grain harvest would be a disaster, creating a real threat to current consumption. Intellectually, Khrushchev's attention had been drawn back to the multiple applications of chemicals in simultaneously solving problems of current consumption and long-term investment.

Khrushchev had already indicated the need for more rapid development of the chemicals industry at the November 1962 Plenum.[43] But he did not formulate a tentative program for such development until

[43] *Stroitel'stvo kommunizma VII*, pp. 358f.

Summer 1963, when the conditions listed above had fallen into place.[44] By 1963–4 he had come to an intellectual appreciation of the multiple investment needs of agriculture (exclusive of further price increases). Yet, at the same time, he focused on chemicals as the key link in the chain of agricultural needs. Having concluded that mineral fertilizers, once applied, could result in high yields within a short period of time,[45] the First Secretary latched onto the development of a mineral fertilizer industry as a panacea for both short-term and long-term needs. At the same time, chemicals was an investment base that could radically transform the character of both heavy and light industry.

Once these conditions had fallen into place, Khrushchev abandoned his earlier approach and looked to the defense budget as a source of funds. In April 1963 he delivered a hard-hitting speech against waste and inefficiency in heavy industry and defense, declaring that the Soviet economy could not produce "nothing but rockets."[46] At the December 1963 and February 1964 Plenums, he argued vehemently for massive investments in the chemicals industry, paid for by cuts in the defense budget for 1964, possible future troop reductions, and "slowing down the growth of certain branches of industry."[47] In Summer/Fall 1964 Khrushchev went still further, announcing plans for a major new program of investment in means of production for light industry, agriculture, and the sectors of heavy industry which service consumer-oriented sectors of the economy.[48] Little wonder that at this time he was sending his son-in-law, Alexei Adzhubei, to West Germany to sound out the prospect of a further reduction in international tensions. For Khrushchev's investment priorities had by then become sufficiently reallocative that a major international thaw would facilitate the reduction in defense expenditures that the consumer investment program required.

Yet closer inspection of Khrushchev's emphasis on reallocation reveals that the Soviet leader's approach to consumer satisfaction continued to place inordinate emphasis on technology (chemicals, farm machinery, and means of production for light industry) and investments, at the expense of current consumption. Thus, his speeches at the March 1962 Plenum were followed by a variety of statements

---

[44] See his memorandum to the Presidium of 12 July 1963 (*Stroitel'stvo kommunizma VIII*, pp. 23–43).

[45] *Pravda*, 29 June 1963; *Stroitel'stvo kommunizma VIII*, pp. 23–43, 105–13, 181–9.

[46] *Pravda*, 26 April 1963.

[47] *Stroitel'stvo kommunizma VIII*, pp. 273, 376, 459–60; see also his comments on the defense budget in Nikita Khrushchev, "O mire i mirnon sosushchestvovanii" (On peace and peaceful coexistence), *Kommunist* (May 1964). See also note 27, above.

[48] *Pravda*, 2 October 1964.

indicating that Khrushchev considered the main task in agricultural machine-building still to be the design and development of new models that would economize on metal.[49] His speech at the November 1962 Plenum called for increased mineral fertilizer production and continuation of the "Leninist line of priority development of the means of production." (Hence, Khrushchev's criticism of "steel" advocates at the same Plenum appears to have been directed at those who monopolized scarce funds that could better be invested in chemicals and means of production for agriculture and light industry.) His April 1963 speech against wastage in the defense establishment was accompanied by the appointment of a chemist as deputy to the Supreme Council of the National Economy, thereby suggesting that, when Khrushchev proclaimed that the Soviet economy could not produce "nothing but rockets," he had in mind the diversion of resources to development of the chemicals industry.[50] Khrushchev's program for development of the chemicals industry speaks for itself. And his last-minute program of Summer/Fall 1964 for expanded investment in light industry called again for more rapid development of means of production for those industries.[51] Thus a restricted range of new technologies, with chemicals in the lead, became the cornerstone of Khrushchev's new-found approach to long-term consumption.

But the short-term consumption situation remained critical, and this, too, explains Khrushchev's fascination with chemicals. Chemicals could serve dual purpose, bringing quick results. Here was the quick fix Khrushchev was searching for.

At the same time, Khrushchev adhered to his traditional price policy in the face of rising pressures for a change, and despite the fact that procurement price rises during 1961–3 still left those prices too low to cover the cost of production of most agricultural products. Thus, in February 1964, he told a convention of agricultural officials that price rises would not be tolerated, and that "if anyone now farms at a loss, it is not due to prices."[52] Nor was this simply political rhetoric for public consumption. In a memorandum to the Presidium in April 1964, he expressed his dissatisfaction with several recent laws that had increased financial assistance to backward farms. Coming so late in his tenure in office, and following the disastrous harvest of 1963, Khrushchev's justification for his opposition to these laws provides striking proof of his continued adherence to a traditional approach: "Material resources, credits and so forth have great import-

[49] See *Stroitel'stvo kommunizma VII*, pp. 126–42.

[50] The personnel change is reported in Tatu, *Power in the Kremlin*, p. 345.

[51] Katz (*Politics of Economic Reform*, p. 95) points out this important difference between the Khrushchev and Malenkov approach to consumer satisfaction during Khrushchev's last months in office.

[52] *Stroitel'stvo kommunizma VIII*, p. 468.

ance, but they do not decide the essence of the matter. As they say, you can receive money, consume it, and still not raise production."[53] Instead, Khrushchev called upon the authorities to lift restrictions on the amount individuals could earn for extraordinary performance, and to "spare neither funds nor material means" to spur effort by the best officials, specialists, and equipment operators.[54]

Thus, even during the last year of his administration, when Khrushchev came closest to becoming the embattled consumer advocate that some scholars claim he had been all along, the First Secretary stood for a mix of approaches to fostering consumer satisfaction.

Administrative Reform

A broadly similar pattern of response on the part of the First Secretary can be found with respect to issues of administrative reform and control. Khrushchev began by abandoning his earlier posture of reconciliation with officialdom. He then forced through measures that would increase centralism, intervention, and pressure. As these solutions proved ineffective, Khrushchev became increasingly erratic in his search for an administrative panacea. Even as he intensified the pressure for quick results, he became increasingly receptive, intellectually and politically, to proposals for technocratic reform or decentralization of the economy. As in other issue-areas, however, his tenure in office ended with the First Secretary espousing a mix of contradictory approaches that he never succeeded in synthesizing.

The period of the late 1950s provided a test of Khrushchev's claim that high pressure could lead to unprecedented levels of plan fulfillment. By Fall 1960, however, reports were accumulating of widespread dissimulation, deception, and formalism within the party and state apparatuses. Rather than admit that his assumptions were flawed, Khrushchev reaffirmed the perspective and intensified the pressure. He returned to the earlier practice of leveling charges of "anti-state" behavior at officials, and expanded that practice by now leveling the charge at both state *and party* officials. "Only enemies of the socialist state could act in this way," was his response to the revelation that, in order to meet their quotas, local cadres were confiscating collective farmers' seed supplies.[55] "An anti-state tendency" was the way he referred to attempts by some officials to secure a lower plan for the

---

[53] *Pravda*, 24 April 1964.
[54] ibid.
[55] *Stroitel'stvo kommunizma IV*, p. 366.

next year.[56] And Khrushchev was determined to get rid of such people: between October 1960 and October 1961, 55 of the 114 provincial and territorial party first secretaries were either replaced or transferred.[57]

But even their replacements were not to be trusted. During 1961–2, Khrushchev raised the pressure on local cadres for extraordinary results, and continued his efforts to pinpoint responsibility for failures, complaining in conspiratorial terms of his inability to get a straight answer from anyone as to who was responsible for a given task.[58] His solution for dealing with this problem was a direct reflection and extension of his established perspectives: expanded mass control as a precondition for increased administrative visibility.

At the January 1961 Plenum, where he railed at length against anti-state behavior, Khrushchev reiterated the basic principle of his problem-solving strategy: "Absence of control can turn even an honest man, if he is unstable, into a thief. There must be public control or some other kind of inspection."[59] Nor was this merely rhetoric for public consumption. Khrushchev reiterated the perspective two months later in a private memorandum to his colleagues in the Presidium. In that memorandum, he discussed at length the need for increasing central control and surveillance over local party organs, and for expanding mass surveillance of local officialdom.[60]

It would be a mistake, however, to view Khrushchev's behavior during these years as static and one-dimensional. For even as he reaffirmed the role of political intervention in his search for an immediate improvement in policy effectiveness, he was also searching for, and espousing, alternative approaches to administrative efficiency.

In the industrial realm, Khrushchev spoke on four occasions of the need to change the bases for evaluating managerial behavior. At the Twenty-Second Party Congress (October 1961), he called for enterprises to "be given greater opportunity to determine the use of their profits."[61] At the November 1962 Plenum, he made favorable mention of the discussions then taking place in central journals and newspapers over the decentralizing proposals of Evsei Liberman.[62] By December

[56] ibid., p. 367; for other cases of Khrushchev's resurrection of the accusation of anti-state behavior and crimes against the people during 1960–4, see ibid., pp. 168, 436; *Stroitel'stvo kommunizma V*, p. 350; *Stroitel'stvo kommunizma VII*, p. 479; *Pravda*, 26 April 1963, and 29 June 1963.

[57] Merle Fainsod, *How Russia Is Ruled*, 2nd edn (Cambridge, Mass.: Harvard University Press, 1963), p. 226.

[58] *Stroitel'stvo kommunizma IV*, p. 347.

[59] ibid., p. 311.

[60] *Stroitel'stvo kommunizma V*, pp. 349–50; also, at the November 1962 Plenum: *Stroitel'stvo kommunizma VII*, p. 407.

[61] Gruliow, *Current Soviet Policies IV*, p. 100 (report on the Party Program).

[62] *Stroitel'stvo kommunizma VII*, pp. 369–71.

1963 his statements included advocacy of formal accountability to the consuming masses on the part of enterprise managers:

> Evidently we should introduce a system whereby factories and firms are directly responsible to the consumer for the quality of their output, must do everything so that enterprises and firms do not work for the stores but for the consumers through the stores . . .
> Wherever possible we must broadly introduce a principle whereby the consumer could make claims against the producer of the goods —that is, so that responsibility is borne not only by the intermediary but by the one who sews poorly or who puts out inferior equipment, instruments and so on.[63]

And the First Secretary struck a similar note in his speech to the Supreme Soviet in July 1964.[64]

Thus an element of "consumer sovereignty" had entered into Khrushchev's public statements. Nor should this be entirely surprising, for his earlier strategies had been based upon a rejection of bureaucratic centralization, concern to stimulate local initiative by new methods, and demands for greater official responsiveness to criticism from below. Moreover, Khrushchev had a political interest in incorporating new themes into his speeches. As Party leader, he had built his authority in part by continually seizing the initiative, cultivating the image of a man who would show the way. When Khrushchev's program began to fail, the climate of opinion within the political and specialist establishments began to shift, and economic reform proposals began to surface in party publications.[65] Khrushchev therefore had an interest in preempting these issues in ways that would keep him looking like a leader who was "out in front."

Yet we may be skeptical as to whether Khrushchev would have instituted a genuine industrial decentralization had he had the time and power. For he never came to an intellectual or practical reconciliation of his reliance on high pressure and political intervention from above with his new-found statements on ways to redirect managerial behavior toward demands from below.

In the agricultural realm, however, Khrushchev nearly arrived at such a synthesis—at least intellectually. During 1963–4 Khrushchev engaged in a process of search for a solution to the agricultural problem during which he successively rejected almost all of the social and political objections to genuine decentralization of managerial initiative and redirection of the interests toward which local state

---

[63] *Pravda*, 15 December 1963 (*CDSP*, vol. 15, no. 48).

[64] *Pravda*, 14 July 1964.

[65] The economic reform proposals of Evsei Liberman were published in *Pravda*, 7 September 1962.

officials would respond. This process led Khrushchev to embrace the idea of the "link" (*zvenevaya*) system as a cure to the ills of both short-term and long-term consumption.

The link system differs from the prevailing brigade system in several important ways.[66] Mechanized brigades on Soviet collective farms are charged with such tasks as rowing and sowing all the fields on the farm. They are paid, not according to the productivity or profitability of the farm as a whole, but simply according to the number of hectares or fields sown or worked. This gives them a built-in incentive to work as quickly as possible, and with little regard for whether their methods of operation will perhaps frustrate the ultimate goal of rational and high-yield cultivation. The system appeals to local and central planners, because it is easily monitored and fits in with the post-Stalin trend in the direction of very large-scale farming. Yet its irrationalities can become obvious to anyone trying to relate intermediate operations to final results.

The "link" system is based on quite different premises. It delegates to a relatively small number of skilled machine operators, specialists, and line personnel the task of cultivating a given piece of land year-round. The "team" is responsible for all the operations, from sowing to reaping.

Payment is a function of the final results, not the intermediate operations, encouraging group efforts to find the most rational and productive means of working the land. Not all crops are amenable to cultivation by these methods, but when introduced experimentally in selected places during the post-Stalin period, the link system has produced phenomenal results. Not only has production increased markedly, but it has done so with far less labor and far fewer tractors than farms working under the mechanized brigade system.

Yet the very bases of the link system's successes have provided some of the main philosophical and political objections to its wider use. Using far fewer workers would mean that large numbers of field hands would be dismissed from work, threatening the sense of job security that Soviet leaders assure the masses is a distinguishing virtue of socialism. Producing far greater quantities of goods, and making the pay of remaining workers a reflection of those quantities, would vastly increase the degree of material inequality and social differentiation in the countryside. And giving autonomy to on-farm teams to run their fields as they see fit would diminish the interventionist prerogatives of local and central planners.

[66] For discussion of the link system in Soviet agriculture, see Dimitry Pospielovsky, "The 'link system' in Soviet agriculture," *Soviet Studies* (April 1970), pp. 411–36; and Alexander Yanov, "Social contradictions of the countryside in the sixties," in *International Journal of Sociology*, special issue (Summer/Fall 1976), pp. 13–74.

Yet Khrushchev's embracing of the link system can be traced to his increasing disregard for these social and political values as he searched for ways to bolster his effectiveness during 1961–4. We have already seen that Khrushchev strongly endorsed elitist approaches to labor payment during this period. In addition, during June 1962, he called for reducing the costs of labor by *releasing redundant workers* on the farms and relocating them for work elsewhere.[67] Throughout these years, he bemoaned the fact that, despite increasing supplies of technology, agricultural production was not keeping pace.[68] Could not great advances be made through more rational use of existing technology? And given Khrushchev's resistance to continual increases in procurement prices, he was led to search for ways to increase on-farm productivity through manipulation of the incentive structure.

As Khrushchev searched more deeply for the causes of the problem, his attention was drawn to the ways in which collective farms distribute their income. In a memorandum to his colleagues on 31 July 1963, he grappled with the problem of how to raise up lagging farms to the level of the advanced.[69] Khrushchev pointed out that further price rises were not needed since farms would only distribute the additional monies equally among all workers, regardless of their level of productivity. Moreover, he went on to argue that the system of pay was so organized as to leave skilled machine operators without a material interest in the "final results" of their work. On 16 September 1963 Khrushchev spoke to a meeting of officials and specialists in Volgograd, and reiterated his dismay that farmers are not rewarded for final results, complaining that Comrade Svetlichny's teams spend 11·7 minutes to produce a centner of sugar beets, while others spend 2½ hours—yet there is little difference in pay between the two![70]

Khrushchev was now starting to meet more people such as Svetlichny and to praise them in his speeches. Comrade Pervitsky and his "team" came in for praise on 26 September 1963, along with calls for broader use of the link system in cultivating rice, and for the broader material differentiation it would require: "Of course, the labor of such masters of their jobs as V. Svetlichny and V. Pervitsky must be well paid for."[71] Khrushchev expanded the praise at the February 1964 Plenum, noting pointedly that one of the many advantages of the link system was that it measured people's contributions by the "results achieved."[72]

[67] *Stroitel'stvo kommunizma VII*, p. 67.
[68] *Stroitel'stvo kommunizma VI*, p. 452; *Stroitel'stvo kommunizma VII*, pp. 196, 215, 298–9; *Stroitel'stvo kommunizma VIII*, pp. 63, 132.
[69] ibid., pp. 62–87.
[70] ibid., p. 131.
[71] *Pravda*, 27 September 1963.
[72] *Stroitel'stvo kommunizma VIII*, pp. 419–22.

Khrushchev's next step on the way to full conversion to the link system was to recognize and express its implications for the costs of administration. In his April 1964 memorandum (the same one in which he expressed opposition to higher prices and credits), Khrushchev pointed out that Svetlichny's team had the benefit of receiving direct payment for results.[73] This, he noted, makes more direct the tie between labor and reward, and would reduce the size of the bureaucratic apparatus required to monitor local behavior and plan fulfillment. Indeed, this was a crucial consideration for Khrushchev had already abolished the district party committee which, among other things, had the most to lose from on-farm autonomy for teams. Raikom officials could have had many reasons for opposing the link system—though the exact distribution of attitudes among them is a question for research. Some might have resented the diminution of their interventionist prerogatives, viewing it as a blow to their political status. Others might have genuinely believed that systematic pressure by local party officials remained the only way to induce a lazy, recalcitrant mass of peasants to work hard. Still others might have defined the mission of local party organs as protection of precarious social values against the "technocratic" forces of economic efficiency. To these officials, the material differentiation and job insecurity caused by widespread introduction of the link system would have raised the greatest objections.

Khrushchev had been raised in the same political culture as these officials, but his political position, his close identification with agricultural affairs, his learning process, and his authority crisis had led him to fall back upon a different mix of values. Achievement was now more important to him than equality; economic results more important than political status. The political status of local party officials, he concluded, was now an impediment to authentic initiative. Unremitting pressure as a spur to initiative, it is true, had been one of his rules of thumb, but Comrades Svetlichny and Pervitsky were teaching him otherwise. Material differentiation was not a social value that he considered repugnant in a time of crisis; he could always fall back on the notion that citizen obligation dictated a higher material payoff to the productive. And the question of job layoffs could also be taken care of easily enough. Could not these people be transferred to work elsewhere, just as the authorities had transferred hundreds of thousands of young people to the Virgin Lands by a combination of pressure and inspiration?

By 5 August 1964 Khrushchev had become a vocal public advocate of the link system. He summarized his views in a speech to grain

[73] *Pravda*, 24 April 1964.

growers in Saratov Province.[74] His speech lauded the potential inherent in such a system, and criticized the shortcomings of the existing system. There was only one thing missing from the speech, though: criticism of the principles of high pressure and central intervention in farm affairs. This may have been an effort to save face; or it may have been a product of his authority crisis and his search for a quick win through high pressure to buttress his credibility. Or, intellectually, it may have been a reflection of his failure to appreciate the contradiction between detailed intervention and farm-team autonomy. Whether for political or intellectual reasons (or both), this was another contradiction that Khrushchev never resolved before his dismissal.

Political Participation

In response to the setbacks of 1960, and the authority crisis that ensued, Khrushchev also redefined his approach to political participation. He now sponsored doctrinal and structural changes that would extend populism throughout middle and lower levels of the state *and party* apparatuses. He encouraged a high level of generalization of criticism, status equalization between the apparatchiki and the masses, and an adversarial relationship between full-time officials and their subordinates.

Khrushchev's behavior at the Twenty-Second Party Congress (October 1961) was indicative of this turn. There he resurrected and intensified the anti-Stalin campaign, and touted a number of doctrinal innovations. Thus, in defining the "State of All the People," Khrushchev indicated that this new form of state was being transformed into a nonpolitical organization of the working people.[75] Similarly, in proclaiming the emergence of a "Party of All the People," he sought to upgrade the ideological status of the party rank-and-file (vis-à-vis the apparatchiki) by predicting that, as an expression of the transition to "communist public self-government . . . the apparatus of the Party agencies will steadily shrink, while the ranks of Party *aktivists* grow."[76]

Such calls for de-politicization and de-bureaucratization could only be legitimized by a consensual image of society. Accordingly, Khrushchev proclaimed that "in our times non-Party people too are actively building communism arm in arm with the Communists, *and*

---

[74] ibid., 5 August 1964 (as translated in *CDSP*, vol. 16, no. 32, p. 5).
[75] Gruliow, *Current Soviet Policies IV*, p. 102.
[76] ibid., pp. 71–2.

the overwhelming majority of them reason like Communists" (italics added).[77] For similar reasons, Khrushchev also needed to downgrade the notion that existing class differences warranted the continuation of an elitist pattern of decision-making at the local levels: "the distinctions between the working class and the peasantry have been eliminated in their major, decisive aspects; the final eradication of class differences will now proceed at an ever-faster pace."[78]

Of course, Khrushchev remained thoroughly committed to the notion that the New Man was still to be created, but the locus of resocialization, he argued, had to shift. Accordingly, he tried still further to downgrade the formal, educational function of party and state officials, in a statement that would be repudiated by Brezhnev ten years later: "the molding of the new man is influenced not only by the educational work of the Party, the Soviet state, the trade unions and the Young Communist League, but by the entire pattern of society's life . . . All economic, social, political, and legal levers must be used to develop people's communist consciousness . . ."[79] And the concept of official "ties with the masses" found its way into the speeches of the First Secretary far more so than in any major speech to a party congress before or since.

In line with this populist thrust, Khrushchev used the Party Congress as a forum for generating an adversarial relationship between officials and masses. His renewal and intensification of the anti-Stalin campaign was justified as an effort to exorcise the "cult of personality" from contemporary Soviet political life and to "erect reliable guarantees" against its return.[80] In outlining proposals for the prospective new Soviet constitution, in a speech six months after the Party Congress, Khrushchev noted that the constitution should "create still stronger guarantees of the democratic rights and freedoms of the working people, and guarantees of the strict observance of socialist legality."[81] Khrushchev was thus raising the level of generalization of permissible criticism to heights not seen since 1956, if even then.

In a similar vein, Khrushchev campaigned during these years to reduce the size of the secretariat within party organizations, so as to force party officials to rely more on non-apparatchiki in decision-

---

[77] ibid., p. 114. Stalin, in his election speech of February 1946, also denigrated the party–nonparty distinction (*Pravda*, 10 February 1946), but this must be interpreted in terms of Stalin's effort at the time to reassert the primacy of his personal authority over all institutions. It was not accompanied by the pervasive Khrushchevian concern for transforming the authority relationship between officials and the masses.

[78] Gruliow, *Current Soviet Policies IV*, p. 66.

[79] ibid., p. 104.

[80] ibid., p. 114.

[81] *Pravda*, 26 April 1962.

making.[82] And he campaigned as well for formal measures that would "ensure the growth of the authority" of agricultural specialists, and protect them from official "arbitrariness."[83] All of which, when coupled with the diminished relative political status of officials resulting from Khrushchev's public statements and doctrinal reforms, created an atmosphere in which citizens might feel freer to challenge their superiors.

The crucial word in this last sentence, however, is "might," for Khrushchev's relationship with a variety of social groups was still dualistic. His intensification of pressure in the economic realm led him to force through measures that defied the advice of sober thinkers in the scientific community.[84] In the cultural realm, bursts of de-Stalinization alternated with harsh crackdowns on the nonconformist, as Khrushchev sought to balance his conflicting commitments to populism and political cohesion. He would press for further revelations to continue the "struggle against the old," but insist that all Soviet citizens follow his lead in "a single monolithic labor collective."[85] In the course of the cultural crackdown of Winter 1962–3, he would revert to vulgarity and neo-Stalinist threats against the nonconformist; but he would do so without making a single use of the terms "discipline" or "vigilance."[86] Similarly, in dealings with workers and employees, he would call upon Soviet officials to treat people tactfully, emphasizing human solidarity rather than commandism;[87] but he would simultaneously lead the witchhunt against "parasites" and sanction widespread use of the death penalty for economic crimes.

Khrushchev's dualistic pattern of behavior on this issue was not a product of intellectual confusion. It was rather a response to his authority crisis. On the one hand, he was only doing what he had been doing since 1953: attempting to demonstrate that political transformation could be made consistent with political stability, and could be used as a substitute for radical budgetary reallocation. On the other hand, his impulsive personality, when combined with his felt-need to recoup lost authority and keep potential rivals off balance,

[82] William Conyngham, *Industrial Management in the Soviet Union* (Stanford, Calif.: Hoover Institution Press, 1973), p. 148.

[83] *Stroitel'stvo kommunizma IV*, pp. 299–300, 347; *Stroitel'stvo kommunizma VII*, pp. 139, 153, 389.

[84] For examples of Khrushchev's attacks on specialists during this period, and the awkward position this often placed him in, see *Pravda*, 16 December 1961 (*CDSP*, vol. 13, no. 50, pp. 7, 8); *Stroitel'stvo kommunizma VI*, pp. 162, 283–4, 321, 464–7.

[85] *Pravda*, 8 March 1963.

[86] ibid. (there is one use of the term, "self-discipline"); for Khrushchev's sense of guilt, while in retirement, about his crackdowns on certain members of the intelligentsia, see Khrushchev, *Khrushchev Remembers*, Vol. 2, pp. 68, 76–7, 80, 98.

led him toward more extreme behavior in pursuit of each goal—populism and enforced cohesion.

An additional clue to Khrushchev's dual motives during this period appears in the semi-annual slogans of the Central Committee. In October 1961, for the first time in the entire postwar period, all reference to "labor discipline," "technological and production discipline," and "state discipline" disappeared from the slogans, not to appear again until after Khrushchev's overthrow.[88]

Yet, in light of the interpretation offered in this chapter, this should not be entirely surprising. The concept of "discipline" is a Soviet euphemism for hierarchical controls, and the reinforcement of discipline is usually done by increasing the discretionary powers of officials vis-à-vis their constituents. Since this was precisely what Khrushchev was trying to move away from, it is understandable that he was trying to decouple the traditionally paired concepts of "organization" and "discipline" in order to further his calls for cohesion based upon new patterns of social leadership.

Authority-Building and Policy Effectiveness: Khrushchev as Politician

As his authority eroded, Khrushchev moved fast to consolidate his formal power. By means of the purges of 1960–1 and the party bifurcation of 1962, he was able to expand his patronage base. By means of the personnel rotation system enacted in 1961, he created a mechanism whereby he might restore a variant of the "permanent purge" to Soviet politics. In the Party–State Control Commission he had an institution geared toward disciplining party officials that would allow the central party secretariat to expand its leverage against members of the regional elite.

Beyond power consolidation and problem-solving, Khrushchev's authority-building strategy reverted, as in other realms of policy, to the methods he had used so effectively during 1953–6. In his initial counterattack of October 1960–July 1961, Khrushchev resurrected the earlier practice of attempting to intimidate the political elite through allusions to a threatening mass mood and the conscious raising of mass consumer expectations. "If the necessary measures are not taken," he warned his colleagues in the memorandum of October 1960, "we may slide back to the situation that obtained in 1953."[89]

[87] *Stroitel'stvo kommunizma VII*, p. 377 (November 1962 Plenum).

[88] The word "discipline" was entirely dropped from the slogans during the period October 1962 through April 1965. In October 1961 and April 1962, it appeared only with reference to "military discipline."

[89] *Stroitel'stvo kommunizma IV*, p. 164.

He went on to allude to the fact that mass expectations had been raised by the Seven-Year Plan, and that these could only be met if production always exceeded demand. At the January 1961 Plenum he raised this last principle to the level of a doctrinal revision, pointing out that the gap between supply and demand "conceals dangerous consequences."[90] And, as if to make clear his willingness to mobilize the masses against local officials, Khrushchev warned that those officials, not he, would be held responsible by the masses for shocks to the standard of living.[91]

Yet Khrushchev was no longer the self-confident leader he had been in earlier years. Even at the height of his counteroffensive after October 1960, the First Secretary's pronouncements sounded like those of a politician who was on the defensive politically. Thus, Khrushchev's demands for extraordinary results began to coexist in his speeches with the intermittent defense of his approach to the calculation of targets: "These are not daydreams but workable plans"; "You know, comrades, that I am an optimist . . . "; "Some may say that Khrushchev takes individual, leading economic units and generalizes their results to the entire . . . zone. But what do you want, comrades?"[92] Moreover, Khrushchev's behavior during these months was that of a leader who felt the need for a quick win to buttress his shaken authority and to demonstrate anew his policy effectiveness. His intensification of pressure in the rural sector was linked to his call for "a sharp increase in production . . . in the immediate future."[93] He proclaimed a "second stage" in the development of the Virgin Lands, hoping to generate mobilizational fervor on behalf of duplicating past successes in that area. As he was at the same time calling for a limited reallocation of funds to the benefit of agriculture, it would appear that his simultaneous intensification of pressure was geared toward preventing a further loss of authority through additional failures, and toward demonstrating to the skeptical that his policies *per se* were not the root cause of the problem.'

For Khrushchev was out on a limb. He had helped to build his authority during earlier years by launching grandiose projects and promising unprecedented results. His detailed supervision of agricultural affairs wedded his personal authority closely to results in that sector. And now the agricultural slowdown was casting doubt on his ability to deliver. Or so it would appear from his behavior at the time. For in all forums during 1961–3—in memoranda to the Presidium, speeches at plenary sessions of the Central Committee,

[90] ibid., p. 286.
[91] ibid., p. 363.
[92] *Pravda*, 9 July 1961; *Stroitel'stvo kommunizma IV*, p. 377; *Stroitel'stvo kommunizma V*, p. 77.
[93] *Stroitel'stvo kommunizma IV*, pp. 297–8.

exhortative speeches before local personnel—Khrushchev both defended his authority in the face of doubters ("political bankrupts") and attempted to augment his authority with big promises of extraordinary results. "Best possible case" analysis pervaded many of his memoranda to the Presidium, proving that, even at this late date, such a line of reasoning was not merely exhortative rhetoric to advance the cause of public mobilization.[94] Rather, it represented the very promise of Khrushchev's administration and the results pledged to the political elite by a First Secretary who simply demanded that they let him show them the way.

But campaignism was no solution to Khrushchev's dilemmas. Rather than contribute to broader horizons and risk-taking among local officials, Khrushchev's pressures reinforced tunnel vision, exclusive focus on single goals at the expense of others, and dissimulation. Moreover, Khrushchev's search for agronomical panaceas both defied agronomic rationality and alienated many of the specialists whose cause Khrushchev was otherwise championing in the de-Stalinization campaign. Heightened pressure also undermined Khrushchev's participatory goals. It was incompatible with a new leadership orientation based on tact and persuasion, and it reinforced the tendency of party secretaries to make decisions rapidly and *in camera*.[95]

Nor is it likely that Khrushchev's authority was reinforced by his renewed efforts to mobilize mass expectations against the political elite, for these were taking place in an entirely different context from that which obtained in 1953–6. Worker riots had broken out in 1959–60. Hence, rather than representing a diffuse warning that the masses might become nasty should their needs at some point not be met, Khrushchev's statements of 1960–1 represented a threat of imminent disorder or retribution should those needs not immediately be met.

This is a crucial distinction. It is conceivable that the first type of allusion to the mass mood could have been received as legitimate (though intimidating) by many officials in 1953–6, for it was not inconsistent with that strand of the ideological tradition which emphasized the responsibility of party officialdom to adopt policies that would respond to the "ever-growing needs and requirements of the people." However, a prediction of imminent disorder on the part of the First Secretary, in a context in which workers had already taken to the streets, would not find legitimation in the ideological tradition, for it

---

[94] ibid., pp. 162–86; *Stroitel'stvo kommunizma V*, pp. 313–52, 418–41.

[95] The generalizations in this paragraph are based on: Waedekin, *The Private Sector*, pp. 304–15; Conyngham, *Industrial Management*, p. 203; Alec Nove, "Peasants and officials," in Jerzy F. Karcz (ed.), *Soviet and East European Agriculture* (Berkeley, Calif.: University of California Press, 1967), pp. 57–72.

would violate the injunction against "tailism": the practice of letting the masses dictate policies to the party. And it could have been viewed in that context as encouragement to the masses to be rebellious, not just demanding.

There are other reasons as well to doubt the effectiveness of Khrushchev's efforts. First, with the passage of time, it would be increasingly difficult to use such allusions to good effect, if only because the initial lack of self-confidence about the political elite's ability to govern without terror (and without Stalin) would wear off rather quickly as the years went by. Second, to the extent that a situation of economic crisis in 1960 was viewed by members of the political elite as a product of policies sponsored by the First Secretary himself, rather than as a regrettable inheritance from Stalin, Khrushchev's efforts to create a sense of elite dependence on his leadership could be turned against him.

Khrushchev, too, was apparently becoming aware of the limits of his ability to recoup policy effectiveness and political authority based on traditional approaches. A perceptible change in his public statements took place after Summer 1961. We have already seen that, from mid-1961 to early 1963, Khrushchev ceased public criticism of the defense budget, acknowledged more often his personal ambivalence and befuddlement about how to handle the agricultural problem, and conceded the need to search for more technocratic or decentralist approaches to public administration. At the same time, the First Secretary revised his approach to authority-building. For during this same period we find that Khrushchev eliminated from his public speeches references to anti-state behavior, put an end to publicly warning the Presidium or Central Committee about the threatening mass mood and began, in February 1963, to try to dampen mass expectations of consumer affluence, thereby also attempting to alter the standard by which his leadership would be judged. Thus, in his February 1963 election speech, Khrushchev played down cross-national comparisons of Soviet accomplishments, and reverted to systematic comparisons of agricultural and other achievements with the levels attained in 1953. And in the same speech, he pleaded with his constituents for patience: "just give us time, because it is impossible to do everything at once."[96]

But the very selectivity of Khrushchev's retreats in all realms became the basis for still another dilemma faced by the First Secretary. Harried local officials who belonged to the Central Committee seized upon Khrushchev's limited endorsement of budgetary reallocations to attempt to push him still further. Or so it would seem from the sudden intrusion into Khrushchev's speeches during these

[96] *Pravda*, 28 February 1963.

years of efforts to hold off a rush of demands for expanded delivery of machinery, fertilizer, and credits.[97] In like manner, Khrushchev's intermittent defensiveness about the realism of his targets apparently unleashed demands from below that the pressure be reduced. Or so it would seem from Khrushchev's warnings that local cadres should not use his statements as excuses for failing to fulfill the plan, or as excuses to slacken their efforts until the arrival of promised material assistance.[98] The change in Khrushchev's public position undoubtedly encouraged these behaviors, even as the limits of his retreat from earlier approaches caused him to try to hold them within bounds.

A most striking manifestation of these dilemmas surfaced at the March 1962 Plenum. In Khrushchev's opening-day speech, he outlined a vast program for expanded investment in agricultural machine-building.[99] In his closing address some days later, we learn by implication what kind of lobbying had intervened: "Comrades, let us agree to talk less of the shortages of machinery and to show more concern for making fuller and better use of the machines that are already on the collective and state farms. It does not take much brains to say 'Give, give give' . . ." The point was to mobilize all resources at hand and not sit in wait for promised resources from the state. "This, comrades, is very important. Otherwise people may be lured by hopes of additional aid, of new machinery: when they give us such-and-such a number of new machines, everything will go smoothly."[100] Indeed, the rush of demands from below must have been such as, cumulatively, to require a degree of budgetary reallocation that Khrushchev was not willing or able to countenance, for in his closing address Khrushchev pointedly advised regional cadres of the limits of his new commitment:

> agricultural workers, and *above all the leaders of republics, terri-*
> *tories, provinces, and districts,* must fully realize that the planned
> measures for increasing aid to agriculture do not mean that re-
> sources will now be diverted to agriculture at the expense of the
> development of industry and the strengthening of the country's
> defenses.[101] (Italics added)

[97] See *Stroitel'stvo kommunizma IV*, pp. 389–91; *Stroitel'stvo kommunizma V*, pp. 50, 230, 310; *Stroitel'stvo kommunizma VI*, pp. 89, 158; *Pravda*, 29 June 1963. Moreover, the content of these demands paralleled the evolving content of Khrushchev's calls for redistribution. During October 1960 through Spring 1961 the demands from below mentioned by Khrushchev were confined largely to requests for machinery. After that, the list expanded to include fertilizers, credits, and capital investments in infrastructure.

[98] *Stroitel'stvo kommunizma IV*, pp. 333f.; *Stroitel'stvo kommunizma V*, pp. 107, 309–10; *Stroitel'stvo kommunizma VI*, pp. 350, 443.

[99] *Pravda*, 6 March 1962.

[100] ibid., 11 March 1962 (*Stroitel'stvo kommunizma VI*, p. 448).

[101] *Stroitel'stvo kommunizma VI*, p. 441.

At this same Plenum of the Central Committee, Khrushchev apparently also faced intense pressure from below to reduce plan targets to more realistic levels. In his opening address, the First Secretary defended the realism of his targets.[102] In his closing address, he confronted his critics:

> The rates of growth of agriculture must conform with the tasks posed in the Party Program . . . [Otherwise] we may reproach ourselves for failing to take anything like full account of our potentials for developing agriculture. In the future some young people may even accuse us of not making a realistic estimate of the potentials of our country and our people, and therefore of posing tasks that are beneath our enormous potentials. We agree with this criticism.[103]

[102] ibid., p. 350.

[103] ibid., p. 443. Be it noted that this is not the standard Western interpretation of events at this plenum (see above, note 25). But in light of the documentation of Khrushchev's policy advocacy presented in this chapter, as a result of distinguishing among the audiences he was addressing, and as a result of factoring Khrushchev's authority-building dilemma into the interpretation of his statements, an important pattern in the evidence has now emerged. Both Ploss and Linden employ as a major component of their evidence during 1961–3 the alleged tendency for Central Committee plenary sessions to deny Khrushchev the demands he had advocated in his opening speeches. This pattern is then used as evidence of the First Secretary's political weakness in the face of opposition within the Presidium. The present study cannot comment on the extent of Presidial-level opposition to Khrushchev. But as we assemble wider bodies of evidence regarding Khrushchev's problem-solving and authority-building dilemmas, the pattern just noted tends largely to evaporate. That the January 1961 Plenum passed a resolution calling for expanded investments in agriculture, but ignoring the needs of light industry, was hardly a defeat for Khrushchev; it was in keeping with his stated position at the time. That the Twenty-Second Party Congress allocated little to consumer needs may not have pleased the First Secretary, but it was in keeping with his balanced speech at the congress and with his view of the relationship between international tensions and defense needs. The failure of the March 1962 Plenum to pass a resolution calling for higher prices for agricultural procurement was in keeping with Khrushchev's position at the time. Moreover, the same Plenum's failure to direct large sums to expanded output of agricultural machinery was in keeping with Khrushchev's demand that the emphasis be placed on developing new technologies that would economize on metal. Then, too, Khrushchev's "backtracking" in his closing speech to the Plenum was not inconsistent with his stated position on investment priorities in his opening speech, and was consistent with the larger tendency during this period for Khrushchev to try to dampen a rush of demands from below whenever he advocated expanded funding. The December 1963 Plenum's paring down of Khrushchev's original targets for chemicals-industry expansion may be counted as a setback for the Soviet leader—or it may be seen as a product of his having been persuaded during the days of the Plenum of the economic impossibility of his original, fantastic targets. In this connection, it is vital to bear in mind that even 75 percent of the original target was an immense undertaking, and that the chemicals industry was unable to absorb even those investments on such short notice.

Khrushchev was caught in a bind. To the extent that he maintained campaignist approaches to problem-solving, he simply compounded the precarious food situation, threatened the realization of his participatory goals, and highlighted the fact that he himself had largely created the existing situation. To the extent that he retreated only partially from these approaches, he sacrificed policy coherence and unleashed a rush of demands from various quarters to go still further. But to the extent that he went still further, he would be admitting the bankruptcy of his distinctive approaches to problem-solving, and would be highlighting his dispensability as a leader. Khrushchev therefore became increasingly erratic during 1963–4, returning to attacks on anti-state behavior and "crimes against the people" at precisely the time he returned to criticism of the defense budget and began to press for the most rapid development of the chemicals industry.[104] The First Secretary's behavior at this time is often explained by his long-term effort to reduce the defense budget for the sake of the consumer, but the evidence assembled in this book does not support such an interpretation. Alternatively, Khrushchev's behavior could be seen as a product of his impatient personality and ingrained susceptibility to panaceas. This explanation has a basis in fact, but is surely incomplete. For Khrushchev's behavior during these years was a joint product of his intellectual, emotional, and political inability to go beyond a selective retreat from his earlier approaches, and of the dilemmas of policy effectiveness and authority-building that these selective retreats created.

Moreover, events were compounding the dilemmas. The drought of 1963 caused a harvest disaster that forced the regime into the unprecedented act of purchasing large volumes of grain from other countries. The price system, even after the incremental price rises of 1961–3, still failed to make economically profitable the production of most agricultural goods. Hence, by the time the dimensions of the 1963 harvest failure were becoming evident, Khrushchev's promises must have been ringing hollow as he tried to rebuild his crumbling authority. One can hardly, for example, imagine anything but skepticism in the minds of most Central Committee members when, at the February 1964 Plenum, Khrushchev declared: "If we set about the job with still greater energy and persistence, we will be able to reach and surpass the United States' level of agricultural production in a few years. And this will happen!"[105] And one might also wonder about the reaction of members of the Presidium to Khrushchev's memorandum of April 1964, in which he declared that all farms could

---

[104] *Stroitel'stvo kommunizma VII*, p. 479; *Pravda*, 26 April 1963, and 29 June 1963.
[105] *Stroitel'stvo kommunizma VIII*, p. 411.

be raised to the level of the advanced in a "maximum of two or three years."[106] Such declarations, we may assume, no longer had the capacity either to mobilize popular energies, inspire official initiative, or protect Khrushchev's authority within the political elite.

There may not have been within that elite any single crystallized conception of what needed to be done to solve the problems of economic development, consumer satisfaction, administrative efficiency, and political participation. And there may have emerged increasingly staunch and disaffected groupings willing to articulate their opposition to Khrushchev's assaults on their institutional interests. These circumstances would have complicated Khrushchev's political and social learning processes. They would have augmented the intellectual difficulty of even discerning, let alone the political difficulty of forging, a stable majority coalition. By October 1964, however, the varied political interests and their representatives in the Presidium had agreed upon one thing: that Khrushchev's leadership had become counterproductive at worst, unnecessary at best. In their eyes, Khrushchev was no longer an effective problem-solver, or an indispensable politician. His authority had crumbled.[107]

---

[106] *Pravda*, 24 April 1964.
[107] The felicitous term, "the crumbling of authority," appears in Tatu, *Power in the Kremlin*, p. 364. Unfortunately, Tatu does not define the term, or explore the relationship between "power" (the title of his book) and authority.

7 How Strong the Leader?: Khrushchev's Power over Policy

One of the questions that has consistently intrigued historians of the Khrushchev era is: "how strong was the leader?"[1] Yet controversy over the extent of Khrushchev's power has never been resolved. At present, we have no clear answers to the crucial empirical questions: (1) How often did Khrushchev push for a significant policy and have to back down; and on which issues? (2) How inclined was Khrushchev to go beyond the policies he settled for? (3) How often did he defer from pushing policies, in anticipation of their rejection? (4) How often did he veto the policy proposals of others? (5) How often did Khrushchev have to pull rank in order to get his policies adopted?

It may be possible to answer these questions through a detailed, issue-by-issue study of the Soviet decision-making process; that is, through a methodology quite different from that embraced in this book. Yet I would not hold out high hopes. Twenty years of decision-making studies have done little to reduce controversy about these matters, or to answer the key empirical questions. Scholars have found that, in order to examine decision-making processes in great detail, one must focus on the less politicized issues. And those issues do not occupy much of the attention of the Politburo.[2]

Building upon the methodology employed in this book, let me propose a somewhat different approach to the study of Khrushchev's power. To what extent was the First Secretary able to control the policy agenda by seeing to it that his policy priorities were adopted by the Politburo; or, conversely, by seeing that priorities he opposed were not adopted? Adapting a phrase from the work of Archie Brown, let us call this "power over policy."[3] In this book, I have been using a methodology that allowed us to discern the policy priorities of the

---

[1] Thomas H. Rigby, "How strong is the leader?" *Problems of Communism* (September–October 1962); see also the debates among Rigby, Richard Lowenthal, Carl Linden, and Robert Conquest on this question, in *Problems of Communism* (July–August 1960) and *Problems of Communism* (September–October 1963).

[2] An important, partial exception to these generalizations may be Joravsky, *The Lysenko Affair*.

[3] Brown, "The power of the General Secretary," p. 151.

Party leader at given points in time. I searched for the language of insistence, accusation, urgency, and defensiveness as indicators of conditions under which Khrushchev was either pushing hard for his priorities, defending his shaken authority, or both. And I engaged in selective kremlinological analysis of political conflict in order to validate the claim that Khrushchev engaged in policy advocacy in his speeches, embracing a distinctive program for implementing the post-Stalin regime consensus.

One way to specify the extent to which Khrushchev exercised power over policy is to examine the correlation over time between his distinctive policy priorities and regime policies actually adopted. That is the purpose of this chapter.

Let us be clear as to what a "policy" means. In this book, I am dealing with the grand issues of Soviet domestic policy, and usually with the basic direction of policy, not the tactical details. Khrushchev might often have "lost" on matters of tactical detail (or might have willingly conceded the points), but if he won on questions of basic priorities and direction, that is the important datum. It is the more important indicator of power over policy. Moreover, policy is not the same as results. Regimes may adopt policies that get frustrated in the course of implementation. A Soviet leader may have sufficient power or authority to gain Politburo acquiescence in the adoption of major policies, but may not choose or be able to apply sufficient power to get those policies faithfully implemented. In this chapter, I am examining only adopted policy, not the ultimate fate of policy. The latter is an important indicator of power and authority, but would require another volume.

My documentation of policy trends is pieced together from a large body of secondary literature on Soviet policy during the Khrushchev years. It does not represent original research, and is not put forth as the final word on the subject. For example, our knowledge of Soviet defense budgeting is far from complete; responsible scholars remain in great disagreement about Soviet defense allocations during 1959–1964. I have tried to make good use of much of what is available, alerting the reader to holes in the evidence. I have not tried to quantify policy trends in a rigorous, tabular fashion. Instead, I have characterized and specified policy changes in prose form, referring the reader to the secondary literature on which the assertions are based.

Several conclusions emerge from the analysis. First, the evidence suggests that Khrushchev enjoyed a high level of power over policy, especially during 1955–62. Second, changes in policy follow the same rhythm as changes in policy advocacy. That is, the study of policy change reinforces our discovery of three distinct stages of the Khrushchev administration. Finally, this chapter suggests a methodological conclusion. In contrast to those who argue that Soviet leaders' speeches are nothing but propaganda and rhetoric, we have found that "what he said" did not diverge very greatly from "what he did." Properly interpreted, Khrushchev's speeches can be a reliable guide to policies adopted, assuming we know how to distinguish standardized rhetoric from policy advocacy.

Investment Priorities and Incentive Policy

Policies enacted during the years of political succession after Stalin reflected the regime's "new deal" consensus, calling for budgetary reallocations that would benefit the consumer. At the same time, those policies mirrored the vagaries of the power struggle between Khrushchev and Malenkov. Malenkov leaned toward policies that would eventually cut deeply into the heavy-industrial and defense budgets in order to fund increases in consumer satisfaction. Khrushchev, in contrast, stood for a relatively low-cost approach to increasing consumer satisfaction. Malenkov's biases defined the thrust of much policy during 1953 and part of 1954. But as Khrushchev gained political strength so, too, did policy shift. Policies enacted during 1955 and much of 1956 largely reflected the biases associated with Khrushchev.[4]

During 1953–4, a variety of measures sharply increased the monetary incomes of workers and peasants. The authorities reduced by 50 percent the amount of state bonds citizens were required to purchase. Prices paid by the state for collective-farm produce were raised sharply, collective-farm debts were written off, various charges, taxes, and costs borne by the rural producer were either cancelled, reduced, or assumed by the state, and restrictions on the private sector in Soviet agriculture were eased, permitting peasants to earn substantially more from the sale of their produce on the private collective-farm market.

In addition to putting more money into the hands of the population, the regime moved to increase the availability of food, soft goods, and consumer durables on which to spend the money. During 1953–4, the authorities launched major programs of investment in agricultural development, and also launched the Virgin Lands Program. At the

---

[4] My description of policy trends regarding budgetary priorities and incentive policy during the succession struggle after Stalin is based on: Schwartz, *Soviet Economy since Stalin*, pp. 55–73; Leonhard, *Kremlin since Stalin*, pp. 79–100; Nove, *An Economic History*, pp. 322–33; Bloomfield, Clemens, and Griffiths, *Khrushchev and the Arms Race*, pp. 50–5.

same time, the state tapped its grain reserves, converted a number of heavy-industrial plants to the production of consumer goods, and raised investment in the food-processing, soft-goods, and consumer-durables industries. To help pay for these investments, the regime cut back the defense budget, and cut back or abandoned many of the grandiose projects Stalin had initiated in the name of progress and security.

All of which pointed in the direction of a potentially far-reaching transformation of values. This raised political questions, and fed into the power struggle—as we have seen in Chapter 2. It also raised practical problems, for, by late 1954, concern about the inflationary impact of these measures had increased within the Soviet leadership. Monetary incomes had increased by 25 percent in two years, outstripping the rate of increase in the availability of goods on which to spend the money. After Khrushchev's disgrace of Malenkov in January 1955, significant changes in policy could be noted. True, a large boost in pensions, minimum wages, and income-tax exemptions was enacted. But this must be weighed against the direction of most other policies adopted.

Thus, the retail price cuts of 1955 and 1956 were fewer and smaller than earlier, and compulsory state bond purchases were reexpanded to their levels of 1952. Procurement prices for agricultural produce rose at a slower rate. Most significantly, in 1955, in spite of a major reduction in the size of Soviet ground forces, overall military expenditures were suddenly increased, at the expense of investment in light industry. The cause of this turnabout was a decision to launch a crash program for modernizing the military establishment with the latest in missiles, submarines, airplanes, and nuclear warheads. As one observer put it, "the decision had been taken to put rockets and the virgin lands program ahead of consumer goods."[5]

Khrushchev's conservative bias also found reflection in the Sixth Five-Year Plan, published in early 1956. That plan did not greatly advantage the consumer, for it emphasized building up the industrial capacity of Central Asia, Siberia, and the Far East, a huge buildup in Soviet atomic power generating capacity, and the modernization of Soviet transportation facilities and energy bases. Indeed, in December 1956, an anti-Khrushchev coalition in the national leadership, taking advantage of Khrushchev's authority crisis after the Hungarian Revolution, pushed through a revision of the Five-Year Plan that would reduce budgetary strain by lowering targets for heavy-industrial production. But Khrushchev counterattacked in Spring 1957, announcing that the Five-Year Plan would be scrapped, and a new Seven-Year Plan would be drawn up. That plan reflected

[5] Schwartz, *Soviet Economy since Stalin*, p. 69.

Khrushchev's growing power over policy during his stage of ascendancy.[6]

The Seven-Year Plan was hardly "pro-consumer." The lion's share of investment was channeled toward growth and defense: development of Siberian and Central Asian energy and mineral sources; conversion of industry to an advanced technological footing; defense modernization. Moreover, most of the sectors deprived of investments to pay for these programs were those benefiting the urban and rural consumer. Thus, the following measures were adopted: (1) a reduction in the rate of increase in real wages; (2) a halt to the practice of annual retail price reductions; (3) a reduction in welfare benefits for certain categories of pensioners; (4) a salary reduction for engineers and administrative employees; (5) postponement for twenty years of interest and amortization payments to the citizenry for state bonds in their possession; (6) suspension of the construction of many clubs, circuses, and stadiums; (7) a cut in procurement prices paid for higher-priced agricultural products (tea, cotton, sugar beets, and citrus fruits); (8) deep cuts in state agricultural investments, as well as demands that collective farms pay in full for the machinery delivered to them as a result of the abolition of Machine Tractor Stations.

In order to reconcile Khrushchev's strategy for growth with his strategy for increasing current consumption, very high pressure would have to be applied in the industrial sector as well. Although investments in heavy industry were high, the campaign to overtake and surpass the USA in per capita output, and the agreement within the leadership to channel above-plan accumulations to agricultural and light-industrial development, required extraordinary results from the privileged sectors as well. Accordingly, institutional measures were adopted in 1958–9 to raise the pressure on managers and workers in industrial enterprises to overfulfill their plans (about which more below). The wage reforms of 1957–8 were geared toward making bonuses more manipulable and effective as a spur to achievement. Introduction of collective piece-work scales served ideological ends, but was also part of an effort to tighten work norms and properly match up the costs and benefits of work effort. Disciplined members

[6] Sources for policy trends in these issue-areas during 1957–60 are: Schwartz, *Soviet Economy since Stalin*, pp. 74–87, 93–125; Leonhard, *Kremlin since Stalin*, pp. 272–9, 311–17, 323–6, 346–50, 369–72; Nove, *An Economic History*, pp. 333–42, 345–8, 352–68; Bloomfield, Clemens, and Griffiths, *Khrushchev and the Arms Race*, pp. 51–8, 106–14; Leonard Kirsch, *Soviet Wages: Changes in Structure and Administration since 1956* (Cambridge, Mass.: MIT, 1972), pp. 4–8, 23–43; Janet Chapman, *Wage Variation in Soviet Industry: The Impact of the 1956–1960 Wage Reform* (Santa Monica, Calif.: RAND Corporation, 1970), *passim*; Waedekin, *The Private Sector*, pp. 270–302.

of the collective would thereby have an incentive and the legitimacy to exert peer pressure on the less disciplined among their workmates. In addition, at the end 1958, the authorities launched a program for establishing Brigades of Communist Labor in all factories, which would act as rate-busters and contribute, among other things, to the campaign against "wastefulness, laxity, and lack of discipline."[7] Thus, Khrushchev's perspectives on the relationship between pressure and productivity had been extended to the industrial sector as well.

Sources of funding from nonconsumer sectors included campaigns to cut back construction of new plants, summer homes, and administrative buildings, a reduction in the level of atomic power plant and hydroelectric power construction, and a search abroad for credits to finance development of the chemicals industry. Moreover, consumer-oriented sectors were not entirely deprived, for a large-scale housing program was launched (something Khrushchev had long been touting), investment in light industry was marginally increased, hospital and educational construction was sharply expanded, and procurement prices for livestock products were raised significantly (though still not enough to cover the costs of production). But much of this could be viewed as consistent with the post-Stalin consensus. For, on balance, it was the consumption-oriented sectors, and agriculture in particular, that bore the greatest brunt of the ambitious investment program in the Seven-Year Plan. Khrushchev was obviously expanding his commitments to appease as many political interests as possible, but he did so within the confines of his larger commitment to demonstrating that his inexpensive approach to increasing consumer satisfaction could work. One gets the impression that Khrushchev was in charge, for the correlation between policies adopted and his stated priorities was very strong indeed.

When it became obvious to Khrushchev that his program was unworkable, his response was to insist that the regime recontract its budgetary priorities, raising investment in agriculture at the expense of other consumer-oriented sectors. But, at the same time, he advocated intensified pressure and campaignism to vindicate his earlier claims. The policies ultimately adopted in 1961 and 1962 suggest that Khrushchev was successful in getting his way.[8] Thus, the regime

[7] For the initial editorial launching the movement, see *Pravda*, 25 November 1958. For the appeal for a campaign against "wastefulness, laxity, and lack of discipline," following the June 1959 Plenum, see ibid., 30 June 1959.

[8] Sources for budgetary and incentive policy trends during 1960–4 are: Schwartz, *Soviet Economy since Stalin*, pp. 121–288; Strauss, *Soviet Agriculture in Perspective*, pp. 166–227; Tatu, *Power in the Kremlin*, pp. 214–19; Bloomfield, Clemens, and Griffiths, *Khrushchev and the Arms Race*, pp. 106–15.

voted measured increases in funds to relieve the financial burden of collective and state farmers, decided that agriculture would henceforth have priority over light industry in the receipt of accumulations resulting from above-plan fulfillments in heavy industry, and voted a 25–30 percent increase in procurement prices for meat and dairy products. This last measure may have been enacted above Khrushchev's objections; or it may have represented a concession to reality on his part.

These policy shifts were balanced off, in turn, by policies that pointed in the other direction. Thus, the authorities cut the percentage of total state investment going to light industry, housing, and the chemicals industry, sharply increased the defense budget, raised targets for heavy-industrial output, sharply increased urban retail prices to pay for the agricultural procurement price increases, cancelled plans to abolish the income tax, and launched campaigns to extend Virgin Lands cultivation, and to plow up fallow grasslands in order to increase current consumption without a large investment of funds.

In 1963 a more ambiguous picture emerges and a more "proconsumer" pattern appears. Procurement prices for potatoes, cotton, and sugar beets were increased, and a supplementary allocation of 1 billion rubles was voted for light industry. In December, in response to the harvest failure of that year, the regime announced a revised plan for 1964–5, which provided for 11·5 billion rubles of investment in agriculture for the two-year period (compared with 10 billion rubles for all of the previous four years combined). Khrushchev's policy advocacy at the time was contradictory and defensive, as he tried to fathom the complexity and recoup lost authority. Some of these measures may have been sponsored by him, or by others with his consent (grudging or otherwise). It is difficult to say. But Khrushchev had not lost his ability to rig the policy agenda by pulling rank. For in December 1963 he marshaled his political resources and forced through a huge diversion of capital into the chemicals industry (his panacea for a quick win), to be paid for by a cut in the defense budget for 1964, further reduction in plans for housing construction, and a reduction of targets for the production of coal and steel.[9]

In 1964 we have clear evidence that Khrushchev was not even able to veto certain policies on procurement price rises that he opposed.[10] Yet we also have evidence that, in Summer 1964, he was preparing to shift gears and force through a major diversion of funds from the heavy-industrial and defense sectors to light industry and agriculture.

[9] For further substantiation of Khrushchev's power over policy during 1961–3, see Chapter 6, note 103, above.
[10] See Chapter 6, note 53, above.

Before he could mobilize his political assets, however, he was removed from office.

In sum, the following observations emerge from this section. Other than the Virgin Lands Program, Khrushchev apparently did not control the budgetary policy agenda during the first year-and-a-half after Stalin's death. Thereafter, he was apparently able to determine the basic approach to increasing consumer satisfaction embraced by the regime during 1955–62. True, some policies during these years ran counter to his stated approach. But these reflected, in part, Khrushchev's adherence to the post-Stalin consensus, in part his evolving recognition of economic reality, and in part his felt-need during the stage of ascendancy to accommodate as broad a spectrum of political interests as possible. Khrushchev was no Stalin; he could not use terror against the political elite. But that does not mean he was simply a broker among political interests. For Khrushchev's response to an evolving political and economic reality was not to foresake his earlier priorities, so much as to supplement them with real, but restricted, sops to previously excluded interests. His power and authority were apparently sufficient to allow him usually to have his way through 1962—though it remains unclear whether defense budget increases in 1961–2 were imposed over his opposition.

In 1963–4, however, Khrushchev's credibility and authority were evaporating. His control over the policy agenda on agricultural issues appeared to be slipping. But he still had substantial formal power that he could draw upon to force through far-reaching policy changes. Lacking authority, however, it is difficult for any leader to pull rank very often before his power base crumbles as well. Khrushchev was able to get away with it in December 1963, but not in September/October 1964.

Administrative Reform

A rather similar pattern emerges when we examine the evolution of Soviet administrative policy under Khrushchev. The post-Stalin consensus called for rationalization of public administration through measures to deburden the center of excessively detailed planning, and to reduce terroristic pressures on managers. Beyond that, the leadership split between those for and against a high pressure approach to administration that called for frequent party intervention in managerial affairs.

Policies enacted during the years of succession struggle reflected both the majority consensus and leadership conflict among advocates of divergent policies.[11] In both industry and agriculture, efforts were made to deburden the center of excessive numbers of detailed decisions. In the rural sector, local offices of the Ministry of Agriculture were closed, and decrees were issued against detailed tutelage of farms by the ministry. In the urban-industrial sector, responsibility for a number of economic branches and functions was transferred to the republic level, while somewhat greater responsibility and flexibility was devolved to the ministers and their deputies.

Beyond these measures, however, administrative reforms in agriculture were primarily interventionist in character, while administrative reforms in industry were not. Thus, in agriculture, reforms sought to increase the degree of local party penetration, supervision, and direction of on-farm affairs. Within each zone of the rural districts, "instructor groups" of three or four individuals were established, with each instructor assigned to mobilize resources in one or two collective farms. These "zonal party secretaries" were supposed to have considerable technical expertise on agricultural affairs, and to live in rural zones rather than district centers, in order to facilitate their interventionist activities. Although the authorities restricted the rights of the Ministry of Agriculture, they simultaneously required collective farms to submit their detailed plans to the local authorities for approval. All this, along with campaigns to further strengthen party cells on the collective farms themselves, reflected a trend toward improving the local party's capacity for intervention and mobilization.

The same cannot be said for policy trends in the industrial sector. Ministries and state committees were merged, consolidated, and redivided, but nothing was done to encourage significantly greater local party intervention in industrial decision-making. In December 1956, in fact, at a meeting of the USSR Supreme Soviet, prevailing industrial targets were reduced in order to relieve excessive pressure, a State Economic Commission with broad powers to allocate resources and eliminate waste was established, and the party apparatus was assigned no special interventionist role in this latest search for administrative efficiency. Indeed, Khrushchev and his supporters in the Presidium played a subordinate role in the deliberations of the session. But this was a shortlived phenomenon, for two months later Nikita Khrushchev mobilized support for dismantling the ministerial struc-

[11] For sources used to identify administrative policy trends during the years of succession after Stalin, see: Schwartz, *Soviet Economy since Stalin*, pp. 55–7, 87–92; Leonhard, *Kremlin since Stalin*, pp. 97–100; Katz, *Politics of Economic Reform*, pp. 53–66; Strauss, *Soviet Agriculture in Perspective*, pp. 210–17; Hough and Fainsod, *How the Soviet Union Is Governed*, pp. 210–13; Robert F. Miller, "Continuity and change in the administration of Soviet agriculture since Stalin," in James R. Millar (ed.), *The Soviet Rural Community* (Urbana, Ill.: University of Illinois Press, 1971), pp. 80–7.

ture, regionalizing industrial administration on the basis of "regional economical councils" (*sovnarkhozy*), and vastly increasing the party's interventionist role in industrial administration. This turnabout was a prelude to the series of confrontations within the leadership that would result in the purge of Khrushchev's rivals and the ascendancy of the Party leader.

In the area of budgetary priorities, we found that political conflict led to policy reversals in 1955–6. With respect to administrative reform, the sequence is somewhat different. Sectoral interdependencies did not require immediate choices among approaches that would be applicable to all sectors—as was the case in trade-offs regarding budgetary questions. To increase investments in light industry required cutting investments elsewhere. Not so in the administrative realm, where direct confrontation among approaches was avoided by a division of labor. Khrushchev took responsibility for agriculture, and imposed a high-pressure interventionist approach to problem-solving in that sector. Only later, when he expanded his power base, and extended his role into the industrial sector, did he seek to impose his distinctive approach there as well.

During his stage of ascendancy, Khrushchev forged a program that intensified interventionism in the rural sector, and extended it into the industrial.[12] Thus, in the rural sector during 1957–8, the zonal district secretaries were abolished as an institution, as were the Machine Tractor Stations. Since the agricultural department of the district party organization had been abolished years earlier, these changes shifted the burden of coordinating affairs in the locales to the collective farms themselves, a circumstance which, in turn, fostered a policy of building up the on-farm party organizations as instruments of mobilization, penetration, and coordination. The locus of political control, then, was being brought "closer to production," at a time when Khrushchev was also pushing for higher targets, pledges, and results through extraordinary efforts at local mobilization. Consistent with the First Secretary's policy advocacy at the time, local initiative was to be unleashed through a combination of high pressure from the center, a reduction of bureaucratic intermediaries between the center and the farm, and a rise in pressure from horizontal sources of control.

Greater party intervention in the industrial sector was also Khrushchev's solution to the task of overfulfilling the Seven-Year Plan. The ministerial structure was largely abolished, in favor of regional

---

[12] On administrative policy during 1957–60, see: Strauss, *Soviet Agriculture in Perspective*, pp. 215–18; Miller, "Continuity and change," pp. 86–92; Schwartz, *Soviet Economy since Stalin*, pp. 87–93; Conyngham, *Industrial Management*, pp. 98–118; Leonhard, *Kremlin since Stalin*, pp. 233–41, 265–8, 272–82, 306–9, 342–4.

economic councils that would coincide with provincial party jurisdictions, thereby facilitating supervision and intervention by regional party authorities. On top of this, central planners sharply increased pressures on industrial officials for cost-cutting and technological innovations. A decree of April 1958 set criminal penalties for managerial failure to fulfill the plan. Local party organs were ordered to tighten up production and investment plans, and to mobilize hidden reserves at enterprises within their jurisdictions. The June 1959 Plenum made pressure for innovation into "everybody's business."[13] Specialists were organized into "technical committees"; specialists and workers were drawn *en masse* into "permanent production conferences"; and all social organizations were charged with agitating on behalf of technological innovation. Thus, Khrushchev's policies were not anticentralist. Rather, they sought to reduce bureaucratic layering between the center and the locales, and to increase pressure on managers from above and below. They amounted to high-pressure interventionism. By this standard, the policies enacted by the regime in both the agricultural and industrial sectors were the measure of Khrushchev's power over policy.

By these standards, it is also striking to discover how very much power over administrative policy Khrushchev retained during 1961–4.[14] For centralism, interventionism, and pressure remained the guiding spirits of policy, even though Khrushchev was increasingly erratic and uncertain about the forms these might take.

During 1961, the level of administrative centralization was increased, with the establishment of state committees for the coordination of a variety of agricultural functions, including a State Committee for Procurements, whose inspectors were charged with detailed supervision of all aspects of agricultural production and procurements.

By early 1962 these measures were already superceded by further reforms to increase party penetration of the rural economy, and also to increase the personal responsibility of regional secretaries for the performance of agriculture. An All-Union Agricultural Committee was established, with subunits at the republic, territorial, and provincial levels, all of which were supposed to be headed by party apparatchiki. At the local levels, every three to four districts were placed under "territorial-production administrations," headed by

[13] This apt characterization appears in Gregory Grossman, "Soviet growth: routine, inertia, and pressure," *American Economic Review* (May 1960), p. 70.

[14] Administrative policy during 1960–4 is outlined in: Miller, "Continuity and change," pp. 92–7; Hough and Fainsod, *How the Soviet Union Is Governed*, pp. 222–5; Conyngham, *Industrial Management*, pp. 128–60, 180–249; Paul Cocks, "Controlling communist bureaucracy" (unpublished, 1975), pp. 501–9; Schwartz, *Soviet Economy since Stalin*, pp. 140–75.

plenipotentiaries appointed from above, and staffed with inspector-organizers whose main function was to force collective and state farms to comply with detailed directives from higher instances. The district party organization was abolished, in order to ensure full concentration of authority at the district level in the party organization of the territorial-production administration.

Eight months later, a still more far-reaching reorganization was superimposed on these changes. In November 1962 the party apparatus was divided, at all levels, into separate industrial and agricultural hierarchies. Party apparatchiki were now to specialize in one or the other sector of production and to intensify their detailed supervision of the sector for which they were responsible. At the same time, a Party–State Control Commission was established to draw the broadest masses into the task of monitoring and publicizing the administrative behavior of both party and state officials. And complementing these reforms were laws promulgated in 1961 and 1964 that raised criminal penalties for managerial corruption and dissimulation.

Division of the party apparatus, and establishment of the Party–State Control Commission, affected both the agricultural and industrial sectors. More specifically in the industrial sector, a succession of additional measures reinforced the gradual trend toward reversing the *sovnarkhoz* reforms of 1957. Thus, in May 1961, the regime established seventeen centralized Councils for Coordination and Planning, each charged with integrating the regional plans of six or seven regional economic councils. In November 1962 the original 105 regions were amalgamated into less than 50 regions, and centralized state committees assumed control over many functions previously exercised by the *sovnarkhozy*. In March 1963 the centralizing trend continued, with the establishment of the Supreme Council of the National Economy, and additional centralized state agencies charged with co-ordinating, and mobilizing reserves in, the industrial sector. But the culmination of this trend came in the agricultural sector. In April 1964 a central commission for livestock production was created, chaired by Presidium-member N. I. Podgorny, and including among its members no less than five other representatives of the Presidium.

Many of the trends just outlined were contradictory in conception and in practice.[15] But they had in common an intensification of intervention in managerial affairs, in some instances by superiors in the state or party bureaucracies, in others by local party organs. Similarly, some of these centralizing reforms may have been opposed by Khrushchev for they had ambiguous implications for bureaucratic authority at the top. But given the coincidence of centralism, intervention, and pressure in the policy trends of these years, it would be difficult to

[15] As argued in Hough and Fainsod, *How the Soviet Union Is Governed*, pp. 223–4.

argue that Khrushchev's power over policy had substantially weakened.

One policy trend in the opposite direction stands out during these years. In November 1962 *Pravda* published, and legitimized discussion of, the reform proposals of Evsei Liberman, a Kharkov economist. In 1964 limited experiments were introduced into light industry, based upon the premises argued by Liberman. This may have been a Khrushchevian defeat, a Khrushchevian concession to reality, or an attempt on his part to keep pace with an evolving climate of opinion that was not crystallized in Presidium-level challenges. We do not know. But it seems probable that, had he stayed in power, Khrushchev would have maintained veto power (if he chose to use it) over broader introduction of such reforms.

Political Participation

During the first years of the succession struggle (1953–5), Khrushchev had little to say about political participation and cultural policy outside the agricultural sector. What he said there had reformist implications; what Malenkov and his associates said about political participation in the urban and industrial sectors implied a conservative conception of what needed to be done. Yet significant policy changes were enacted, consistent with a post-Stalin consensus on behalf of expanding four types of political participation: (1) expanded involvement of the citizenry in the administration of public policy; (2) expanded input by citizens and specialists before decisions are made; (3) transferral of certain minor functions performed by executive organs of the state bureaucracy to the jurisdiction of social activists and mass organizations; and (4) expanded rights for citizens and mass organizations vis-à-vis executive authority.

The policies enacted during 1953–5 made progress in each of these directions.[16] Public involvement was fostered by a campaign to elect more workers and peasants to bureaus of primary party organizations, by efforts to build up the substructure of shop-level party organizations, and by a vast expansion in the number of rural party cells and primary party organizations. With respect to expanded input, the authorities moved to reduce the hold of dogma on the social and natural sciences, to encourage critical feedback from the scientific, technical, and cultural intelligentsia, and to organize conferences of specialists that would explore previously forbidden topics. Limited

[16] On policy toward political participation during the succession struggle, see Leonhard, *Kremlin since Stalin*, pp. 63–79, 90–2, 113–19, 127–30; Cocks, "Controlling communist bureaucracy," pp. 472–89; Hough and Fainsod, *How the Soviet Union Is Governed*, pp. 205–6, 211–13, 226–7; Conyngham, *Industrial Management*, pp. 65–89.

progress in the direction of functional transfer began in 1955, with cuts in the full-time staff of local party and state organizations, and encouragement of the use of larger numbers of unpaid staff.

The most dramatic changes, however, took place in the expansion of rights, especially popular and party rights vis-à-vis the security organs. Thus, the years immediately following Stalin's death were characterized by: campaigns for "socialist legality"; a narrower definition of political crime; amnesties for several categories of political prisoners; judicial reforms and liberalization of the legal code; the establishment of party and state committees to supervise and control secret police activities; abrogation of the laws of 1934 and 1937 which had given the police special powers to deal with "sabotage" and "terrorism."

It is difficult to know whether these changes caused controversy within the leadership (other than dissents by Beria and Molotov). They may have been products of the post-Stalin consensus. Or some of them, such as functional transfer, may have begun in 1955 only because that was when Khrushchev outflanked Malenkov. What is clear, however, is that this measured reconciliation created unresolved tensions between those in the establishment and society-at-large wishing to push still further, and those seeking to keep the reconciliation within strict limits. Khrushchev's secret speech and de-Stalinization campaign decided the issue, and led not only to the tacit legitimation of cultural dissent during 1956, but also to other measures consistent with the thrust of his speeches at the Twentieth Party Congress: efforts to resuscitate and reactivate the local soviets, the Young Communist League, and the trade unions; the establishment of new research institutes in the social sciences, and the revitalization of several social science disciplines; and the initiation of a process that would lead eventually to a virtual emptying of the labor camps of millions of political prisoners.

When Khrushchev re-seized the initiative in 1957, his distinctive program for political participation came into bloom. Khrushchev's stated conception of what needed to be done to foster the "full-scale construction of communism" correlated almost perfectly with the policies actually adopted.[17] Thus, with respect to expanded involve-

---

[17] On policy toward political participation during 1957–60, see Leonhard, *Kremlin since Stalin*, pp. 251–3, 296–305, 340–2, 352–5; Cocks, "Controlling communist bureaucracy," pp. 477–89; Conyngham, *Industrial Management*, p. 68, 73–89; Mary McAuley, *Labor Disputes in Soviet Russia, 1957–1965* (Oxford: Clarendon Press, 1969), pp. 66–73; Ellen Mickiewicz, *Soviet Political Schools* (New Haven, Conn.: Yale University Press, 1969), pp. 9–12; Aryeh Unger, *The Totalitarian Party* (London: Cambridge University Press, 1974), pp. 34, 69–71, 128; Jan S. Adams, *Citizen Inspectors in the Soviet Union* (New York: Praeger, 1977), ch. 3.

ment, there began in 1957 a vast and sudden expansion in the size of the party, in the size of party and nonparty *aktivs*, and in the role of social organizations in the discussion and implementation of policy. The party's adult political-education program suddenly began to emphasize the training of nonparty, nonofficial members of society; the program also ballooned in size and sharply reduced the importance of ideological study in the curriculum. From 1958 onward there took place a big push to expand mass-political work by party and Communist Youth League organs, to extend party agitation to residential areas and to categories of the populace not previously touched. At the same time, primary party organizations, run by retired military personnel and pensioners, were established in nonproduction, areal units. And from 1959 onward millions of workers and specialists were drawn into the work of newly created social organizations geared toward propagandizing technical achievements and diffusing technical innovations. Thus, Khrushchev was drawing "all the people" into the process of "building communism."

This goal also found reflection in the composition of the various activist strata. Under Stalin, the so-called "social activists" (*obshchestvenniki*) were, in practice, the officials themselves. In the late 1950s, however, the term came to refer to a new stratum of mobilizers drawn from all groups in society. Efforts were made to enlist these activists from among the more technically competent "opinion leaders" in society.[18] The hope was that the didactic relationship involved in mobilization would be based upon interaction between social peers and would thus be less susceptible to considerations of ego, status, or formal position in the hierarchy. Thus, rather than simply call upon Soviet officials to adopt a less heavy-handed leadership orientation, the redefinition of participation during the late 1950s involved the creation of a stratum of mobilizers that would mediate the relationship between officials and the masses. Here was a concrete manifestation of the search for new methods of social control to replace administrative methods and political control. "All the people" would be drawn into the process of monitoring the behavior of their immediate hierarchical superiors; however, they would also be mobilized *en masse* to monitor each other. Expanding the size and responsibility of the party and nonparty *aktivs* was part of a process of making the mobilization process more palatable and effective. But it was also a process of penetrating social networks among the masses so as to activate energies and channel them toward the tasks of building communism.[19]

[18] Conyngham, *Industrial Management*, p. 84.

[19] For an insightful reconceptualization of the role and status of the *aktiv* in Leninist regimes, see Kenneth Jowitt, "National, state and civic development in Marxist–Leninist regimes," unpublished paper presented to the American Political Science Association, San Francisco, September 1975.

With respect to the expansion of specialist input and the expansion of citizen's rights vis-à-vis their hierarchical superiors, policy trends represented a continuation and codification of trends begun earlier, rather than a sharp acceleration or change of direction. But as concerns the other type of political participation—transfer of functions—real change took place. During 1957 a resolution of the Central Committee forced local party organs to reduce their full-time staffs and to transfer the performance of functions more and more to members of the party committee and to nonstaff instructors. In 1958 there began a broad campaign to recruit thousands of unpaid activists into the party apparatus. And in 1959 a campaign was launched to reduce the number of full-time staff in the trade-union hierarchy. Simultaneous with all these efforts was the initiation of a movement for the transfer of some administrative functions of the state to public corporations or mass organizations that would have independent jurisdiction over the performance of these functions. The organizations in question are familiar to students of recent Soviet history: comrades' courts, citizens' militia, the Federation of Public Sports Societies, and the transfer of urban and rural health services to the jurisdiction of trade unions and local soviets respectively.

Khrushchev's policy advocacy during the stage of ascendancy was not yet fully populist. True, it threatened the political and bureaucratic prerogatives of state officials, and it sought to dilute elitism in party recruitment policies. But it also toned down the anti-Stalin campaign, did not challenge the leading role of apparatchiki in public affairs, did not stand for an adversarial relationship between party officials and the masses, and was based on Khrushchev's reconciliatory unity platform of 1959. All this changed, however, when Khrushchev faced his authority crisis after 1960. He then formulated a fully populist program for political participation. And that program was enacted into policy.[20]

In October 1961, at the Twenty-Second Party Congress, a renewed, more public, and more far-reaching anti-Stalin campaign was launched. This led to, and encouraged, the public flowering of anti-Establishment poets, the publication of Aleksandr Solzhenitsyn's *One Day in the Life of Ivan Denisovich*, the coalescence of an anti-Establishment coterie around the journal, *Novy Mir*, and a period of

---

[20] On policy toward participation during 1960–4, see Cocks, "Controlling communist bureaucracy," pp. 473–512; Conyngham, *Industrial Management*, pp. 76–86, 129–209; Dina Spechler, "Permitted dissent in the decade after Stalin," in Paul Cocks, Robert Daniels, and Nancy Heer (eds), *The Dynamics of Soviet Politics* (Cambridge, Mass.: Harvard University Press, 1976), pp. 41–7; Kenneth Kerst, "CPSU History Re-Revised," *Problems of Communism* (May–June 1977), pp. 18–22; Rothberg, *Heirs of Stalin* pp. 41–133; Adams, *Citizen Inspectors*, chs 3–4.

freedom in research and writing about party history unparalleled since the early 1930s. In addition, a variety of political reforms during this period were inspired by anti-official biases. Elected production committees were set up in the factories as a means of broadening worker participation in decision-making. A campaign was launched to encourage factory union committees to protect workers against illegal overtime, dismissals, and underpay for work done. Within the party, there took place a vast expansion in the number of nonstaff instructors, the newly formed Party–State Control Commission was given the mandate to see to it that "those who spoke critically of party leaders in report meetings received equal time with other speakers,"[21] and a rotation system was set up to limit the number of years or terms a party secretary at any level could remain at his post. In the same spirit, rules changes made it easier for the party masses to reject nominees for the position of secretary of the primary party organization. And during 1963–4 there took place a large-scale recruitment of specialists into line positions within the apparat, by-passing the standard practice of requiring training in a party school before appointment to such a position.

But, consistent with Khrushchev's policy advocacy, populism was complemented during these years by intensified intolerance of certain types of social and individual "deviance." The death penalty for economic crimes was restored in May 1961, during which month anti-parasite campaigns were also given national scope. New laws provided for five years' exile from one's town of residence if convicted of being an "idler," and comrades' courts were given summary rights to deal with "idlers" in this fashion. The citizens' militia was unleashed to enforce criteria of "socialist morality" in public conduct. And in cultural affairs, bursts of de-Stalinization alternated with harsh crack-downs on the cultural intelligentsia when the latter went too far in trying to stretch the limits of the permissible.

Nikita Khrushchev was not controlling these processes in detail, but there is every indication that almost all of the policies just noted were either a product of his personal political initiative or a reflection of his problem-solving strategy.

Concluding Reflections on Khrushchev's Power over Policy

Khrushchev appears to have exercised a high degree of power over the basic direction of policy. Thus, his long-term association with a low-cost approach to agricultural development, an expensive program for modernization of the defense establishment, a high-pressure, inter-

---

[21] Cocks, "Controlling communist bureaucracy," p. 491.

ventionist approach to public administration, and an increasingly
populist approach to political participation bear striking resemblance
to the content and direction of basic policy adopted during 1955–62.
The exceptions to these trends are relatively few in number—research
and development for the chemicals industry in 1958; marginally
increased investment in light industry during 1957–9; a brief lull in
the rate of increase of defense spending during 1959–60; and modest
increases in agricultural investment (including procurement price increases) in 1961–2. Moreover, these exceptions are noteworthy for
their modesty. They constitute supplements to the basic trend of
policy during these years, rather than reversals of direction.

During 1963–4 the picture is a mixed one. The supplements to
Khrushchev's previous policy biases become larger in both number
and significance. Yet Khrushchev continues to enforce his priorities in
many issue-areas. Some policy changes may have been defeats for
him; others may have reflected his increasing concessions to economic
reality. But from the larger number of policies he succeeded in defending or newly pushing through, one suspects that he retained a great
deal of power over policy at this time as well. Indeed, such a conclusion is reinforced by the fact that Khrushchev's successors moved
quickly to reverse or reconsider so many of his policies after his overthrow. While Khrushchev played the role of broker throughout his
years in office (a role which distinguished his leadership from that
of Stalin), he also played the roles of initiator of policy trends and
protector of those biases when they became less effective in solving
problems. And he appears to have gotten his way, for the most
part—even during 1963–4, though probably less so during these years
than before.

Those scholars who emphasize the limits of Khrushchev's power
over policy make a weak case. Of course, if they are only seeking
to prove that Khrushchev was not a Stalin, that he had to consult,
face criticism of specific policies, bargain, and adjust, they are undoubtedly correct; but they are also not saying very much. For their
definition of "power over policy" is so broad as to be a meaningless
test. If power over policy is instead defined as the ability to define
and defend the basic direction of policy, then the case put forth by
"conflict theorists" is probably wrong.

Indeed, Khrushchev's memoirs may do the best job of conceptualiz-
ing the nature of his power over policy. As Grey Hodnett has noted,
those memoirs contain many contradictory statements on this score.[22]
Yet, closer inspection of those statements indicates that, in noting the
limits of his power, Khrushchev was typically referring to his obligation or need to consult or persuade others in the collective leadership—

[22] Hodnett, "Succession contingencies in the Soviet Union," p. 2.

rather than referring to manifest opposition to his leadership or policies.[23] Statements pointing in the opposite direction are still more revealing. Thus, he refers to his tenure in office as "the years when the direction of our policies depended largely on me."[24] In a similar vein, he reveals: "I held a post that gave me a voice which was to a certain extent decisive, as long as I had the support of others",[25] and "When I was in the leadership, I set both internal and foreign policy to a considerable extent."[26] Those who claim otherwise would appear to bear the burden of proof.

[23] See Hodnett's display of quotations from Khrushchev, *Khrushchev Remembers*, Vol. 2, in ibid., p. 2, fn. 14.

[24] *Khrushchev Remembers*, Vol. 1, p. 512.

[25] ibid., Vol. 2, p. 27.

[26] ibid., Vol. 2, p. 344.

Part Three
The Brezhnev Years

8 Political Succession and Consumer Satisfaction, 1964–8

Khrushchev never resolved the contradictions among the various components of his approach to planning. The adjustments he made during the last years of his administration served largely to deepen those contradictions. He came to threaten the interests of the military-heavy-industrial complex without even a compensatory increase in productivity and consumer satisfaction. His program for development of the chemicals industry, as a panacea for both current and long-term consumption, upset the balance of the entire economy, at a time when his restrictions on the private sector in agriculture, and his rural campaignism, were aggravating the consumer situation. Ultimately, Khrushchev's big promises and his race with the West proved incapable of inspiring popular initiative or sustaining a sense of elite dependence upon him for direction.

After Khrushchev: The Majority Consensus

Just as Stalin's successors in 1953 were in some agreement that a rise in material incentives and consumer satisfaction had to be placed on the political agenda, so Khrushchev's successors drew some common lessons from their experiences of 1957–64. These lessons represented a degree of consensus on basic perspectives capable of forging at least a majority coalition within the leadership. For if we examine speeches by Leonid Brezhnev and Alexei Kosygin during 1964–66, anniversary speeches of April and November, as well as *Pravda* editorials following Khrushchev's overthrow, we discover a convergence of certain themes.[1] These themes indicate a collective reevalua-

---

[1] Generalizations about the majority consensus after Khrushchev are based on the following speeches: Brezhnev, in *Pravda*, 7 November 1964, 27 March 1965, 11 July 1965, 30 September 1965, 18 May 1966, 28 May 1966, and 11 June 1966. Brezhnev at the Twenty-Third Party Congress (Gruliow, *Current Soviet Policies V*, pp. 4–31). Kosygin, in *Pravda*, 10 December 1964, 12 July 1965, 18 July 1965, 28 September 1965, 9 June 1966, and 4 August 1966. Kosygin, in *Planovoe khoziaistvo*, no. 4 (April 1965). Kosygin at the Twenty-Third Party Congress (Gruliow, *Current Soviet Policies V*, pp. 93–112). Demichev, in *Pravda*, 23 April 1965 (Lenin Day speech); Poliansky, in ibid., 7 November 1965 (Revolution anniversary speech); Yegorychev, in ibid., 23 April 1966 (Lenin Day speech); Pel'she, in ibid., 7 November 1966 (Revolution anniversary speech).

tion of Khrushchevian conceptions of the capacity of the system, the benefits obtainable from the use of pressure, and the appeals likely to elicit authentic popular initiative. The new consensus reflected a sorting through of the pros and cons of various approaches to budgetary and incentive policy as means of increasing consumer satisfaction. Whereas Khrushchev had attempted to modify his policies somewhat in the last year or two before his dismissal, his successors shed much of the intellectual baggage and political promises with which Khrushchev had burdened himself, and made a decisive shift in their approach to increasing consumer satisfaction.

Thus, the *Pravda* editorial on 17 October 1964 criticized Khrushchev for "actions based on wishful thinking, boasting, and empty words," taking him to task for his "voluntarism" and "subjectivism." Speeches by Soviet leaders now came to include ceaseless repetition of the need for "realism" in planning, and for an approach that appreciated the "complexity" of the environment, in contrast to early-Khrushchevian calls for a "struggle" to exploit "inexhaustible reserves." Target-setting was no longer to be a process of anticipating the unprecedented, so much as a process of judging possibilities on the basis of past performance. As Brezhnev put it in September 1965 : "everything must be done to put an end to voluntarism and subjectivism in planning. Workers in the planning agencies must be guided in their work exclusively by objective economic calculations, and they must have the means for this."[2]

A rather broad coalition was apparently also in agreement on the need to dampen the consumer expectations generated by earlier plans and visions. References to the "full-scale" (*sploshnoe*) construction of communism dropped precipitously, and almost entirely disappeared from leaders' speeches within a year after Khrushchev's overthrow. The standard of comparison expressed in public speeches also shifted in such a way as to dampen expectations of imminent abundance or imminent victory in overtaking US levels of agricultural and consumer goods output. Thus, specific targets in leaders' speeches tended to remain within the context of the current Five-Year Plan, while general targets came to be stated in more diffuse and open-ended form. Official speeches came to measure progress in the consumer field with respect to levels reached since some previous point in Russian or Soviet history, be it 1913, 1940, 1953, or the years of the previous Five-Year Plan.

In addition to reevaluating the capacity of the system and attempting to lower consumer expectations, a majority coalition appears to have agreed upon an expanded emphasis on scientific and technological innovation—relative to the mobilization of popular energies—as the

2 *Pravda*, 30 September 1965.

harbingers of eventual affluence. For cross-national standards of comparison did not disappear from leaders' speeches; instead, they were redirected toward the realm of technological innovation. As Alexei Kosygin put it in September 1965: "the center of gravity of world economic competition between socialism and capitalism is shifting precisely to these aspects of production."[3]

But, in the absence of a vision of abundance, how could the regime elicit initiative from the mass of workers and peasants? Khrushchev's efforts had been in part instrumental: the vision of abundance would make up for current scarcity, and thereby make material incentives effective at their relatively low levels. Brezhnev and Kosygin abandoned this tack when it proved counterproductive, but they could not ignore the problem that had spawned the approach in the first place. In part, their response was budgetary, as we shall see below. In part, however, their response was to continue the emphasis on material incentives and to revise the structure of those incentives in a more inegalitarian direction. Alexei Kosygin echoed the new consensus at the Twenty-Third Party Congress when he proclaimed a decisive shifting of weights in the doctrine: "*the chief thing in our labor-payments policy* is a steady rise in the stimulating role of wages in solving the major production tasks of the five-year plan" (italics in original).[4] By further sacrificing ideals of social transformation in favor of economic achievement, the regime signalled its intention to create conditions under which minimal and rising levels of material security, private material gain, and individualistic economic pursuits would be assured to most Soviet citizens. In return, the authorities demanded that the grandiose promises of 1959 and 1961 be forgotten.

Finally, whatever their manifold differences over investment priorities, most of Khrushchev's successors appear to have drawn the conclusion that decisions as to resource allocation would have to be acutely sensitive to the implications for current consumption. This was the common line of argumentation in major speeches by Brezhnev and Kosygin in November–December 1964. Brezhnev noted the problem of repressed inflation and called for heavy industry to set its sights on dealing with the problem:

> With the growth in the earnings of Soviet people, the demand for consumer goods is increasing . . . We must take this into account and utilize all the possibilities and achievements of scientific and

3 ibid., 28 September 1965.
4 Gruliow, *Current Soviet Policies V*, p. 105; see also analogous declarations by Brezhnev in *Pravda*, 7 November 1964; by Kosygin, in ibid., 10 December 1964; and by Demichev, in ibid., 23 April 1965.

technical progress to develop mass production of consumer goods . . .
The development of heavy industry must be subordinated to the
requirements of constant technical reequipment of the whole
economy, the needs of defense, and also the interests of rapid
advance in agriculture, light industry and food industry.[5]

In like manner, Kosygin emphasized the need "to expand substantially the output of agricultural products and consumer goods . . . to
bring the rates of growth of the production of consumer goods closer
to the rates of growth of the production of the means of production," and he discoursed at length on heavy industry's obligations to
the consumer.[6] Thus, one of the lessons drawn from the Khrushchevian
experience by a majority coalition within the leadership was the need
simultaneously to meet and depress consumer expectations of current
consumption.

This consensus, however, left considerable room for political conflict and differences of perspective. Specifically, it left unresolved
many of the issues which had divided the Soviet leadership after
Stalin: (1) the concrete approach to solving the agricultural problem;
(2) the relative priority of light industry and agriculture; (3) the relative priority of the rural and urban consumer in efforts to increase
"consumer" satisfaction; (4) the cost to heavy-industrial and defense
budgets of such efforts; and (5) the relative role of party activism
versus material incentives as spurs to initiative.

Policy Trends

Budgetary decisions during the years following Khrushchev's dismissal
were consistent with a decisive shift away from Khrushchevian
problem-solving strategies.[7] Targets for the Eighth Five-Year Plan
(1966–70) stood in sharp contrast to the Seven-Year Plan (1959–65)
and the Third Party Program (1961), for those targets markedly
reduced the gap between aspirations and capacity. In addition, at the
March 1965 and May 1966 plenary sessions of the Central Committee, expensive, long-term programs of investment in agricultural
machinery, irrigation, chemicals, land reclamation, and procurement

[5] *Pravda*, 7 November 1964 (*CCPSP*, vol. 16, no. 43).
[6] *Pravda*, 10 December 1964.
[7] These paragraphs are based on the following sources: Alec Nove,
"Economic policy and economic trends," in Alexander Dallin and Thomas
Larson (eds), *Soviet Politics since Khrushchev* (Englewood Cliffs, NJ:
Prentice-Hall, 1968), pp. 84–109; Alec Nove, "Agriculture," in Archie Brown
and Michael Kaser (eds), *The Soviet Union since the Fall of Khrushchev*
(New York: The Free Press, 1975), pp. 1–15; Keith Bush, "Soviet capital
investment since Khrushchev: a note," *Soviet Studies* (July 1972).

price rises were adopted. The programs called for an immediate doubling of expenditures on agriculture during the Five-Year Plan. The March 1965 Plenum on agriculture came well in advance of preparation of the Five-Year Plan, though, and its allocation of 71 billion rubles to agriculture established this level of funding as a fixed constraint, leaving heavy industry, defense, light industry, and other sectors to compete for the remainder of the budgetary pie. Defense was the winner, in a big way.

The funds to pay for these varied expensive programs were drawn largely from sources that would not threaten planned increases in current consumption: the bloated chemicals industry; housing; foreign investment; and, especially, a planned reduction in the growth rate of heavy industry and transportation. Herein lay the reallocative emphasis of the new regime. Khrushchev's successors felt the need to sacrifice long-term growth in heavy industrial capacity to the short-term requirements of agriculture and current consumption.

During this period of political succession, and within a new elite environment of consensus and conflict, Leonid Brezhnev developed his positions and strategies regarding investment priorities and incentive policy. The evolution of Brezhnev's strategy as problem-solver and politician in these realms of policy is the focus of the remainder of this chapter.

Leonid Brezhnev: Investment Priorities and Developmental Perspectives

Five months after the overthrow of Khrushchev, Leonid Brezhnev came forth with an expensive, long-term program of agricultural development that would attempt to sharply upgrade both short-term and long-term consumption.[8] But there was nothing foreordained about the advancement of such a program. Although Khrushchev's campaignism had been discredited in the eyes of the majority coalition in the leadership, the precise character of alternatives to that approach was by no means self-evident. Any number of approaches to the agricultural dilemma would have been consistent with a rejection of Khrushchev's. And judging from policy enacted during this period, the nature of Brezhnev's defense of his program, and the terms of the policy debate at the time, it would appear that varied interests within the political elite favored varying approaches to the problem.

One approach might have emphasized the extension of Khrushchev's move toward decentralization and the link system, with or without heavy funding of rural development. A second approach might have opted for a moderate program of expenditures, cautiously allocated,

8 *Pravda*, 27 March 1965.

in the belief that a return to organizational stability and more rational use of pressure would spur the authentic initiative and growth of production required to get agriculture back on its feet. A third approach might well have been urban and anti-peasant, making the following kind of argument: "Let's not invest very much in agriculture, because the rate of return doubtless will be very low, compared to what we might get from light industry. Agriculture's problems are organizational, in part; but let's admit, our peasants are ill-educated and lazy. You raise their incomes, they work less and get by on the same. They would rather exert themselves on their private plots in any case. So why pour money into the public sector, where the peasant will find ways to avoid hard work whatever the incentive? On the other hand, investment in light industry—if it is tied closely enough to consumer demand—could prove a great source of expansion and rising productivity well into the future. Our urban producers—working class and intelligentsia alike—are far more self-disciplined and conscious of the public interest than is the peasantry. Moreover, the availability of attractive consumer goods (and, perhaps, rising urban affluence in the face of a more slowly growing rural sector) may be just the right spur to much greater rural effort and productivity."

In contrast to all these approaches, Brezhnev's program rejected the drift toward the link system and rejected the anti-peasant rationalization for restricting the scope of investment in agriculture in favor of light industry. In all forums during October 1964–6 Brezhnev insisted that a capital-intensive approach to solving the agricultural problem was a *sine qua non* for both the advancement of the economy and the improvement of socio-political relations among classes:

> *We understand that an upsurge in agriculture is something that is vitally necessary to us for the successful construction of communism. In order to resolve this nationwide task, we must put a firm economic foundation under agriculture. V. I. Lenin regarded this question as one of the most important questions of the Party's economic policy, since it touches upon the very foundation of the Soviet state— the relationship of the working class and the peasantry.*[9] (Italics in original)

During the next year-and-a-half, Brezhnev followed up on this commitment to struggle against anti-rural biases. Speaking in Leningrad in July 1965, he urged enterprises to recognize their obligation to help solve the agricultural problem by giving priority to tasks oriented toward that sector.[10] At the September 1965 Plenum, which

[9] ibid., 27 March 1965 (*CDSP*, vol. 17, no. 12); for additional examples before this date, see Brezhnev, *Leninskim kursom*, pp. 42, 108.
[10] *Pravda*, 11 July 1965.

was convened to discuss industrial–administration reform, Brezhnev devoted a major portion of his speech to discussion of the agricultural situation.[11] At that same Plenum, he warned against forces within the political and administrative elite that would "balance the books" to the disadvantage of agriculture when resources are tight, and he defined this as an unjustified "infringement on the interests of the collective and state farms." At the May 1966 Plenum on land reclamation, he scolded representatives of heavy industry for failing to contribute their share to the resolution of agricultural problems and proposed structural reforms to remedy the situation.[12] And in his May 1966 speech to the Young Communist League, Brezhnev dwelled at length on the need for urban youth and urban workers to upgrade the level of culture and mechanization in the countryside, and to exercise patronage (*shefstvo*) over collective farms.[13]

Brezhnev's expensive agricultural program was approved in March 1965; the Five-Year Plan was not approved until 1966. In the interim, the remainder of the budgetary pie was being divided and Leonid Brezhnev made it clear that, along with agriculture, budgetary redistributions ought to benefit the defense sector. Thus, in all major speeches during April–December 1965, Brezhnev condemned the "aggression" of the USA (for escalating the war in Vietnam), and linked this condemnation to the proposition that the Soviet Union would have to build up its defense might to repel potential aggressors and to be taken seriously as a defender of its allies: "The Soviet people well understand the need for these expenditures and fully support the measures of our party and government to strengthen the defense might of our fatherland."[14]

In contrast to this unwavering advocacy of rising defense expenditures, Brezhnev was almost silent on the question of expanded investment in light industry. In major speeches during 1965, the number of sentences he devoted to that subject could be counted on the fingers of one hand.[15] And when he did mention light industry, it

---

[11] ibid., 30 September 1965.

[12] ibid., 28 May 1966.

[13] ibid., 18 May 1966; and for additional examples, see also Brezhnev, *Ob osnovnykh voprosakh ekonomicheskoi politiki KPSS na sovremennon etape*, 2 vols (Moscow: Politizdat, 1975), Vol. 1, pp. 99–111; Gruliow, *Current Soviet Policies V*, pp. 16, 19; *Pravda*, 11 June 1966.

[14] Brezhnev, *Leninskim kursom I*, pp. 152–3; see also ibid., pp. 156–7, 160, 161, 165, 224–5, 248, as well as *Pravda*, 11 July 1965.

[15] There was no discussion of light industry in his March 1965 Plenum report (*Pravda*, 27 March, 1965), July 1965 speech in Leningrad (*Pravda*, 11 July 1965), September 1965 Plenum report (*Pravda*, 30 September 1965), October 1965 speech in Kiev (*Leninskim kursom I*, pp. 233–50), or his 8 May, 1965 speech on the twentieth anniversary of victory in World War II (ibid., pp. 118–55). One passing reference appeared in his speech to graduates of the military academy, on 3 July 1965 (ibid., p. 159).

was either a passing reference or, more significantly, emphasized the need to raise the quality of mass consumer goods. This would be accomplished through broader introduction of "the achievements of scientific and technical progress," which, in turn, would result from greater efficiency and innovation in the industrial sector.[16]

But the evidence regarding Brezhnev's position is ambiguous. At the December 1965 Plenum, and again at the Twenty-Third Party Congress, Brezhnev announced a commitment to further "convergence of the rates of development of the production of means of production and the production of consumer goods."[17] Moreover, at the Party Congress he indicated that this convergence of growth rates would be a result of both the expanded production of consumer goods at heavy-industrial enterprises and the channeling of above-plan accumulations into light industry.[18] And in his election speech after the Party Congress Brezhnev reendorsed the commitment, adding that "this task has become urgent and immediate."[19]

We may legitimately wonder about the depth of Brezhnev's commitment to this task, however. He made no mention of it in his May 1966 speech to the Young Communist League or his November 1966 speech to officials in Georgia.[20] And in his May 1966 speech on land reclamation, he expanded his commitment to finding "funds and material resources for agriculture in hitherto unprecedented amounts," and suggested that these might come from the very source expected to contribute to expanded consumer goods development: above-plan fulfillment.[21] Given this pattern of evidence, one suspects that investment in light industry ranked a poor third in Brezhnev's order of preferences regarding resource allocation. He did not begin to endorse light-industrial investment until after nearly one year of unequivocally calling for budgetary redistributions to the benefit of agriculture and defense. And when he began to endorse it, the pattern of his statements suggests a political compromise in which the General Secretary did not have a very great stake. This is not to say that he was anti light industry in principle. It is rather to argue that for reasons of politics, preference, or both, Brezhnev chose to reconcile national security and material security for the population through costly programs in the defense and agricultural sectors. These initial choices in turn limited the funds available for other sectors.

---

[16] These comments, moreover, came in 1964: *Pravda*, 7 November 1964; and *Leninskim kursom I*, p. 43 (20 November 1964).

[17] Brezhnev, *Ob osnovnykh voprosakh*, Vol. 1, pp. 100–1; Gruliow, *Current Soviet Policies V*, p. 16.

[18] Gruliow, *Current Soviet Policies V*, pp. 16, 21.

[19] *Pravda*, 11 June 1966.

[20] ibid., 18 May 1966; *Leninskim kursom I*, pp. 458–75.

[21] *Pravda*, 28 May 1966.

Leonid Brezhnev: Incentive Policy and Popular Initiative

Brezhnev's expensive approach to agricultural development found expression in his position on price policy as well, and reflected a decisive break with Khrushchevian incentive policy in the rural sector. Shortly after Khrushchev's overthrow, Brezhnev announced that "fuller use of the principle of the material interest of collective farms and collective farmers acquires particular importance."[22] That this was not simply a reference to the structure of material incentives within existing price levels was made clear at the March 1965 Plenum. There the First Secretary argued at length that adequate prices are, indeed, a necessary condition for agricultural development. When prices go up, Brezhnev observed, so do deliveries of produce; when they go down, deliveries go down as well.[23] Delegates who had listened to Khrushchevian discourse on price policy could hardly have failed to notice the striking change in perspective.

Brezhnev's position on price policy, when coupled with his claim that it was imperative to "harmoniously combine the interests of the state as a whole and of the individual farms" (a new doctrinal formulation),[24] was an affirmation of his contention that the regime could do business with the peasantry; that higher prices would yield greater initiative and higher productivity. To the extent that voices within the political elite were arguing that ingrained peasant orientations would nullify the impact of these costly expenditures, Brezhnev was claiming the opposite.

Although Brezhnev was substantially increasing the relative role of material incentives, it would be a mistake to characterize his orientation as purely pragmatic or agnostic, or to view his approach as the very antithesis of Khrushchev's. For Brezhnev's approach to incentive policy included a good dose of political mobilization as well. Party activism remained as an important supplement to higher material rewards. Brezhnev was similar to Khrushchev in his claim that people could be inspired through political appeals to be other-regarding, if party activists more rationally demonstrated to them the material and moral payoffs to be had thereby. Where the two Soviet leaders differed was in the content of their mobilizational appeals and in the relative weight of material incentives and party activism as spurs to initiative.

Brezhnev was "political" in his approach to mass mobilization in two senses. First, he did not claim that material incentives alone could or should be relied upon to spur initiative. Thus, even at the March 1965 Plenum, where so much of his report dwelled on the new price

22 ibid., 7 November 1964.
23 ibid., 27 March 1965.
24 ibid.

policy, Brezhnev pointed out that "a permanent plan does not reduce but on the contrary raises the responsibility of party and soviet agencies for increasing the output of farm products and for fulfilling the state's assignments. If we say that the plan has the force of law, then it should be mandatory for everyone. It cannot be changed and it cannot go unfulfilled!"[25]

But Brezhnev was political in a second, more positive, sense than simply an emphasis on citizen obligation would suggest. He also stood for civic pride and Soviet nationalism as integrating myths to rally the populace and spur unselfish behavior. Although Khrushchev had expressed great pride in Soviet social and political accomplishments, his Seven-Year Plan and Third Party Program had explicitly coupled communism with material affluence, as defined by the standards of the USA and the West. Brezhnev was specifically trying to break the link established by Khrushchev, and to firmly establish the feeling or belief that Soviet society and the value thereof are not defined by a comparison with the USA or any other country, that life in the USSR had become rich and fulfilling on its own account, and that the spiritual or other qualitative differences between the socialist and capitalist worlds made comparisons based primarily on material standards invalid.

Thus, if we examine Brezhnev's speeches during 1964–6, we find him constantly comparing Soviet past and present accomplishments to the West, but largely in order to emphasize Soviet superiority: "the average annual increase in industrial output in the years of Soviet rule has been 10 percent. By way of comparison we might note that in the same period it has been only 3·4 percent in the chief country of capitalism, the United States of America."[26] In addition to these indicators, such boasting was applied to steel production, space exploration, output of specific commodities, national income, welfare benefits, natural resources, and stability of growth.[27] The basic message being conveyed was "we've got nothing to be ashamed of; we've got it made." Such a message had also appeared in Khrushchev's speeches, but was overshadowed at the time by Khrushchev's simultaneous claim that "we've got a long way to go."

Another type of "we've got it made" message that runs through Brezhnev's speeches is the image of "capitalist hell."[28] Brezhnev continually reminded his audiences of the social and political decay of advanced capitalist society, with its alleged high rates of inflation

[25] ibid.
[26] ibid., 7 November 1964.
[27] See speeches by Brezhnev listed in note 1, above; in addition, these generalizations apply to other speeches given by the Soviet leader during 1964–6 (*Leninskim kursom I*, pp. 36–45, 56–65, 118–55, 156–66, 233–50, 458–75).
[28] My thanks to Alexander Yanov for suggesting this term.

and unemployment, crime, and social injustice. In some cases the implication was that "state-monopoly capitalism" was on its last legs; in others, that, despite the decay, "imperialism" continued to have immense staying power and military capacity. But in all cases an image of the West was presented that would impress upon the audience the inherent undesirability of alternatives to socialism, regardless of relative aggregate levels of consumer goods or agricultural production.

As an overlay to all of this was the constant theme of Soviet patriotism, stated explicitly, and often in lyrical tones. About half of Brezhnev's major speeches to domestic audiences during 1964–6 were devoted largely to patriotic themes: the greeting of cosmonauts, celebrations connected with the twentieth anniversary of victory in World War II, awards to republics and cities for their enthusiasm in contributing to national efforts.[29] His speech to the Young Communist League in May 1966 dwelt at length on the need to "train youth in revolutionary traditions" and "to rear every young person to be an ardent patriot of our great country."[30] And in Kiev, or Tbilisi, he would emphasize Soviet nationalism, accomplishments reached under Soviet power, and common trials in building and defending the "socialist fatherland" as the cement binding the federation.[31]

We may never know just how deeply Brezhnev adhered to these beliefs, or how much ambivalence he might have experienced about the ability of these appeals to elicit authentic popular initiative. Yet it would be difficult to argue that the political thrusts of Brezhnev's speeches (citizen obligation, pride in accomplishment, and patriotic pride) were merely symbolic rhetoric. They had deep roots in the regime's ideological traditions, as well as in Brezhnev's personal background. And these perspectives were consistent with Brezhnev's position on resource allocation. A harmonious view of inter-class and inter-ethnic relations, based on the unifying force of being a single "Soviet people," would be consistent with investment priorities that sought to ensure that all classes should have material and physical security through higher defense expenditures, massive investment in rural development, and subsidization of urban retail prices. Herein lay Brezhnev's strategy for fashioning his appeal as a problem-solver, and for generating national unity, élan, and fervor as well.

---

[29] The body of speeches on which this generalization is based is listed in notes 1 and 27, above.

[30] *Pravda*, 18 May 1966.

[31] Brezhnev, *Leninskim kursom I*, pp. 233–42, 465; see also *Pravda*, 11 July 1965.

Brezhnev as Politician

In fashioning his image as a leader, Brezhnev manipulated his rhetoric on budgetary policy in ways that would appeal to deep yearnings within the political establishment for both an improvement of economic performance and an atmosphere of tranquility.[32] On the one hand, he tried to impress upon members of the political elite the urgency of the agricultural situation, calling his program an "urgent, nationwide need," without which it would be impossible to build communism.[33] On the other hand, Brezhnev appealed to current yearnings, not for a sense of dynamism, but for a sense of stability. Thus, at the March 1965 Plenum, Brezhnev pointed out that his program would allow the regime "to manage agriculture confidently and according to plan."[34] At the September 1965 Plenum, he played upon elite fears, not of the masses, but of the weather, adding that his program would ensure "a *steady* increase in the ouput of all agricultural products"[35] (italics added).

This was turning out to be the basic promise of his leadership in agriculture. At the Twenty-Third Party Congress he promised "the steady expansion of production at high and, most important, stable rates," as well as a land-reclamation program that would "ensure high, stable harvests in zones with unfavorable natural conditions."[36] Two months later, at the Central Committee Plenum on land reclamation, Brezhnev made this theme the very title of his speech: "Land Reclamation is a Fundamental Problem in the Establishment of Stable Agricultural Production in the Country."[37]

Beyond the promise of a sense of security in the agricultural sector, however, Brezhnev sought to decouple his personal authority from short-term fluctuations in the agricultural situation. It is true that, at the March 1965 Plenum, he demanded a "radical improvement in the development of animal husbandry in the next two or three years."[38] But this was the only statement of its kind on the part of the First Secretary during this two-year period. Instead, it was typical of Brezhnev to point out that a decisive solution of the agricultural problem would "require time and much concentrated effort," or "immense efforts and large capital investments and material and

[32] On the Brezhnev regime's ethos of "tranquility," see Archie Brown, "The power of the General Secretary," in T. H. Rigby, Archie Brown, and Peter Reddaway (eds), *Authority, Power and Policy in the USSR* (London: Macmillan, 1980), pp. 146–7.

[33] *Pravda*, 27 March 1965.

[34] ibid.

[35] ibid., 30 September 1965.

[36] Gruliow, *Current Soviet Policies V*, pp. 18, 20.

[37] *Pravda*, 28 May 1966.

[38] ibid., 27 March 1965.

technical resources."[39] Indeed, at the May 1966 Plenum on land reclamation, Brezhnev appeared to go out of his way to protect his own authority from premature criticism should the payoffs from his program be slow in coming. The results he was now willing to promise amounted to little more than learning from experience and trial by error:

> Of course, quite a few questions will arise about methods of irrigation, varieties of crops, systems of engineering installations, etc. But we figure that within the next few years we shall accumulate a great deal of experience in these matters . . .
>
> Perhaps we shall not avoid certain shortcomings and mistakes in planning, in the approach to the assimilation of individual expanses of land. I don't believe they will be very significant, and the experience acquired will help us to eliminate them in subsequent years . . .
>
> When we have done some work and acquired broader experience . . . the essence of this problem will be exposed in even greater diversity and depth.[40]

This was in striking contrast to Khrushchev, who had immediately claimed to be privy to agronomical panaceas that would radically improve production without heavy expenditures. Khrushchev had thereby attempted to increase elite dependence on his expertise, by coupling his authority to both big promises and detailed personal intervention. Brezhnev instead called for leaving agronomic detail to the real agronomists, and for moderating elite expectation of results.

An equally striking contrast to Khrushchev's authority-building strategy was Brezhnev's total abstention from allusions to the mass mood. Although he would warn of the importance of his capital-intensive approach to the agricultural problem, he made no effort to appeal over the heads of the national leadership to the masses, and never warned the elite of possible mass disorder or retribution in the event that they failed to follow his lead. Nor did he make an effort to raise consumer expectations in order to intimidate the local elite. In short, whereas Brezhnev sought to mobilize elite support for his program by appealing to perceived yearnings for a reliable program of agricultural development, he never allowed this authority-building strategy to appear to be supportive of a move toward personal rule.

[39] ibid., 11 July 1965, and 28 May 1966; Brezhnev, *Ob osnovnykh voprosakh*, Vol. 1, pp. 107–9; *Leninskim kursom I*, p. 468.
[40] *Pravda*, 28 May 1966 (*CDSP*, vol. 18, no. 23).

Elite Strategies and Political Conflict

Brezhnev's positions on resource allocation and incentive policy differed significantly from those of his colleague, Chairman of the Council of Ministers and Politburo-member Alexei Kosygin.[41] It is unclear just how Kosygin proposed to solve the agricultural problem, but it is clear that the Prime Minister's stated preferences and perspectives did not dovetail with those of the First Secretary. The existence of this divergence may explain the temporary challenge to Brezhnev's agricultural program during the one-year period, early 1967–early 1968.[42] For Kosygin appears to have spoken for forces within the political elite that did not accept the contention that there was no alternative to an extremely expensive approach to rural development.

At the Twenty-Third Party Congress, Kosygin endorsed some of the major features of Brezhnev's speech: priority allocations for defense and agriculture, and efforts to direct the attention of priority sectors toward the needs of the urban consumer.[43] Yet within the context of this consensus, there were differences between the speeches of Brezhnev and Kosygin that highlighted both the lower order of priority Brezhnev placed on light industry, and the higher order of priority Kosygin attached to that sector.

Thus, Brezhnev referred to an upsurge in agriculture as a "highly important task for our entire Party and people,"[44] whereas Kosygin avoided this socio-political definition of the problem. In addition, the Prime Minister advocated the use of *public* pressure to further the cause, whereas the General Secretary called for pressure from above and within-channels:

Brezhnev[45]	Kosygin[46]
Party and Soviet agencies, ministries, associations, and enterprises must regard the production of consumer goods as an important state task.	The production of consumer goods is an important and honorable task. Its fulfillment must be under the constant control of Party, Soviet, trade union and Young Communist League organizations—of the general public.

[41] They also differed from the apparent policy advocacy of others in the Politburo, most notably Nikolai Podgorny and Alexander Shelepin. As this book is meant to highlight the strategies of the General Secretary, it is not a comprehensive examination of the gamut of leadership conflict over policies. Documentation of conflict is confined to similarities and differences between the Party leader and the Chairman of the Council of Ministers.

[42] See Hahn, *Politics of Soviet Agriculture*, pp. 189–99, for a description of this challenge.

[43] Gruliow, *Current Soviet Policies V*, pp. 95–7, 101, 102.

[44] ibid., p. 18.

[45] ibid., p. 21.

[46] ibid., p. 100.

Finally, Kosygin went further than Brezhnev in describing the importance of expanded consumer-goods production, linking it to the broader
issue of incentives and productivity:

> . . . acceleration of the growth of consumer goods production is a
> necessary prerequisite for the further successful development of the
> economy. Only given this condition is it possible to put into opera-
> tion all the material incentives for an upsurge in production.[47]

Divergent statements by the two Soviet leaders continued after the
Party Congress. In their election speeches of June 1966, Brezhnev
emphasized agriculture's need for "large-scale capital investments,"
whereas Kosygin appeared to endorse the notion that agriculture's
problems were mainly organizational, not financial: "The necessary
reserves have been created for normal food supplies. And if there
are still bottlenecks in food deliveries . . . these are not related to
food shortages but to poor organization of deliveries."[48] In November
of that year, after the record harvest, Brezhnev made a speech in
Georgia in which he warned against complacency "easy paths" and
"magic formulae" in solving the agricultural problem.[49] Nonetheless,
in his election speech of March 1967, Kosygin repeated his rosy
assessment of the situation in agriculture, and pointed to the rising
purchasing power of the population, concluding that only the accelerated development of light industry could relieve inflationary pressures.[50]

During most of 1967 Brezhnev did not speak out publicly against
the political tide in favor of reallocations to the advantage of light
industry.[51] But the crop failure of 1967 afforded him the opportunity
to go back on the counteroffensive. In his November 1967 address on
the fiftieth anniversary of the October Revolution, Brezhnev declared
that "our country is now able to put more resources into the development of agriculture."[52] This was a tune Brezhnev had not sung since
October 1966. But there was a new note to this tune as well. Just as
Brezhnev had used the crop failure of 1965 to press for an expanded
commitment to land reclamation and irrigation, so he used the crop

[47] ibid., p. 97.
[48] *Pravda*, 11 June 1966, and 9 June 1966.
[49] *Leninskim kursom I*, p. 468.
[50] *Pravda*, 7 March 1967.
[51] Thus, Brezhnev made no major pitch for agricultural investments in
his election speech (*Pravda*, 11 March 1967), his speech to the military
academy graduates (ibid., 6 July 1967) or his speech to the plenary session
of September 1967 (Brezhnev, *Ob osnovnykh voprosakh*, Vol. 1, pp. 244–
50).
[52] *Pravda*, 4 November 1967.

failure of 1967 both to reassert the basic premises of his program and to expand the commitment still further to include a costly program of rural construction: "we consider this a matter of statewide importance and are tackling it in earnest."

Alexei Kosygin, however, had not spoken his last word on the subject. Speaking in Minsk in February 1968, Kosygin ignored the crop failure of 1967 and again repeated his optimistic assessment of the agricultural situation, concluding: "We have the possibility of completely meeting the country's foodstuff needs and maintaining our grain reserves."[53] And in reference to the growing movement for capital investment in rural construction, Kosygin struck a Khrushchevian posture, advocating that such construction be financed out of local resources, "from the earnings of the farms themselves."

Brezhnev accepted the challenge to polemicize. Speaking in Moscow one month later, Brezhnev argued that it was time to shift attention back from light industry to agriculture.[54] Whereas Kosygin presented a rosy picture of the agricultural situation, Brezhnev painted a rosy picture of the situation in light industry: "The party's course toward bringing together the rates of growth of production of consumer goods and the production of the means of production is being successfully realized." In contrast to Kosygin's suggestion that the grain problem had been solved, Brezhnev argued that "a great deal of work remains to be done." And in contrast to Kosygin's emphasis on light industry, Brezhnev suggested a different road to consumer satisfaction: "The better things go in our industry and agriculture, the greater possibilities will open up for further raising the well being of our people."

Shortly after these polemics, the forces pushing for expanded agricultural investments made a comeback, restoring many of the cuts of the previous year. Brezhnev was having things done his way.[55]

Nor was this pattern of elite consensus and conflict unique to the realms of policy examined in this chapter. A very similar pattern was in evidence on the issues of administrative reform and political participation.

---

[53] *Sovetskaia Belorussiia*, 15 February 1968 (*CDSP*, vol. 20, no. 7, pp. 11–17).

[54] *Pravda*, 30 March 1968 (*CDSP*, vol. 20, no. 13, pp. 3–7).

[55] A similar analysis of the polemic between Brezhnev and Kosygin over agricultural investment in 1967–8 can be found in Hahn, *Politics of Soviet Agriculture*, pp. 189–97.

9 Political Succession and Administrative Reform, 1964-8

The overthrow of Khrushchev created conditions under which a fundamentally new approach to administrative efficiency could be adopted by the Soviet leadership. Khrushchev's efforts to ensure administrative responsibility through unremitting pressure from above and below had placed impossible demands on local officials. This contributed to an economic crisis that undermined Khrushchev's authority, to which he responded by increasing the pressure for immediate results and purging the administrative elite. In the end, he had achieved neither administrative efficiency nor the successful defense of his authority.

Khrushchev's successors may not have been united and certain about the full panoply of policy changes required in the administrative realm, but at least a majority coalition appears to have agreed on some fundamental premises and perspectives underlying their approach to administrative efficiency.[1] In this respect, their perspectives were far more consensual than had been the case among Stalin's successors. Specifically, a broad coalition appears to have agreed upon the following: (1) the desirability or necessity of reconciling the search for administrative efficiency with a posture of accommodation and consensus-building toward Soviet officialdom; (2) the desirability or necessity of administrative stability; and (3) the need to rationalize pressures placed on Soviet officials, in order to ensure a closer correspondence between the demands on officials and the resources available for meeting those demands.

The consensus on adopting a posture of reconciliation toward Soviet officialdom expressed itself in constant refrains to the effect that deviance would not be equated with corruption or sabotage, and that Soviet officials would enjoy physical security and job security so long as they proved honest and competent. These refrains took many forms. At the Aesopian level, few cadres could have failed to note that accusations of anti-state behavior were entirely absent from speeches by Brezhnev and Kosygin during the period under review in this chapter. But the leadership did not rely solely on Aesopian indicators of its new posture. Three weeks after Khrushchev's overthrow, Brezhnev spoke on the forty-seventh anniversary of the Bolshevik Revolution, and ensured cadres of their security against arbitrary,

---

[1] For the sources upon which generalizations about the majority consensus after Khrushchev are based, see Chapter 8, note 1.

personalistic rule.[2] Brezhnev endorsed the Twentieth Party Congress, promised the "restoration of genuinely Leninist norms," and called this "the general line of our party," a statement that was greeted by "stormy applause." At the September 1965 plenary session, Kosygin described the regime's changing posture toward its managerial executives, by reassuring them that "the party and the people value the country's experts and executives whom they fully trust and support in their difficult work for the good of society."[3] The two critical words in this statement are "trust" and "difficult." The concept of trust indicated a formal rejection of the earlier notion that mistakes by officials would be taken as indications of their lack of social consciousness. Moreover, the recognition that their work was "difficult" accorded cadres the assurance that some mistakes were acknowledged to be in the nature of the task, and that these would not be interpreted simply as gross incompetence. At the Twenty-Third Party Congress, Brezhnev gave similar assurances to party cadres when he declared that "the development of the principle of democratic centralism has found expression in . . . the manifestation of complete trust in cadres . . ."[4] Indeed, the notion of "trusting the cadres" became a virtual by-word of the Brezhnev regime, receiving obeisance or discussion in most articles and books on cadre policy and administrative affairs.[5]

Broad agreement on the need for administrative stability and predictability was also communicated quickly after Khrushchev's overthrow and frequently thereafter. Thus, the *Pravda* editorial on the occasion of the reunification of the party apparatus, just one month after Khrushchev's dismissal, noted that local officials during 1962–4 had done their best in an impossible situation, but that the reorganization had "*objectively* led to confusion in the functions, rights, and obligations of the Party, Soviet, and economic agencies" (italics added).[6]

In addition, Brezhnev and Kosygin regularly criticized the Khrushchevian penchant for "hasty reorganizations," "subjectivism," "voluntarism," and "hare-brained schemes," promising instead to improve management "cautiously and without fuss or haste."[7] Further, in outlining programs for administrative reform in the agricultural and industrial sectors during 1965, both Soviet leaders dwelled at length

[2] *Pravda*, 7 November 1964.
[3] ibid., 28 September 1965.
[4] Gruliow, *Current Soviet Policies V*, p. 25.
[5] See T. H. Rigby and R. F. Miller, *Political and Administrative Aspects of the Scientific and Technical Revolution in the USSR* (Canberra: Australian National University, 1976), p. 35.
[6] *Pravda*, 18 November 1964 (*CDSP*, vol. 16, no. 45, p. 4).
[7] *Pravda*, 7 November 1964.
[8] See ibid., 27 March 1965, and 28 September 1965.

on the need for executive personnel to be given stable plans in order to diminish the uncertainty in their work environments.[8] In the absence of such predictability, they explained, officials could hardly be expected to perform up to their capabilities: "an atmosphere of nervousness and bustle deprived managers of a long-range perspective and undermined their faith in their abilities."[9] Frequent reorganizations "prevented [officials] from fully demonstrating their abilities and created the soil in which irresponsibility could grow."[10] This was a far cry from Khrushchev's complaint that too many executives wanted to spend their days "in complete calm."

A similar theme was evident in the new regime's perspectives on the degree to which individuals should—or could—be held responsible for behavior forced upon them by contradictory pressures and demands. Khrushchev's response had been to search for "the culprit" and, when frustrated in this search, to call upon the masses to help ensure total visibility of official behavior. "Absence of control," he had argued, "can turn even an honest man, if he is unstable, into a thief. There must be public control or some other kind of inspection."[11] Alexei Kosygin implicitly rejected this approach in his major address of December 1964.[12] Leonid Brezhnev, however, later formally revised the official party line:

> . . . the system of management that has existed until now, under which the same questions were dealt with simultaneously by several organizations . . . created conditions under which some officials were tempted to place the blame for their own failures and short-comings on some other agency and to explain all difficulties by "objective" factors.

Now this might sound like a typically Khrushchevian perspective on administrative control, were it not for the fact that, in the very next breath, Brezhnev reversed the traditional explanation, adding that, "under such circumstances, even good managers often began to lose a sense of direct responsibility for the job entrusted to them."[13]

[9] ibid., 27 March 1965.

[10] Gruliow, *Current Soviet Policies V*, p. 25. (Note: The quotations cited are illustrative; the same message can be found, in one form or another, in most of the speeches by Brezhnev and Kosygin during this period.)

[11] *Stroitel'stvo kommunizma IV*, p. 311. This was an important statement of perspective under Khrushchev, and it echoed the traditional Stalinist dictum about bureaucracy: "even good officials begin to grow spoiled and bureaucratic when left to themselves with no control or check on their activities" (Malenkov, at the Nineteenth Party Congress, in Gruliow, *Current Soviet Policies I*, p. 119).

[12] *Pravda*, 10 December 1964.

[13] ibid., 30 September 1965 (*CDSP*, vol. 17, no. 39).

Finally, broad agreement on the need to reduce the pressure on Soviet officials to attain the unprecedented results expressed itself in the constant refrain in favor of greater "realism" in planning and greater respect for "proportions." Beyond these Aesopian indicators, however, Brezhnev and Kosygin indicated their agreement on a doctrinal change in this area. Rather than demand simply, as had Khrushchev, that local officials pay greater attention to the "interests of the state" or the "interests of the people," the new Soviet regime supplemented these ritualistic injunctions with a recognition of the difficult position of the local official in the command economy: "We came to the firm conviction that in the area of production it is necessary to strive for a more harmonious combination of the interests of the state, on the one hand, and the interests of the enterprise and the immediate producers, on the other."[14]

All of these changes reflected a reevaluation of the requirements for administrative responsibility in the command economy. They indicated an appreciation of conflicting pressures at the local level, and of the official's inability to calculate the consequences of his behavior for other units in the system. Hence, they conceded the difficulty of holding officials responsible for behavior which was virtually predetermined by contradictory or unrealistic demands. Thus, the leadership was conceding its obligation to find new methods of planning that would appreciate these dilemmas. And, from a political standpoint, it was assuring the cadres that administrative control and reform would not be accompanied by a purge of the administrative or political elite.

Yet the consensus on behalf of reducing pressure and intervention left unresolved several key questions: (1) what would be the role of party activism and political intervention in a rationalized administrative system? (2) What would be the relative roles of intervention (from above, below, and/or from horizontal sources of control) versus material incentives as spurs to administrative initiative? (3) What would be the role of the market in proposals for administrative reform? Would the consensus evolve in the direction of decentralized market socialism, or would it settle for a combination of more rational central planning, reduced pressure, and selective political intervention? (4) What social costs would be borne in the search for administrative and economic efficiency? Would a reduction in political intervention result in managers being allowed to sacrifice welfare and equity considerations in rationalizing production within economic enterprises?[15]

As had been the case during 1953–7, the years of political succession were marked by competing biases with respect to administrative reform. After Stalin's death, Khrushchev had supported approaches

[14] *Pravda*, 11 June 1966; see also ibid., 7 November 1964, 27 March 1965, 12 July 1965, and 30 September 1965; Gruliow, *Current Soviet Policies V*, p. 105.

to the problem that relied on party intervention in managerial affairs. Leonid Brezhnev was to do much the same, but within the context of a very different elite consensus. Hence, Brezhnev's definition of the scope and nature of party intervention would differ significantly from the Khrushchevian conception. What the two leaders had in common, however, was a willingness to struggle against technocratic and decentralist approaches to administrative reform. Brezhnev, like Khrushchev, would attempt to build his authority by projecting the image of a problem-solver who would increase administrative efficiency without sacrificing the leading role of the party in administrative affairs.

Leonid Brezhnev: On Party Activism and Administrative Reform

We have seen that, in his approach to incentive policy, Brezhnev was not a pure pragmatist. Although more inclined than Nikita Khrushchev to rely on the private sector and material rewards as a spur to productivity, he was political in his approach to party mobilization in several important respects. Similarly, with respect to administrative reform, Brezhnev was less interventionist than Khrushchev, but more so than those advocating formal restraints on the party's right to intervene in economic affairs. Brezhnev was "political" in this realm as well, for he argued that administrative initiative could not be channeled in desired directions without a regular role for party intervention. Similarly, Brezhnev did not endorse the decentralist alternative, offering instead a combination of centralism, deconcentration, and selective party interventionism as the prescription for administrative efficiency.[16] These orientations found expression in his speeches on agricultural and industrial affairs during 1965–6.

At the March 1965 Plenum, Brezhnev had a great deal to say about the sources of administrative initiative in the rural economy.[17] His views were in striking contrast both to Khrushchev's use of unremitting pressure and to Khrushchev's eventual advocacy of the link

[15] Western analyses of the functions served by party intervention in managerial affairs often saw this as motivated solely by power considerations, and as antithetical to efficiency (for example, Conyngham, *Industrial Management*). Jerry Hough, in contrast, argued that a positive coordinative function was performed by party intervention (*The Soviet Prefects* [Cambridge, Mass.: Harvard University Press, 1968]). But only very recently has party intervention been interpreted in terms of the social values protected by such acts (George Breslauer, *Five Images of the Soviet Future* [Berkeley, Calif.: University of California, Institute of International Studies, 1978] and Jerry Hough, *Soviet Leadership in Transition* [Washington, DC: Brookings Institution, 1980], pp. 134–8).
[16] For the formal distinction between "decentralization" and "deconcentration," see Chapter 1, note 5.
[17] *Pravda*, 27 March 1965.

system. The very first paragraphs of Brezhnev's speech were devoted to discussion of the leading role of the district party organization (raikom) in the countryside, while his failure to even mention the link system in his long address signaled his intention to rely upon the brigade system, and upon broader consultation among local party officials and farm chairmen, for results.

Although restoring the political status of the rural raikom, Brezhnev did not echo the Khrushchevian claim that the way to stimulate initiative among local state officials was through a combination of detailed guidance of the rural economy by local party officials and mobilization of the masses against their administrative superiors. Rather, Brezhnev's was a call for more rational, regulatory leadership, and the creation of a more stable environment for local administrators. He called upon local party and soviet agencies to work out plans that would avoid "mistakes" by being assigned "objectively," and by taking into account the distinctive capabilities of each farm. He indicated in no uncertain terms that the goal was to "grant more economic independence" to the collective and state farms, and to "put an end to the practice of command and administration by fiat, to petty tutelage, to the usurping of the functions of the leaders and specialists of the collective and state farms."

And what of the social costs to be borne in the pursuit of economic efficiency? Would Brezhnev countenance the broad material differentiation and social insecurity that Khrushchev had eventually come to advocate? Brezhnev had little to say on the issue at this point. Perhaps he assumed that the new system of procurement norms and prices, coupled with more differentiated and realistic plans, would obviate the need for drastic measures. Moreover, Brezhnev may have viewed his egalitarian policy of raising the level of rural life to that of the urban as a satisfactory alternative. On the other hand, Brezhnev's noncommittal posture on the issue was reflected in his call for proposals on how to rationalize the structure of material incentives: "We have many unresolved questions here. The system of remunerating labor on the collective and state farms is still far from perfect."

And what of the role of the rural party organs? Other than co-ordinating district affairs in general, would they have a distinctive interventionist function within a rationalized planning structure? Brezhnev was calling for the party to revert to a more coordinative posture, exercising more selective intervention, but toward what ends? When would such intervention be appropriate?

For one thing, Brezhnev called upon party organs to pay more attention to culture and welfare in an era when the "production mentality" could easily lead to an overemphasis on economic concerns —and following a leader, Khrushchev, who had allowed just such an overemphasis to develop.[18] Thus, in his March 1965 Plenum address, Brezhnev coupled his endorsement of a more regulatory role for the rural district party organization with a warning to raikom officials that, at a time when "the decisive role belongs to production," it would nonetheless, "be wrong to forget questions of the culture and everyday life of the rural workers."[19]

A second interventionist function articulated by the First Secretary was to protect the national interest against parochial decisions made by rural officials in response to an imperfect planning and incentive structure. On this score, Brezhnev's position was analogous to that of Khrushchev, though not as extreme. Thus, at the December 1965 Plenum, Brezhnev criticized deviant practices on the farms, in particular the tendency of collective farmers to reduce the size of fields devoted to the less profitable crops, and to produce only for local needs during a bad year.[20] He demanded that local party and soviet agencies exercise close supervision of on-farm decision-making, and ensure that collective farm officials respond to the current price structure in ways consistent with the public interest. Brezhnev was trying to make the current, higher levels of crop prices "work," and one way to do that was to combine those prices with party intervention to plug the loopholes and to prevent formally deviant behavior. That pressure, he made clear, would be selective, and would not be allowed to degenerate into confiscation. But it would be real:

> The March Plenum . . . affirmed that the procurements plan is fixed, that no one has the right to change it. But no one has the right not to fulfill it either . . . At the March Plenum it was stressed that the grain procurement plan of 3·4 billion poods is a minimum, that the state plans to procure a significant amount of grain above the plan at elevated prices.[21]

At the May 1966 plenary session on land reclamation, Brezhnev turned his attention to the relationship between central party and state officials, and defined still a third interventionist function for the party: breaking through bureaucratic routine in order to infuse new values, redefine missions, and ensure the introduction of new programs.[22] Pointing out forcefully that greater funding of agriculture must be

[18] The concept, "production mentality," appears in Kenneth Jowitt, "An organizational approach to the study of political culture in Marxist–Leninist Systems," *American Political Science Review* (September 1974), p. 1,185.

[19] *Pravda*, 27 March 1965.

[20] Brezhnev, *Ob osnovnykh voprosakh*, Vol. 1, pp. 108–9.

[21] ibid. Brezhnev's March 1965 speech had devoted some half-dozen lines to such warnings about deviant practices; his December 1965 report devoted some fifty-eight lines to such warnings.

[22] *Pravda*, 28 May 1966.

combined with "high responsibility and exactingness toward cadres," Brezhnev launched into an attack on the Ministries of Agriculture and of Land Reclamation, demanding that the ministers henceforth "answer fully to the party and the state."

Here, too, Brezhnev's position was analogous to Khrushchev's, though with important differences. In the years immediately following Stalin's death, Khrushchev had sharply criticized various agricultural ministries and ministers for bureaucratic inertia, obsolete programs, and an inability to adjust to new tasks. He demanded that they change their ways or face dire consequences. Brezhnev did much the same, but within the context of restoring the ministerial structure that Khrushchev had eventually abolished, and within the context of demanding increased party penetration of central ministerial decision-making, rather than demanding resignations. In sum, Brezhnev's stated conception of the central party's interventionist function was shaped by a new commitment to reconciliation with officialdom.

In the industrial sector, Brezhnev's statements on administrative reform also reflected both the new consensus and the First Secretary's definition of the party's distinctive functions in such a context.[23] Neither a recentralizer nor a decentralizer, Brezhnev called for deconcentration of operational decision-making within the new ministerial structure. He demanded a reduction in bureaucratic layering, overlapping jurisdictions, and overly detailed controls over the managers. None of which distinguished his position from that adopted by Khrushchev in the years immediately following Stalin's death. Where they differed was in Khrushchev's regional perspective, which presaged his eventual abolition of the ministerial structure, in contrast to Brezhnev's acceptance of the ministerial-branch system, which he coupled with efforts to deconcentrate administration within that system.

In fact, Brezhnev at times sounded like N. Bulganin or G. Malenkov, rather than N. Khrushchev, in phrasing his demand that ministerial officials expand the decision-making latitude of managers. At the September 1965 Plenum, for example, he praised the "remarkable commanders of production."[24] At the December 1965 Plenum he insisted that the years of Soviet rule had created a corp of competent and trustworthy enterprise directors who could be counted on to exercise initiative in the national interest without detailed ministerial control.[25] The First Secretary apparently was claiming that detailed

---

[23] Brezhnev's major statements on industrial administration during October 1964–April 1966 are clustered in the latter half of this period: *Pravda*, 30 September 1965; Brezhnev, *Leninskim kursom I*, pp. 243f.; Brezhnev, *Ob osnovnykh voprosakh*, Vol. 1, pp. 102f.; Gruliow, *Current Soviet Policies V*, pp. 15, 16, 22.

[24] *Pravda*, 30 September 1965.

[25] Brezhnev, *Ob osnovnykh voprosakh*, Vol. 1, p. 102; see also Gruliow, *Current Soviet Policies V*, p. 15.

central control was a habit infused in the central ministerial structure before 1957, and that it was likely to recur after 1965, frustrating efforts toward an efficiency-oriented rationalization of public administration.[26]

But Brezhnev was equally unambiguous in his opposition to genuine decentralization of the economy. Thus, in his statements on administrative reform, Brezhnev never mentioned the idea of "direct ties" between enterprises, or between scientific institutes and enterprises, and he made only one passing reference to the need for further thought about the character and role of "economic contracts."[27] Moreover, at the September 1965 Plenum, Brezhnev pointed out that "all questions related to the acceleration of technological progress [must] be resolved through the plans."[28] And at the December 1965 Plenum he followed his call for ministries to cease overprescription with an equally insistent call for the avoidance of decentralization:

> But for the condition of a given branch of industry as a whole; for the level of its technological development; for the smoothness of work of all enterprises of this branch—for these the minister and apparat of the corresponding ministry answer to the Central Committee of the Party and the government. And no one can substitute for them on this matter.[29]

In his opposition to genuine decentralization and marketization, Brezhnev's position was similar to Khrushchev's. Khrushchev had wanted to foster a horizontal focus on the part of local officials, but not the kind of horizontal focus that a market would require. Instead, Khrushchev worked to increase horizontal control over state institutions by party organizations. By 1965, however, those advocating decentralization had recognized the need to break both the vertical and horizontal controls over managerial personnel, and the substitution of a market as a coordinating mechanism. Such a conclusion was rejected by Brezhnev, as it had been by Khrushchev.

What distinctive functions for party interventionism did Brezhnev envisage in a less centralized ministerial structure? Those functions paralleled the three distinctive functions indicated in Brezhnev's

[26] This conclusion is also reached in Katz, *Politics of Economic Reform*, p. 147.

[27] See *Pravda*, 30 September 1965: "In the course of communist construction many acute problems constantly arise whose practical resolution requires profound theoretical preparation. Advancing to the forefront today, for example, are such questions as socialist economic accountability, the use in planned economic management of profit, prices, credit, economic contracts, etc. . . ."

[28] ibid.

[29] Brezhnev, *Ob osnovnykh voprosakh*, Vol. 1, p. 102; see also Gruliow, *Current Soviet Policies V*, p. 22.

speeches on rural administration: breaking through bureaucratic routine and redefining operating procedures in the ministries; protecting the national interest against parochial local decisions; and protecting precarious social values in the quest for economic efficiency.

Thus, at the September 1965 Plenum, Brezhnev called for raising the role of party committees within the ministries, and for regular reportage by those committees to the Central Committee about the inner workings of the ministries.[30] At the December 1965 Plenum he called upon party organizations in the ministries, as well as Central Committee departments, to intensify their attention to certain inertial and persistent problems, and to break through administrative obstacles to their resolution: the problem of frozen assets resulting from constantly starting up new projects before ongoing projects are even near completion; the problem of partial-capacity use of new construction; and the problem of bloated staffs.[31] At the Twenty-Third Party Congress he declared his preference for the selective application of party pressure as a stimulus for technological innovation.[32] Thus, he noted that questions of material incentives for innovation remained up in the air. In addition, he followed praise for the industrial reforms with the observation that "conditions of themselves do not guarantee success." If conditions did not ensure success, then something else was needed, either greater incentive and autonomy, or greater pressure. Brezhnev's conclusion was predictable: "Therefore it is necessary that the ministries and party and state agencies pay more attention to science and the application of its achievements in the national economy." Thus, Brezhnev's conception of the selective use of vertical and horizontal intervention to overcome administrative resistance to risk-taking complemented the commitment to avoiding excessive reliance on material inducements.

In this respect, Brezhnev's conception of the party as a protector of precarious social values merged with his conception of the party as a mechanism for breaking through bureaucratic inertia. This may have been what he had in mind in October 1965 when, in discussing the industrial reforms before an audience in Kiev, he averred that the entire system of party organizations must "stand in guard of state and societal interests," that it must help state officials to solve problems, but also "not allow the activities of individual economic administrators to contradict the interests of the state and the interests of our society."[33] It may also have been on his mind while making his June 1966 election speech, in which he called improvements in the assortment and quality of goods "a matter of honor" for all party and state organs, and "simultaneously a major economic and a major

[30] *Pravda*, 30 September 1965.

[31] Brezhnev, *Ob osnovnykh voprosakh*, Vol. 1, pp. 103–7.

[32] Gruliow, *Current Soviet Policies V*, pp. 15, 22.

[33] Brezhnev, *Leninskim kursom I*, pp. 244–5.

political issue."[34] For to the extent that arguments were being made within the political elite and attentive public for achieving the goals of economic efficiency, technological innovation, and improved quality through genuine decentralization or through rationalization of the organization of production at the expense of egalitarian social values, this *was* a political issue.

Thus, in both the agricultural and industrial sectors, Brezhnev, like Khrushchev before him, advocated an important role for party interventionism as a spur to initiative. Their conceptions of the scope, purpose, and character of party intervention, however, were quite different. Brezhnev's positions were shaped in part by a consensus that emerged as a result of the Khrushchevian experience. Specifically, Brezhnev defined the role of party organs to be more coordinative than had Khrushchev, and defined its interventionism as more selective. Brezhnev also worked within a spirit of reconciliation with officials of the state bureaucracy which, in turn, implied acceptance of the ministerial-branch system, mechanisms of accountability that did not imply large-scale purges of the state bureaucracy, and mechanisms of administrative control that did not foster unregulated mass surveillance of the bureaucrats.

Brezhnev's public statements do not reflect a clear conception of the precise functions of party intervention in ministerial and managerial affairs, or of the relationship between intervention and economic efficiency. Those statements do, however, indicate a clear opposition to further development of administrative policy in a decentralist direction. On this score, Brezhnev differed notably from Alexei Kosygin.

Elite Perspectives and Political Conflict

Just as Brezhnev and Kosygin differed in their approach to investment priorities, so they differed over questions of administrative reform. The two Soviet leaders may not have been as far apart in their positions as the economists in the Academy of Sciences who were debating the alternatives of deconcentration versus decentralization.[35] And the two leaders may have been ambivalent or uncertain about how to control the bureaucracy, or about the social and political costs they were willing to pay for the sake of economic efficiency. But the

34 *Pravda*, 11 June 1966.
35 For those discussions, see Katz, *Politics of Economic Reform*; also, Richard Judy, "The economists," in H. Gordon Skilling and Franklyn Griffiths (eds), *Interest Groups in Soviet Politics* (Princeton, NJ: Princeton University Press, 1971). Neither Katz nor Judy conceptualizes the differences among these economists using the terms "deconcentrators" and "decentralizers."

differences in their speeches were real nonetheless. Moreover, just as Brezhnev and Kosygin polemicized over resource allocation during 1967–8, so they engaged in a similar polemic over questions of administrative reform.

Brezhnev's speeches during 1964–6 were noteworthy for their avoidance of decentralist terminology; Kosygin's were not. Kosygin called for "raising the role of enterprises as the basic economic cell of our economy."[36] The Prime Minister spoke often of the need for "direct ties" and "contracts" between suppliers and consumers of both inputs and outputs.[37] He called for "firm legal guarantees of the expanding rights of enterprises" against interference by higher instances.[38] In addressing the relationship between scientific institutions and enterprises that might be able to introduce their innovations, Kosygin called for "direct relations of economic accountability," rather than a directive or interventionist approach to the matter of reducing the gap between science and production.[39] Unquestionably, Kosygin was not advocating market socialism, but his endorsement of concepts associated with further movement in a decentralizing direction distinguished his speeches from those of Brezhnev, who was apparently satisfied to concentrate on realizing a combination of deconcentration and selective party intervention.[40]

Moreover, differences between these two leaders were evident from the ways in which they legitimized the need for administrative reform. Each of them acknowledged that the focus of economic competition between capitalism and socialism had switched to the realm of technological progress. However, in the context of the elite dialogue taking place at the time, to the extent a leader emphasized the inferiority of Soviet products or technology, he buttressed the case for selective emulation of the market-oriented methods employed by the main competitor: capitalism. Hence, it is noteworthy that Kosygin was far more negative about Soviet accomplishments than was Brezhnev. Brezhnev, for example, had this to say: "Now that we have entered the world market on a broad scale and are engaged in competition with the most highly developed capitalist countries, *it is very important that Soviet machines, machine tools and equipment . . . not only are*

[36] *Pravda*, 28 September 1965.
[37] ibid., 10 December 1964, and 28 September 1965; Gruliow, *Current Soviet Policies V*, p. 96.
[38] *Pravda*, 28 September 1965, and 12 July 1965.
[39] Gruliow, *Current Soviet Policies V*, p. 96.
[40] Indeed, some years later, when Kosygin apparently no longer wished to be associated with this terminology, the version of his 11 July 1965 speech was substantially doctored in the reprinted form in Kosygin, *A. N. Kosygin: izbrannye rechi i stat'i* (Moscow: Politizdat, 1974), p. 257. Compare new paragraphs one and two on this page with the original version in *Pravda*, 12 July 1965.

not inferior to but are better than foreign models (italics added)."[41] In contrast, when speaking to officials of the State Planning Committee in March 1965, Kosygin repeatedly harped on the inferiority of Soviet machinery vis-à-vis American machinery.[42] And when speaking in public, though not as explicit as before a closed audience, he was significantly more negative than Brezhnev: "The products of Volgograd enterprises . . . do not always survive competition with goods of the best foreign firms."[43]

From mid-1966 through October 1967 differences between Brezhnev and Kosygin on industrial reform were muted in public. But by early 1968 the positions of the two Soviet leaders had become increasingly polarized. Whether this reflected philosophical differences or solely an effort by Brezhnev to outflank and discredit Kosygin is unclear. But the polemics were real nonetheless.

Thus, in his anniversary speech of November 1967, Brezhnev revised earlier formulations about the need to combine the interests of the state with those of the enterprise and the individual worker.[44] The "interests of the enterprise" were now missing from Brezhnev's statement of the main tasks in the realm of administrative reform. In contrast to this retreat from basic principles of the 1965 reforms, Kosygin was calling for their further elaboration.

Speaking in Minsk in February 1968, Premier Kosygin lamented the fact that the gap between science and production remained huge, that the level of technological innovation in the enterprise remained low, and that the organization of production in the enterprises remained so inefficient.[45] His prescription for dealing with the situation was to further extend the principles of the 1965 reform: "On the whole it is correct and economically advantageous and is yielding very good results . . . the new system is viable and correct . . . and meets the interests of the enterprises and the collectives of their workers."[46] Moreover, Kosygin backed up this line of argumentation in characteristic fashion, invoking the capitalist experience as a positive referent: "In the capitalist countries the monopolies are obliged to wage a sharp struggle for profits and must react quickly to the consumer's demands, produce up-to-date types of goods and seek the most rational forms of organizing and managing production."[47] In

[41] Gruliow, *Current Soviet Policies V*, p. 16. This kind of muted notation of Soviet inferiority on the world market can also be found in his speeches in *Pravda*, 30 September 1965 and Brezhnev, *Ob osnovnykh voprosakh*, Vol. 1, p. 106.
[42] Kosygin, *A. N. Kosygin: izbrannye rechi i stat'i*, pp. 213–14, 217–18.
[43] *Pravda*, 12 July 1965.
[44] ibid., 4 November 1967.
[45] *Sovetskaia Belorussiia*, 15 February 1968 (*CDSP*, vol. 20, no. 7, pp. 11–17).
[46] *CDSP*, vol. 20, no. 7, p. 14.
[47] ibid., p. 13.

addition to improving and expanding the reform as a means of generating domestic sources of technological innovation, Kosygin argued that the country should seek to obtain and diffuse foreign sources of technology: "it would be short-sighted of us not to make use of the latest foreign scientific and technical achievements."[48]

The two Soviet leaders were about to lock horns on still another set of issues. One month later, speaking at the conference of the Moscow City Party organization,[49] Brezhnev took a swipe at Kosygin's reference to the importation of foreign technology and also, by implication, at Kosygin's praise of decentralist methods of advancing technological innovation: "In discussing scientific-technological progress, some workers obviously underestimate the achievements of scientific-technical thought in our country and other socialist countries. By the same token, these people are inclined to overestimate the achievements of science and technology in the capitalist world." In addition, Brezhnev lamented the slow progress in introducing scientific innovations into production, but his proposed solution further undermined, rather than reaffirmed, the thrust of the decentralist alternative. Thus, whereas Kosygin in Minsk had praised the 1965 reforms and called for their further development, Brezhnev in Moscow implied that a new stage had been reached and that new policy premises were called for: "The period of the organizational establishment of the ministries has ended, and the time has come to make increasing demands on their work. The ministries bear primary responsibility for the technical level in their respective branches of industry." And whereas Kosygin had spoken only of the acceleration of scientific and technical progress, Brezhnev reinforced an interventionist approach by emphasizing speed in the introduction of new technology in the era of the "scientific and technical revolution."

How did Brezhnev propose to "make increasing demands" on the work of the ministries? Through greater Party intervention in, and supervision of, the work of state institutions—an option that Kosygin had not discussed in his address a month previous. Thus, Brezhnev called for "raising the role of the Party and of all communists in deciding *economic and political tasks*" (italics added; note the order); in reference to the state of affairs in capital construction, the General Secretary observed that "it is the duty of the party organizations to exercise control over this important sector in our economic construction and *not only* to criticize it, *but also* to give practical help in accelerating the improvement of capital construction" (italics added). Toward this end, party cadres would have to upgrade their technical skills (recall Khrushchev in 1956!) and tighten intra-party discipline. The goal was to increase "the combat capacity of the party organiza-

[48] ibid.
[49] *Pravda*, 30 March 1968 (*CDSP*, vol. 20, no. 13, pp. 3–7).

tions." Brezhnev was not calling for "substitution"—that is, over-absorption of party organs in operational detail. Rather, he was demanding that party organs raise their capacity for selective intervention in administrative affairs, in order to break through bureaucratic inertia: "The party organizations are obligated to look into all this. However, this is not a matter for the party organizations alone, but first and foremost for the ministries, the economic, planning, and supply agencies and all our specialists."

Brezhnev capped his rejection of the Kosygin approach by formally revising the rhetoric of earlier years with respect to incentive policy. Repeating the obligatory notion that it is necessary "correctly to combine material and moral stimuli," the General Secretary then went out of his way to add a new twist: "it would be incorrect to reduce everything only to material self-interest, for this would impoverish the inner world of Soviet man." Clearly, the implication was that an augmentation of party activism was required as a supplement to material incentives.

Brezhnev had seized the initiative. Whether or not Kosygin actually stood for the things of which Brezhnev accused him remains unclear. Brezhnev's polemics may have been tailored to discrediting Kosygin by pinning the extremist label on him, just as Khrushchev had done to Malenkov. Whatever the case, Brezhnev was now coming to the fore as spokesman for an alternative approach to technological innovation—one that explicitly rejected "automatic levers" or managerial autonomy toward that end. Implementing such an approach would require a tightening of both party and state discipline. The sanctions for failure to innovate would have to be sufficiently predictable and severe to induce such innovation despite the unfavorable balance of positive and negative rewards. This had important implications, in turn, for the expressed relationship of accommodation and reconciliation between the General Secretary and Soviet officialdom. The job security of state and party officials would have to hinge on their responsiveness to new demands. It should come as no surprise, therefore, that at the March 1968 Moscow City Party Conference, the General Secretary also explicitly revised the doctrine of "trust in cadres":

> . . . it would be wrong to think that placing increased trust in the workers and giving them greater independence signify a weakening in the control exercised over their activity. Trust in and respect for cadres must invariably be combined with high exactingness toward them. The party, while trusting its cadres . . . will stringently penalize any violation of party or state discipline, regardless of positions held or past services."

Brezhnev was not accusing anyone of "anti-state" behavior; his remarks did not presage a purge, and they were not tailored to equate bureaucratic inertia or deviance with corruption or sabotage. They were, however, an effort to expand the definition of deviance beyond that which it possessed during 1964–7. This indicated a greater reliance on sanctions, monitoring, and intervention as mechanisms for ensuring administrative responsiveness to demands emanating from the center. It served further to undermine the premises that had informed the reforms of 1965. It upgraded the relative role of pressure as an instrument for ensuring administrative initiative. It conferred top-level legitimacy on those forces within the administrative and political elite that were pushing in these directions all along.

And it fashioned for Brezhnev a revised image as politician, somewhat analogous to that fashioned by Khrushchev in 1956. The General Secretary had stolen the issue of administrative reform from Kosygin, and was ready to offer an alternative. He now presented himself as the leader best suited to combining measured administrative reform with selective political security—that is, political security for those cadres who followed his lead.

10 Political Succession and Political Participation, 1964–8

In seeking to expand mass political participation, Nikita Khrushchev operated on the basis of a claim that the stimulation of authentic popular initiative was incompatible with excessive bureaucratization. This claim informed his embracing a populist approach to the problem. At the same time, he launched campaigns for social and attitudinal transformation based, not on Stalinist methods, but on intensified social control. In the end, this combination of populism and enforced cohesion did not produce the kinds of changes Khrushchev had promised, failed to improve economic performance, and contributed to the erosion of Khrushchev's authority.

Khrushchev's successors rejected his commitments to radical political and social transformation. They toned down or halted the de-Stalinization campaign and the anti-official policies, reasserting the bureaucratic and political prerogatives of state and party officials. They reduced pressure for social transformation and the arbitrariness of social controls, permitting a greater measure of individual autonomy from political mobilization. They sought to reduce dogmatic controls in the social sciences, expand input from the specialist community on matters of public policy, and improve the regime's awareness of public opinion. The new consensus thus sought not only to reassert official prerogatives, but also to improve the responsiveness of officialdom to societal moods. And repression of those who refused to accept this consensus—that is, dissenters—was expanded and intensified.

The Consensus Emerges

The new consensus emerged in stages. During the six-month period October 1964–April 1965 the majority coalition broke with several of Khrushchev's more far-reaching doctrinal changes.[1] No critique of Joseph Stalin by name appeared in any of the literature under review. Nor was there mention of the "Party of All the People." On the other hand, many of Khrushchev's populist revisions continued to appear

[1] *Pravda*, 7 November 1964, 10 December 1964, 27 March 1965, and 23 April 1965; Brezhnev, *Leninskim kursom I*, pp. 36–45; Kosygin, *A. N. Kosygin: izbrannye rechi i stat'i*, pp. 209–19.

in regime statements. Thus, the concept of "discipline" was still excluded from the Central Committee slogans published in April 1965.[2] And those slogans still paid obeisance to the Khrushchevian definition of the "State of All the People," as did the anniversary speeches of November 1964 and April 1965.[3] Brezhnev's anniversary speech of November 1964 continued the Khrushchevian call for a "struggle against bureaucracy," a call which was echoed in Kosygin's December address to the Supreme Soviet, in which the Prime Minister demanded the replacement of all officials found guilty of failing to respond to criticism.[4] Further, Brezhnev's anniversary speech echoed the Khrushchevian definition of the nature of the era: that socialism had been fully and finally victorious, and that the nation was now in the period of the full-scale construction of communism.

All of which may explain the fact that no speech by Politburo-member Mikhail Suslov was published in *Pravda* during this six-month period, and no speech from this period was reprinted in his collected speeches when these appeared some years later.[5] The leading regime ideologist may well have been uncomfortable with the continuing coexistence of competing premises.

During Spring/Summer 1965, however, Mikhail Suslov went public and a shift in the majority consensus took place, further purging the populist elements from regime conceptions of political participation. Speeches by Brezhnev, Kosygin, Suslov, and anniversary spokesmen during the entire period May 1965–December 1966 excluded all reference to the "State of All the People," struggle against bureaucracy, or a definition of the era which linked the full and final victory of socialism with the full-scale construction of communism.[6] The concept of "discipline" returned to regime slogans in October 1965.[7]

[2] See *Pravda*, 22 April 1965.

[3] See ibid., slogan 101; ibid., 7 November 1964, and 23 April 1965.

[4] ibid., 10 December 1964.

[5] The two volumes consulted are M. A. Suslov, *Izbrannoe: rechi i stat'i* (Moscow: Politizdat, 1972); and M. A. Suslov, *Na putiakh stroitel'stva kommunizma* (Moscow: Politizdat, 1977), Vol. 2.

[6] The speeches in question are (1) Brezhnev: 8 May 1965 (*Leninskim kursom I*, pp. 118–55); 3 July 1965 (ibid., pp. 156–66); *Pravda*, 11 July 1965, and 30 September 1965; 23 October 1965 (*Leninskim kursom I*, pp. 233–50); 22 December 1965 (Brezhnev, *Ob osnovnykh voprosakh*, Vol. 1, pp. 99–111); Gruliow, *Current Soviet Policies V*, pp. 4–31; *Pravda*, 18 May 1966, 28 May 1966, and 11 June 1966, 1 November 1966 (*Leninskim kursom I*, pp. 458–75). (2) Kosygin: *Pravda*, 10 December 1964; Kosygin, *A. N. Kosygin: Izbrannye rechi i stati*, pp. 209–19 (19 March 1965); *Pravda*, 12 July 1965, 18 July 1965, and 28 September 1965; Gruliow, *Current Soviet Policies V*, pp. 93–112; *Pravda*, 9 June 1966, and 4 August 1966. (3) Suslov: 2 June 1965 (Suslov, *Na putiakh*, Vol. 2, pp. 3–19); 17 July 1965 (ibid., pp. 20–6); 30 October 1965 (ibid., pp. 27–37); 13 May 1966 (ibid., pp. 47–56); *Pravda*, 8 June 1966.

[7] *Pravda*, 23 October 1965.

And October 1965 was the last time that the "State of All the People" appeared in regime slogans (though it would reappear years later in redefined form).[8]

The significance of this shift was that it delegitimized anti-official and anti-elitist approaches to political participation. But within this context, the new regime consensus also demanded an expansion of mass and specialist input into regime decision-making. Thus, three weeks after Khrushchev's dismissal, Brezhnev spoke on the anniversary of the Revolution and promised that the new regime would base its decisions on "objective appraisals, exact information, correct utilization of the economic laws of socialism and the achievements of science, a scientific approach."[9] His comments were echoed by Alexei Kosygin one month later.[10]

This was a new theme in Soviet elite discourse. The leaders of the Communist Party had always claimed special insight into the laws of historical development, based upon their ideological legacy in Marx's "scientific socialism." Hence, throughout Soviet history, leaders have claimed that their decisions are made on a scientific basis.[11] However, used in that way the term was basically a cover for the leading role of party officials who would provide the direction and basic goals for policy. What was now occurring after Khrushchev, however, was something different: a redefinition of the meaning of "scientific decision-making" in the direction of a more open-ended, empirical approach that did not excessively prejudge conclusions. The majority consensus, then, appeared to entail a commitment to regularization of consultation with those members of the scientific community who were committed both to empiricism[12] and to respecting the political status of Soviet officialdom.

Leonid Brezhnev: Political Participation and Political Status

During the honeymoon period October 1964–April 1965, Brezhnev's speeches were characterized by a spirit of national reconciliation. Major institutional interests were assured that "collective leadership"

---

[8] Compare *Pravda*, 23 October 1965, slogan 99, with ibid., 17 April 1966, slogan 97.

[9] ibid., 7 November 1965; see also Brezhnev's exceptionally strong statements on this score in ibid., 27 March 1965.

[10] ibid., 10 December 1964; see also Kosygin, *A. N. Kosygin: izbrannye rechi i stat'i*, pp. 211, 216, 217 (speech of 19 March 1965).

[11] See the discussion of "scientific decision-making" in Jerry Hough, "The Brezhnev era: the man and the system," *Problems of Communism* (March–April 1976), pp. 15–16.

[12] Strictly speaking, this should read "open-ended empiricism," since Stalinist dogmatism was highly empirical in outlook.

would replace "subjectivism" and "voluntarism" in the national leadership's approach to policy-making. The workers and peasants were assured that their interests in material, physical, and national security would now receive real attention, in place of the Khrushchevian propensity for "ballyhoo" and "empty words." Specialists were accorded extensive recognition and praise ("our brilliant scientist compatriots"), and were assured that their advice would be heeded by decision-makers.[13] In short, all major groups were assured by the First Secretary that the new regime would be responsive to their interests.

Honeymoons, whether political or marital, are by definition periods when sources of conflict are ignored or denied, and this one was no exception. Brezhnev's generalizations about expanded responsiveness ignored the fundamental dilemmas inherent in the post-Stalin commitment to expanded political participation: Which "interests" in society would be catered to in cases of conflict among them? Which strata in the scientific community would have greatest access to, and responsiveness from, Soviet officials? What would be the balance between the desire to respond to interests in society and the simultaneous desire to reshape the individual's definition of his interests through political socialization? How does one draw the line between constructive criticism and criticism that challenges the competence or authority of those being criticized?

These were the kinds of tensions that came to the fore as the honeymoon of 1964–5 gave way to the conservative reaction of 1965–6. And as this reaction gathered steam, Brezhnev's definition of the terms of political participation became more concrete.

Brezhnev's speech to the Twenty-Third Party Congress, his address to the Young Communist League, and his election speech of June 1966 are noteworthy as major statements of the Party leader's position—all the more so because, in his election speech, Brezhnev called for the rapid completion and publication of a new constitution that would ostensibly formalize his approach to authority relationships in the system.[14] Brezhnev reasserted in his speeches the pre-1958 language and arenas of politics. He engaged in no discussion of transferring functions from state to mass organizations. And when he discussed the "expansion of rights," this referred to the process of administrative deconcentration to enterprises and republics, rather than to expanding the rights of mass organizations vis-à-vis their hierarchical superiors.

Moreover, Brezhnev explicitly rejected doctrinal innovations with anti-official implications. In place of the "Party of All the People,"

[13] For these varied assurances, see Brezhnev in *Pravda*, 7 November 1964, and 27 March 1965; and in Brezhnev, *Leninskim kursom I*, pp. 36–45.

[14] *Pravda*, 11 June 1966; the call for a new constitution was later excised from the speech as published in Brezhnev, *Leninskim kursom I*, p. 434.

Brezhnev referred to the Communist Party as the "political leader of the entire Soviet people."[15] Whereas Khrushchev at the Twenty-Second Party Congress had declared that "the overwhelming majority" of the Soviet people "think like Communists," Brezhnev at the Twenty-Third Party Congress merely pointed out that "the victory of socialism has wrought a most profound change in the consciousness of the Soviet people."[16] And whereas Khrushchev had argued that "essential differences" between town and country had been eradicated, Brezhnev averred that in future "essential differences will disappear."[17] In sum, Brezhnev rejected the consensual and largely homogeneous image of society through which Khrushchev had sought to legitimize his attack on elitism among party officials.

Consistent with this position was Brezhnev's approach to cultural affairs. Speaking one month after the trial and sentencing of the dissidents Andrei Sinyavsky and Yuli Daniel, Brezhnev indicated clearly that he did not share Khrushchev's largesse regarding the level of generalization at which criticism would be considered political deviance:

> Unfortunately, one also encounters those tradesmen in the arts who, instead of helping the people, select as their speciality the denigration of our system and slander against our heroic people . . . The renegades do not cherish what is most sacred for every Soviet man—the interests of the socialist homeland. It is perfectly obvious that the Soviet people cannot overlook the disgraceful activity of such individuals. They treat them as they deserve.[18]

For Brezhnev, the existence of such "renegades" was not only an intolerable disgrace; it was dangerous as well. For, in contrast to Khrushchev who claimed that a form of systemic criticism was required to advance the "struggle of the new against the old," Brezhnev argued that what was now needed was greater civic pride in the old as a condition for constructing the new. Hence, the regime now needed simultaneously to crack down on the dissenters and intensify political socialization. Speaking to the Young Communist League, Brezhnev spoke at length about the need for pride in Soviet accomplishments and revolutionary traditions, called for a "resolute struggle against bourgeois ideology," and insisted that "the main thing in the work of the Young Communist League is the upbringing of

---

[15] Gruliow, *Current Soviet Policies V*, p. 24.
[16] Compare Gruliow, *Current Soviet Policies IV*, p. 114, with Gruliow, *Current Soviet Policies V*, p. 29.
[17] Compare Gruliow, *Current Soviet Policies IV*, p. 66, with Gruliow, *Current Soviet Policies V*, p. 22.
[18] Gruliow, *Current Soviet Policies V*, p. 23.

young people."[19] Similarly, at the Twenty-Third Party Congress Brezhnev called for the intensification of "Marxist–Leninist training" among natural and social scientists, even as he praised them and their scientific work.[20] Such political socialization would ensure that specialists compartmentalize their critical faculties, exercising them in the public interest in their fields of specialization, but not generalizing them to larger questions of political organization.

Yet even as he was stating a conservative conception of authority relationships, Brezhnev insisted that Soviet officials encourage expanded input from the scientific intelligentsia and that they heed those inputs in the course of making decisions.[21] Moreover, Brezhnev made clear that a return to political elitism did not imply a return to traditional methods of relating to various social groups—quite the contrary. In return for a rejection of Khrushchevian populism, Soviet officials would have to demonstrate their ability to generate more subtle and differentiated approaches to mobilization: "the primary party organizations should give proper consideration to the individual peculiarities in people's characters, to their needs and demands, their capabilities and attitudes towards the cause."[22] Or when speaking to the Young Communist League: "those who work with youth must not fail to take account of this diversity of interests and needs of young men and women."[23] Or in his election speech: "the party also takes into account the entire array of political interests and spiritual demands of the working people."[24]

This was a new theme in Soviet political discourse. The discussion of "social interests" under Stalin had identified but a few such interests—personal, class, and state, for the most part—and had emphasized the subordination of personal to state interests.[25] Under Khrushchev, the goal of radical social transformation had legitimized a simplified view of society that did not accord recognition to the "interests" of social groups within classes. On the other hand, Khrushchev's populism had led him to counterpose social interests to the interests of officialdom. After Khrushchev, the rejection of populism required the revival of a harmonious conception of the relationship between official and social interests, but was accompanied by a more

---

[19] *Pravda*, 18 May 1966.
[20] Gruliow, *Current Soviet Policies V*, p. 29.
[21] ibid.
[22] ibid., p. 25.
[23] *Pravda*, 18 May 1966.
[24] ibid., 11 June 1966.
[25] See G. E. Glezerman, *Polnoe sootvetstvie proizvodstvennykh otnosheniy i proizvoditel'nykh sil v sotsialisticheskom obshchestve* (Moscow: Gosizdat, 1951); "Interes," in *Bol'shaia sovetskaia entsiklopediia*, Vol. 18 (Moscow: Gosizdat, 1953), p. 280.

complex image of the nature and plurality of social interests.[26] Brezhnev's formulations reflected his contention that the regime could not manipulate social groups effectively without taking into account the existing level of consciousness among various groups within classes. And this required learning more about how people themselves defined their interests. Thus, while reasserting the pre-1958 language and arenas of politics, Brezhnev also demanded efforts to raise the responsive capacities of each.

And whereas Brezhnev argued that there was no longer a need to struggle against bureaucracy, he also reassured Soviet citizens that the return to political elitism would not signal a return to political arbitrariness. Thus, in his speech to the Twenty-Third Party Congress, he pointed out the importance of observing "socialist legality" and of creating an atmosphere of stable expectations in society, such that those who were politically conformist would not be alienated from the regime.[27] In his June 1966 election speech,[28] he called for raising the role of the soviets at all levels and "strengthening their day-to-day ties with the masses of working people," improving the work of mass organizations, "perfecting legislation and strengthening legality . . . combatting bureaucratism and formalism in all their manifestations." At the same time, Brezhnev emphasized that socialist legality and stable expectations for the politically conformist would be accompanied by the strictest enforcement of law and order:

> But rule by the people is at the same time a strict rule, inconceivable without conscious discipline and a high level of organization. And it does not wax sentimental over those who harm society be they hooligans or criminals, bureaucrats or idlers, parasites or plunderers of the public wealth. There must be no place for them in Soviet society—such is the firm will of the party and the people.

[26] See Murray Yanowitch and Wesley A. Fisher (eds), *Social Stratification and Mobility in the USSR* (White Plains, NY: International Arts and Sciences Press, 1973), pp. xviii–xxiv; Ts. A. Stepanian and V. S. Semenov (eds), *Klassy, sotsial'nye sloi i gruppy v SSSR* (Moscow: Nauka, 1968); *passim*; and G. E. Glezerman, "Sotsial'naia struktura sotsialisticheskogo obshchestva," *Kommunist*, no. 13 (1968), pp. 28–39. For a summary of changes taking place in the philosophical literature, see the article by A. S. Aizikovich, "Vazhnaia sotsiologicheskaia problema," *Voprosy filosofii*, no. 11 (1965). For a representative example of the effort to synthesize this approach with the reassertion of political elitism, see S. S. Vishnevskii, "Interesy i upravlenie obshchestvennymi protsessami," in V. Afanas'ev (ed), *Nauchnoe upravlenie obshchestvom*, 8 vols (Moscow: Mysl', 1967–74), Vol. 1, pp. 173–217. For a dissent from this trend, see B. V. Kniazev, *et al.*, "O prirode interesa kak sotsial'nogo iavleniia," *Vestnik MGU* (*Seriia Filosofii*), no. 4 (1968), pp. 11–20.

[27] Gruliow, *Current Soviet Policies V*, p. 26.

[28] *Pravda*, 11 June 1966 (*CDSP*, vol. 18, no. 23).

Thus, Brezhnev's position presumed that authentic popular initiative could be stimulated without a fundamental change in authority relationships. He claimed that such initiative could be elicited through a combination of private material rewards, appeals to patriotism and party traditions, repression of dissenters who might infect the masses with anti-official ideas, and a more subtle approach to dealing with the politically conformist. In contrast to Khrushchev, Brezhnev's position also presumed that official responsiveness to specialist input could be achieved through regular channels. In sum, Brezhnev's approach to political participation squared with his claim that policy effectiveness required a more responsive bureaucratic regime. And each of these claims was consistent with his authority-building strategy during these years, for that strategy catered to yearnings among Soviet officials for political status, job security, and stable expectations. Brezhnev had forged his own program for synthesizing "socialist legality" with political control.

Elite Perspectives and Political Conflict

In each of the issue-areas already investigated in this book, we have discovered a common pattern of evolution of political conflict between Brezhnev and Kosygin. Within the context of a post-Khrushchevian consensus, the two Soviet leaders staked out conflicting positions. These positions became increasingly polarized over time until, during the period November 1967–March 1968, Brezhnev and Kosygin engaged in a multi-issue polemic. Kosygin attempted to defend the policies for which he had stood all along. But Brezhnev behaved somewhat differently. He selectively retreated from previous positions, became increasingly rigid in his stance, and attempted to present himself as the protector of traditional social and political values against "extremists" such as Kosygin.

An analogous pattern is evident in the realm of political participation. Between mid-1966 and late 1967 Brezhnev became increasingly the defender of the privileged political status of party officials, and less the defender of those who would pressure the apparatchiki to improve their responsiveness to various societal demands. Thus, in his anniversary speech of November 1967,[29] rather than calling the Communist Party the "political leader of all the Soviet people," Brezhnev referred to it as "the militant vanguard of the Soviet working people." And while he acknowledged the importance of appreciating diverse interests in society, he insisted in the same breath that societal complexity should not be taken as a sign of the need for new political institutions: "We do not and cannot have any political

[29] *Pravda*, 4 November 1967.

organization other than the CPSU that would take into account the interests and the specific features of the classes and social groups in our country, of all nations and nationalities, and of all generations, and that would combine these interests in its policy."

Within four months, however, Brezhnev was going much further in his defense of traditional values. In his March 1968 address at the Moscow City Party Conference,[30] Brezhnev called pointedly for "iron party discipline," and quoted Lenin to emphasize the point. This was the first time since the overthrow of Khrushchev that Brezhnev had spoken in these terms. Moreover, the General Secretary's references to "scientific decision-making," and to the "scale and complexity" of problems, now avoided all mention of their implications for empirical science and expanded input, instead coupling them with normative references: "Only a party that is united by a unity of views and actions, having great experience of political and organizational activity, is able to give to all the work of communist construction a purposive, scientifically-based and planned character." And Brezhnev escalated the critique of cultural dissent by referring to the offenders, not as individual renegades, but as "individual groups of Soviet people [whom] bourgeois ideologists still hope somehow to influence."

The contraction of Brezhnev's commitments was accompanied as well by a polemic with Kosygin, though within the context of the consensus outlined earlier. That is, there was no significant difference between them as to the desirability of more closely enforcing law and order, a crackdown on cultural dissent, the need for expanded input, and restoration of the prerogatives of Soviet officialdom. However, some differences emerged over the extent to which executive or specialist authority ought to be protected from political intervention by party officials. Thus, when speaking in Minsk in February 1968,[31] Kosygin demurred from Brezhnev's evolving definition of authority relationships. In contrast to Brezhnev's endorsement of a normative definition of scientific decision-making, Kosygin warned that "it is impossible to dispense with careful social and economic analysis." And in contrast to Brezhnev's stress on party intervention in managerial affairs, Kosygin warned that "only thoughtful, genuinely scientific organization of production can yield the necessary results." Differences between the two Soviet leaders on this set of issues were not nearly as extensive as their differences on investment priorities, incentive policy, and administrative reform. Moreover, polarization on participatory issues after Khrushchev was not nearly as large as was the case after Stalin. This circumstance may have contributed to the much greater intensity of political conflict during the rise of

[30] ibid., 30 March 1968 (*CDSP*, vol. 20, no. 13, pp. 3–7).
[31] *Sovetskaia Belorussiia*, 15 February 1968 (*CDSP*, vol. 20, no. 7, pp. 11–17).

Khrushchev, as contrasted with the rise of Brezhnev. Yet, while conflict may not have been as intense it was there during 1964–8, and it spanned the gamut of issues, from investment priorities through the terms of political participation within the Establishment.

11 Brezhnev Ascendant, 1968-72

During 1957–60, having discredited and discarded his main rivals in the leadership, Nikita Khrushchev forged and presented a comprehensive program for progress in all realms. That program bore Khrushchev's distinctive stamp, for it was based on the extension of approaches he had been advocating all along. But the program also selectively reincorporated elements of the approaches advocated by Khrushchev's defeated rivals.

An analogous pattern emerged during the second stage of the Brezhnev era. After Brezhnev seized the initiative from Kosygin during 1968, the Party leader reexpanded his political coalition by forging and presenting a comprehensive program of his own. That program emphasized Brezhnev's priorities, for it sharply expanded investment in agriculture, increased party mobilization and intervention in the industrial and agricultural sectors, and increased the status of party officials vis-à-vis all other groups. At the same time, Brezhnev retreated from the extreme positions he had adopted during the polemic with Kosygin, identifying himself with a program that not only extended the applicability of his preferred approaches but selectively reincorporated approaches that Kosygin had earlier advocated. Thus, Brezhnev's was a "compromise" program—far more so than Khrushchev's had been. And the Party leader sought to project himself as the individual best suited to synthesize the political interests required to forge and implement such a program.

Investment Priorities: Brezhnev as Artful Synthesizer

Brezhnev had seized upon the failure of Khrushchev's agricultural policies to propose a very expensive program for rural development in March 1965 and May 1966. However, the record harvest of 1966 left Brezhnev on the defensive, and strengthened forces pushing for expanded funding of light industry. The crop failure of 1967 then afforded Brezhnev the opportunity to regain the initiative, and to restore the cuts of the previous year.[1] Thus, at the October 1968 Plenum, Brezhnev secured the funds he was demanding for the "all-out strengthening of the material base of agriculture" and "the further technical re-equipping of agriculture in the shortest possible time."[2]

[1] Hahn, *Politics of Soviet Agriculture*, pp. 197–9.
[2] *Pravda*, 31 October 1968.

Unusually severe weather conditions during Winter 1969 contributed to an acute shortage of meat in Soviet cities by the end of that year. Brezhnev's response was to take to the offensive once again. In his April 1970 speech at the Kharkov tractor plant he twisted the traditional definition of "consumer goods" (usually a reference to light industry) to include "animal-husbandry products."[3] In his June 1970 election speech, he directly confronted those who were not willing to pay the opportunity costs of a large and immediate diversion of funds to agriculture: "The creation of an up-to-date material and technical base for agriculture can be stretched out to twenty-five years. It can also be substantially accelerated. We favor this latter path . . . We intend to hold firmly to this course, comrades."[4]

Brezhnev continued this line of argumentation one month later at the July 1970 Plenum: "This is now the decisive factor"; "we have no other way."[5] But there was a new twist to Brezhnev's argumentation. As before, he was demanding a heavily capital-intensive approach. But Brezhnev now came armed with promises from the heads of seven ministries associated with the military–heavy-industrial complex that they would produce agricultural equipment at their plants "without reducing the volume of production of their basic output." Thus, Brezhnev's synthesis of political interests and values was becoming apparent. He would project himself as the leader best suited to solving the agricultural problem by persuading the most powerful and productive economic forces in the system to work toward that end. As a leading spokesman for the interests of the military–heavy-industrial complex, he would use their strengths to advance the interests of the consumer.

This is precisely the political posture that Brezhnev struck on the issue of consumer-goods production as well. After the matter of agricultural investment had been settled, Brezhnev turned his attention to consumer goods. A careful examination of his speech at the Twenty-Fourth Party Congress (March 1971) suggests that the General Secretary simply transferred his leadership strategy from one sector to the other.

In his speech to the Party Congress, Brezhnev demanded that economic officials "saturate the market with consumer goods."[6] Yet at the same time he insisted that such a commitment "by no means signifies that we are reducing our attention to heavy industry."[7] Was this contradiction a sign of either hypocrisy or demagoguery? Not according to Brezhnev, for the synthesis he was proposing resolved the

3 ibid., 14 April 1970.
4 ibid., 13 June 1970.
5 ibid., 3 July 1970.
6 Gruliow, *Current Soviet Policies VI*, p. 22.
7 ibid., pp. 19–20.

contradiction. A section of his speech was entitled: "Heavy Industry is the Foundation of the Country's Economic Might and of a Further Rise in the People's Well-Being."[8] Several paragraphs later he gave the details as to how this could be, arguing that heavy-industrial enterprises would have to expand the production of means of production for consumer-oriented sectors ("this is precisely the ultimate function of heavy industry") and expand the production of consumer goods directly in those enterprises. And he singled out the defense industry as one particularly suited to the latter task.[9]

We do not know how the elite representatives of heavy industry and defense interests felt about Brezhnev's demands, but from the remarks of the General Secretary we become privy to his anticipation of their objections. Recognizing that the Soviet political and administrative systems are shot through with considerations of status and prestige, and aware that the production of consumer goods had for long been considered a low-prestige task, Brezhnev endeavored to change this ethos. Demanding "a substantial change in the very approach to the production of consumer goods," Brezhnev threatened with unspecified punishment any cadres and officials of the heavy-industrial sector who failed to internalize the message. He provided a convenient rationalization for those squeamish about a potential loss of status: "at the present stage the role of heavy industry is not only not diminishing but growing, since the range of immediate practical problems it resolves is expanding." And he offered a revision in Soviet Party Congress lexicon that would increase the status of consumer-goods production at industrial enterprises. Throughout the post-Stalin period, Soviet leaders had regularly spoken of progress in the production of consumer goods at industrial enterprises. But no speech by a First Secretary or Prime Minister at a Party Congress, and no resolution of a Party Congress, had ever used the term *"industrial* consumer goods." Leonid Brezhnev at the Twenty-Fourth Party Congress not only introduced this term, but included it in the title of a section of his speech as well.[10]

In addition to these efforts to exercise leadership through the synthesis of domestic political interests, Brezhnev sought to demonstrate that his foreign-policy leadership could improve consumer satisfaction and industrial productivity. In his speech at the Twenty-Third Party Congress (1966), Brezhnev had made almost no linkage between foreign capital and Soviet domestic economic development. In con-

---

[8] ibid., p. 19.
[9] ibid, p. 20.
[10] ibid., pp. 18–22. Contrast the interpretation of the type of leadership offered by Brezhnev, and of the depth of his commitment on the issue, to the interpretations in Yanov, *Detente after Brezhnev*, pp. 16–19, and in Hahn, *Politics of Soviet Agriculture*, pp. 246–8.

trast, at the Twenty-Fourth Party Congress, he spoke at great length on the matter.[11] He pointed out the economic and political benefits to be derived from "the expansion of international exchanges." He demanded structural reforms in the foreign trade system to facilitate "mutually advantageous economic deals" with East Europe, West Europe, Japan, and the USA. And he made explicit the linkage between politics and economics by including the task of "deepening relations of mutually advantageous cooperation in all fields with states that seek to do so" in the six-point "Peace Program" he put forth at the Party Congress as the basis for détente.

As for Siberian development, the General Secretary said almost nothing about the topic in his speech, and even eliminated from the economic section of that speech the customary subsection on the "correct distribution of productive forces," in which questions of Siberian development are usually treated. Instead, the entire economic section of his speech was devoted to problems of intensive development (management, incentives, planning, squeezing heavy industry for the sake of the consumer, etc.), which was consistent with Brezhnev's effort to demonstrate that the system, under his leadership, could be made to work.

Brezhnev's position on defense budgeting is much more difficult, if not impossible, to discern. As we have seen, he did state his intention to lean on ministerial officials and enterprise directors in the military–industrial complex to induce them to produce more consumer durables above-plan. But on other issues—the total level of funding for defense, and the relative emphasis to be placed on funding of strategic versus conventional forces (or on funding priorities within these sectors)—the General Secretary had nothing to say at the Party Congress or in speeches before domestic audiences. Moreover, Western analysts are in profound disagreement as to policy at the time: the size of the total budget and the distribution of funds within it.[12] Nonetheless, the convergence of two trends that can be documented may provide a clue to Brezhnev's position. Even scholars who disagree about trends seem to agree that a distinct reduction in the rate of deployment of strategic weaponry took place during 1970–2.[13] This was in part

[11] Gruliow, *Current Soviet Policies VI*, pp. 7–8, 14, 15, 25.

[12] The most sharply contrasting positions can be found in Franklyn Holzman, *Financial Checks on Soviet Defense Expenditures* (Lexington, Mass.: Lexington Books, 1975), on the one hand, and Steven Rosefielde, *Underestimating the Soviet Military Threat* (New Brunswick, NJ: Transaction Press, 1981) or William Lee, *The Estimation of Soviet Defense Expenditures for 1955–1975* (New York: Praeger, 1977), on the other. An intermediate position is struck in United States Central Intelligence Agency (CIA), *Estimated Soviet Defense Spending in Rubles, 1970–1975* (Washington, DC: CIA, May 1976).

[13] See CIA, *Estimated Soviet Defense Spending*, p. 8, and Rosefielde, *Underestimating the Soviet Military Threat*, fig. 13.3.

a product of the rhythm of technological development, but it was also a product of political intervention, for there were alternatives and the Soviet leadership apparently decided to defer certain weapons deployments and tests at the time. In addition, there is considerable evidence of a debate during 1969 about détente and the nature of Soviet commitment to arms control. The "pro-détente" and "pro-arms control" forces apparently won out, ostensibly at the December 1969 Plenum.[14] If we assume that Brezhnev was among those ascendant forces, we may also tentatively draw the inference that the political choice to defer certain strategic developments at the time was part of a political decision to further the cause of arms control in the hope of avoiding future excessive budgetary strain. If such was the case, it would lend support to the hypothesis that Brezhnev adopted such a position as part of his compromise program at the Twenty-Fourth Party Congress—a program that was being forged during 1969–70.

Administrative Reform: Brezhnev as Artful Synthesizer

At the December 1969 Plenum of the Central Committee, Brezhnev buried the hopes of decentralizers once and for all, in terms that stood in marked contrast to Kosygin's more optimistic assessment of the potential of the 1965 reforms: "In general, these measures have yielded good results. But, naturally, they still have been unable to solve the problem of increasing the efficiency of the economy as a whole."[15] As proof of the proposition, Brezhnev dwelt at great length on the manifold inefficiencies, bottlenecks, and technological lags still typical of the Soviet economy. He railed against bureaucratic inertia in the ministries, waste of resources, and ministerial lack of responsibility. He took the ministries to task for failing to struggle for the advancement of technological innovation. And he took enterprise directors to task for failing to exercise creative initiative and risk-taking within their domains.[16] He repeated many of these criticisms in speeches during 1970, and at the Twenty-Fourth Party Congress. And he made clear that henceforth such bureaucratic maladies would be fought resolutely through an increase in central and local party intervention.

But Brezhnev did not see augmented intervention *per se* as the answer to the problems of administrative efficiency. Having outflanked Kosygin, he now indicated his intention to propose a reform that

---

[14] For an analysis of this debate, see Lawrence T. Caldwell, *Soviet Attitudes to SALT*, Adelphi Papers no. 75 (London: Institute of Strategic Studies, 1971).

[15] Brezhnev, *Ob osnovnykh voprosakh*, Vol. 1, pp. 417–18.

[16] ibid., pp. 416–17, 420–4.

would rationalize central planning and streamline public administration. Thus, at the December 1969 Plenum, he announced, vaguely but significantly, that "important corrections will be introduced into the structure of administration, allowing us to make it more rational, eliminating unnecessary links, establishing a correct correspondence of rights and duties, powers and responsibilities on all levels."[17] What type of streamlining he had in mind remained unstated. Four months later, Brezhnev heightened the anticipation by revealing that "major new decisions" in the realm of administrative reform were in the offing, but he did not reveal details of the plan.[18]

Brezhnev chose the forum of the Twenty-Fourth Party Congress to outline his program. In his main report to the Party Congress, he announced that new "forms of the organization of industry" were required that would "correspond to the requirements of the times."[19] And what did the General Secretary have in mind? The answer came quickly, and indicated that the production association had now become Brezhnev's cause:

Naturally all this is possible only with large-scale associations and combines, and this makes their creation especially urgent . . . The intensified concentration of production is becoming a necessity. Accumulated experience shows that only large associations are able to concentrate a sufficient number of skilled specialists, to ensure rapid technical progress and to make better and fuller use of all resources. The course aimed at the creation of associations and combines must be pursued more resolutely—in the long run, they must become the basic economic-accountability links of social production.[20]

The production association is a combination of enterprises, research and development organizations, and experimental factories, engaged in related production activities, though not necessarily located in close proximity to each other.[21] The idea behind this reform was to bring three or four enterprises, and their associated scientific organizations, under one administrative roof, give the association director considerable leeway to define the division of labor within the association, and

[17] ibid., p. 421.
[18] *Pravda*, 22 April 1970.
[19] Gruliow, *Current Soviet Policies VI*, p. 23.
[20] ibid., pp. 23, 27.
[21] The following discussion of the production associations is based on: Alice Gorlin, "Socialist corporations: the wave of the future in the USSR?", in Morris Bornstein and Daniel Fusfeld (eds), *The Soviet Economy: A Book of Readings*, 4th edn (Homewood, Ill.: Irwin, 1974); and "Industrial reorganization: the associations," in US Congress, Joint Economic Committee, *Soviet Economy in a New Perspective* (Washington, DC: US Government Printing Office, 1976).

thereby both reduce the burden on central planners and increase efficiency at the micro-level. The State Planning Committee and the various ministries would concentrate on improving their capacity for long-term planning of critical decisions through computerization, while devolving responsibility for much current operational planning to the association directors. From the standpoint of the individual enterprise director, such a reform constituted a recentralization relative to the hopes and practices of 1965–7. But from the standpoint of both central planners and association directors, the reform represented a new form of deconcentration, with potential for eventual, further steps in the direction of decentralization.

All of which sounds good in principle, but in practice there were multiple political obstacles in the way of getting the production associations established and operative—obstacles that indeed arose in subsequent years. First, the production associations would entail the abolition of "main departments" (*glavki*) within the ministries, power-ful and established administrative agencies that employed some two-thirds of the ministerial staff. Second, production associations would, for the sake of economic efficiency, combine enterprises subordinate to different ministries, thereby reducing the influence of individual ministries over the operations of the enterprises involved. Third, the associations would often combine enterprises from different regional jurisdictions, thereby reducing the influence of local party and governmental organs over the enterprises which would now have only the association director as their common superior. Fourth, many managers of successful factories would resist incorporation into associa-tions, since they were likely to be forced to subsidize less successful enterprises within the same association. Finally, from the standpoint of making the associations operative once they were established, association directors would have to ensure accountability and control over their member enterprises, rationalizing indicators and improving information-processing. Otherwise, bottlenecks would develop that would foster a reconcentration, as ministries seized the opportunity to intervene and reassert their control with a proliferation of rules. Thus, two forms of political entrepreneurship would be required to get the production association movement off the ground: (1) breaking through political obstacles to setting up production associations according to criteria of economic efficiency; and (2) preventing excessive inter-ference in operational decision-making within the associations once they were established.

In his speech to the Party Congress, Brezhnev indicated his sen-sitivity to the need for such political entrepreneurship. He also demon-strated his intention to coopt the production association issue and use it to augment his authority as both problem-solver and politician. First, Brezhnev demanded that the ministries and local party organs should not interfere with the establishment of associations that cut across their traditional political jurisdictions: "In creating associations, it is especially important that administrative boundaries and the departmental subordination of enterprises not serve as obstacles to the introduction of more efficient forms of management . . . The improvement of the structure of management requires a consistent struggle against all manifestations of a narrowly departmental or localistic approach."[22] Second, Brezhnev indicated that, once established, associations could not meet their potential for efficiency unless their directors were freed from excessive operational interference in their work:

> At all levels of management, it is important clearly to define the extent and relationship of rights and responsibility. Extensive rights with few responsibilities create opportunities for administrative high-handedness, subjectivism, and ill-considered decisions. But extensive responsibility with few rights is no better. In such a situation, even the most diligent official frequently finds himself powerless, and it is difficult to hold him fully responsible for the job assigned.[23]

Although Brezhnev's vision was more deconcentrating than decentralizing, it nonetheless had significant, potential political implications for the long-term evolution of Soviet public administration.[24] Thus, Brezhnev's demand that neither "administrative boundaries" nor "departmental subordination" impede the establishment of associations was a challenge to the bureaucratic prerogatives of the most powerful administrative forces in the system and, if successful, would create an administrative unit freer to avoid detailed control by those forces. Moreover, Brezhnev's call for clarification and codification of jurisdictions, rights, and responsibilities could, if taken to its logical conclusion, constrain the interventionist prerogatives of ministries and local party organs alike. True, it is unlikely that Brezhnev had thought through all these implications, or that he would have favored them had he done so—especially in light of his simultaneous endorsement of increased party activism at the time. But the fact that Brezhnev was willing to make these public commitments with such force indicates three things about his authority-building strategy. First, as a problem-

[22] Gruliow, *Current Soviet Policies VI*, p. 27.
[23] ibid.
[24] Yanov (*Detente after Brezhnev*, pp. 35ff.) discusses the political potential of the production associations. In my opinion, his discussion overstates Brezhnev's commitment to a decentralist vision by failing to distinguish between statements by the General Secretary geared towards establishing the associations in ways that would cut across jurisdictions and statements geared toward improving the deconcentrating potential of the associations.

solver, he placed great emphasis on the benefits to be obtained from large-scale organization and the concentration of resources. Second, as a problem-solver, he did not claim interventionism *per se* to be the answer to Soviet administrative problems—that, in line with the post-Khrushchev consensus, he proposed the rationalization of planning procedures as a necessary context for selective political intervention, and, in line with his intention to coopt the reform issue, he was willing to sponsor limited reform that contained important political implications. And, third, he wanted the production association to be identified as another example of an issue on which he demonstrated his skill as an artful political broker. For, as on matters of resource allocation, Brezhnev was attempting to build his authority by demonstrating his willingness to try to induce the most powerful political interests in the system to mend their ways, without leading a frontal assault on their institutional autonomy.

Incentive Policy: Brezhnev as Artful Synthesizer

During the early years of his administration, Brezhnev had supported the shift toward genuinely expanded material rewards, but had demurred from overemphasis on such rewards. Instead, he had sought to supplement utilitarian emphases with equal emphasis on civic pride, citizen obligation, and party activism as modes of spurring initiative and labor productivity. During his polemic wth Kosygin, he became still more critical of overemphases on material incentives. But after seizing the initiative from Alexei Kosygin, Brezhnev proposed a compromise in this realm of policy as well.

Brezhnev's approach to agricultural incentive policy crystallized during the period, late–1968 through mid–1970. At the October 1968 and December 1968 Plenums, he advocated increasing material incentives for the most productive workers on the farms, while simultaneously cracking down on "consumerite tendencies", that is, situations in which a rise in pay to the collective farmers was nonetheless accompanied by a failure of production indices to keep pace with the rise in earnings.[25] The General Secretary's complaint was not based on ideological qualms. Rather, it was based upon a perception that rising material incentives were often not stimulating commensurately higher production and sale to the state of those goods the regime wanted. "Automatic levers," as they had been defined in 1965, were apparently not working. Accordingly, the regime had four choices: (1) to decentralize public administration and allow freer play for

[25] *Pravda*, 31 October 1968; Brezhnev, *Ob osnovnykh voprosakh*, Vol. 1, pp. 371–6.

market forces to determine prices and payments; (2) to return to a Stalinist, confiscatory approach to procurements; (3) to maintain the centralist pattern, but to increase sharply the level of investment, raising prices until production and procurement of all important products reached satisfactory levels (other factors being equal); or (4) to combine measured increases in material incentives with measured increases in party pressure and intervention. Having rejected both confiscation and decentralization, and lacking the budgetary slack, personal will and, perhaps, political clout to attempt option number three, Brezhnev opted for the fourth alternative. This combination of approaches was reflected in his illuminating statement to the December 1968 Plenum, where he averred that the "working people" have a "civic responsibility" for the "profitability of production."[26] In seeking to strike a balance among coercion, exhortation, and material incentives, and in opposing Stalinist-confiscation, decentralization, as well as overinvestment in procurement price increases, Brezhnev echoed perspectives enunciated by Khrushchev in his last years in office. But Brezhnev did so at a much higher level of material rewards than Khrushchev had ever been willing to countenance, and therefore remained within the consensus of the post-Khrushchev era.

Brezhnev continued to press for this combination of higher prices, more differentiated material incentives, and expanded pressure at the important July 1970 Plenum.[27] He announced that prices for animal-husbandry products would be increased dramatically in the interests of the profitability of production. He declared that a major problem had been high turnover among skilled machine-operators, and that the regime would improve their pay and living conditions, "sparing no efforts" to induce them materially to stay in the countryside. However, having announced a vast expansion of investments in agriculture, Brezhnev went far beyond his earlier calls for "civic responsibility" for the "profitability of production," now calling for augmented pressure, monitoring, and obligations in return for those investments. If the state was to continue to pour large sums into rural development, Brezhnev declared, "we are not indifferent as to how this money will be used on the farms." Therefore, he explained further, "Party, soviet, and agricultural agencies are obliged to take under strict supervision the use of all the additional money that the collective farms and state farms will receive in connection with the raising of purchase prices." The rationale for this demand, according to Brezhnev, was the state funding in a socialist society is a privilege, not a right, and the peasant, therefore, has an obligation to use state funds judiciously. If the state continues to increase agricultural appropria-

26 ibid., pp. 372–3.
27 *Pravda*, 3 July 1970 (*CDSP*, vol. 22, no. 27).

tions each year, "it has the right to expect that the collective farms and state farms will correspondingly increase their sale of agricultural products to the state."

Finally, Brezhnev backed up these demands with a doctrinal adjustment that was bound to affect the perceptions and behavior of local cadres:

> Today one rarely encounters the slogan about one's first commandment, which was once well known. But after all, this is a perfectly correct slogan. The delivery and sale of grain and other products to the state had always been and must now be the paramount obligation of every collective farm and state farm.

Now when the "first commandment" had been the rule (under Stalin), it was a synonym for confiscation and impoverishment. Under Khrushchev the term fell into disuse, but the procurement prices for most products were so far below costs of production that pressure for deliveries amounted to a policy of confiscation. By the end of 1970, Brezhnev's message was that prices had now been raised to levels that would more than cover the costs of production, and that investments in agricultural technology and infrastructure were consistently lowering the costs of production. Hence, no excuses would be accepted for failure to deliver, and the authorities would crack down on such deviant practices as hoarding, luxury expenditures, or concentrating on the most profitable crops only, at the expense of other delivery obligations.

The effort to supplement higher material incentives with increased pressure became a component part of Brezhnev's approach to increasing labor productivity in the industrial sector as well. A new mix of approaches became ever more salient in the speeches of the General Secretary during 1969–71, especially in his report to the December 1969 Plenum, and in his April 1970 Kharkov speech, wherein he railed against "disorganizers of production, absentees, drunkards, and slipshod workers," even as he called for expanding material rewards for the most productive workers.[28] What Brezhnev was proposing was a compromise: the regime would maintain its commitment to raise wages, bonuses, current consumption, and investment in consumer-oriented sectors. In return, however, the authorities would demand that the consumer keep his expectations within bounds, and that he respond with labor contributions to the existing level and structure of material incentives. Political and social pressure, then, would be counted on to serve a dual purpose: (1) to supplement material incentives and make them effective; and (2) to expose the "undisciplined" and deprive them of undeserved rewards.

[28] *Pravda*, 14 April 1970.

This approach was consistent with Brezhnev's compromise on resource allocation. Moreover, it was a not illogical response to secular trends in the economy that were coming to a head in the late 1960s. The failure of industrial reform markedly to increase aggregate economic efficiency; the acute capital shortage of the late 1960s; and the meat shortage of 1969 all combined to complicate the task of improving consumer satisfaction. Getting heavy industry to work for the consumer without neglecting its own plan obligations would require special efforts to improve labor productivity. Yet improving labor productivity in the absence of sufficient consumer goods to make material incentives effective was the dilemma in which the Soviet leadership found itself. The response was to increase both material incentives and pressure.

As we noted earlier, Kosygin had already spoken of this dilemma at the Twenty-Third Party Congress,[29] in contrast to Brezhnev. This had been one of his arguments for increasing production of industrial consumer goods. When Brezhnev proposed a synthesis of interests at the Twenty-Fourth Party Congress, therefore, it was not surprising that he would coopt this issue as well. In his main report, the General Secretary pointed out that increasing the availability of consumer goods had become a necessary incentive for increasing labor productivity and social mobility.[30]

Brezhnev also strongly endorsed expanded intra-class material differentiation in his speech at the Party Congress. Devoting an entire subsection of his speech to the need for "intensifying economic incentives," the General Secretary proposed that changes be made that would "place in a more privileged position" those collectives that struggle to overfulfill the plan and sponsor technological innovation.[31] There must have been considerable support among the delegates for such an approach, for the statement was met by "prolonged applause." Moreover, Brezhnev chose the occasion of the Party Congress to endorse expanded emulation of the Shchekino experiment for the first time in a public address since Khrushchev's overthrow.[32]

While challenging one social value, however, Brezhnev defended another. The General Secretary was willing to challenge the sanctity of job security and wage equalization for the sake of economic efficiency. But the subsidization of prices on basic consumer needs

[29] Gruliow, *Current Soviet Policies V*, p. 97.
[30] Gruliow, *Current Soviet Policies VI*, p. 18.
[31] ibid., p. 23.
[32] ibid., pp. 27–8. The Shchekino experiment was first introduced in 1967 at the Shchekino Chemical Combine. It called for the release of redundant labor, and the distribution of wages saved by that release among the remaining skilled workers. Thus, it threatened "egalitarian" social values in two ways: (1) by threatening job security; and (2) by increasing material differentiation within and between enterprises.

remained untouchable: "The important and complicated task of saturating the market with articles of consumption must be accomplished with a stable level of state retail prices."[33]

Thus, on matters of incentive policy as well, Brezhnev presented himself during 1969–71 as an innovative consensus-builder who would synthesize conflicting approaches to labor productivity.

Political Participation: Brezhnev as Artful Synthesizer

Khrushchev's overthrow was eventually followed by a conservative reaction against his policies of political transformation. The elite consensus supporting such a reaction was apparently rather broadly based. But that issue also got caught up in the power struggle, as the question of the relative political status of party officials vis-à-vis state officials and specialists became an object of polemics between Brezhnev and Kosygin. Brezhnev fanned the ongoing conservative reaction for apparently political reasons. For, by the time of the Twenty-Fourth Party Congress, he had retreated to an intermediate, conciliatory posture that fitted well with the comprehensive, unity platform he presented at the congress.[34]

Before the assembled delegates, Brezhnev began by identifying himself with the further elevation of the political status of party and state officials vis-à-vis specialists and the masses. His call for strengthening the state was now included in the title of a subsection of his speech.[35] He officially rejected the doctrinal revision introduced at the Twenty-Second Party Congress, according to which societal activity would be the principal arena within which popular consciousness would be raised.[36] He condemned party members "who do not show themselves to be genuine political fighters," and those "whose activeness is only for show," demanding expanded mobilization of the *aktiv* into the performance of party assignments.[37] He extolled the workers' collective as "the basic cell of socialist society," thereby elevating the political status of an institution controlled by party

[33] ibid., p. 22.

[34] A Soviet émigré who claims to have been involved in the drafting of Brezhnev's speech contends that this address was meant to suggest alternatives to Khruhchev's doctrinal and historical perspectives at the Twenty-Second Party Congress (Boris Rabbot, "An open letter to Leonid Brezhnev," *New York Times Magazine Section*, 6 November 1977).

[35] Gruliow, *Current Soviet Policies VI*, p. 30.

[36] Compare Gruliow, *Current Soviet Policies IV*, p. 104, with Gruliow, *Current Soviet Policies VI*, p. 32; or see the quotations and discussion in Breslauer, "Khrushchev reconsidered," p. 31.

[37] Gruliow, *Current Soviet Policies VI*, pp. 36–7.

officials and geared toward social pressure and political socialization.[38] And he approvingly announced the new rights of party organizations in research institutes.[39]

But, in the same speech, Brezhnev retreated from his extremist terminology of 1968, sought to slow the movement of the conservative reaction, and insisted that the process of activating social energies be based upon a new leadership orientation. Thus, whereas in 1968 he had called the CPSU the "militant vanguard of the working people," he now went back to dubbing it "the political leader of the working class and of all the working people."[40] Whereas in 1968 he had made a special note of pointing out that no institution could compete with the CPSU in performing the function of reconciling competing interests, he now endorsed the "competing interests" image of Soviet society without this caveat.[41]

Nor was this all. In his address to the Party Congress, Brezhnev also demanded that Soviet officials exercise "tact," "restraint," and lack of arbitrariness.[42] He demanded the complete observance of rights and laws, adding that "this applies especially to the activity of officials."[43] He entitled a section of his speech, "strengthening legality and law and order," thereby placing these concepts on an equal plane.[44] He noted the need for state security agencies that would exercise "unremitting vigilance . . . against the actions of hostile elements, against the intrigues of imperialist intelligence services." But he pointed out that the security agencies had been "strengthened with politically mature cadres," who possessed "the spirit of Leninist principles, unswerving observance of socialist legality"[45]—thereby reaffirming his administration's commitment to drawing a clear line between political and non-political crime (and punishment). Then, too, Brezhnev indicated that intra-party discipline would not be based upon Salinist methods, criticizing both "the anarchic lack of discipline" and "bureaucratic centralization," and dubbing them *equally injurious to the Marxist-Leninist Party*" (italics added).[46] In light of this balance, there was some truth to Brezhnev's remark in his closing speech that his administration had made it possible for nondissenters to "breathe easily, work well, and live tranquilly."[47]

[38] ibid., p. 31.
[39] ibid., p. 36.
[40] ibid, p. 34.
[41] ibid., p. 28.
[42] ibid., pp. 30, 35–6.
[43] ibid., p. 31.
[44] ibid.
[45] ibid.
[46] ibid., p. 36.
[47] ibid., p. 176.

Indeed, on the issue of culture, Brezhnev had characteristically tough words for dissenters, but his remarks now indicated an effort to check the snowballing conservative reaction and to prevent a further strengthening of Stalinist-restorationist tendencies. Brezhnev criticized both the personality cult and subjectivism in political leadership, and added harsh words both for those who criticize the entire Stalinist period and those who propagate "dogmatic notions that ignore the great positive changes that have taken place in the life of our society in recent years."[48] In like manner, Brezhnev placed on an equal plane as slanderers of Soviet reality both the right and the left wings of the cultural intelligentsia:

Some people tried to reduce the diversity of today's Soviet reality to problems that had irrevocably receded into the past as a result of the work the Party had done to overcome the consequences of the personality cult. Another extreme that had some currency among certain men of letters was the attempt to whitewash phenomena of the past that the Party had subjected to resolute and principled criticism, to conserve ideas and views at variance with the new . . .
The Party and the people have not tolerated and will not tolerate attempts—no matter what their origin—to blunt our ideological weapons, to stain our banner.[49]

While cracking down on these elements within the cultural intelligentsia, however, Brezhnev proposed simultaneously to raise the status of groups within the scientific and technical intelligentsia that could contribute to the realization of his program—and that accepted its limits: mathematical economists, systems analysts, and so on.[50] In addition to insisting that they play a more active role in decision-making, Brezhnev sponsored doctrinal innovations that elevated the ideological status of science and scientists. First, Brezhnev argued that the intelligentsia would grow in size more rapidly than other social groups as a logical result of the party's emphasis on the scientific and technological revolution.[51] Second, Brezhnev introduced the doctrine that the main task was now "organically to combine the achievements of the scientific and technological revolution with the advantages of the socialist economic system"[52]—a doctrine that rejected market

48 ibid, p. 38.
49 ibid., pp. 33–4.
50 ibid., pp. 26–7; already at the December 1969 Plenum, Brezhnev had introduced this theme, and had reverted back to an empirical definition of scientific decision-making (Brezhnev, *Ob osnovnykh voprosakh*, Vol. 1, p. 421).
51 Gruliow, *Current Soviet Policies VI*, p. 29.
52 ibid., p. 23.

socialism, but simultaneously called for an alliance of party officials, state officials, and empirical scientists to improve the quality of central planning and to foster technological innovation within production associations. And third, Brezhnev restated the doctrinal notion that science was becoming a direct productive force (first introduced at the Twenty-Second Party Congress), but rephrased it in such a way as to add ambiguity as to whether science, in some respects, had perhaps already become a direct productive force: "the role of science as a direct productive force is being manifested on an increasing scale."[53]

Thus, on issues of political participation, Brezhnev proposed to synthesize political privilege with expanded input, involvement, and rights, based upon a spirit of national reconciliation and harmony for the politically conformist.

Brezhnev as Politician

The first four years of the Brezhnev era had been ones of relatively balanced collective leadership. But during the subsequent years, as he seized the initiative in policy formulation, Brezhnev also expanded his power base and his personal role in the leadership.[54] From 1969 onward, there took place a sharp increase in the Party leader's visibility and adulation in the mass media. At the December 1969 Plenum, he decisively expanded his policy-making role into the industrial–administrative sphere. In June 1970 he supplanted Kosygin by delivering the main speech to the Council of Ministers, and later in the year he alone signed the "Directives" of the Ninth Five-Year Plan. During 1969–70 Brezhnev also seized the initiative in foreign affairs, personally supervising the furtherance of rapprochement with West Germany, while in 1971 he assumed personal direction of Soviet–US relations. Moreover, at the Twenty-Fourth Party Congress, the size of the Central Committee was expanded by forty-six (in contrast to twenty in 1966), affording Brezhnev larger opportunities for patronage allocation. And at the same Party Congress, four new members were added to the Politburo, of which at least three (Kunaev, Shcherbitsky, and Kulakov) could be counted as likely supporters of both Brezhnev and his policies.

As Brezhnev's visibility and stature increased during this period, so his authority-building strategy shifted from what it had been during

---

[53] ibid.
[54] This paragraph is based on: Hodnett, "Succession contingencies in the Soviet Union"; Peter M. E. Volten, *The Soviet 'Peace Program, and its Implementation towards the West* (Amsterdam: Foundation for the Promotion of East–West Contacts, Free University, 1977).

the earlier years. During the first stage of his administration, Brezhnev had conspicuously avoided Khrushchevian tactics. He had rejected the practices of turning mass consumer expectations against Soviet officials, of appealing to the masses over the heads of his colleagues, and of attempting to increase elite dependence on his leadership by making grandiose promises and warning of mass retribution for failure to fulfill those promises. Clearly, this was a prudent course, given official memories of the Khrushchev experience.

During the second stage of his administration, while struggling with a variety of political interests to forge his comprehensive program, Brezhnev shifted his authority-building strategy. Thus, as Brezhnev pushed the initiative on agricultural affairs during Spring/Summer 1970, he increasingly tried to use the spectre of the mass mood to increase his political leverage. His speech in Kharkov in April 1970 was broadcast on national television, and appealed for "frankness" in the public revelation of shortcomings.[55] In the same month, speaking on the anniversary of Lenin's birth, Brezhnev spoke for the first time of the spectre of mass consumer expectations: "People's requirements grow constantly as society develops and culture increases. Lenin spoke very aptly on this point. 'When we see new demands on all sides,' he emphasized, 'we say: "This is as it should be . . ."'"[56] In his June 1970 election speech, he became more specific still:

But for a fuller and therefore more correct evaluation of the state of affairs in agriculture, it is necessary to take into account not only how agriculture has grown in comparison with the past, but above all how much this growth satisfies the population's current need for food products, and industry's needs for raw materials.[57]

And at the July 1970 Plenum, when pressing for large-scale investments, Brezhnev alluded to "greater difficulties" that would result from failure to allocate the necessary resources.[58] Similarly, while pushing for a new program of administrative reform, Brezhnev escalated the threats against cadres. During 1965–7, he had spoken about the new doctrine of "trust in cadres" in conciliatory terms. In 1968, when he tried to steal the initiative from Kosygin, Brezhnev coupled trust in cadres with greater "exactingness" toward them, indicating that the party would "stringently penalize any violation of party or state discipline."[59] At the December 1969

[55] *Pravda*, 14 April 1970.
[56] ibid., 22 April 1970.
[57] ibid., 13 June 1970.
[58] ibid., 3 July 1970; see also Brezhnev's warnings at the December 1970 Plenum (Brezhnev, *Ob osnovnykh voprosakh*, Vol. 2, p. 109).
[59] *Pravda*, 30 March 1968.

Plenum, the General Secretary broadened the definition of exacting-ness still further: "Such demandingness, of course, also includes what are called 'organizational conclusions.' "[60]

Once Brezhnev's program had been formulated and accepted for ratification by the Twenty-Fourth Party Congress, the General Secretary retreated from the aggressive posture of 1969–70. Thus, in terms consistent with his "unity" platform of 1971, Brezhnev omitted allusions to the threatening mass mood from his speech at the Party Congress. Moreover, in that same forum, he struck a more balanced posture toward the cadres. Although he averred that "executive posts are not reserved for anyone forever," he also reaffirmed the theme of "trusting the cadres," and made this theme a component of his closing remarks after the discussion of his report.[61] And he placed great emphasis on the task of retraining cadres whose skills had become obsolete, rather than purging them.[62]

The overall pattern of evidence during this period—Brezhnev's role and power expansion, his increased visibility and stature, his selective and temporary reincorporation of Khrushchevian components into his authority-building strategy, and his retreat from such components at the Twenty-Fourth Party Congress—is entirely consistent with the evolution of Brezhnev's policy program. In effect, Brezhnev was arguing that programmatic innovation was compatible with collective leadership, but that it would require some concentration of power within those confines. Brezhnev was offering himself as the leader best suited to combine dynamism in policy with physical and job security for the cadres—if only they followed his lead.

Conflict and Consensus: Kosygin's Acquiescent Posture

Brezhnev's unity platform generated few complaints from Alexei Kosygin at the Twenty-Fourth Party Congress. In sharp contrast to their polemic of 1967–8, the two Soviet leaders now exhibited a high level of consensus on the issues.

The Brezhnev synthesis on matters of resource allocation may have been less than fully satisfying to Alexei Kosygin, but if it was the Prime Minister did not indicate as much in his speech. At the Party Congress, he echoed almost all the themes of Brezhnev's earlier address on this score. Thus, in contrast to his statements at the Twenty-Third Party Congress, Kosygin now accepted agriculture as a "concern of all the people."[63] He fully endorsed the suggested approach to making

[60] Brezhnev, *Ob osnovnykh voprosakh*, Vol. 1, p. 428.
[61] Gruliow, *Current Soviet Policies VI*, p. 37; *XXIV s"ezd II*, p. 216.
[62] Gruliow, *Current Soviet Policies VI*, p. 37.
[63] ibid., p. 125.

heavy industry contribute to the expansion of both consumer goods and means of production for consumer-goods industries. He echoed verbatim the formulae in Brezhnev's speech regarding the "main task of the five-year plan" and regarding the status of heavy industry as the "foundation of the country's economic might."[64]

Moreover, Kosygin specifically endorsed almost all the features of Brezhnev's administrative program: the need to establish production associations that would break down structural barriers between science and production; the need to improve information-processing and central planning technologies; the need to expand specialist input toward these ends; the need to upgrade the quality of monitoring from both above and below; and the need to retrain executives in special courses.[65] In like manner, he echoed Brezhnev's remarks about the need to restructure material incentives in ways likely to spur innovation, calling this "now the most important thing."[66]

Brezhnev's ambiguous definition of the degree of independence production associations might eventually enjoy also found expression in Kosygin's remarks. Although the Prime Minister avoided the terminology of 1965 ("direct ties"; "contracts"), he affirmed some very basic principles and premises of that reform: "As resources increase, we shall be able to develop wholesale trade in the means of production. This will expand the independence and initiative of enterprises and associations in the selection of rational economic ties and will facilitate savings in material resources, improvements in work and cutbacks in the supply apparatus."[67] In sum, it would appear that Kosygin had acquiesced in the redirection of the 1965 reforms, possibly because Brezhnev's vision of the significance of the new reform did not rule out eventually expanding the autonomy of associations to develop horizontal, contractual ties.

Yet there were shades of difference between Brezhnev and Kosygin that force us to revise any conclusions of unqualified consensus between the two. It is noteworthy that Kosygin did not echo the urgency and unqualified remarks of Brezhnev regarding the importance of the rapid establishment of production associations. The furthest he went was to concur that "the ministries must resolutely embark on the path of introducing this form of the organization of management. This has been correctly stated at the Congress." But the force of this statement was decidedly diminished by the fact that it was sandwiched between two caveats regarding the advisability of rapid and uniform establishment of associations: "We must approach the formation of associations thoughtfully and in an economically

[64] ibid., pp. 118, 119, 122, 124, 135.
[65] ibid., pp. 130–1.
[66] ibid., pp. 128, 129.
[67] ibid., p. 130.

valid manner . . . Needless to say, the organizational structure and forms of associations cannot be identical in all branches, and we still need creative searches here."[68] Nor did Kosygin echo Brezhnev's prediction that the associations would ultimately become the basic economic-accountability units of society. Instead, the Prime Minister's emphasis on a "go-slow" approach implied the long-term existence of an economy based primarily on "autonomous" enterprises, and it may well have been in this spirit that Kosygin complained of too much ministerial interference in "the economic-accountability rights of *enterprises*" (italics added).[69] Finally, Kosygin buttressed the "go-slow" approach by excluding from his remarks any mention of the expanded role of primary party organizations in the ministries.

This point of difference between Brezhnev and Kosygin may have been resolved by a political compromise reached at or after the Party Congress. The very people who had the most to lose from the establishment of production associations according to criteria of economic rationality rather than political jurisdiction—officials of the ministries and their main administrations—were put in charge of drawing up the plans for the transition.[70]

It is unlikely that Kosygin's acquiescent posture was purely a product of his satisfaction with the compromise nature of Brezhnev's program. After all, the Prime Minister's stature was diminished by Brezhnev's role expansion, emerging personality cult, public effort to portray Kosygin as an extremist in 1968, and by Brezhnev's selective cooptation of positions previously associated with his rival. Moreover, there is clear evidence in Kosygin's speech to the Party Congress that the Prime Minister was forced to engage in self-criticism. For one

---

[68] ibid.

[69] ibid., p. 128.

[70] This interpretation of consensus and conflict over the production association experiment differs from that suggested by Katz (*Politics of Economic Reform*, pp. 120, 130, 144–5, 162, 172, 185, 186, 190). Katz barely mentions Brezhnev's name in discussing the politics of the 1971 reform. He sees "mergers" as a feature of the Kosygin reforms of 1965 that was discussed and legitimized at the time, but which only received full expression in 1970–1. Seeing relatively little difference of principle between the reforms of 1965 and 1971, Katz sees Kosygin as the motive force behind each, and posits a very low level of conflict within the leadership over both the 1965 and 1971 versions.

Katz's interpretation is a useful corrective to tendencies in Soviet studies toward overstating the degree of elite polarization whenever differences between leaders become apparent. However, Katz seems to go too far in the opposite direction. His interpretation cannot explain the manifold evidence of political and programmatic divergence between Brezhnev and Kosygin outlined in this book. In part, this is a result of Katz's research strategy; his chapters examine the 1965 reforms through 1966, and then skip to 1971 in something of a postscript.

thing, he rejected "all erroneous conceptions that substitute market regulation for the leading role of state centralized planning."[71] For another thing, he criticized the behavior of some managers during the economic reform as "antistate practice."[72] This was the first time since Khrushchev's overthrow that either Soviet leader had resorted to such terminology in his public speeches. In as much as Kosygin was criticizing his own nominal constituents (enterprise managers), and since Kosygin himself had earlier been accused of inordinate fascination with market-oriented solutions to economic problems, these statements can hardly be interpreted as efforts to steal the initiative from Brezhnev. Rather, they read more like self-critical indications of Kosygin's political weakness.

The precise weight of political coercion versus political compromise or persuasion in Kosygin's inducements to acquiesce cannot be determined at this time. Nor can we weigh the possible impact of his failing health on his political ambitions, and the effect this might have had on his behavior at the Party Congress. (Such failing health, however, would not prevent Kosygin from engaging in a broad polemic with Brezhnev at the following Party Congress, in 1976). What is significant, however, is that Kosygin was no longer engaging in public polemics on a range of issues. Nor was he feeling either the need or the ability to mollify a constituency that might be disgruntled with the compromise.

Kosygin had retreated from the limelight. This was Brezhnev's show.

[71] Gruliow, *Current Soviet Policies VI*, p. 129.
[72] ibid.

12 Frustration and Reaction, 1972-5

Brezhnev's program was ambitious: it would require both good luck and political leadership to sustain the momentum. It was based on the assumption that the unusually good weather conditions that had prevailed during 1966–70 would be repeated during 1971–5. It further assumed that arms-control agreements would be reached before a new generation of weaponry had been developed, awaiting a costly process of production and deployment that would begin about 1973. And it assumed that Western capital, credits, and technology for the development of Siberia would become available before a shortage of energy forced Soviet capital to try to do the job on its own—thereby forcing a reconsideration of the investment program of 1971. Thus, the fragility of Brezhnev's program derived from the fact that three of the foundations on which it rested were either out of the control of the leadership (the weather), or were only partially under its control (Soviet–US governmental relations and Soviet relations with Western and Japanese business interests).

Brezhnev's behavior during the eighteen months that followed the Party Congress indicated his willingness to supply the leadership required by his program. In domestic affairs, Brezhnev used the November 1971 Plenum of the Central Committee as a forum toward this end. There he harshly criticized lags in the completion of construction for the food industry and light industry in general. To emphasize the point, he warned of "significant difficulties" in the absence of a "turning-point" (*perelom*) on the question. Similarly, with respect to administrative reform, he candidly accused the ministries of having little "desire to organize work in a new way," criticized "elements of conservatism" in the state bureaucracy, called for increased party control over the matter, and indicated that the solution would be to "decisively punish disruptions of party and state discipline."[1]

In the foreign-policy realm Brezhnev assumed personal direction of Soviet–US relations, and made some key concessions in Spring 1971 to further negotiations with the USA. Later in the year further concessions were forthcoming, and President Nixon received an invitation to visit Moscow during Spring 1972. At the November 1971 Plenum Brezhnev secured the Central Committee's formal endorse-

[1] Brezhnev, *Ob osnovnykh voprosakh*, Vol. 2, pp. 207–10.

ment of his détente policies. And in May 1972 the Soviet Union and the USA signed the first Strategic Arms Limitation Treaty, as well as a series of collateral treaties and statements of principle.

Brezhnev was apparently supplying the political leadership, but luck was not fully on his side. The weather did not cooperate. The year 1972 brought to crucial agricultural areas of the Soviet Union the worst combination of winterkill and drought in fifty years. The targets of the Ninth Five-Year Plan were under threat even before that plan had been in existence for a year. Soviet negotiators quickly went onto the international markets to purchase large quantities of grain to sustain the livestock program. But even larger questions were looming, for Leonid Brezhnev would have to make some hard choices. How would he defend his image as effective problem-solver and indispensable politician? Would he redefine his socio-economic program? Would he shuffle the dominant coalition in the leadership and ally with new forces? If so, which ones, and at whose expense?

The parallels with Khrushchev were striking. He, too, had presented an ambitious, comprehensive program at a Party Congress, only to have it frustrated by circumstances at home and abroad over which he had little control. Khrushchev's response had been to launch a counteroffensive against the most powerful interests in the system. Brezhnev chose to respond quite differently. He accomodated to those interests while seeking new measures at home and abroad to improve consumer satisfaction and increase the efficiency of the economy. Moreover, he did so within a context (both domestic and international) that differed significantly from that faced by Khrushchev in 1960–1.

The period 1973–6 encompassed the remainder of the Ninth Five-Year Plan, and the first year of the Tenth. During this period, both new opportunities and new constraints arose. On the positive side, 1973 brought a record harvest. The same year also ushered in the heyday of détente, and the consummation of trade agreements with the USA, West Germany, and France (Japan was to follow a year later). In 1973–4 the OPEC oil embargo of Western economies led to a five-fold increase in the price of oil and gold on world markets, in both of which the USSR was rich. And 1976 brought still another record Soviet harvest.

But the constraints were equally severe. The availability of Western capital and credits was limited by both commercial and political considerations, the latter exemplified by US efforts to link credit and trade to Soviet emigration policies. In 1975, moreover, a drought of unprecedented intensity helped to produce the most disastrous agricultural situation in decades. The peasantry engaged in large-scale slaughter of livestock due to the shortage of feed grain. Light industry and heavy industry suffered also from the impact of the rural setback.

The Ninth Five-Year Plan, in consequence, suffered the highest degree of underfulfillment of any plan since the First Five-Year Plan of 1928–32. All of which led one Western observer to suggest that the crop failure of 1975 "may well be . . . the largest single blow suffered by the Soviet economy since the German invasion of 1941."[2]

This combination of gains and setbacks created a highly fluid decision-making environment for Soviet leaders. It effectively scuttled the ambitious, expanded program of 1971. And it reopened the fundamental questions with which the Brezhnev–Kosygin regime had been grappling since 1964. Where would they find the resources to maintain consumer satisfaction? Should those resources be purchased from domestic sources? Or should the search focus primarily on foreign sources? And what of the relationship between consumer satisfaction and administrative efficiency? Should the regime sacrifice precarious social values in order to spur labor productivity? Should it sponsor decentralization of the economy in order to relieve the tight budgetary situation? In this connection, what would become of Brezhnev's capital-intensive approach to agriculture? Would decentralization in the agricultural sector (for example, the link system) increase productivity without requiring a large new infusion of funds? Would those advocating greater investment in the urban–light-industrial sector now hold sway? And what of Siberia? With the high prices now fetched on world markets for oil, natural gas, gold, and other minerals, would the development of these resources in Siberia and the Soviet Far East allow the nation to satisfy its need for consumer goods, grains, and technology through foreign trade and barter? Would this approach also obviate flirtation with administrative decentralization? But how to develop the resources of Siberia? Through domestic resources, or primarily with foreign capital, credits, and expertise? This, in turn, raised the issue of political participation. If détente and expanded trade implied expanded interaction between Soviet and foreign citizens, would this interaction contaminate Soviet citizens with Western standards of consumer affluence, decentralization, and political participation? Finally, there remained the option of abandoning the commitments of the post-Stalin period and reverting to a form of Stalinism—based upon insulation from the West, economic autarky, extreme consumer austerity, more pervasive political controls, and reconcentration of the planning mechanism.

The strategy likely to be chosen, and the answers to these specific questions, were by no means self-evident, either to Western observers or to harried Soviet leaders. The choices were real and were being discussed within the Soviet establishment. But the consequences of

[2] Gregory Grossman, "The Brezhnev era: an economy at middle age," *Problems of Communism* (March–April 1976), pp. 21–2.

specific choices were only dimly perceived. Moreover, the situation was continually evolving, creating new opportunities and constraints. During 1973–4 the program of 1971 was officially redefined. After the drought of 1975 it was redefined once again. In each case, Brezhnev retreated further from the commitments he had embraced in 1971, making his peace with the military–industrial complex and with the centralist—but not with the autarkic—forces in the system.

Investment Priorities: Brezhnev's Retreat and Redefinition

Brezhnev was quick to retreat from his commitments to light industry and industrial consumer goods after the full dimensions of the 1972 harvest failure became evident. In his December 1972 address, commemorating the fiftieth anniversary of the founding of the USSR, he dwelled at length on questions of consumer satisfaction, but made no special appeal for the interests of Group B industries.[3] In the same speech, when enumerating regime successes in improving the well-being of the populace, he listed only increased earnings and housing as indicators of such improvements. Moreover, in Summer 1973 Brezhnev went on a barnstorming tour of Central Asia and the Ukraine, during which he delivered four major addresses.[4] Although this tour was devoted primarily to augmenting pressure for grain deliveries, it is nonetheless curious that, in the four speeches in question, the General Secretary did not once mention Group B industries. At the December 1973 Plenum Brezhnev devoted considerable attention to Group B industries, noting the setback caused by the drought, and rhetorically reaffirming his commitment. But this was apparently a case of symbolic rhetoric, for Brezhnev's statements shifted the emphasis from what it had been at the Twenty-Fourth Party Congress. At that time he had called for "saturating the market with consumer goods." Now he called for doing "significantly more . . . with respect to both the quantity of consumer goods *and especially their quality*" (italics added).[5]

This was the line Brezhnev developed in his speeches of 1974–5 to the extent that he mentioned light industry, which was rare. Thus, in his June 1974 election speech, he indicated clearly his opposition to expanded funding of that sector: "The key to success lies in the

[3] *Pravda*, 22 December 1972
[4] See ibid., 27 July 1973, 28 July 1973, 16 August 1973, and 25 September 1973.
[5] Brezhnev, *Ob osnovnykh voprosakh*, Vol. 2, p. 353.

mobilization of all forces, the improvement of economic management, high output, enhanced discipline, and organization."[6]

Moreover, Brezhnev's pledge to pressure heavy industry to produce consumer goods above-plan also fell by the wayside. In his public addresses he simply ignored the pledge.[7] In his speeches to the Central Committee plenary sessions of December 1972 and December 1973, he diffused responsibility for the task away from the military–heavy-industrial complex. Thus, in December 1972, he called upon "all economic, soviet, and party organs" to overfulfill their plans and thereby increase the possibility for expanded consumer-goods production.[8] And in December 1973 he retreated still further, suggesting that executives in light industry itself would be the first to answer for consumer-goods availability.[9]

Brezhnev's proposed solution to the problem of consumer satisfaction was to concentrate on putting things in order in the rural sector. Thus, at the December 1972 Plenum, he seized upon the setback of that year to argue for still heavier investment in agriculture.[10] One year later, after the record harvest of 1973, Brezhnev argued that his approach to the agricultural problem had been vindicated. But rather than give in to the forces pushing for a diversion of funds to light industry, he called for further expansion of agricultural investment, geared toward the specialization and concentration of agricultural production, enterprises for the production of feed grains ("the question of feed grains is moving to center stage"), and grain storage facilities.[11] In March 1974 he went public to criticize those who had not yet "overcome the temptation to borrow money for solving . . . problems from funds allocated for achieving an upswing in agricultural production."[12] And he then went on immediately to further increase those funds. In the same speech, he outlined and praised a massive (35 billion ruble) program of long-term investment in the Non-Black-Earth Zone. The following month he convened a meeting of party and state officials of the zone, delivering a long, detailed speech on the new program.[13] And he touted the program in

---

[6] *Pravda*, 15 June 1974; note also Brezhnev's silence on the needs of light industry in speeches published in ibid., 8 September 1974, 12 October 1974, and 14 June 1975.

[7] "Public addresses" are defined as speeches published in *Pravda*.

[8] Brezhnev, *Ob osnovnykh voprosakh*, Vol. 2, p. 251.

[9] ibid., p. 353.

[10] ibid., pp. 243, 245.

[11] ibid., pp. 343, 346–8.

[12] *Pravda*, 16 March 1974; this was a major address in Alma-Ata which was televised nationally.

[13] The speech was not published in Soviet newspapers at the time, but was reprinted (apparently in full) in Brezhnev, *Ob osnovnykh voprosakh*, Vol. 2, pp. 390–418.

subsequent public speeches as a major step on the path toward stable and dependable agricultural procurements in spite of weather conditions.[14] His major speeches of 1974–5 contained numerous pitches for expanded agricultural investments, even as they all but ignored the investment requirements of light industry.[15]

In addition to expanding his program of agricultural development, Brezhnev responded to the drought of 1972 by suddenly pushing for expansion of programs for Siberian development to lengths that had not been provided for in the Ninth Five-Year Plan (1971–5). In his December 1972 anniversary speech, he placed "development of the northern and eastern regions" on a par with "the early five-year plans, post-World War II reconstruction," and the Virgin Lands Program.[16] That this was more than just a rhetorical flourish was made clear by a doctrinal shift introduced by Brezhnev in this speech. Previously, the standard formulation on nationalities policy had called for combining the "interests of the republics" with All-Union interests. While this slogan was not dropped, it was superceded. Brezhnev now stressed that, for purposes of distributing investments among the republics, the Soviet Union would henceforth be treated as a "single economic mechanism." More pointedly, he proclaimed:

Now, when the task of evening out the level of economic development of the national republics in our country has been accomplished in the main, it is possible for us to approach economic questions primarily from the standpoint of the interests of the state as a whole, of improving the efficiency of the USSR's entire national economy—needless to say, with consideration for the specific interests of the Union and autonomous republics.

Such an alteration in approach, Brezhnev insisted, would allow greater "freedom of economic maneuvering."[17]

This is the rhetoric of a regime that is trying to free its hands of political constraints and to gain greater flexibility to allocate resources among the republics as it sees fit. Siberia, the Far East, the "northern regions," and the Non-Black-Earth Zone are all located in the Russian Republic. If Brezhnev was throwing his political weight behind massive programs for the development of precisely these regions, he would have to face objections from officials in those union republics deprived of actual or potential resources in the budgetary competition. By 1974, and throughout that year and the next, Brezhnev's public speeches

---

[14] *Pravda*, 24 April 1974, 15 June 1974, and 8 September 1974.

[15] ibid.; also ibid., 14 June 1975.

[16] ibid., 22 December 1972.

[17] See the discussion in Robert Osborn, *The Evolution of Soviet Politics* (Homewood, Ill.: Dorsey Press, 1974), pp. 431–2, 465–6.

included frequent high praise of development projects in these regions of the Russian Republic, including new-found calls for accelerated construction of the hugely expensive Baikal–Amur railway through Siberia. His doctrinal shift on the terms of Soviet federalism was a natural adjunct.

And where else did Brezhnev propose to find the capital for such projects? Apparently not from the defense budget, though Brezhnev's public comments on this subject were infrequent, forcing us again to be cautious in drawing conclusions. The comments he did make, however, all pointed in the same direction. Thus, on 20 March 1972, he pointed to increased US defense spending as justification for a Soviet response in kind.[18] In his election speech of June 1974, he made clear that Soviet defense spending would increase until formal agreements were reached to cut it back.[19] And in May 1975 he made an analogous statement in his speech on the thirtieth anniversary of the end of World War II.[20] All of which was being said at a time when Soviet strategic deployments were suddenly accelerating, and when a decision was apparently made to maintain defense expenditures at high levels despite slowdowns in the rate of growth of GNP.[21]

Surely the cutbacks in plans for consumer-goods production were not sufficient to fund simultaneous sharp increases in funding of agriculture, Siberian development and, apparently, defense spending. Brezhnev's proposal was to look abroad for new sources of capital. In his rare speeches on questions of foreign trade during 1972 Brezhnev continued to invoke the terminology of 1969–72, which had expressed the desire for "expanded, long-term economic relations and trade."[22] But after the Central Committee Plenum of April 1973 (which had been devoted to "strengthening foreign economic ties," and in which Brezhnev played a leading role),[23] the General Secretary's behavior changed. He visited West Germany in May, and signed a long-term economic agreement. He visited the USA in June, meeting with the President, with senators and congressmen, and with business

---

[18] *Pravda*, 21 March 1972.

[19] ibid., 15 June 1974.

[20] ibid., 9 May 1975.

[21] The alleged testing and deployment of new rocketry is not a controversial point among historians of the period (for details, see CIA, *Estimated Soviet Defense Spending*, pp. 10f.); on the decision of 1975 to insulate military spending from the effects of the slowdown in rate of growth of GNP, see Myron Rush, "Underestimating Brezhev's political strength," *Wall Street Journal* (20 August, 1981), p. 22.

[22] See *Pravda*, 15 September 1972, and 1 December 1972; see also the communiqué after Richard Nixon's visit to Moscow (ibid., 31 May, 1972).

[23] See Christian Deuvel, "An unprecedented Plenum of the CPSU Central Committee," *Radio Liberty Research Bulletin*, RL 145/73 (New York: Radio Liberty, 3 May 1973); also see *New York Times*, 8 May 1973, p. 3.

leaders. In October he hosted Japanese Prime Minister Tanaka in Moscow. And throughout the year his definition of the situation was different from that which had characterized his speeches the year previous. He now linked political détente with economic détente, and called constantly for "broadening the international division of labor" through "mutually advantageous, large-scale, and long-term economic ties," of both a bilateral and multilateral kind.[24] The implication of the change in terminology was clear. The General Secretary was in effect saying, "You have things we need; we have things you need. Let us expand the interdependence of our economies on equitable terms, and we can each advance the realization of our domestic economic goals, while fostering the cause of détente and arms control as well."

The link with Siberian development in Brezhnev's speeches was not yet explicit, and understandably so, for Brezhnev's big "push to the East" did not begin until early 1974. But at that time his public statements on the nature of foreign economic ties changed as well. His speeches to both foreign and domestic audiences now came to include incessant mention of "large-scale projects" and "product payback arrangements,"[25] which is precisely what the Soviets would need to finance large-scale projects in Siberia and the Far East. Nor was the General Secretary speaking only to Western governments (and Japan); throughout 1973–5 Brezhnev was unusually active in also inducing East European governments to increase their contributions to Soviet development projects.[26]

The impression is unmistakable, then, that Brezhnev had decided to balance his retreat from pushing the consumer-goods program with advances in pushing "big projects" in the industrial, agricultural, and defense sectors. At the same time, he sought to expand economic and political détente in directions that would increase Soviet economic interdependence with capitalist economies, but enlist the resources of those economies in Soviet efforts simultaneously to advance their level of technological development, increase consumer satisfaction, guard against shocks to the standard of living, and exploit the increasingly valuable resources of Siberia.

[24] *Pravda*, 20–30 June 1973 (*passim*), 28 July 1973, 1 August 1973, 16 August 1973, 9 October 1973, and 27 October 1973.

[25] ibid., 4 July 1974 (the communiqué after Richard Nixon's visit), 16 October 1974, 29 October 1974, 6 December 1974 (text of trade agreement with France), and 19 March 1975.

[26] See ibid., 22 December 1972 (we "must take into account such a favorable feature of the present international situation as the broad development of the international division of labor—first of all, the economic integration of the socialist countries"), 21 July 1974, 7 October 1974, and 19 March 1975.

Incentive Policy: Brezhnev's Redefinition, 1973–4

Brezhnev was a leading figure in raising mobilizational pressure as the magnitude of the setback of 1972 became evident. In August/September 1972 he toured Central Asia and Siberia, conferring with local leaders about ways to cut losses, and increasing the pressure on Central Asian (especially Uzbek) leaders to compensate for the grain losses with a large cotton harvest.[27] By December 1972 the General Secretary's redefinition had crystallized. In his anniversary speech of that month, military terminology became standard for the first time in his years in office. Grain procurement was no longer a problem, or even a struggle; it was now a "battle" (*bitva*). Reports on grain fulfillment were no longer statistical compilations of glorious achievements in the struggle for plan fulfillment; they were now "communiqués from the field of a gigantic battle."[28]

During Summer 1973 Brezhnev turned up the pressure for a big, quick win—a record grain and cotton harvest that would vindicate his approach to the agricultural problem. He toured Central Asia and the Ukraine, touting the "struggle for grain," and pressuring party leaders to adopt ambitious pledges of overfulfillment.[29] In Kiev, for example, he induced the party leadership to promise to deliver 1 billion poods of grain in 1973, and then demanded in public that this become "in the future the minimum norm for the Ukraine's farmers."[30] He extracted analogous pledges from the leaders of Uzbekistan, Kazakhstan, Kirgizia, Turkmenia, Tadzhikistan, and Azerbaidjan.[31]

Brezhnev was also a leader in the call for expanded mobilizational pressure in the industrial sector. Campaigns for "socialist competition" had been going on since 1969. But during 1969–72 Brezhnev had only echoed the call for increased labor discipline; his endorsement of socialist competition *per se* was muted at best. On this issue as well, December 1972 was a turning-point. In his anniversary address, Brezhnev for the first time engaged in a laudatory discussion of socialist competition.[32] In various speeches during 1973–4 he followed this up with calls for making increased labor discipline "the central

[27] See *Pravda* for the following dates in 1972: 26 August, 28 August, 29 August, 30 August, 31 August, 1 September, 2 September, 3 September, and 5 September.

[28] ibid., 22 December 1972.

[29] See ibid., 27 July 1973, 16 August 1973, 25 September 1973, 13 November 1973, and 16 November 1973.

[30] ibid., 27 July 1973.

[31] He announced success in these efforts in a speech in Tashkent (ibid., 25 September 1973).

[32] ibid., 22 December 1972; the point is made in Constantin Olgin, *Socialist Competition under Brezhnev* (New York: Radio Liberty Research Supplement, 16 May 1975).

task," with calls for greater use of "counterplans" in industry and agriculture, and with praise of Stakhanovism.[33] Overfulfillment of the plan, he told an audience in Novorossiisk in September 1974, must become the "militant [*boevym*] slogan" of all workers, with Communist Labor shock workers in the forefront.[34]

But Brezhnev was contradictory on the issue of incentive policy. For even as he was calling for increased coercion against unproductive workers, he was imprecise about the kinds of measures required to buttress the pressure with positive inducements. In his anniversary speech of December 1972 Brezhnev declared that, as far as the agricultural sector was concerned, the material incentive issue had been solved. Prices had been raised to levels that well exceeded the costs of production; current investment would emphasize technology and infrastructure.[35] Hence, he could justify the rise in pressure of 1973 as a legitimate "public interest" measure designed to ensure that the peasantry in fact pursued its economic self-interest as the regime defined it.

But by March 1974 Brezhnev was no longer claiming that the problem was simply one of prices. As advocates of both the link system and the Shchekino experiment had long been insisting, the problem was one of relating material rewards to the final results of production. Otherwise, workers and peasants would simply perform routine, intermediate operations that, more often than not, undermined the goal of high-quality, high-quantity output—and they would still receive bonuses for having fulfilled their norms. This is the position that Brezhnev adopted, for the first time since he came to power, in his speech of March 1974: "economic levers . . . must be improved still more, and we must orient ourselves toward an increasingly direct dependence between the pay of individual workers and whole collectives and the end results of their activity. Only in this way can we achieve the efficient utilization of land and equipment and the accelerated growth of labor productivity."[36]

But the Soviet party leader was apparently not ready to force the matter: "Quite a few new proposals are being put forth in this field, and interesting initiatives are being carried out—all of this deserves serious study."

Similarly, Brezhnev was turning up the pressure in the industrial sector. Augmented pressure was precisely the way in which the planners were undermining the Shchekino experiment. Yet, at the December 1973 Plenum, Brezhnev made statements that pointed in a

[33] See *Pravda*, 25 September 1973, 24 April 1974, and 8 September 1974; also Brezhnev, *Ob osnovnykh voprosakh*, Vol. 2, p. 359.
[34] *Pravda*, 8 September 1974.
[35] ibid., 22 December 1972.
[36] ibid., 16 March 1974 (*CDSP*, vol. 26, no. 11).

different direction. He praised the rationalization of labor taking place in the oil-refining industry, which had made possible the release of 70,000 redundant workers.[37] This observation provided the backdrop for Brezhnev then to praise the Shchekino experiment for the first time since the Twenty-Fourth Party Congress, and to demand that it be emulated and diffused throughout the economy "more boldly and more quickly."[38]

It would be irresponsible to make too much of these isolated statements over a period of sixteen months. On the other hand, it would be a missed opportunity if we ignored them, for these comments touched upon fundamental issues in ways that were either rare or unprecedented for Brezhnev. Moreover, Brezhnev's comments on Shchekino are analogous to his statements about the need to relate pay to final results in the rural sector. In each case the consequence would be broader material differentiation between the productive and unproductive workers, release of redundant workers, and an expanding wage "fund." In each case, the experiment can only be successful if higher wages for higher productivity are matched by attractive goods on which to spend the money.[39] Coming on the heels of the record harvest of 1973, the recovery of industry in general during that year, and sharply expanded prospects for foreign trade and credits, Brezhnev's statements may have reflected his claim that the consumer situation could be salvaged through his new strategy.

Such an interpretation assumes that Soviet leaders perceive a direct link between the success of anti-egalitarian experiments and a bullish consumer situation. Although Soviet leaders have never said so in public, there are patterns in Soviet policy that support this assumption. Thus, the Shchekino experiment was launched in 1967—precisely the year when, after a record harvest, investment in light industry was being expanded. The Shchekino experiment was endorsed by a decree of the Central Committee in 1969, at a time when funds for agricultural development were being sharply expanded. It was publicly endorsed by the General Secretary in 1971, in the same Party Congress address in which he spelled out an expanded program for both agricultural and consumer-goods production. Moreover, it was endorsed in the same speech in which Brezhnev, for the first time, acknowledged the linkage between consumer goods' availability and

37 Brezhnev, *Ob osnovnykh voprosakh*, Vol. 2, p. 358.
38 ibid., p. 359.
39 A former Soviet economist who, while in the USSR, was a specialist on economic experiments such as the Shchekino experiment, has informed me that his extensive research under the auspices of the Academy of Sciences convinced him that the main obstacle to these experiments was the lack of consumer goods on which to spend extra wages, and consequent regime resistance to expansion of the wage fund (personal communication from Professor Aron Vinokur, Haifa University, Israel).

the effectiveness of material incentives as spurs to production initiative. It was endorsed again by the General Secretary only after the record harvest of 1973. Its progress was consciously impeded by the planners during 1972, when prospects for improving the consumption situation had suddenly darkened. Thus, one interpretation of Brezhnev's comments would be that his optimistic claims of 1973–4 led him, as in 1971, to be willing to challenge egalitarian social values for the sake of economic efficiency.

Another interpretation would be quite different. It would see Brezhnev's comments as largely demagogic. Given the increased struggle for investment funds between the light-industry and agriculture advocates after the 1973 harvest, it is quite probable that support for inegalitarian experiments in both sectors would increase among those seeking ways to hold down investments in either sector. Brezhnev's comments, then, could be viewed as a demagogic effort to ally rhetorically with both sets of forces in order to maintain his position as principal definer of the direction of policy, without exercising the power required to force through new directions. The fact that the planners were undermining the Shchekino experiment at precisely this time, the fact that Brezhnev was turning up the pressure for results at the same time as he was advocating experiments that presupposed a reduction of pressure, and the fact that Brezhnev called only for "further study" of "interesting proposals" in his comments of March 1974, would all support this interpretation.

A third interpretation would view Brezhnev as a leader who, at the time, did not choose to retreat too far from his commitments of 1971, and sought to balance his augmentation of pressure (which, based on the Khrushchevian experience, he must have realized could have only limited positive results) with "progressive" initiatives in the realm of incentive policy. This need not be viewed as entirely demagogic. For one thing, Brezhnev may not have clearly perceived the workability of these experiments and proposals. For another, he may have been trying to keep them on the political agenda in the form of limited experiments—rather than giving in to forces seeking to scuttle them entirely—so as to test their practicability.

One of the last two interpretations is probably closer to the truth. The first interpretation contends that Brezhnev was being self-assertively reformist at the time, vowing to push through any structural reforms that the Shchekino experiment would require. Yet there is no evidence that political intervention took place at the time, geared toward forcing the ministries to desist from subverting the experiments. The third interpretation may be closest to the mark. It would square both with Brezhnev's career background and with his commitment—restrained but real—to foster structural change in the Soviet economy on a limited, experimental basis. Moreover, there was little political cost involved in keeping such experiments on the policy agenda, and considerable potential cost involved in appearing to retreat too far from "realism" about the need for structural changes to improve the functioning of the economy. Finally, such an interpretation would be consistent with analogous behavior by Khrushchev at a corresponding stage of his administration. Just as Khrushchev incorporated endorsement of economic reform proposals into his speeches in the early 1960s, so Brezhnev might be expected to attempt to maintain his image as an innovative problem-solver by coopting issues and redefining their thrust.

Administrative Reform: Brezhnev's Retreat and Redefinition

Just as Brezhnev retreated from his expanded commitments on investment priorities, so he retreated from his aggressive posture of 1971 regarding the production association movement. No mention of these administrative forms appeared in his December 1972 anniversary speech.[40] At the December 1972 Plenum, Brezhnev offered but one tepid afterthought: "we must also more quickly go over to large associations and combines as the basic production unit in our economy."[41] In public speeches during 1973, Brezhnev did not once mention the production associations. And at the December 1973 Plenum, Brezhnev struck the pose of a political leader who had retreated from his assertive posture of two years earlier:

> Bearing in mind completely the complexity of such a task, and the fact that one must approach it in a well thought-out manner, with sufficient care, we must also see another side of the question— that its resolution must not be postponed for long.
> . . .
> The process of creating large associations in industry raises more than a few questions. Warnings are being expressed: are not certain ministries approaching this important matter in a formal manner, is not the reorganization being reduced to a change in signposts?[42]

At the December 1971 Plenum he had been fully prepared to answer this question; now he let it lie.

But, as if to compensate for his retreat on this issue, Brezhnev now became a leading advocate of regional and project planning. This was

---

[40] *Pravda*, 22 December 1972.
[41] Brezhnev, *Ob osovnykh voprosakh*, Vol. 2, p. 254.
[42] ibid., p. 355.

not an entirely new theme in Brezhnev's speeches. At the Twenty-Fourth Party Congress, he had pointed to the development of the "fuel and power complex," space research, and agriculture as examples of Soviet experience with programmed planning of inter-branch projects.[43] In his election speech after that congress, he had made a big pitch for integrated planning of territorial complexes in Siberia.[44] But it was only during the period of redefining his program that Brezhnev addressed the political-organizational aspects of the matter, and became insistent about the need to break through constraints.

Thus, at the December 1972 Plenum, Brezhnev demanded that the State Planning Committee improve its ability to solve inter-branch problems.[45] At the December 1973 Plenum, he dwelled at length on the need for improvements in the "branch system of administration," such that it would "take territorial aspects more fully into account," and he proposed structural changes in the State Planning Committee to further this goal.[46] At the December 1974 Plenum, he declared his frustration with the pace of change, pointing out the need to "free ourselves from the prison of inertia," and to "liquidate bottlenecks that are holding up the growth of our economy."[47] And in his June 1975 election speech, he extolled the Baikal–Amur railway, indicated the need for comprehensive planning of the region that railway was opening for exploitation, and made a pitch for improving the work, and raising the role, of planning and designs agencies toward that end.[48]

In the agricultural realm as well, Brezhnev seized the initiative on matters of administrative reform. At the eventful December 1973 Plenum, he pushed suddenly for agro-industrial complexes, inter-collective farm construction organizations, and other cooperative endeavors among collective and state farm units: "I think that the time has come, as they say among us, to lay out the red carpet for inter-collective farm enterprises."[49]

After the December 1973 Plenum, Brezhnev quickly followed up the initiative seized. In his major, lengthy, and nationally televised speech in Alma-Ata in March 1974,[50] he proclaimed the specialization and concentration of agricultural production, and the expansion of inter-farm cooperation, to be the "third stage" in the development of agriculture since Khrushchev. He declared these questions "urgent and fundamental." He devoted eleven lengthy paragraphs to a discus-

[43] Gruliow, *Current Soviet Policies VI*, pp. 24, 27.
[44] *Pravda*, 12 June 1971.
[45] Brezhnev, *Ob osnovnykh voprosakh*, Vol. 2, pp. 252–3.
[46] ibid., p. 356.
[47] ibid., pp. 447–8.
[48] *Pravda*, 14 June 1975.
[49] Brezhnev, *Ob osnovnykh voprosakh*, Vol. 2, p. 347.
[50] *Pravda*, 16 March 1974.

sion of the problem, far more attention than he had ever accorded it in any speech since 1964.[51] Moreover, he explicitly linked the issue of agricultural concentration, and agro-industrial integration, to the theme of inter-branch planning, criticizing "the persisting features of the multibranch, fragmented structure of production [which are] retarding the intensification of agriculture." From this he concluded that the urgent, new processes under way in the realm of agricultural administration would require a new system of management based on closer inter-departmental coordination, clear-cut definition of rights and jurisdictions, deconcentration of more operational decision-making to the farms and districts, and the elimination of extraneous links in the administrative hierarchy.

In sum, the vigor with which Brezhnev had advocated political-organizational changes to facilitate production associations in his speech to the Twenty-Fourth Party Congress died down during 1973–4. But it was replaced by still greater vigor in his advocacy of inter-branch planning reforms in both the industrial and agricultural sectors. On the other hand, those planning reforms may have had fewer decentralist implications in peoples' minds than had the ambiguous production association movement at the Twenty-Fourth Party Congress. If so, Brezhnev's program change constituted a retreat from reformism, rather than just a shift of focus, a retreat consistent with his behavior on other issues as well.

Political Participation: Brezhnev's Redefinition

At the Twenty-Fourth Party Congress, Brezhnev had struck the posture of a moderator. He endorsed the conservative reaction, but sought to prevent it from going further than it already had. During 1973–4, however, Brezhnev appeared to endorse a further extension of the reaction, as well as an intensification of political socialization. But

[51] Brezhnev had had absolutely nothing to say about such cooperative endeavors in his major addresses at agricultural plenums of March 1965, May 1966, and October 1968. In November 1969, at the Collective Farm Congress that approved a hierarchy of kolkhoz councils, Brezhnev made a short pitch for agrarian-industrial associations (*Pravda*, 26 November 1969). In his plenum address of July 1970, he endorsed the needs of rural construction, concluding that "the development of inter-collective farm construction organizations should be promoted in every way" (*Pravda*, 3 July 1970). And at the Twenty-Fourth Party Congress, he noted that "the rapid development of agriculture is leading to the ever broader dissemination of inter-collective farm and state-collective farm production associations and the creation of agro-industrial complexes . . . The Party will support these forms of production in rural areas" (Gruliow, *Current Soviet Policies VI*, p. 21). But all these were akin to passing references compared with the discussion in Brezhnev's March 1974 speech.

at the same time, Brezhnev continued to advocate a balance between conservative reaction and the creation of a less arbitrary environment for the politically conformist.

Thus, speaking in Alma-Ata in August 1973, Brezhnev reminded his audience that détente would mean expanded contacts with foreigners, and he dubbed this a good thing. But he then went on immediately to qualify the endorsement: "At the same time, and this cannot go unmentioned, a more thorough approach to questions of the communist upbringing of our country's working people is now required . . . The Party Central Committee attaches paramount importance to . . . this."[52] Similarly, in his address to the Young Communist League in April 1974, Brezhnev praised the inter-generational tutelary movement (*nastavnichestvo*), called for it to become a nationwide movement, demanded the intensification of patriotic education and mobilization of youth, and criticized egoism, money-grubbing, and a consumer attitude to life as "negative phenomena" the "danger" of which should not be "underestimated."[53]

In the same speech, Brezhnev lent his stamp to an intensified crackdown on dissidents, in effect accusing them of treason: "Certain renegades and deluded people in our country have tried to sing in tune with our class and ideological enemies." In 1968 Brezhnev had defined dissenters as susceptible to influence by bourgeois ideologists. In 1971 he had tempered his remarks relative to those of 1968. Now he was accusing dissidents of trying to aid the enemy—of conscious intent.

But Brezhnev was careful to differentiate among his constituencies. He did not want the intensification of political socialization to lead to official arbitrariness and lack of responsiveness that would alienate the nominally conformist. Thus, two months later, in his election speech,[54] he offered a definition of "strengthening socialist legality" that was strikingly similar to his admonitions at the Twenty-Fourth Party Congress, including his admonitions against "arbitrariness on the part of officials." And in the same speech, he criticized "bureaucratism" on the part of officials who seek to evade responsiveness to public complaints.

In like manner, Brezhnev continued to call during these years for the elevation of official responsiveness to specialist input that would advance official goals. Thus, at the December 1972 Plenum, he pointed out that the drought had done least damage to those regions in which officials heeded the advice of agricultural specialists.[55] Three days later, on the fiftieth anniversary of the establishment of the

[52] *Pravda*, 16 August 1973.
[53] ibid., 24 April 1974.
[54] ibid., 15 June 1974.
[55] Brezhnev, *Ob osnovnykh voprosakh*, Vol. 2, p. 244.

USSR, Brezhnev gave strong support to the empirical definition of scientific decision-making, criticized "dogmatism," and called for a creative approach to theory.[56] In July 1973 Brezhnev offered just such a creative approach: "Not long ago we spoke about science **becoming** a direct productive force. We even wrote it into our program. Now we can say that science has already **become** a direct productive force, the significance of which is growing from day to day" (bold in original).[57]

Brezhnev as Politician

Brezhnev's coalition-building strategy was becoming clear. Support for increased interdependence with the world economy could be traded for further insulation of the population from nonconformist ideas. Support for strategic arms limitation talks could be traded for the increased defense spending taking place during the talks. Support for diverting scarce capital to Siberia and the Far East could be traded for the prospect of limits to the Soviet share in financing the venture. Support for Soviet financing of the Baikal–Amur railway could be won by arguing that the West needed to be shown that the Soviets would develop Siberia on their own if Western politicians tried to drive too hard a bargain. Support for the intensification of mobilizational pressure in industry and agriculture could be won by pointing to the record results of 1973, and could be mitigated by Brezhnev's simultaneous recognition of reform proposals in the realm of incentive policy. Support for retreat on the issue of production associations could be traded for a push toward other types of centralist reforms in the agricultural and industrial sectors. Support for the crackdown on dissidents and liberal sociologists could be traded for expanded opportunities for input by those who accecpted the new priorities (for example, project planners, mathematical economists, and regional planners). And support for a program that was so critically dependent on the success of détente could be purchased through cooptation of the Foreign Minister, Minister of Defense, and KGB Chairman into the Politburo (as happened in April 1973). Moreover, Brezhnev's strategy could satisfy a wide range of noninstitutional interests, for by leaning on, and developing, the strengths of the traditional system (military capacity, natural resources, grandiose projects, large-scale administrative organization, industrialization of agriculture, and the concentration of resources on priority goals generating mobilizational fervor), Brezhnev could publicly reconcile Soviet nationalism and

---

[56] *Pravda*, 22 December 1972.
[57] *Brezhnev, Leninskim kursom IV*, p. 218.

pride in Soviet accomplishments with the pursuit of both national security and popular material security.

In redefining his program, and retreating from previous commitments, Brezhnev did not mirror Khrushchev's confrontational approach to politics. No allusions to a threatening mass mood appear in his speeches. No effort to appeal to the masses over the heads of officials, and no augmentation of threats against the cadres, appeared in the published versions of those speeches.[58] It is possible, of course, that they were there, but were excised by the censors—but such censorship in itself would require explanation, since a Khrushchevian strategy requires publicity to be effective. Other, more plausible, explanations might be advanced. First, it may be that after the Polish riots of December 1970, followed by the Soviet drought of 1972, allusions to the mass mood, or appeals to the consumer, on the part of the General Secretary would have been viewed as encouraging the masses to act upon their disaffections. This would have been viewed as threatening and illegitimate on the part of many members of the political elite (akin to Khrushchev's strategy during 1961), rather than merely intimidating but legitimate (which had been Khrushchev's strategy in 1954). Brezhnev could lean toward such a strategy during 1970—as he did in seeking to expand the scope of his agricultural program—but not in 1973.

A second possible explanation would simply be that Brezhnev did not need to take such an approach in 1973 because his new program represented a withdrawal of challenges to the most powerful institutions in the system. By falling back on a program that used the strengths of those institutions to work for grandiose projects, he was attempting to redirect their missions, but not redefine their character.[59] He was reverting to traditional mobilizational appeals. Hence, the politics of private coalition-building would be sufficient.

[58] With the possible exception of the following: "It is very bad if party, soviet, and economic leadership cadres are unstable, if they are changed often. We must try to avoid this. However, it is still worse when people who work poorly and do not cope with their duties are kept in their posts too long" (*Pravda*, 28 July 1973). If this does indeed constitute an escalation of threats, it may have been situation-specific, rather than a change in general policy orientation. For this statement was made in Kiev, during the tour of Central Asia and the Ukraine, when Brezhnev was turning up the pressure for a quick win.

[59] Philip Selznick, in his classic *Leadership in Administration*, defines "institutional leadership" as a process of redefining the character of organizations—their commitments and basic orientations. In 1971 Brezhnev was apparently calling for a redefinition of the character of Soviet heavy-industrial organization, by attempting to change basic orientations and statuses. In 1973, in turning to the strengths of heavy industry (for example, in building railways in Siberia), Brezhnev was redirecting the mission of Soviet heavy industry, but was no longer seeking to redefine its character.

A third explanation would point to the fact that Brezhnev's program of 1973 was heavily dependent on the success of détente—for keeping alive the promise of future cuts in defense spending; for developing Siberia; for satisfying consumer expectations. This was a tenuous base upon which to rest the success of one's domestic political program. To encourage mass consumer expectations, or to appeal to the masses, on a programmatic revision that increased Soviet dependence on foreign countries would have been unwise on two counts. For one thing, it would have raised consumer expectations at a time when Brezhnev's ability to meet those expectations hinged on success in an arena over which he had, at best, partial control. For another thing, it would have raised eyebrows within a political elite that considers foreign affairs the last realm of policy over which the masses should have a say.

We need not make a choice among these explanations. They are mutually reinforcing, and add up to the conclusion that a strategy of public confrontation was neither necessary, desirable, nor wise in light of what Brezhnev was attempting to do: redefine his domestic program in a conservative direction.

Nonetheless, the entire history of policy change since Stalin had been premised on the notion that a conservative program might not be sufficient to attain post-Stalin goals of economic betterment and administrative efficiency. Hence, Brezhnev would be likely to face skepticism (if not criticism) from within segments of the political elite that had earlier supported his compromise program of 1971. We might therefore expect to find evidence that Brezhnev found it problematic to redefine his program in 1973–4. Indeed, we do.

Eschewing a confrontational strategy did not mean that Brezhnev simply settled for using closed Central Committee Plenums as private forums in which to mobilize support for his new program. There is evidence to suggest that Brezhnev manipulated the arenas of politics in a more public direction (as he had done in 1970) in order to increase his political leverage and intimidate potential critics. The sequence unfolds during the period Summer 1973 through Summer 1974. First, Brezhnev went on a public tour of Central Asia and the Ukraine, publicly demanding from republican leaders ambitious pledges of overfulfillment, raising their targets to unprecedented heights[60]—all, ostensibly, to secure a quick win of great proportions, to vindicate his agricultural program, and to use these results to justify expanding the scope of his program at the December 1973 Plenum of the Central Committee. Second, his speech of March 1974, delivered prior to the announcement of his expensive program for developing the Non-Black-Earth Zone, extolled such a program in a nationally televised

[60] See sources noted in note 29, above.

address from Alma-Ata.[61] Third, Brezhnev followed this up with two public speeches (to the Young Communist League in April 1974, and to his electoral constituents in June 1974) in which he summarized, extolled, and insisted on support for his grand projects of agricultural and Siberian development.[62] This strong association between Brezhnev's use of intimidating language or arenas of politics and his efforts of 1970 and 1973–4 to forge programs bearing his stamp suggests that Brezhnev's authority-building strategy had to contend with a variety of powerful forces within the political elite. As we shall see in the next chapter, the failure of his program in 1975 was to throw Brezhnev onto the defensive.

[61] *Pravda*, 16 March 1974.
[62] ibid., 24 April 1974, and 15 June 1974.

13 The Twenty-Fifth Party Congress, 1976: Brezhnev's Authority Challenged

To be successful, Brezhnev's new program required good luck on both the domestic and foreign scenes. But such luck was not forthcoming. The Jackson–Vanik amendment to a US–Soviet trade bill required formalized guarantees of emigration for Soviet Jews in exchange for a relatively modest sum of US economic credits voted by Congress, a combination of conditions that proved unacceptable to the Politburo, and that led to its repudiation of the trade agreement in January 1975. In addition, both commercial and political considerations led Japanese negotiators to balk on large-scale investment of capital in Siberian development. And the drought and crop failure of 1975 all but scuttled Brezhnev's hopes for a major breakthrough toward sharply increasing the proportion of meat and milk, vegetables and fruits in the diet of Soviet citizens.

On the heels of the setbacks of 1975, the draft of the new five-year plan was published.[1] That document reflected both the frustrated hopes of 1971–4, and Brezhnev's decision to stick with his new program of 1973–4. Growth targets for both productive and nonproductive investment in heavy industry, light industry, and urban welfare were moderated substantially. In contrast to the Ninth Five-Year Plan, the growth rate of heavy industry was once again slated to be greater than that of light industry and industrial consumer goods. Indeed, still lower rates of growth of consumption were projected than had in fact been realized during 1971–5.

The big winners in the competition for funds were defense, Siberian development, agriculture, nuclear power, automobiles-for-export, pollution control, and the food industry. From the directives of the Tenth Five-Year Plan, it would appear that Brezhnev was standing up for the key components of his redefined program, despite the setbacks. But by the time the Twenty-Fifth Party Congress convened in February 1976, many of the delegates must have wondered what the new situation implied for the credibility of Brezhnev's program, for the level of political conflict within the Politburo, and for the evaluation of Brezhnev's policy effectiveness by members of the broader political elite.

[1] For an analysis of that draft, see Grossman; "The Brezhnev era: an economy at middle age."

The Twenty-Fifth Party Congress:
Where Do We Go from Here?

Brezhnev's speech at the Twenty-Fifth Party Congress provides insight into the positions he adopted after the drought of 1975.[2] With a few marginal revisions, he chose to stick with his new program of 1973–4, and to concentrate primarily on defending his policy effectiveness against skeptics, parrying challenges to his authority by shifting responsibility for failure, augmenting his personality cult, and increasing the threats against the cadres. For, in contrast to 1971, Brezhnev did not strike the pose of a self-confident, artful synthesizer. Rather, the language of insistence, accusation, and urgency pervaded his speech. Even as he was reaffirming his conservative program, he was warning skeptical members of the political elite that his was the only way. If they wished to avoid *immobilisme*, a return to Stalinism, or market-oriented alternatives, they would have to follow his lead.

Brezhnev reaffirmed his strategy of industrializing agriculture, calling it a "state task of all the people," and adding that the success of the program "will require time, labor, and enormous investments." Lest any comrades question the wisdom of the program, Brezhnev used very strong language to underscore his commitment. The current approach, he asserted, "completely accords with the fundamental interests of the collective-farm peasantry and the working class, has passed the test of time, and has received the approval of all the people. This means it is correct. This means the party will, in the future as well, follow this line." Of course, efficient use of agricultural investment will require that the party "improve the organization and administration of agricultural production." But, either in response to those favoring decentralization, or in response to those challenging Brezhnev's leadership capacity in light of the crop failures, the General Secretary added that "this is a complex matter; there are no ready recipes."

Brezhnev admitted that the slow development of light industry gave cause for concern. But he dismissed the arguments of those who placed the blame on the agricultural crisis: "It is not just a question that because of the shortage of agricultural raw materials caused by the poor harvest, light industry and the food industry failed to meet planned indices for a number of products. We must raise this question more broadly and more pointedly." More broadly and more pointedly, Brezhnev laid the blame on attitudes rather than on objective conditions, and pointed a finger of accusation at "central planning and economic organs," the ministries, and all those who "plan and direct

---

[2] *Pravda*, 25 February 1976 (*CDSP*, vol. 28, no. 8). All citations from Brezhnev's address are from these sources.

this sector of the economy" (italics added). Rather than calling for expanded investments in Group B industries, the General Secretary emphasized the existence of "huge reserves" that could be brought to bear to improve the efficiency of this sector.

Brezhnev's speech reflected both the changed economic situation and the General Secretary's decision to fall back upon the military–heavy-industrial complex for support. Raising the standard of living was now explicitly relegated to the status of a "long-term goal," while heavy industry was no longer called upon primarily to serve the consumer. Quite the contrary, Brezhnev now defined "the essence of the party's economic strategy" to be **"a further buildup of the country's economic might, the expansion and fundamental renewal of production assets, and the ensuring of stable, balanced growth for heavy industry—the foundation of the economy"** (bold in original).

Moreover, Brezhnev spoke about Siberian and Far Eastern development at this Party Congress in terms not present in his speech at the Twenty-Fourth Party Congress, and in terms consistent with his redefinitions of 1973–4. He promised "new life to vast areas of Siberia, the North, Central Asia, and the Far East." He pointed out that planners are "now going farther and farther to the east and north for petroleum, gas, coal, and ore," and that "a fundamentally new stage in the development of East Siberia's productive forces has been planned." And as for the "big projects" in agriculture, Brezhnev proclaimed that "land reclamation in the Non-Black-Earth Zone will get under way on a broad scale. Major new irrigation systems will be constructed in the southern and southeastern sections of the European part of the country and in Central Asia and Kazakhstan."

Despite the setbacks of 1975, Brezhnev was also determined to push forward with an increasing dependence on foreign sources of capital, technology, and consumer goods. He devoted more than twice as much space to the subject than he had in 1971. He raised the status of the subject by addressing it in the context of a subsection of the speech entitled, "The development of foreign economic relations" (previously, no such subsection existed in speeches of the General Secretary at party congresses). And he emphasized the linkage of such relations to the solution of Soviet domestic economic problems by locating the subsection in the economic section of the report (previously, such ties were discussed in the section on international relations). Moreover, Brezhnev unambiguously legitimized the vital role of such relations in the realization of his program: "Like other states, we strive to use the advantage that foreign economic ties offer with a view to mobilizing additional possibilities for the successful accomplishment of economic tasks and gains in time . . ."

Nor was this all. Brezhnev also made a point of noting the potential of these ties for improving consumer satisfaction at home. Then, too, he placed great emphasis on the importance of product-payback agreements for the exploitation of Siberian wealth. And finally, Brezhnev went much beyond his statements of 1971 in advocating the use of East European sources for the realization of Soviet goals, and demanded that the planners take "the next step forward" toward "the elaboration and implementation of long-term, special-purpose programs" with Comecon partners.

On the issue of production associations, Brezhnev's speech confirmed his retreats of 1973–4. He mentioned, for example, that "more and more production and industrial associations are being created," adding later that "we must . . . remove the burden of inconsequential matters from the upper echelons of management . . . complete work on the creation of production associations and improve their activity." But that was all. Brezhnev had acquiesced in a "go-slow" approach that would augment the deconcentrating, but not decentralizing, potential of the association movement. Brezhnev did not laud the productive potential of the associations as he had in 1971; he did not refer to them as the "basic economic-accountability links of social production"; and he did not criticize the ministries or local party officials for frustrating their establishment according to criteria of economic efficiency.

However, as had been the case in 1973–4, Brezhnev sought to compensate for retreats by pushing harder for other elements of his program. At the Twenty-Fifth Party Congress, he dwelled at length on inter-branch coordination problems in the West Siberian complex; he lent his support to the need for further development of mathematical economics, systems analysis, and automated control systems for inter-branch planning; and he demanded political-organizational changes toward these ends: "What we need here is a united, centralized program embracing all stages of work . . . It is important that in every case there should be specific organs and people to carry the whole weight of responsibility and to coordinate all efforts in the framework of this or that program."

Moreover, the rhetoric that Brezhnev employed in justifying the need for such reforms was far more assertive than any he had used previously. He characterized reforms geared toward project planning as "an unpostponable matter," which must "take effect in the immediate future." He dubbed clarification of jurisdictions "the essence of organizational questions" and the "foundation of foundations of the science and practice of administration."

Of course, Brezhnev then reassured his listeners that he was no hare-brained schemer à la Khrushchev: "The Central Committee is against hasty, impulsive reorganizations of the administrative structure, of existing methods of economic administration. It is necessary to measure the cloth not seven times, as the saying goes, but eight or even ten times before cutting." But this much said, Brezhnev immediately went on to indicate that there had already been enough experimenting and that the time for instituting genuine administrative changes had come: "But once we have done the measuring, once we have understood that the existing economic mechanism has become too tight for the developing economy, we must fundamentally improve it." And lest his words be forgotten in the interval between his main report on 24 February and his short concluding statement on 1 March, Brezhnev returned to the theme in his concluding remarks: "We shall act correctly, in a Leninist fashion, if, having acknowledged our achievements, we concentrate attention on the remaining shortcomings, on unresolved tasks."[3] Although the injunction to concentrate on unresolved problems and tasks had been a constant one throughout Brezhnev's tenure in office, this was the first Party Congress of the Brezhnev era at which the General Secretary had included the caveat in his usually optimistic, concluding statement.[4]

On questions of political participation as well, Brezhnev stuck with his new approach of 1973–4. His statements on cultural dissent indicated endorsement of the lengths reached by the conservative reaction. He was not whipping it on any longer, for by 1976 it had gone quite far beyond the level of 1972. Nor, however, was he making special efforts to restrain it. Rather, the General Secretary went back to the practice of balancing his comments. Thus, when speaking of the secret police, Brezhnev praised the "Chekists" who work in the finest tradition of "Felix Dzherzhinsky" (thereby indicating what happens to dissenters), but also assured his listeners that the secret police work under strict party control and in complete observance of socialist legality (thereby indicating that the politically conformist, as far as he was concerned, had nothing to worry about).

In like manner, Brezhnev continued to defend those groups whose specialized input was required for the success of his socio-economic and administrative programs. The empirical definition of scientific decision-making received considerable attention by the General Secretary. In contrast to the Twenty-Fourth Party Congress, discussion of empirical scientific research was now placed toward the very start of the section on the ideological-upbringing work of the party.[5] Brezhnev noted the increasing "scope and complexity" of tasks, concluding that, under such conditions, "a critical approach to all matters acquires special importance." He also reiterated his support for economic science, mathematical economics, and for their more rapid introduction into planning methods. And Brezhnev criticized Soviet

---

[3] *Pravda*, 2 March 1976.
[4] Compare *XXIII s"ezd II*, pp. 291–8; and *XXIV s"ezd II*, pp. 213–18.
[5] I am grateful to William Haidiger for drawing this to my attention.

officials for their failure to respond to specialist input. The scientific-technological revolution, he pointed out, requires "a determined struggle against stagnation and the rigidities of routine, genuine respect for science, and the ability *and desire* to seek advice and to take it into consideration" (italics added). Brezhnev was not calling for responsiveness to scientific input that ran counter to his program. But by upgrading the status of specialists in the context of questioning the motives of officials who failed to heed scientific advice, he appeared to be reducing the gap in relative political status between intransigent officials and conformist specialists.

Finally, Brezhnev noticeably escalated threatening rhetoric against the cadres, either to push his program or to defend himself against accusations of lack of policy effectiveness, or both.

A solicitous, considerate attitude toward cadres has become firmly established in the party. An end has been put to the unwarranted shuffling and frequent replacement of personnel, a question that was raised back at the Twenty-Third Congress . . . However, this does not at all mean that, under the pretext of consolidating our pool of cadres, those who, as they say, do not pull their own weight, do not fulfill their duties, can remain in their leading posts . . .
We cannot have Party leaders who have lost the ability to evaluate their own activity critically, who have lost touch with the masses, who engender flatterers and toadies, who have lost the trust of the Communists. I think that the congress will support this statement of the question.

This was not yet a call for a purge, but it was a step closer to such a call than any of Brezhnev's earlier rhetoric. It lacked the balance and spirit of conciliation toward the cadres of Brezhnev's remarks at the Twenty-Fourth Party Congress. Moreover, it was accompanied at the Twenty-Fifth Party Congress by a remarkable escalation of the adulation heaped upon Brezhnev by the speakers.[6] The message being conveyed, on this as on other issues, was "Follow me! There is no other way! The alternatives could be much worse!"

In sum, during 1973–6 Brezhnev retreated to a conservative program at home and an innovative program abroad. He would maintain a high rate of growth of defence expenditures, and a highly centralized administrative system. He would search for arms-control agree-

[6] For a comparison of this adulation to that accorded Khrushchev, see Hough, "The Brezhnev era: the man and the system"; for an analysis of variations among speakers in the amount and type of praise extended to Brezhnev at the Twenty-Fifth Party Congress, see George Breslauer, "The Twenty-Fifth Party Congress: domestic issues," in Alexander Dallin (ed.), *The Twenty-Fifth Congress of the CPSU* (Stanford, Calif.: Hoover Institution Press, 1977).

ments that promised to contain the rate of growth of the defense budget. And he would seek foreign economic ties that would, among other things, alleviate the plight of the Soviet consumer and improve the quality of central planning.

Alexei Kosygin: "There Must Be a Better Way!"

Premier Kosygin had largely acquiesced in Brezhnev's definition of the situation in 1971. In 1976 this was no longer the case. With respect to Brezhnev's efforts to parry responsibility for the situation in light industry, and with respect to questions of resource allocation, incentive policy, and administrative reform, Kosygin had very different things to say.[7]

For one thing, Kosygin tried to counter Brezhnev's efforts to shift responsibility for difficulties, emphasizing the seriousness of the agricultural situation, the nonobjective causes of that situation, and its impact on consumer-goods production. Thus, Kosygin was far more explicit than Brezhnev in enumerating the shortfalls in agricultural production. And whereas Brezhnev had devoted an entire paragraph to the decisive role of the weather in explaining agricultural difficulties, Kosygin followed his enumeration of problems in that sector with: "Of course, unfavorable weather conditions also had an effect. But everything cannot be attributed solely to the weather." In like manner, Kosygin contradicted Brezhnev in his explanation of difficulties in Group B industries. In Kosygin's speech we find no attempt to blame the ministers charged with directing Group B industries. Instead we find the Soviet Premier arguing that current agricultural problems "could not but reflect on the rates of growth of the food and light industries."

Moreover, in defining the investment priorities of the regime, Kosygin did not echo Brezhnev's conception of the main task, and never referred to heavy industry as the "foundation of the economy." Instead, Kosygin underscored the formulation that had been written into the "Basic Guidelines" for the Five-Year Plan:

> The principal task of the Five-Year Plan is the consistent implementation of the Communist Party's course aimed at an upswing in the people's material and cultural living standard on the basis of the dynamic and proportional development of social production and an increase in its efficiency, the acceleration of scientific and technical progress, the growth of labor productivity and every possible

[7] *Pravda*, 2 March 1976 (*CDSP*, vol. 28, no. 10).

improvement in the quality of work in all units of the national economy.[8] (Italics in original)

Nor, for that matter, did Kosygin endorse Brezhnev's assertion that agriculture is a "task of all the people" (though he did support a "continuation of the line in favor of real redistribution of accumulated resources to the advantage of agriculture.")

Finally, Kosygin apparently went out of his way to emphasize the importance he attached to consumer-goods production. Whereas Brezhnev had claimed that it was agriculture that required assistance from all branches of the economy, Kosygin argued that "there is practically not a single branch of the national economy that does not take part in producing *consumer goods*" (italics added). Whereas Brezhnev's only revelation about the December 1975 Plenum (the major address of which had not been published) was that it stressed the importance of using "material and financial resources . . . more rationally and solicitously," Kosygin's sole revelation was that "Leonid Ilyich Brezhnev noted at the December plenary session [that] the priority growth of heavy industry does not mean any relaxation of attention to the all-round expansion of consumer-goods production." Whereas Brezhnev had used his discussion of foreign economic relations to point out the importance of importing consumer goods, Kosygin's discussion of that subject made but a passing and vague reference to the use of importation to "meet the interests of the fuller satisfaction of Soviet people's requirements for various goods."

For the Soviet Premier would appear to have preferred the augmentation of consumer-goods availability through domestic sources of production. This conclusion is also suggested by Kosygin's much greater emphasis on the urgency of the consumer-goods situation. Brezhnev had made but one reference to the mass mood, and only in the context of shifting blame to the shoulders of leaders of Group B industries. Kosygin invoked the spectre of mass expectations in more generalized and far-reaching terms:

. . . the demands on our industry to produce not merely more goods for the people but high-quality goods that will fully satisfy growing consumer demand are becoming more and more urgent. Persistent demands with respect to the quality, convenience and novelty of articles are being made not by some restricted circle of consumers but by virtually the entire urban and rural population.

[8] In fairness, we should note that Brezhnev included a paragraph in his speech in which he communicated these same ideas, but without boldface and without dubbing them "the main task of the five-year plan." Thus, in contrast to the Twenty-Fourth Party Congress, where Brezhnev and Kosygin used identical phraseology and emphasis in noting the "main task," the two Soviet leaders now diverged in their formulations.

With respect to the production associations, Kosygin's comments indicated endorsement of the pace of reform to that point. And well it might, for his earlier appeals for a "go-slow" approach had apparently carried the day. But in addition to this note of satisfaction, we now find a reversal of roles between Brezhnev and Kosygin. At the Twenty-Fourth Party Congress, Brezhnev had coopted the issue of production associations, while Kosygin, recognizing their long-term potential for movement toward measured decentralization, nonetheless urged a cautious approach to their conception and establishment. At the Twenty-Fifth Party Congress, Brezhnev redefined the associations as just another measure of deconcentration, while Kosygin began to laud them and to push for defining them as a first step toward decentralization. Announcing that the establishment of associations would be completed by 1980, Kosygin proclaimed them to be "a qualitatively new phenomenon in the management of industrial production . . . in keeping with the special features of the present stage of the development of the economy." This much said, Kosygin then resurrected the terminology of the 1965 reforms—terminology he had conspicuously avoided in his speech at the Twenty-Fourth Party Congress. He discoursed on the need for "signed contracts," "direct long-term ties" among enterprises and associations, and he called for the broader extension of "long-term credits."

Analogous differences between the two Soviet leaders emerged in their conception of the requisites for project and regional planning. Brezhnev had spoken of centralized programs; Kosygin proposed that "an active role should be played by the local Soviet organs and the Councils of Ministers of the Union Republics."[9]

With respect to the social costs of administrative reform, Kosygin also appears to have embraced causes abandoned by the General Secretary. Both Brezhnev and Kosygin called for a system of indicators that would relate intermediate efforts on the part of workers and managers to the "final results" of production. But Brezhnev's comments along this line spoke primarily of relating *indicators* to final results, whereas Kosygin spoke more fully of relating *incentives* to final results. Moreover, while Kosygin did not mention the Shchekino experiment by name, he did endorse reforms that would fire redundant labor. Kosygin's position on material differentiation and job insecurity as spurs to efficiency is summed up in the following excerpt from his speech:

---

[9] The difference between these formulations has been pointed out in Violet Conolly, "The territorial-production complex in Siberia and the Far East," *Radio Liberty Research Bulletin*, RL 339/76 (New York: Radio Liberty, 6 July 1976).

Progressive forms of material incentives, particularly pay for end-products or finished facilities, result-oriented systems and incentives for increasing the output of high-quality products with a smaller number of employees, will be employed more widely . . .

[We must] intensify the incentive role of wages, salaries, and collective farmers' pay, making them more dependent on the end-results of production and its increased efficiency.

This was precisely the terminology Nikita Khrushchev had used in advocating the link system in agriculture during 1963–4.[10]

These differences do not necessarily imply that Kosygin was personally challenging Brezhnev's leadership. All that we know about Kosygin's personality, ambitions, and health at the time suggest that he was not of a mind to lead a cabal to force Brezhnev from office. What these differences do suggest, however, is that, when Brezhnev's conservative program began to falter, a climate of opinion became more salient within segments of the political elite that questioned Brezhnev's effectiveness as a problem-solver. That climate of opinion found expression at the very top in the person of Alexei Kosygin. It also had an impact on Brezhnev's behavior, for the General Secretary apparently felt the need to parry responsibility for failure. His authority, after all, was under challenge, and he did not have very many concrete successes to point to.

[10] See above, Chapter 6, notes 69–74.

14 Shedding the Skeptics, 1976–81

Like Khrushchev before him, Brezhnev had faced multiple frustrations. First, his comprehensive program proved unworkable, and he responded with a new, more conservative program linked closely to détente. Then events of 1975 undermined his new program, and before he could reassess his priorities, the Twenty-Fifth Party Congress was upon him, with clear signs of skepticism about Brezhnev's problem-solving abilities. Brezhnev parried those challenges at the Party Congress, but the observer concerned to predict how Brezhnev would recoup lost authority, and buttress his power, might have expected some new twists in the years following the Party Congress.

The observer would have been proven right. In 1976–8 Brezhnev sought to buttress his authority in three ways: (1) by seizing the initiative and adding new features to his policy program—typically, features geared toward securing a quick improvement in consumer satisfaction; (2) by preempting, coopting, and redefining issues previously associated with Alexei Kosygin, shaping those issues in ways that would reinforce his image as a leader capable of generating a spirit of national élan; and (3) by altering his strategy as politician to expand the public dimension, sharply escalate threats against ministerial officials, and thereby keep potential rivals off balance. In addition, Brezhnev took unprecedented steps to consolidate his formal power. In all, Brezhnev's strategy may have worked. For by the time of the Twenty-Sixth Party Congress, Brezhnev's authority was no longer under public challenge by the Prime Minister. On the other hand, this circumstance may not have resulted from Brezhnev's revised authority-building strategy so much as from an accidental event: months before the Party Congress, Alexei Kosygin had died, and been replaced by a Brezhnev loyalist: Nikolai Tikhonov.

Power Consolidation

In Spring 1977, much to the surprise of foreign observers, Politburo-member N. Podgorny was purged from the leadership, and Brezhnev took over Podgorny's position as Chairman of the Presidium of the Supreme Soviet. This was the first time in the Brezhnev era that a member of the inner core of the collective leadership (Brezhnev,

Kosygin, Suslov, Kirilenko, and Podgorny) had been ousted. It was also the first time in the Brezhnev era that the Party leader combined in his person two of the top positions in the leadership. Moreover, Brezhnev installed V. Kuznetsov as First Deputy Chairman of the Presidium of the Supreme Soviet and, for the first time, accorded Politburo status to the occupant of that post. All of which came on top of Brezhnev's being made a "Marshal of the Soviet Union," (in 1976) a military rank that fitted with his earlier-announced role as Chairman of the Defense Council. Indeed, Brezhnev's accretion of power was so great, and so sudden, that the General Secretary felt constrained to assure Central Committee members that he would not abuse his power.[1]

Brezhnev's next major blow on behalf of power consolidation came in November 1978. At that time, K. Mazurov, one of the most likely pretenders to Brezhnev's position, was purged from the leadership. K. Chernenko, an old crony of Brezhnev, was given full Politburo membership, while N. Tikhonov, another Brezhnev associate, was made a candidate member. These, along with other personnel changes at the Plenum, led one Western observer to describe this (somewhat exaggeratedly, perhaps) as, for Brezhnev, "a substantial victory, perhaps the most impressive in his political career."[2]

In 1980 Brezhnev enjoyed still another sharp accretion of formal power, due to the resignation and death of Kosygin. His replacement by N. Tikhonov assured Brezhnev of near-total consensus of perspectives within the inner core of the leadership.

Brezhnev as Problem-Solver: Some New Wrinkles

Just as Brezhnev responded to the political challenges of 1976 by seizing the initiative through power consolidation, so he reacted to the policy frustrations of 1975 by seizing the initiative with new policy proposals. In October 1976, at the annual Central Committee Plenum, he launched a campaign for greater assistance to the private sector in Soviet agriculture.[3] He followed this up with still stronger endorsement of that campaign in a speech to the trade union congress in March 1977.[4]

In December 1977 Brezhnev sponsored another significant change,

---

[1] *Pravda*, 5 June 1977.
[2] R. Judson Mitchell, "The Soviet succession: who, and what, will follow Brezhnev?" *Orbis*, vol. 23, no. 1 (Spring 1979), p. 32.
[3] *Pravda*, 26 October 1976.
[4] ibid., 22 March 1977; and later: *Pravda*, 5 October 1977 (speech on new Constitution), 4 July 1978 (CC Plenum), and 28 November 1978 (CC Plenum).

this time in energy policy. Until then, Brezhnev's cause had been a generalized commitment to the development of Siberian resources. But energy priorities specifically had been Kosygin's bailiwick and, at the Twenty-Fifth Party Congress, the Soviet Prime Minister had indicated that coal extraction remained the centerpiece of a long-term, balanced policy.[5] December 1977 changed all that. At the Central Committee Plenum of that month, Brezhnev delivered a speech that voided certain features of the Tenth Five-Year Plan (1976–80), substituted oil for coal as the centerpiece of energy policy, reduced targets for steel production to pay for the shift, and shortened the time horizon on energy policy, calling for sharply increased extraction from Tiumen' oil fields.[6] The decision had been made "to settle for short-run solutions to long-term problems," concentrating scarce resources on short-term, high-priority, narrow goals.[7]

Indeed, when we examine Brezhnev's speeches from December 1977 onward, we find that such a strategy informs a new theme in his public statements. The Party leader now advocates concentrating resources on overcoming specific, vital bottlenecks within the budgetary sectors on which he places priority: oil extraction; agricultural machine-building; construction of storage facilities for grain; feed-grain processing; and transportation.[8] Transportation itself was also a new theme, apparently spurred by widespread bottlenecks, and by the great importance of reliable transport for Brezhnev's energy and agricultural programs. And to promote the cause of unbalanced concentration of resources on priorities, Brezhnev announced the creation of several new commissions within the centralized state bureaucracy, charged with coordinating inter-branch projects of the sort he was advocating.[9]

Thus, all of these changes in Brezhnev's program—a campaign to improve performance of the private sector in agriculture, rapid oil extraction, and priority concentration of resources on bottlenecks—were consistent with a determination on the part of the General

[5] Thane Gustafson, "Soviet energy policy: from big coal to big gas," in Seweryn Bialer and Thane Gustafson (eds), *Russia at the Crossroads* (London: Allen & Unwin, 1982).

[6] Leonid Brezhnev, *Ob osnovnykh voprosakh ekonomicheskoi politiki KPSS na sovremennom etape: rechi i doklady*, 2nd expanded edn (Moscow: Politizdat, 1979), Vol. 2, pp. 445–57.

[7] F. Douglas Whitehouse and Ray Converse, "Soviet industry: recent performance and future prospects," in US Congress, Joint Economic Committee, *Soviet Economy in a Time of Change*, 2 vols (Washington, DC: US Government Printing Office, 1979), Vol. 2, p. 407.

[8] Brezhnev, *Ob osnovnykh voprosakh* (1979 edn), Vol. 2, pp. 449–52; *Pravda*, 31 March 1978, 2 April 1978, and 26 April 1978; *Leninskim kursom VII*, pp. 530ff. (November 1978 Plenum); *Pravda*, 3 March 1979, and 28 November 1979.

[9] Brezhnev, *Ob osnovnykh voprosakh* (1979 edn), Vol. 2, p. 452.

Secretary to secure a quick improvement in economic performance that would bolster his authority. They were also consistent with efforts to keep potential critics off balance by himself remaining on the offensive.

Such an interpretation seems also to be supported by Brezhnev's statements about consumer goods and about proposals for decentralization of the economy. In contrast to his speech at the Twenty-Fifth Party Congress, from December 1977 onward, Brezhnev suddenly reintroduced some "reformist" themes into his statements. Thus, at the December 1977 Plenum, he endorsed broader introduction of the Zlobin contract-brigade method, the Shchekino experiment, and new forms of agricultural management—themes he reiterated at the April 1978 Congress of the Young Communist League.[10] At the November 1978 Plenum, he renewed calls of 1971 for greater attention to "industrial consumer goods," a theme he developed further at the October 1980 Plenum, where he called upon officials in the military–industrial complex to use excess capacity toward these ends.[11]

There are several ways to interpret these remarks. One interpretation would view them simply as eyewash, a purely symbolic nod in the reformist direction, with absolutely no policy consequences. The trouble with this interpretation is that it cannot explain why Brezhnev endorses these experiments at some times, but not at others. Moreover, it ignores the fact that public statements by the General Secretary willy-nilly add legitimacy to the efforts of those officials and specialists throughout the system who are struggling on behalf of such experiments.

A second interpretation would be that Brezhnev's endorsement of these themes was meant primarily to serve political purposes. Given the limits of the endorsements (they contained nothing of the assertive rhetoric associated with them in 1971), they could have been intended primarily to neutralize potential criticism by preempting the issue of reformism, contributing to Brezhnev's image as a politician who was both taking the lead and recognizing "reality." In this sense, they would have been analogous to Khrushchev's endorsement of industrial reform during 1962–4: an effort to keep up with an evolving climate of opinion to the effect that experimentation with more far-reaching policy changes was simply the obvious and rational thing to do.

A third interpretation would view Brezhnev's remarks in the context of his needs as a problem-solver. This interpretation would posit that Brezhnev struck a posture of highly selective reformism in order to further policies that would complement his search for a quick win. Thus, whatever production of consumer durables could be squeezed

---

[10] ibid., p. 455; *Pravda*, 26 April 1978.
[11] *Leninskim kursom VII*, p. 534; *Pravda*, 22 October 1980.

from above-plan fulfillment in the military–industrial complex would ostensibly contribute to the goal of improving consumer satisfaction. Similarly, in encouraging limited forms of industrial and agricultural decentralization experiments, after a poor agricultural harvest (in contrast to 1973), Brezhnev could have been communicating the following message: "We have to concentrate resources on priority tasks. This means that some sectors or regions will be deprived of needed supplies. Those who are so deprived will have to make much more efficient use of available resources. One way to do that is to introduce progressive experiments in those regions or sectors—but with the understanding that they will not be allowed to spread to the system as a whole."

Indeed, there is support for this interpretation in the fact that, during April through July 1978, Brezhnev introduced still another theme into his speeches: a stress on regional self-reliance to reduce transportation costs and to improve local agricultural performance "on the cheap."[12]

A combination of these last two interpretations would appear to be the most plausible explanation for Brezhnev's change in behavior during these years. Highly selective and limited reformism would complement Brezhnev's centralist priorities, hopefully bolster his image as a problem-solver, and contribute to his image as a politician in step with the times. This interpretation would also be consistent with my contention that, during these years, Brezhnev experienced an authority crisis, and responded to it by taking to the offensive and seeking to keep potential critics off balance. An examination of his efforts to redefine his public posture as politician lends further support to this view.

Brezhnev as Politician

Just as new programmatic themes entered Brezhnev's speeches during 1976–9, so new political themes entered as well. Brezhnev sharply escalated his criticism of officials in the ministries and in the State Planning Committee, and, equally important, he did so in public or publicized arenas. Thus, at the December 1977 Plenum, Brezhnev criticized Gosplan and the ministries for conservatism, inertia, and performance shortfalls.[13] He sharply expanded the criticism at the July 1978 Plenum on agriculture and the November 1978 Plenum, where he criticized state officials for opposition to his energy and

---

[12] *Pravda*, 3 April 1978, 7 April 1978, 4 July 1978, and 28 November 1979.
[13] Brezhnev, *Ob osnovnykh voprosakh* (1979 edn), Vol. 2, p. 447.

agriculture programs.[14] The trend continued. Castigating ministers by name, and naming lots of names, Brezhnev used the November 1979 and October 1980 plenary sessions as forums from which to deliver "bombshell" speeches, enumerating shortfalls in all sectors, and blasting the individuals ostensibly responsible.[15] Equally important, in a break with previous policy, the speeches of November 1978, November 1979, and October 1980 were immediately published in daily newspapers. Nothing quite so frank and threatening had been published in the name of the General Secretary since the Khrushchev years. The similarities lay in the specification of guilt, the demand for replacing the guilty, and the publicity given the charges. The differences were that Brezhnev made no accusations of "anti-state" behavior, and that he leveled charges only against officials of the state bureaucracy, not against party officials.

Nor was this all. Another Khrushchevian tactic also received more prominent attention in Brezhnev's speeches at this time: encouragement of the masses to criticize their hierarchical superiors within the state bureaucracy:

> . . . it is necessary to continue, and to impart still more vigor to, the resolute, uncompromising struggle against instances of lawbreaking, suppression of criticism, red tape, formalism, and bureaucracy. More publicity. More attention to people's needs and opinions. More direct, concerned contacts with the masses. That's how the party poses the question.[16]

This new theme may have been mere eyewash: manipulation of the masses at a time of economic hardship. Alternatively, it may have been motivated by a desire to turn mass disaffection against local cadres, build up dossiers critical of those cadres, and thereby increase the political leverage of the central party secretariat with the continuing threat of purge. Genuine mass criticism of state bureaucrats would serve that end.

Tentative support for this second interpretation can be found in provisions of the new Soviet constitution, which unexpectedly was finalized in 1977, precisely when Brezhnev was consolidating his

[14] *Pravda*, 4 July 1978, and 28 November 1978.
[15] ibid., 28 November 1979, and 22 October 1980. The concept of a "bombshell" speech was used by a Soviet source to characterize Brezhnev's address to the November 1978 Plenum (reported in Jerry Hough, *Soviet Leadership in Transition* [Washington, DC: Brookings Institution, 1980], pp. 11–12.
[16] *Pravda*, 3 March 1979 (election speech). See also: ibid., 22 March 1977 (to the trade unions), 5 October 1977 (Supreme Soviet address on the new constitution), and 23 September 1978 (in Baku).

power and redefining his authority-building strategy.[17] Article 58 gave citizens the right to file complaints against officials, and to seek recourse in a court of law against those officials, up to and including the "right to compensation for damages." Article 49 prohibited persecution for criticism, a provision that was upgraded in the final, ratified constitution through inclusion of a second sentence: "Persons who persecute others for criticism will be called to account."[18]

It is possible that these articles reflected existing social and political forces involved in drawing up the constitution, and that they were not a product of intervention by the staff of the General Secretary to further his authority-building strategy. That is, the articles may simply be an expression of a secular trend toward providing a less repressive and arbitrary environment for the politically conformist. On the other hand, a power-political interpretation would be supported by an examination of published commentary on the proposed constitution during 1971–6. It is curious to note that one feature of Khrushchevian discussions of the proposed constitution that did not reappear in official statements under Brezhnev was the need for a mechanism to formally guarantee citizens extra-bureaucratic recourse against arbitrary official behavior.[19] Yet just such a provision suddenly appeared in the constitution, was upgraded still further in the final draft, and appeared co-terminously with a major power expansion on the part of Brezhnev.

Of course, the contrast with Khrushchev's populism is still substantial. Khrushchev established a Party–State Control Commission, encouraged an adversarial definition of the relationship between officials and the masses, and campaigned personally to foster status equalization in the public political arena. The measures taken under Brezhnev were much less far-reaching. But they were real nonetheless, and their inclusion in the constitution at a time when Brezhnev was further consolidating his power suggests a possible interconnection between the authority-building needs of the General Secretary and encouragement of the masses to criticize their hierarchical superiors.

---

[17] The draft of the new constitution appeared in *Pravda*, 4 June 1977; the finalized version was published in ibid., 7 November 1977; see also Robert Sharlet, *The New Soviet Constitution of 1977: Analysis and Text* (Brunswick, Ohio: King's Court Communications, 1978).

[18] *Pravda*, 7 November 1977, as noted in Sharlet, *The New Soviet Constitution*, p. 53.

[19] See Brezhnev's remarks on the constitution in *Pravda*, 22 December 1972, and in Gruliow, *Current Soviet Policies VII*, p. 31. Also see the authoritative article by V. Kotok and N. Farberov, "Konstitutsiia SSSR–razvivaiushchiisia osnovnoi zakon obshchestva i gosudarstva", *Sovetskoe gosudarstvo i pravo* (June 1973), pp. 3–12. Then compare their formulations with those of Khrushchev in *Pravda*, 26 April 1962.

Complementing the trend toward encouraging the masses to criticize was Brezhnev's oblique turn back toward warning the political elite about the consequences of ignoring the mood of the consumer. This was implicit in his candid and public delineation of economic bottlenecks, as when he warned the October 1980 Central Committee Plenum that "a food program must be drawn up" because "we still encounter difficulties in supplying the cities and industrial centers with such foodstuffs as meat and milk."[20]

Thus, with respect to both policy and politics, Brezhnev felt the need after 1976 to seize the initiative in order to build his authority, or prevent it from further eroding, as an adjunct to his power consolidation. By the time of the Twenty-Sixth Party Congress (February/March 1981), we might have had the opportunity to see whether Brezhnev's images as effective problem-solver and indispensable politician had been restored, or whether Kosygin and Brezhnev would once again be parrying responsibility for failure. For by then, Soviet agriculture was in a sorry state, having suffered two harvest failures in a row, and US–Soviet détente was dead. The cornerstones of Brezhnev's program were crumbling once again. Hence, we might have expected to find indications of defensiveness in his address to the congress. But we do not, for Kosygin's death, and replacement by a "Brezhnev man," apparently decisively changed the political landscape. Whatever skepticism or hostility toward Brezhnev's program existed within the political elite, it no longer found expression in the advocacy of a member of the inner core of the leadership. As a result, we find that Brezhnev stuck with his new program, and no longer appeared to be on the defensive about it.

The Twenty-Sixth Party Congress, 1981

Brezhnev's address to the Party Congress confirmed his support for the new program forged since 1976.[21]

Agriculture remained a priority sector. After the harvest failures of 1979 and 1980, Brezhnev was candid about the difficulties, but reiterated that further elaboration of his approach to the problem—not an alternative approach—was required. He called for the development of a "special food program," for a comprehensive rural development program, and for speedier development of the Non-Black-Earth Zone. He also made a big pitch for easing restraints on the private sector as a contribution to improving the food-supply problem.

But while agriculture remained a priority, it was, as far as results

[20] *Pravda*, 22 October 1980.
[21] ibid., 24 February 1981.

were concerned, nothing to brag about. Brezhnev instead chose to identify himself most closely with energy policy, and to treat it as the heroic campaign of the decade. Energy simply dominated the speech. In his discussion of economic progress, territorial production complexes for oil, gas, and coal received first attention. In discussing the importance of heavy-industrial development, energy provided the first examples. When outlining bottlenecks to be overcome, he cited heavy industry, "especially, and in the first place, the fuel and energy branches," as well as the need for a rise in expenditures in connection with the development of the east and north. In his section on the "more efficient use of production potential," much of the discussion dealt with the need to reduce wastage of energy resources, adding that "successes in the entire national economy will greatly depend on raising the efficiency of the extraction industry." When he discussed concrete administrative changes in the national economy, his examples of models to be followed were the inter-branch departments and commissions created to coordinate development of the West Siberian oil and gas complex. The high priority given to energy development in Brezhnev's speech is summed up in the following quotation from that address:

> I consider it necessary to single out the rapid increase in extraction of Siberian gas as a task of primary economic and political importance. The deposits of the West Siberian region are unique. The largest of them—Urengoi—has such a gigantic amount that it could, for many years, meet the internal needs of the country as well as export needs—including exports to capitalist countries.
>
> I would like only to emphasize that the task of improving the structure of the fuel and power balance is becoming more and more pressing.
>
> The extraction of gas and oil in West Siberia, and their transport to the European section of the country, will have to be considered the most important links in the energy program of both the Eleventh and even the Twelfth Five-Year Plans. Such is the aim of the Party's Central Committee, and, I hope, it will be supported by the congress.

On top of these commitments, Brezhnev reaffirmed the priority development of heavy industry as the main task of the Eleventh Five-Year Plan. When coupled with a slowdown in the rate of increase in capital available for investment, and assuming that Brezhnev is not pushing behind the scenes for defense budget cuts, it would be a great surprise to find Brezhnev realistically advocating much expanded investment in light industry and consumer services.

Indeed, Brezhnev's statements about the consumer sector (over and above agriculture or the food program) echoed his statements of 1977–80, which were aimed at eking out marginal gains, keeping the issue on the policy agenda, and bolstering his image, rather than at assigning a very high priority to the sector. Thus, Brezhnev announced that the rate of growth of Group B industries would exceed that of Group A in the Eleventh Five-Year Plan. He called on heavy-industrial enterprises to produce more industrial consumer goods. And he urged the new Ministry of the Chemicals Industry to "make real strides in the production of synthetics" for use in consumer soft goods. But otherwise, this commitment had all the signs of a very low priority. First, Brezhnev's advocacy of "industrial consumer-goods" production was low-key and brief. It did not even resemble the campaign rhetoric of 1971; nor was it coupled with doctrinal innovations to reduce the political status of traditional heavy-industrial tasks. Second—and again in contrast to 1971—the discussion of these matters was very short, and came at the very end of the section of the speech on matters of public welfare. Third, while Brezhnev spoke of the need for new technologies and better supply for light-industrial enterprises, he reserved the language of insistence for aspects of the problem that do not require increased central funding: "It may be that in no other sphere of the national economy do local possibilities and local reserves play so great a role as in satisfying everyday consumer demand, and in serving the population." Having said this, his subsequent invocation of the threatening mass mood to warn the cadres against poor performance in this area came across as a re-affirmation of the importance of mobilizing local resources, rather than an indication of Brezhnev's commitment to increased central funding. In sum, Brezhnev's stated budgetary priorities of 1981 more closely resembled those of 1976 than those of 1971. And when the inevitable investment crunch arrives, we are not likely to find him defending the cause of light industry and consumer services.

As to foreign economic ties, Brezhnev tentatively abandoned (or substantially toned down) the language of 1976. In the 1981 speech, he decoupled key features of his domestic program from dependence on foreign imports. First, there was no longer a separate section on foreign economic ties. Second, discussion of the matter was moved back from the section on domestic policy to the section on foreign policy. Third, that discussion was both brief and entirely open-ended; he no longer specified the actual or potential benefits of such ties for domestic economic progress. Fourth, when discussing technological development, Brezhnev unexpectedly made a pitch for Soviet industry to concentrate more on producing its own advanced technology, and less on purchasing technology abroad.

On the other hand, Brezhnev appears to be leaving his options open on this issue, a position that is consistent with his collaborative offerings in the foreign-policy section of his address. I detect four indicators that Brezhnev was leaving his options open. First, when specifying the causes of the breakdown of foreign economic ties, Brezhnev expectedly blamed the West, and alluded to Western policies that Washington had touted, but did not mention the USA by name. Second, Brezhnev was optimistic and forthcoming about the possibility of further developing economic intercourse with West Germany and France, though his failure to include this in the discussion of foreign economic ties *per se* may imply that he considered US–Soviet ties to be central. Third, in his discussion of the food problem, Brezhnev, twice in the course of eight column lines, cited trade as a component of the program for alleviating the problem (but he did not link such trade to détente *per se*). Fourth, Brezhnev justified Siberian development in part by noting that it would "for many years" provide natural gas for export to capitalist countries.

On matters of public administration, Brezhnev's speech reaffirmed the centralist bias of 1976. He suggested a regrouping of scientific forces to enhance technological innovation in machine-building. He acknowledged that variants on the structure of enterprises and associations are needed, but seemed to refer the whole issue back to committee: "Great and varied experience has been accumulated. And it is precisely this experience that tells us that the search must be continued (*poiski nado prodolzhat'*). Brezhnev's continued preference was rather for structural alterations within central planning organs to improve inter-branch project planning. As for the rest of the economy, Brezhnev defined the main tasks in public administration primarily as mobilizational tasks. Thus, he devoted an entire subsection to the need for thrift, which he called the "core" (*sterzhen'*) of the party's economic policy. In addition, he defined the main cause of shortcomings in public administration as psychological inertia. In like manner, he proclaimed increased "demandingness" to be the "only path" toward improved administrative efficiency. Finally, he defined "discipline" and "personal responsibility" as the primary current needs, and greatly downplayed the need for more balanced and realistic plans relative to the need for greater managerial effort.

Brezhnev's failure at the Party Congress to endorse experiments with selective decentralization may be suggestive. His earlier endorsement of those experiments came at times when he was either seeking to synthesize reformist and conservative tendencies (1971), or was on the defensive about his policy effectiveness and seeking to maintain his image as capable problem-solver (1973, 1977–8). With Kosygin no longer in the leadership, he may have felt less political need to shore-up his image. Indeed, support for this interpretation can be found in the general tone of Brezhnev's speech. In 1976 we found evidence of defensiveness in the report of the General Secretary. In 1981 we do not. The language of insistence, accusation, and urgency are strikingly diminished compared to the previous Party Congress. To be sure, that language is used at points to buttress the General Secretary's demands for energy development, thrift, local party attentiveness to mass consumer and welfare demands, and a reduction of mass and official corruption. But consider the other side of the ledger:

(1) Agriculture is not referred to as an "all-people's task," and there is no language in the agricultural section comparable to his 1976 insistence that his program "is correct . . . the party will, in the future as well, follow this line . . . there are no ready recipes" (1976).

(2) On light industry, Brezhnev does not lay blame for shortcomings on those "who plan and direct this sector of the economy" (1976).

(3) On administrative affairs, the language is equally timid: nothing about "unpostponable" reform needs; no particular need is defined as the "foundation of foundations of the science of administration"; the language of urgency is gone; and Brezhnev's optimistic closing speech to the congress[22] does not echo the warning of 1976 to "concentrate on the remaining shortcomings, on unsolved problems."

(4) On cadre policy, Brezhnev very much toned down threats against incompetent or dishonest officials (assuming that his greater candor about corruption was not meant to be taken as such a threat). He never even raised the issue of the balance between "respect for cadres" and "exactingness" toward them, much less elaborate on the need for placing greater weight on "exactingness."

What accounts for this decline in the language of insistence and accusation? It would be difficult to argue that Brezhnev's program is now more credible, for the harvest failures of 1979–80, and the demise of détente, were greater shocks to the viability of that program than had been the events of 1975. What has changed, however, is the representation in the Politburo of individuals with independent power bases and prestige who are inclined to propose alternative, more reformist policies than Brezhnev. For a close examination of the address delivered by N. Tikhonov suggests that he did not echo Kosygin's political and policy-oriented dissent.[23]

---

[22] ibid., 4 March 1981. Quotations from 1976 can be found in ibid., 25 February 1976, and 2 March 1976.
[23] ibid., 28 February 1981.

Tikhonov's Acquiescent Posture

On agricultural issues, Tikhonov's stated perspectives were almost identical to those of Brezhnev, and he made no effort to emphasize Brezhnev's personal responsibility for the situation. Kosygin's detailed enumeration of shortfalls, and his insistence that "not everything can be attributed to the weather," found no counterpart in Tikhonov's speech.

On heavy-industrial priority, Tikhonov echoed Brezhnev's definition of the main task of the Five-Year Plan (Kosygin had not), and endorsed Brezhnev's energy development priority: "The Eleventh Five-Year Plan period is the first stage of the implementation of the USSR's energy program, being worked out on the initiative of Leonid Ilyich Brezhnev."

On matters of light industry, on which Kosygin's dissent had been most broad-based, Tikhonov faithfully echoed Brezhnev. He praised the Eleventh Five-Year Plan for projecting higher rates of growth for Group B than Group A, but he, like Brezhnev, then went on to define the requisites of success largely in mobilizational terms. He said nothing about investments *per se*, demanded more "initiative and persistence" in using "all the existing possibilities and reserves," called for the fuller use of "local resources," and called expanded consumer-goods production "a matter of the honor and professional pride of all those who produce consumer goods." In contrast to Kosygin, he did not blame agricultural shortfalls for adversely affecting consumer-goods production.

On issues of public administration, Tikhonov's speech was also an echo of Brezhnev's. He cited subjective "forces of inertia and tradition" as "the main reason for the difficulties, shortcomings, and bottlenecks in the national economy." He called for enlarging and improving the role of central planning organs in setting economic priorities and coordinating interdependencies. In sharp contrast to Kosygin, he did not use any of the decentralist terminology of the 1965 reforms. He spoke of the transition to production associations (as had Brezhnev), but did not speak in the laudatory terms that Kosygin had chosen ("a qualitatively new stage . . ."). He did make one statement with potentially reformist implications. After calling for a struggle to overcome bureaucratic obstacles to the proper functioning of production associations, Tikhonov raised the question: "Are the rights and duties of associations and their constituent units distributed in a sufficiently well-founded way?" If this was meant to be a nod in the reformist direction, it was tepid fare. Not buttressed by the terminology of 1965, nor by any mention of "enterprise rights," and stated as a question rather than an imperative, it does not come across as any less conservative than Brezhnev's analogous statement about the need for further "searches." In other words, it does not indicate a will to incur the political costs of taking action.

On foreign economic ties, there was greater divergence between Brezhnev and Tikhonov than on other issues—though the difference may not be very significant. As we saw, Brezhnev vastly toned down his association with the issue, though he kept open his options. Tikhonov (also in contrast to Kosygin) devoted a headlined section of his speech to the topic. Like Brezhnev, however (but unlike Kosygin), he twice mentioned foreign economic ties as a source of consumer goods. Unlike Brezhnev, he called on planning organs to "constantly work on raising the efficiency of foreign economic ties in the interests of economizing on labor and material resources, accelerating technological progress, and gaining time."

On the grand issues of Soviet policy, then, the gap between the General Secretary and the Chairman of the Council of Ministers, in evidence in 1976, is absent in 1981. Moreover, on issues of political authority, the dissension of 1976, in which both men were trying to parry responsibility for failure, is also gone. This last point can be further substantiated by one final indicator: the terms in which Kosygin and Tikhonov paid homage to Brezhnev. In his opening remarks in 1976, Kosygin had praised Brezhnev, but emphasized the position he occupied: [24]

> The Central Committee and Politburo, headed by the distinguished political figure of our time, the General Secretary of the CC KPSS, Leonid Ilyich Brezhnev . . .
> . . . the progressive tendencies of world development, profoundly laid out by the General Secretary of the CC KPSS Leonid Ilyich Brezhnev in the Accountability Report to the congress . . .

In contrast, Tikhonov's opening remarks gave billing as well to Brezhnev the man, omitting his last name and his title:

> With particular profundity, Leonid Ilyich characterized the multifaceted activity of the Central Committee, the titanic work of the party and people . . .
> In conceiving and realizing this course, the leading role belongs to Leonid Ilyich Brezhnev. The party and people see in Leonid Ilyich a wise and experienced leader . . .

In like manner, Kosygin's opening praise of Brezhnev's report lauded it as a "distinguished contribution to the theory and practice of communist construction," whereas Tikhonov called it "a distinguished creative contribution to the development and enrichment of Marxist–Leninist teaching."

[24] ibid., 2 March 1976.

But just as tactical differences were in evidence in Brezhnev's and Kosygin's largely agreeable speeches of 1971, so a few tactical differences mark the speeches of Brezhnev and Tikhonov. Those differences appear to transcend matters of political loyalty and philosophical agreement, reflecting Tikhonov's role as spokesman for the planners and ministerial bureaucrats, whose biases are generally in favor of balanced planning—a bias that often clashes with the penchant of Party leaders to bolster their authority by launching campaigns, shortening time horizons, and concentrating resources.

Thus, in Brezhnev's remarks on planning, the concepts of "balance" (*sbalansirovannost'*) and realism in planning received short shrift; they were merely dependent clauses and caveats in a hard-hitting critique of officials who seek lower plans. In contrast, Tikhonov devoted several paragraphs to the importance of balance in planning, introducing the discussion with the statement: "I would like to speak in particular about improving balance."

Analogous differences may be in evidence on the issue of energy policy. Brezhnev had invoked the language of insistence in support of his program for forced extraction of West Siberian natural gas, using terminology suggesting that the issue is controversial. Tikhonov's remarks on energy development, while formally endorsing Brezhnev's programs, do not give to the energy issue the extraordinary centerpiece quality it had in Brezhnev's speech. Then, too, it may be significant that Tikhonov sandwiched his main remarks on energy with introductory and concluding statements that emphasized balanced energy development: "Our duty, however large our supply of natural resources might be, is to search constantly for the most rational means of extracting them and the most economical means of using them . . . We must work more actively to find new and more efficient sources of energy and to use them more rationally" (contrast the spirit of these remarks with the first lines of the Brezhnev quote, p. 238, above). Finally, in his discussion of foreign economic ties, Tikhonov made no mention of Brezhnev's claim that the export of Siberian gas to capitalist countries was a component of regime plans or expectations, much less high hopes.

On balance, though, the elements of harmony far outweighed the elements of discord in the two main addresses at the Twenty-Sixth Party Congress. Through a combination of seizing the initiative, purging certain members of the leadership, and good luck, Brezhnev had succeeded in shedding the skeptics. His authority as problem-solver and politician may still have been in very serious question within the political establishment, but that skepticism no longer found expression at the very top of the political hierarchy when the delegates assembled for the first Party Congress of the 1980s.

15 How Strong the Leader?: Brezhnev's Power over Policy

Western analysts have engaged in much less discussion of the extent of Brezhnev's power than they had earlier of the extent of Khrushchev's power. Despite some differences among them, scholars tend to agree that the restraints of collective leadership have been stronger under Brezhnev than they were under Khrushchev. Khrushchev confronted the major interests within the Soviet political establishment, and temporarily got away with it. Brezhnev, in contrast, sought to strike deals that were innovative, but less threatening to entrenched interests. Moreover, the means he chose to get his way were also less extreme than those of Khrushchev.

Yet we remain in the dark about the precise extent of Brezhnev's potential power. The General Secretary's failure to confront the political establishment leaves us without a clear test of his power. What could he have got away with if he had tried? Was he not inclined to go far beyond the policies he settled for? Or was he hemmed in by political constraints? We cannot say with confidence.

Yet we do know what Brezhnev chose to fight for. This book has highlighted the programs he embraced over time, and those on which he staked his political authority. On the basis of kremlinological analysis, we have also found that these programs, while less alienating than Khrushchev's, were nonetheless controversial within the political establishment. The question then becomes: how much power over policy did Brezhnev enjoy?

A definitive answer remains beyond our reach, given the crucial unknowns. But it would be a missed opportunity to leave it at that. If we examine the correlation over time between Brezhnev's assertive policy advocacy and changes in policies adopted by the Politburo, we can advance our knowledge one step further. That is the purpose of this chapter. The conclusion we shall draw is that Brezhnev was far more than a broker among interests. It is difficult to identify many instances when Brezhnev was rebuffed or defeated on questions of priority and the direction of policy. Conflict on these matters was real and frequent, but Brezhnev almost always won.

Investment Priorities

The new majority consensus after Khrushchev was based on common lessons drawn from the Khrushchevian experience. That consensus rejected Khrushchev's search for panaceas to improve economic performance, and rejected as well his low-cost approach to raising consumer satisfaction. Within the context of this shift, political conflict during the stage of succession centered on the relative priority of agriculture versus light industry in the competition for funds, and on the obligations to be borne by the military–industrial complex for increasing the availability of consumer goods. Brezhnev and Kosygin split on these issues.

Policies enacted during 1964–8 reflected both the regime consensus and the vagaries of the power struggle between Brezhnev and Kosygin.[1] As had been the case after Stalin, policy zig-zags indicated that the power of the General Secretary to control the policy agenda was somewhat circumscribed, but grew as the succession struggle came to a head.

The Eighth Five-Year Plan (1966–70) was being hammered out as the succession struggle got under way. It called for huge investments in agriculture and defense, the very priorities that Brezhnev had embraced. But, in addition, investment in light industry, and in means of production for consumer-oriented enterprises, was raised significantly. These varied, expensive programs required cuts in other sectors, and herein lay the novel emphasis of the new regime. Khrushchev's successors felt the need to sacrifice long-term growth in heavy-industrial capacity to the short-term requirements of agriculture and light industry, in the hopes of increasing current consumption. Hence, the funds to pay for these programs were drawn largely from sources that would not threaten planned increases in short-term consumption: the chemicals industry; housing; East European, West European, and Japanese investments; and 11–12 percent rise in wholesale prices for industry; a switch from grants to loans in state allocations to many enterprises; expected gains from expanded growth and increased efficiency; and a planned reduction in the growth rate of heavy industry and transportation.

Benefits from the agricultural program were not long in coming. Although a poor harvest in 1965 led the regime to import some grain from abroad, the following year brought the largest harvest in Soviet history. Soon thereafter, and amidst signs of political conflict between

---

[1] On budgetary policy during the succession struggle after Khrushchev's dismissal, see: Hahn, *Politics of Soviet Agriculture*, pp. 165–206; Alexander Dallin and Thomas B. Larson (eds), *Soviet Politics since Khrushchev* (Englewood Cliffs, NJ: Prentice-Hall, 1968), pp. 62–6, 84–109, 112–14; Katz, *Politics of Economic Reform*, pp. 105–8, 121, 157–8, 179; Nove, *An Economic History*, pp. 369–70; Archie Brown and Michael Kaser (eds), *The Soviet Union since the Fall of Khrushchev* (New York: The Free Press, 1975), pp. 1–15; Bush, "Soviet capital investment since Khrushchev," pp. 91–6.

Brezhnev and Kosygin, investment priorities were changed to the disadvantage of agriculture. The September 1967 Plenum of the Central Committee adopted a revised national-economic plan for 1968–70. The new plan called for a sharp increase in investment in light industry, an equally sharp increase in pensions, minimum wages, and welfare benefits, and a further boost in funds for the defense budget. The Plenum was followed, in February 1968, by a supplementary one-year allocation of 1 billion rubles to light industry. All of which was slated to be paid for by further cuts in heavy-industrial growth and a 25 percent cut in agricultural investment.

The new program did not stick. As Brezhnev gained political strength so, too, did agricultural investments rise once again. Decrees of May and September 1968 called for sharply higher investment in fertilizer production, agricultural machine-building, and land improvement. The October 1968 Plenum of the Central Committee voted a further sharp increase in agricultural funding. Light industry and heavy industry were the losers.

During Brezhnev's stage of ascendancy, he threw his full political weight behind his expensive approach to solving the agricultural problem.[2] The July 1970 Plenum voted an additional 70 percent increase in funds for agriculture. In January 1971 the regime launched a major new program for the industrialization of animal husbandry. By a decree of April 1971, the targets and funds for these complexes were nearly doubled. And in April 1972 a four-year program was initiated to improve the quality of life in the countryside through expanded and upgraded educational, recreational, health, and analogous facilities.

But, in line with his proposing a compromise program, Brezhnev also advocated increasing investment in light industry, and measures to increase the availability of industrial consumer goods. These were reflected in policy. The managers of heavy-industrial enterprises were given both positive and negative incentives to comply with the demand for increased production of consumer durables in their plants. First, the planners included such extra obligations in the enterprise plan for total output, thus allowing the production of consumer goods to

[2] On investment priorities during Brezhnev's stage of ascendancy, see Hahn, *Politics of Soviet Agriculture*, pp. 189–253; Gregory Grossman, "From the Eighth to the Ninth Five-Year Plan," in Norton T. Dodge (ed.), *Analysis of the USSR's 24th Party Congress and 9th Five-Year Plan* (Mechanicsville, Md: Cremona Foundation, 1971); Donald Green, "Capital formation in the USSR: an econometric investigation of bureaucratic intervention in the process of capital construction," *Review of Economics and Statistics* (February 1978); US Congress, Joint Economic Committee, *Soviet Economic Prospects for the Seventies* (Washington, DC: US Government Printing Office, 1973), pp. 42–4, 71–86, 376–403, 642–50; US Central Intelligence Agency (CIA), *Estimated Soviet Defense Spending*, pp. 8–9.

count toward plan fulfillment. Second, the regime launched a media campaign to pressure officials in heavy industry to pledge increased production of consumer goods. Third, by a decree of October 1971, the regime prohibited officials in light and heavy industry alike from reducing or halting the production of consumer goods in high demand. Over and above these measures, the Ninth Five-Year Plan scheduled a dramatic increase in the production of passenger cars, and a 50 percent increase in investment in light industry.

What sectors were to pay for these consumer-oriented measures, agricultural development in particular? First, in 1970–72 there was apparently a reduction of the rate of growth of expenditures for strategic weapons systems (though not for other categories of the defense budget). Indeed, some analysts argue (though this is controversial) that the military received during these three years the lowest-ever share of the total budget. Second, the Ninth Five-Year Plan placed much less emphasis on Siberian development than had the Eighth Five-Year Plan, at least as far as domestic sources of investment capital were concerned. Third, projected growth figures for heavy industry were still more modest than in the previous Five-Year Plan, some major projects were cancelled in order to free up capital, and a campaign was launched in 1969 for priority completion of selected projects. Fourth, efforts to increase consumer satisfaction, and to increase productivity, were now increasingly linked to foreign trade. The period witnessed a sudden increase in imports of Western technology, food, and consumer soft goods.[3]

What does this tell us about Brezhnev's power over budgetary policy during his stage of ascendancy? With respect to the agricultural budget, this was surely a Brezhnev win, and a big one at that. Beyond that, things become much more ambiguous. The lull in testing new strategic weaponry was probably not a hard choice, as it fitted the rhythm of technological development at the time. But it was felicitous from the standpoint of Brezhnev's détente policy, which may well have been controversial. Hence, if we assume that Brezhnev pushed such a policy for foreign-policy reasons, we may count this as a Brezhnev "win," but a small one. The same might be said about foreign-trade policy, but for the fact that this was Kosygin's bailiwick. Hence, we

---

[3] There is some question about the extent to which the Ninth Five-Year Plan (1971–5) can, on balance, be called "consumer-oriented" because, in addition to the measures noted in this paragraph, investment to benefit the consumer was purchased at the expense of "below-average increases set for non-productive investment, the bulk of which is devoted to housing and to the construction of health, education, welfare and cultural facilities" (Keith Bush, "Resource allocation policy: capital investment," in US Congress, Joint Economic Committee, *Soviet Economic Prospects for the Seventies* [Washington, DC: US Government Printing Office, 1973], p. 44).

cannot demonstrate a Brezhnev win. Policy on industrial consumer goods was fully consistent with Brezhnev's policy advocacy at the Twenty-Fourth Party Congress but, again, this had been Kosygin's issue in 1966. We can assert that Brezhnev coopted the issue in 1971, trying to make it his own. But we cannot determine whether he did so in order to further bolster his image and out of personal choice, or because he perceived that he was not strong enough to prevent the issue from being placed on the policy agenda despite his opposition.

In general, there were considerably more "compromise" features to the comprehensive program advanced by Brezhnev in 1971 than there had been in Khrushchev's program of 1959. In my analysis of Brezhnev's policy advocacy and authority-building strategy, I concluded that the General Secretary had coopted policies previously associated with Kosygin, and had tried to take credit for his unique synthesis of conflicting priorities. By demonstrating that regime policy mirrored this synthesis, I can demonstrate that Brezhnev's words were not merely symbolic rhetoric. But I cannot demonstrate whether Brezhnev's inclusion of so many compromises was a sign of his strength or a sign of his weakness. If power over policy is defined as the ability both to enforce one's priorities and coopt the secondary issues, then Brezhnev appears to have projected considerable power over policy. But if the term is defined only as the ability to prevent having any compromises (either with one's rivals or with economic reality) included in one's program, then Brezhnev's behavior would be viewed as a sign of weakness. I prefer the first definition, for the second assumes a Brezhnev inclination to avoid all political and pragmatic compromises, and posits a higher level of polarization in the Soviet leadership than is consistent with the documented post-Khrushchev consensus. Brezhnev was surely not as powerful in 1971 as Khrushchev was in 1959. But his ability to enforce his priorities and coopt other issues suggests that he was more than just a broker; he was an initiator as well.

Once Brezhnev's program proved unworkable, however, he redefined his program, reducing his commitment to consumer soft goods and durables, but seeking to compensate with a sharp expansion of consumer-oriented foreign trade. He also called for a sharp increase in spending on growth-oriented and agricultural projects. His policy advocacy was reflected in policy.[4]

[4] Investment priorities during 1973–6 are based on: CIA, *Estimated Soviet Defense Spending*, pp. 7–8; Green, "Capital Formation in the USSR"; Grossman, "The Brezhnev era: an economy at middle age"; E. Stuart Kirby, "The Soviet Far East and Eastern Siberia," in *The Far East and Australasia, 1975–1976* (London: Europa Publications, 1975); US Congress, Joint Economic Committee, *Soviet Economy in a New Perspective*, pp. 67–80, 447–59, 575–99, 677–94.

The budgetary policies of 1973–5 abandoned several key features of the program of 1971. Whatever lull in defense spending had taken place during 1970–2 was no longer in evidence. Investments in the development of Siberia also increased sharply. In October 1972 24 billion rubles worth of funds were shifted from other ministries to agriculture to deal with the grain crisis. In April 1974 some 35 billion rubles were earmarked for land reclamation and social development in the Non-Black-Earth Zone. To help pay for these programs, heavy-industrial growth rates were slowed further, investment in light industry was reduced, East European governments were pressed for investment capital, and campaigns were launched (in 1973) to concentrate resources on the completion of unfinished, priority projects. In addition, the Soviet government sharply increased imports of foreign technology, consumer goods, feed-grains, and food, and searched vigorously for foreign credits to help finance large-scale projects. In 1975 the regime signed a long-term agreement with the USA to purchase a minimum annual sum of grain, regardless of short-term need. Also in 1975, the regime initiated large-scale construction work on new sections of the Baikal–Amur railway. Finally, after the harvest failure of 1975, the Soviet leadership decided to maintain the growth rate of defense spending, despite the slowdown in the rate of growth of GNP.

As we saw in Chapter 13, these were also roughly the priorities infused in the Tenth Five-Year Plan for 1976–80. Growth targets for light industry were lowered substantially. The bulk of investments went to defense, Siberian development, agriculture, the food industry, pollution control, nuclear power, and automobiles for export. While some of these decisions may have been grudging concessions to economic or international realities, the polemics between Brezhnev and Kosygin at the Twenty-Fifth Party Congress suggest that there was more than one view in the leadership about what kinds of concessions reality demanded. Our analysis of Brezhnev's policy advocacy during 1972–6 suggests that, when the crunch came, he was able to exercise a great deal of power over policy. This does not mean that he was shoving his program down the throats of the political elite. For, as we have seen, the strategy Brezhnev chose in reaction to frustration was, in contrast to Khrushchev, to accommodate to the most powerful institutional interests in the system. Khrushchev's ability to confront many of those interests, and to get his preferred policies adopted during 1961–3, was a real testimony to his ability to exercise power over policy. Brezhnev needed only to deny the weaker, reformist elements in the Establishment. Hence, we cannot conclude that Brezhnev's extent of power over policy was fully tested during this period. Nor can we conclude that it was the equal of Khrushchev's. But we can be impressed by the fact that the policies behind which

Brezhnev threw his weight during 1972–6 were the policies actually adopted.

As we noted in Chapter 14, however, Brezhnev apparently sponsored a number of policy changes during 1976–80 that were more far-reaching, and more upsetting of plan balance, than his earlier programs.[5] To be sure, he remained committed to the rough priorities of the Tenth Five-Year Plan, but he also called for loosening restraints on the private sector in agriculture, major changes in energy policy, and a pipeline construction program for 1981–5 that could upset the entire balance of the Eleventh Five-Year Plan. Assuming that these measures are controversial, Brezhnev probably had to pull rank to force them through. But he apparently succeeded, partly because he was able to seize the initiative at a time of economic and international uncertainty, partly because his coalition in the Politburo kept expanding as potential skeptics were dropped from the leadership or died. Khrushchev had also succeeded in pushing through a destabilizing chemicals program shortly before his ouster. This is testimony to the substantial power of the General Secretary to exercise power over policy after he has consolidated his leadership, and even in the face of challenges to his problem-solving competence. But it does not ensure that he will stay in office; indeed, it may even shorten his tenure, as Khrushchev discovered. But that is another matter.

Incentive Policy

The majority consensus after Khrushchev called for much greater emphasis on tangible material rewards, in general, and private material rewards, in particular, than Khrushchev had been willing to countenance. In policy debates, Brezhnev and Kosygin then split over how far this trend should be allowed to go, with Brezhnev emphasizing the need to avoid compromising the party's mobilizational activities and values. But during 1964–8 the new consensus prevailed in policy.[6]

[5] On Soviet investment priorities since 1976, including analyses of the Eleventh Five-Year Plan (1981–5), see: US Congress, Joint Economic Committee, *Soviet Economy in a Time of Change*, 2 vols (Washington, DC: US Government Printing Office, 1979), Vol. 1, pp. 164–75, 196–229, 352–68, 402–22, 581–99, and Vol. 2, pp. 55–86; Gustafson, "Soviet energy policy"; Daniel L. Bond and Herbert S. Levine, "The 11th Five-Year Plan, 1981–1985," in Seweryn Bialer and Thane Gustafson (eds), *Russia at the Crossroads: The 26th Congress of the CPSU* (London: Allen & Unwin, 1982); Douglas B. Diamond, "Soviet agricultural plans for 1981–1985," in ibid.

[6] On incentive policy during the succession struggle after Khrushchev, see: sources cited in note 1, above, as well as Waedekin, *The Private Sector*, pp. 316–43.

The agricultural program enacted in 1965 went far to relieve the financial burden on collective farmers. Procurement targets were greatly reduced and made more uniform, and promises were extended that these would remain stable from year to year. Many debts were cancelled, discriminatory rural taxes (the *sel'skaia nadbavka*) were eliminated, prices for goods and equipment purchased by collective farmers were reduced, collective farmers were granted a guaranteed wage, procurement prices on many products were raised dramatically, and a system of higher prices for above-plan deliveries of grain was put into effect. Moreover, these price increases were absorbed by the state budget, rather than being paid for by an increase in urban retail prices. And the increases in procurement prices for most products reflected a much more serious attempt to adjust prices to previous years' costs, in contrast to Khrushchev's adjustment of prices to levels that would become profitable only after major efforts to cut costs, rationalize production, and improve local leadership.

A similar concern for increasing personal material incentive could be found in the regime's industrial incentive policies. Measures connected with the industrial reforms of September 1965 expanded the role of bonuses (versus fixed wages) as spurs to labor productivity, and a variety of special bonuses were established to reward those who resisted the temptation to change jobs. In a similar vein, in 1967 the authorities approved the introduction of the Shchekino experiment in the Shchekino chemical combine.

The emphasis on individual material rewards also found expression in greater reliance on individualistic activities as means of spurring initiative and raising short-term consumer satisfaction. In November 1964 the regime announced the end of Khrushchev's additional restrictions on the private sector in agriculture (significant restrictions remained, of course). In March 1965 it announced a commitment to vastly expanding the production of passenger automobiles. And also during 1965, restrictions on private housing construction were reduced in both town and countryside.

Many of these measures were consistent with the post-Khrushchev consensus, and cannot necessarily be considered defeats for Brezhnev. For the General Secretary was a party to that consensus, and was only arguing against allowing the new policy to go too far. His was a fall-back position, consistent with the role he embraced as protector of threatened political values. At the same time, they cannot be defined as Brezhnev victories, as we may assume that many of them did not meet opposition from Kosygin. But when Brezhnev pushed to the fore in 1968, both his policy advocacy, and regime policy, began to shift. During Brezhnev's stage of ascendancy, we find him advocating a new mix of material incentives and mobilizational pressure, one that would simultaneously increase material rewards for highly productive laborers while increasing mobilizational pressure on the less productive. This also was the new mix of approaches that characterized regime policy during 1969–72.[7]

Intensification of mobilization in the industrial sector resulted in major new campaigns to tighten labor discipline through legal coercion, social pressure, and exhortation. Seven such policy changes may be noted: (1) campaigns for mobilizing reserves, socialist competition, and shock labor; (2) a resurgent role for the agitator in exhorting workers on the job; (3) the spread of a movement geared toward intensifying the paternalistic supervision of younger workers by older ones (*nastavnichestvo*); (4) revival in 1969 of the annual celebration, by means of a day of free labor donated to state projects, of the first *subbotnik* (Saturday work-day); (5) a variety of administrative measures to reduce labor turnover and increase penalties for lax performance; (6) tying of bonuses, personal advancement, and access to collective material rewards more closely to productivity and innovation; and (7) drawing up of personal productivity plans for workers, specifying their responsibilities, and ostensibly expanding the regime's capacity to monitor poor performance.

A similar extension of pressure and restrictions took place in the agricultural sector. From 1969 onward, collective farms were required to channel more money into the reinvestment funds in order to combat "excessive" personal accumulation. The new collective farm charter (adopted in 1969) prohibited collective farm earnings from rising faster than productivity. Then, too, the earlier policy emphasis on "automatic levers" (that is, market incentives) was now formally abrogated. Henceforth, farms would be required to sell to the state (at elevated prices) no less than 35 percent of above-plan production of grain and 8–10 percent of above-plan production of animal-husbandry products.

But policy trends during these years—like Brezhnev's program—were dualistic. While decisively rejecting any thought of making party mobilization and administrative pressure irrelevant, they also sought to increase material rewards for productive, or strategically placed, laborers. Thus, in the agricultural sector, the October 1968 Plenum voted to expand the policy of offering 50 percent bonuses for above-plan deliveries of produce. The July 1970 Plenum voted a sharp increase in bonuses for skilled workers, a further sharp increase in procurement prices for crops and animal-husbandry products, and higher prices for meat purchases from the private sector. Moreover,

[7] On incentive policy during Brezhnev's stage of ascendancy, see US Congress, Joint Economic Committee, *Soviet Economic Prospects*, pp. 30–8, 316–39, 541–53; Cocks, "Controlling communist bureaucracy," pp. 561–6; Aryeh Unger, "Politinformator or agitator: a decision blocked," *Problems of Communism* (September–October 1970); Olgin, *Socialist Competition*.

the collective farm charter permitted a doubling of the size of private plots, which was followed by an official campaign to induce local authorities not to interfere in the workings of the private collective-farm markets.

In the industrial sector, the authorities changed the laws regarding distribution of incentive funds, in order to ensure that a larger proportion of bonus money would be channeled to the more highly productive blue-collar workers. Furthermore, in October 1969, a resolution of the Central Committee gave formal party approval to the Shchekino experiment, urging ministries and enterprises to emulate it. During 1970–1 a press campaign followed up on this commitment, urging workers in industrial enterprises to support such experiments (they called for increased wage differentiation and the firing of redundant labor) for the sake of efficiency and prospective all-round abundance. And during 1970–2, in cities with 100,000 or more population, job-placement bureaus were established and proliferated.

The intensification of pressure on workers during Brezhnev's stage of ascendancy, and the rejection of any drift toward "automatic levers" as the very basis of regime incentive policy, was clearly a victory for the orientation defended by Brezhnev during the stage of political succession, and again during the stage of ascendancy. Increasing procurement prices for certain agricultural products, and raising bonuses for skilled workers in agriculture, was also consistent with Brezhnev's earlier priorities, and with his approach to dealing with the food problem. But the Shchekino experiment, with its manifold socio-economic implications, was not something we would have expected Brezhnev to endorse. Whether he did so because of reformist group pressures, or in order to coopt the issue, or as a concession to economic reality, cannot be answered on the basis of our evidence.

But once Brezhnev's program failed, incentive policies changed as well, in directions consistent with Brezhnev's public advocacy, and in directions that dropped the reformist experiments and reverted back to the combination of intensified pressure and higher material rewards for the productive with which Brezhnev had identified himself all along.[8] Thus, after 1972, campaigns for labor discipline and overfulfillment of plans were intensified. Grain in the countryside was virtually being confiscated. By a law of December 1974, workers who quit their jobs lost their right to a private plot. And beginning in

[8] On incentive policy since 1973, see Olgin, *Socialist Competition*; anonymous, "Further aid to private farms," *Radio Liberty Research Bulletin*, RL 125/77 (New York: Radio Liberty, 25 May 1977); anonymous, "Financial aid for the construction of private homes in rural areas," *Radio Liberty Research Bulletin*, RL 124/77 (New York: Radio Liberty, 25 May 1977); US Congress, Joint Economic Committee, *Soviet Economy in a Time of Change*, Vol. 1, pp. 325–40, Vol. 2, pp. 109ff., 763–82.

1972–3, the ministries began to undermine the Shchekino experiment by cutting back the size of the wage fund in the more productive factories.

This is basically the approach that has been enforced to the present, though with a few new wrinkles in recent years. As we noted in Chapter 14, policy changes in late 1976 and early 1977 called for greater material assistance to the private sector in Soviet agriculture, and legal enactments in Fall 1980 markedly reduced restrictions on that sector, leading one Western observer to muse that it could eventually have the effect of eroding ideological resistance to reconsideration of the entire collective-farm system![9] In addition, Brezhnev's reinclusion in his speeches of a very muted and supplemental endorsement of limited reform experiments in industry and agriculture appears to correlate with policy changes in recent years. Discussion of such experiments in Soviet periodicals suddenly became more widespread in 1977–78. And selected regional experimentation with such approaches has noticeably increased. In the light of Brezhnev's ability to pull rank politically, and in investment policy, since 1977, it seems likely that these two changes, as well as the continuation of the post-1972 party activist bias, are reflections of his control over the policy agenda—with his endorsement of changes in the private sector, and of limited reform experiments, being concessions to economic necessity rather than to group pressures. This conclusion, however, must be tested in further research.

Administrative Reform

The majority consensus after Khrushchev endorsed a shift toward a less interventionist, and less high-pressure, approach to administration. But, as with incentive policy, Brezhnev struck the posture of a protector of party interventionism against the forces of decentralism. The result was that regime policy during the stage of political succession reflected the new consensus as well as a tenuous and unequal coexistence of decentralist and interventionist biases. It was the measure of Brezhnev's power over policy that the direction in which policy evolved was decidedly interventionist.[10]

[9] Keith Bush, "Major decree on private plots and livestock holdings," *Radio Liberty Research Bulletin*, RL 38/81 (New York: Radio Liberty, 26 January 1981), p 6.

[10] On administrative policy during the post-Khrushchev succession, see Rigby and Miller, *Political and Administrative Aspects*, pp. 16–23, 38–44, 78–81; Cocks, "Controlling communist bureaucracy," pp. 525–66; Conyngham, *Industrial Management*, pp. 253–87; Dallin and Larson, *Soviet Politics since Khrushchev*, pp. 23–40, 73–109; Brown and Kaser, *Soviet Union since the Fall of Khrushchev*, pp. 1–15, 196–217.

In November 1964 the division of the party apparatus into parallel industrial and agricultural hierarchies was reversed, and local party officials were ordered to interfere less than had previously been the case with the functions of managers and state administrators. Instead, party officials were told to concentrate on their traditional functions of coordination, personnel control, supervision of implementation, and worker mobilization.

These trends were reinforced by the abolition of the Party–State Control Commission in December 1965. The return to separate institutions for party, state, and people's control, and sustained efforts to clarify and formalize the jurisdictions of each, represented a reaffirmation of the regime's commitment to protect Soviet officials from unregulated mass criticism. The huge numbers of mass control organizations established under Khrushchev were variously disbanded or placed under closer apparat and managerial control. A new emphasis was placed on improving bureaucratic monitoring techniques, and on developing a body of administrative law to effectively regulate and codify administrative relationships.

In the rural sector, more stable administrative relationships were fostered by the reestablishment of the district party committee as the local authority in charge of agricultural affairs, restoration of the Ministry of Agriculture to a position of authority and responsibility for agricultural affairs in general, and a program of stable planning which accorded "greater scope for local officials and farm management to adapt output to local conditions," [11] to consult with specialists, and to work within a relatively predictable environment.

In the industrial sector, the regime consensus found expression in administrative reforms adopted in September 1965. The regime formally abolished the system of regional economic councils, and much of their central coordinative superstructure, replacing them with the centralized production-branch ministries that had existed before 1957. But rather than return fully to the *status quo ante*, the authorities simultaneously introduced measures intended to reduce overcentralization, expand managerial discretion in the use of resources within their domains, and promote technological innovation among enterprise managers. Thus, the planners were now ordered to judge managerial success primarily by criteria of sales and profitability, rather than simply according to whether the gross output plan had been fulfilled. In addition, the ministries were ordered to allow managers the right to adjust the mix of inputs in their production processes as they saw fit to meet demand for their products. Finally, the ministries were ordered to accord managers the right to keep a more substantial proportion of enterprise profits for use as reinvestment funds, funds for the more flexible and differentiated allocation of bonuses to staff

[11] Nove, "Agriculture," p. 5.

and employees, and funds for such collective material rewards as housing and recreational facilities.

But there were also countervailing tendencies in the policies of these years. The very ministries with the most to lose from the industrial-administrative reforms were the ones placed in charge of carrying it out, and they were given a full three years to shift enterprises to the new system. This provided the ministries in question with both the leverage and the time to undermine the progress of a reform that would have diminished their prerogatives and status. Moreover, the reforms, as enacted, neglected to provide enterprise managers with much material inducement to undertake the considerable risks associated with technological innovation in the command economy. Instead, a low ceiling was placed on the bonuses managers might receive for successful innovation. The joint consequence of these varied provisions was that coordinative ministries in Moscow continued during 1966–8 to prescribe in detail the behavior of their managerial subordinates, to expropriate their profits for use elsewhere, and to prevent elaboration of the decentralist alternative, at a time when enterprise managers had little material incentive to contradict the dictates of their ministerial superiors.

Moreover, within this context, the central party apparatus was initiating policies to upgrade the interventionist capacities of party organs. In late 1965–6, a program was launched to activate and strengthen the primary party organizations within ministries and other governmental institutions. These party organs were told to gather regular, critical reports on the internal functioning of the state bureaucracy, and were assured of support by the central party apparatus in the event of conflicts with their ministerial superiors. During 1966–7 a series of decrees further expanded the apparat's supervisory and investigative activities vis-à-vis central and local organs of the state bureaucracy. And in 1967 the party press sharply toned down the post-Khrushchev campaign against excessive party interference in managerial affairs, while increasing the number of critiques of inadequate party supervision of the state bureaucracy. Little wonder that, in May 1968, shortly after Brezhnev had outflanked Kosygin in the leadership, an All-Union conference discussed ways of improving the planning mechanism, and "the conservatives clearly were in control."[12]

Administrative policy during Brezhnev's stage of ascendancy called for an intensification of intervention in managerial affairs from

---

[12] Katz, *Politics of Economic Reform*, p. 180.

central, regional, and mass sources of control.[13] After the December 1969 Plenum of the Central Committee, party intervention in the industrial sector increased. During 1970 the people's control machinery was reactivated and dramatically expanded in size in order to draw the masses more broadly into the struggle against managerial "conservatism." In the same year, a Central Committee resolution demanded the reactivation of party committees in ministries, and promised them support for their interventionist activities. And coextensive with these changes was the initiation of a "tendency to shift primary responsibility for implementing scientific management and structural reform from the state bureaucrats to the party apparatchiki."[14]

These trends were extended further in 1971. The people's control machinery was formally expanded in size and scope, penetrating institutions that had previously not had such groups and "posts" of people's control. At the Twenty-Fourth Party Congress, the party rules were amended to bestow on ministerial party committees the formal right of supervision of ministerial decision-making. And in 1971–2, measures were enacted to provide formal sanctions against managers violating quality standards, along with which a campaign was launched to expose officials responsible for heavy industry and the consumer sector to direct public exposure and criticism regarding the consumer situation.

Similarly, in the rural sector, state procurement organizations were now given the right to intervene at the production planning stage of the agricultural cycle, while district party committees were urged to increase their supervision of on-farm affairs.

At the same time, however, the rationalizing impulse remained strong, and limited the lengths to which interventionism was encouraged to go. Techniques of systems analysis, previously used on a large scale primarily in the defense sector, were now actively developed and propagandized as part of a sustained effort to diffuse their use to other sectors so as to improve the quality of central planning. And a major movement was launched at the Twenty-Fourth Party Congress to set up production associations throughout the industrial economy. As had been the case in 1966, however, the institutions given primary

13 On administrative policy during 1969–72, see: Rigby and Miller, *Political and Administrative Aspects*, pp. 38–44, 81–2; Cocks, "Controlling communist bureaucracy," pp. 537–50; Karl Ryavec, *Implementation of Soviet Economic Reforms* (New York: Praeger, 1976), pp. 158–85; Gorlin, "Socialist corporations", pp. 522–35; Alice Gorlin, "Industrial reorganization: the associations," in US Congress, Joint Economic Committee, *Soviet Economy in a New Perspective*, pp. 162–88; Keith Bush, *Soviet Agriculture: Ten Years under New Management* (Radio Liberty Research Paper, 21 August 1974); Gertrude E. Schroeder, "Recent developments in Soviet planning and incentives," in US Congress, Joint Economic Committee, *Soviet Economic Prospects*, pp. 11–30.

responsibility for designing this reform were the ones with the most to lose.

All of which was consistent with Brezhnev's policy advocacy and administrative priorities at the time. The intensification of interventionism clearly reflected Brezhnev's political ascendancy and power over policy, while the simultaneous strengthening of certain rationalizing tendencies was consistent, both with the post-Khrushchev consensus, with Brezhnev's consistent adherence to that consensus, and with Brezhnev's embracing a compromise program at the Twenty-Fourth Party Congress.

After 1972, however, administrative policy changed once again.[15] New forms of intervention were adopted, pressure for results was increased, and centralizing tendencies were reinforced. Efforts to improve the quality of central planning continued, especially regional planning. But these were set strictly within the limits of the drift toward greater intervention and greater centralization.

In 1973 a campaign was launched to concentrate resources in Soviet industry on completion of priority projects (as opposed to the starting up of new ones), which, in turn, required directive intervention in ministerial and regional affairs by departments of the Central Committee. In agriculture, the "battle for grain" was accompanied by the establishment of operating control groups at procurement centers, with broad powers to do all that was necessary to bring in the harvest. In addition, party organizations in both industry and agriculture were ordered to break through administrative obstacles to the realization of new plans for administrative reform.

One type of reform that was not going to take place was widespread establishment of production associations according to criteria that would challenge party and ministerial jurisdictions. A statute on the production associations was finally published in April 1973, and it revealed a victory for the "go-slow" approach to this reform.[16] It placed inordinate emphasis on careful analytic work before making changes, and on adapting to diversity. Indeed, this was reflected in progress made (or not made) during 1973–5 in establishing production associations. The pace of change was very slow, far behind

[14] Cocks, "Controlling communist bureaucracy," p. 564.

[15] On administrative policy from 1972 to 1976, see: Gorlin, "Industrial reorganization"; Joseph Berliner, "Prospects for technological progress," in US Congress, Joint Economic Committee, *Soviet Economy in a New Perspective*, pp. 431–46; Paul Cocks, "Rethinking the organizational weapon: the Soviet system in a systems age," *World Politics* (January 1980); Cocks, "Science policy and Soviet development strategy"; anonymous, "Agrarian-industrial integration in the Soviet Union," *Radio Liberty Research Bulletin*, RL 351/76 (New York: Radio Liberty, 14 July 1976); Osborn, *Evolution of Soviet Politics*, pp. 431–2; Green, "Capital Formation in the USSR."

[16] *Pravda*, 3 April 1973.

schedule, amidst clear signs that ministries, *glavki*, and managers of enterprises that stood to lose their independence within larger firms were dragging their feet. In all, the progress made during 1973–5 was such as to change the reform from one with potential for genuinely challenging political jurisdictions to one that amounted in good measure to a change in administrative signposts. The authorities as much as acknowledged this in June 1975 when, in response to two years of struggle between factory managers and association directors, they announced plans to codify administrative law in order to clarify jurisdictions.

Meanwhile, other types of administrative reform were coming to the fore. In April 1973 the regime published a new regional planning scheme.[17] That plan divided the country into seven regions which cut across republic boundaries in order to group sections of the country according to their economic potential, rather than according to formal political boundaries. The scheme was not meant to redraw the map of the Soviet Union; it was for use by the planners only. But it had real implications for the ways in which the State Planning Committee would define regional interests in deciding crucial questions of resource allocation and industrial location. It was no coincidence that, during this period, plans for the creation of new "territorial-production complexes" in Siberia and the Far East were being rapidly developed and implemented. For a new focus on regional planning was consistent with the new emphasis both on concentration of resources and on developing Siberia through multinational involvement in large-scale projects.

Concentration of resources and a regional approach to development was also the primary direction of policy in the agricultural sector. The December 1973 Plenum launched a massive program for the concentration and specialization of production, for the establishment of "agro-industrial complexes" (bringing together under a single administrative roof "all the branches and sub-branches engaged in the production, procurement, processing, storage, transportation, and wholesale marketing of agricultural produce,"[18] for the creation of inter-collective farm and collective farm–state farm enterprises and organizations to perform needed tasks with pooled resources, and for the transfer of 70 million peasants to urban-type settlements in rural areas. All of which was to take place under strict district-level centralization. The purpose of the campaign was to integrate the rural economy more closely into the economy as a whole, to facilitate the use of advanced technology in agriculture, to reduce lines of communication and transportation among interdependent components of

[17] See the discussion in Osborn, *Evolution of Soviet Politics*, pp. 431–2.
[18] "Agrarian-Industrial integration," pp. 1–2.

the rural production, processing, and delivery cycle, and to break through departmental barriers to coordination. Although the regional planning called for by such a reform was quite different from the regional planning for Siberian development, the reform nonetheless represented an analogous philosophy: to upgrade the role of the territorial factor at the expense of the branch approach. Moreover, a regional planning approach analogous to the Siberian was called for by the Non-Black-Earth Zone development project announced in April 1974.

Thus, the new mix of policies adopted after 1972 called for improvements in regional and project planning by central authorities, reliance on large-scale organization, concentration of resources, amalgamation of administrative units to simplify the task of central planning, and the activation of party organs to break through administrative obstacles to the realization of these goals. All of which was precisely the kind of policy Brezhnev came to advocate when he redefined his program in 1973–4.

Moreover, these are the kinds of policies that have continued to this day. Brezhnev became more insistent about the need for reforms within central organs to improve central planning (and to concentrate it on his priorities) after 1976. But the bias remained centralist, as has policy since then. There was much fanfare about a resolution of July 1979 that represented the regime's long-awaited policy statement on the issue of administrative reform. That resolution, however, called for a variety of policy changes in the planning process, but it did not indicate a change in regime priorities away from interventionism or in the direction of decentralization. Rather, it called for changes in indicators and incentives to improve the efficiency of central planning.[19] Hence, there is little reason to believe that, in the late 1970s, Brezhnev has lost control of the administrative policy agenda.

Political Participation

The majority consensus after Khrushchev was anti-populist. It called for a return to a regime that protected the political and bureaucratic

[19] On Soviet administrative policy since 1976, see US Congress, Joint Economic Committee, *Soviet Economy in a Time of Change*, Vol. 1, pp. 217, 312–40; Nancy Nimitz, "Reform and technological innovation in the Eleventh Five-Year Plan," in Bialer and Gustafson, *Russia at the Crossroads*; Bundesinstitut für ostwissenschaftliche und internationale Studien, *The Soviet Union 1976–1977: Volume 4* (New York: Holmes & Meier, 1979, chs 7–8); Robert F. Miller, "The politics of policy implementation in the USSR: Soviet policies on agricultural integration under Brezhnev," *Soviet Studies* (April 1980); Timothy Dunmore, "Local party organs in industrial administration: the case of the *ob"edinenie* reform," ibid.

prerogatives of state and party officials. However, it also called for efforts to improve the responsive capabilities of that bureaucratic regime. This dual commitment left unresolved the question of the relative political status of party officials, on the one hand, and executive or specialist authorities, on the other. The issue was joined by Brezhnev and Kosygin in 1967–8, after which a change in policy direction could be discerned.

The conservative reaction expressed itself in policy changes in all four areas of mass and specialist participation.[20] With respect to mass involvement in public affairs, the following measures were taken: (1) the pace of recruitment of new members into the CPSU was slowed down by an order of the Central Committee, expulsions from the party increased, and disciplinary standards were tightened up; (2) a rapid return to greater elitism in recruitment into the adult political education system took place, emphasizing once again the enrollment of party members, and sharply reducing the total enrollment in the system; (3) the authorities restored the emphasis on training in party schools before recruitment into the apparat, purging the "diploma specialists" recruited by Khrushchev in his last years in office; (4) the visibility of national policy-making was reduced by the end of publication of transcripts of Central Committee plenary sessions (after April 1965), the end of "expanded" plenary sessions, and greater discretion by Politburo-members in their public comments about Politburo deliberations.

With respect to expanded input, the conservative thrust was reflected in the end of the de-Stalinization campaign, a police crackdown on cultural dissent, intensification of restrictions on publication about party history (after 1965), and an insistence, enforced in practice, that critical input be formulated at a lower level of generalization than had hitherto been tolerated (for example, "our manager

---

[20] For policy regarding participation during the years after Khrushchev's dismissal, I have used: Conyngham, *Industrial Management*, pp. 253–88; Rigby and Miller, *Political and Administrative Aspects*, pp. 23–43; Cocks, "Controlling communist bureaucracy," pp. 525–50; Mickiewicz, *Soviet Political Schools*, pp. 12–17; Dallin and Larson, *Soviet Politics since Khrushchev*, pp. 41–71; Kerst, "CPSU history re-revised," pp. 22–32; Unger, *The Totalitarian Party*, pp. 105–66; Linda Lubrano Greenberg, "Soviet science policy and the scientific establishment," *Survey* (Autumn 1971); Jerry Hough, *The Soviet Union and Social Science Theory* (Cambridge, Mass.: Harvard University Press, 1977), pp. 109–39; Brown and Kaser, *Soviet Union since the Fall of Khrushchev*, pp. 96–8, 121–56; Joravsky, *The Lysenko Affair*, pp. 182–6; Ellen Mickiewicz, "Policy applications of public opinion research in the USSR," *Public Opinion Quarterly* (Winter 1972–3); Solomon, *Soviet Criminologists and Criminal Policy*, pp. 67–9, 107–25; Peter Juviler, *Revolutionary Law and Order* (New York: The Free Press, 1976), pp. 51–122; Friedgut, *Political Participation*, pp. 65–70, 247–88; Adams, *Citizen Inspectors*, ch. 5.

lauds it over us," rather than "Soviet officials act like bosses"). As for functional transfer, the conservative reaction found expression in an increased number of full-time, paid officials on the staff of party commissions, integration of nonstaff commissions into the local party structure, and a reining in of the people's militia and comrades' courts to bring them under procedural control of the party and state bureaucracies.

Finally, concerning citizens' rights vis-à-vis executive authority, the conservative reaction resulted in a number of important changes: (1) dismantling of the Party–State Control Commission, which deprived citizens of a hierarchy independent of the formal party and state organs to which they could direct grievances against their superiors; (2) a sharp reduction in the level of turnover among primary party organization secretaries; (3) rules changes making it more difficult for party members to block the election of primary party organization secretarial candidates nominated by higher instances; and (4) revision of the Criminal Code to make dissidents eligible for prosecution for anti-state crimes.

Anti-populism was supplemented by efforts to increase the responsiveness of a bureaucratic regime to all groups which accepted the return to a privileged political status for party and state officials: (1) expanded public opinion polling and funding for "concrete sociological research"; (2) the purge of Lysenko from his position in the scientific community, and a further reduction of dogma in many of the social and natural sciences; (3) the establishment of new channels for consultation with specialists (commissions, standing committees, conferences, liaisons with research institutes); (4) increased emphasis on local party attentiveness to formal citizen complaints; (5) a stress on improving information processing within the party apparatus, and on developing more differentiated methods of mobilization (for example, the new institution of the "politinformator"); (6) the development of legal norms to make methods of social control less arbitrary in their application; and (7) the development of new legal norms to protect defendants within the judicial system in cases that did not involve political crime.

During Brezhnev's stage of ascendancy, however, it became clear that the General Secretary's position on the relative political status of party apparatchiki versus officials and establishment specialists had won out.[21] For during 1969–71, the following policy changes were

[21] Policy changes in this issue-area during 1969–72 are discussed in: Cocks, "Controlling communist bureaucracy," pp. 527–50; Rigby and Miller, *Political and Administrative Aspects*, pp. 23–38, 82–102; Juviler, *Revolutionary Law and Order*, pp. 104–16; Brown and Kaser, *Soviet Union since the Fall of Khrushchev*, pp. 218–75; Alexander Yanov, *The Russian New Right* (Berkeley, Calif.: University of California, Institute of International

enacted: (1) initiation of campaigns for "iron discipline" among party members; (2) formalization of the right of primary party organizations in Academy of Science research institutes to supervise the administration of those institutes, both to see that research projects were responsive to regime needs, and to guard against dissidence; (3) expanded programs and pressures for political socialization of the scientific intelligentsia, demanding, for example, that they more regularly and frequently attend philosophical seminars to demonstrate their doctrinal purity; and (4) extension of the crackdown on dissidence to unorthodox journals within the Establishment.

After 1972 the conservative reaction spread still deeper into official science. During 1973–4 a major crackdown in Establishment social science took place, affecting such journals as *Voprosy filosofii* (organ of the Institute of Philosophy of the Academy of Sciences), and including large-scale personnel changes, new watchdog commissions and regulations, and a decisive change in the content of published theoretical discussions.[22]

This is the pattern that has been followed to this day: efforts to increase the responsiveness of official organs to politically unsensitive demands of the conforming population, coupled with continuing affirmation and expansion of the leading role of apparatchiki vis-à-vis others within the political establishment.[23] On the latter point, Brezhnev and Kosygin had divided in their polemics of 1967–8. Brezhnev's power over policy apparently held sway.

Concluding Reflections on Brezhnev's Power over Policy

Although Brezhnev was probably less powerful than Khrushchev, he also appears to have been far more than a broker. He was able to have his way on agricultural investment priorities, the role of party intervention in public administration, the role of party mobilization in incentive policy, aggrandizement of the budgetary claims of the military–industrial complex, the relative status of party officials versus executives and specialists, and the relationship of foreign trade and

---

Studies, 1978); Adams, *Citizen Inspectors*, chs. 5, 7; Aron Katsenelinboigen, *Soviet Economic Thought and Political Power in the USSR* (New York: Pergamon, 1980), pp. 25–7, 78–80, 102, 126–8, 157, 163; in addition, see the running discussion about scientists' obligations, as translated from the Soviet press, and published in *CDSP*, during May 1971–April 1972.

[22] See Elizabeth C. Sheetz, "Stepped-up efforts to curb dissent in the USSR," *Radio Liberty Research Bulletin*, RL 164/77 (New York: Radio Liberty, 12 July 1977).

[23] Bundesinstitut, *The Soviet Union 1976–1977*, chs 1–5; Sharlet, *The New Soviet Constitution, passim*; these assertions are also supported by my reading of *CDSP* since 1977.

détente to Soviet domestic policy. All of these were contentious issues within the leadership, and while we may assume that Brezhnev felt constrained to forge compromises, it is also clear that his basic biases prevailed. Moreover, Brezhnev was able to seize the initiative from Kosygin, coopt, preempt, and redefine issues, and force through changes in direction. It remains an open question whether these successes resulted largely from Brezhnev's alliance with the more conservative political forces, or from his control over the levers of power through the office he occupied.

Part Four
Conclusion

16 Patterns of Leadership since Stalin

The evidence brought forth in this book suggests that Soviet elite politics since Stalin has been marked by substantial continuity and consensus on the need to increase consumer satisfaction, rationalize the administrative structure, and expand political participation (relative to Stalinist levels). However, there has also been continuous and broad commitment to certain key traditional values: military and heavy-industrial progress, as well as a centralist and party-activist approach to spurring initiative. The task of the Party leader has been to devise programs that synthesize new goals with traditional values.

Khrushchev's strategy was to raise initiative, productivity, and political support through campaigns for social and political trans-formation, rather than through budgetary redistributions. When this program failed, he tried to reevaluate his assumptions, but was erratic and on the defensive. His authority and power collapsed before he could devise a resynthesis. Brezhnev, in contrast, rejected campaigns for social and political transformation, relying instead on budgetary redistributions and highly selective political and administrative reforms to achieve the goals of spurring initiative, raising productivity, and increasing mass support for the regime. When Brezhnev's innovative synthesis faltered, he redefined it in a still more traditional direction, and avoided Khrushchev's fate.

Despite the great differences between their authority-building strategies, both Khrushchev and Brezhnev worked within the bounds of "post-Stalinism," avoiding either a return to Stalinism or a break-through toward liberalism. (See Table 1.1, p. 6). Yet Western characterizations and evaluations of Khrushchev's and Brezhnev's orientations have often been misleading, for they have tended to overstate the differences, and to view these leaders as choosing between, rather than synthesizing, egalitarian and elitist values.

Khrushchev and Brezhnev as Problem-Solvers

Nikita Khrushchev is sometimes thought of as a great egalitarian, in that he sought to lead his people out of Stalinism into the promised land depicted in Lenin's *State and Revolution,* a land of peace, prosperity, opportunity, homogeneity, and consensus. To some observers, Khrushchev was a "great reformer" of political authority and political status relationships within the system.[1] Others view him as a dedicated decentralizer of Soviet public administration.[2] And others view him as a "reformist" with respect to budgetary and incentive policy – an embattled advocate of the consumer against the weight of military and heavy-industrial interests.[3] Indeed, a few writers portray him as all of these.[4]

Some of these images are seriously in need of revision; others require qualification to capture the complexity of the issues under investigation. Khrushchev's role as "liberator" of the peasantry accurately reflects his efforts to upgrade the status of peasants in the eyes of party and state officials; but the term fails to capture the Party leader's coercive campaigns against the private sector in Soviet agriculture, and his ready willingness to impose his own agricultural and organizational schemes on Soviet rural producers. Similarly, Khrushchev's role as "great reformer" well captures his populist redefinition of political authority relationships (especially between local officials and the masses), but does not reflect the intolerant and illiberal limits that Khrushchev placed on the expansion of political participation.

Furthermore, in his approach to most other realms of policy, Khrushchev was even closer to his Stalinist roots. His adherence to the post-Stalin consensus demanded increased investment in consumer-oriented sectors and higher material incentives. But beyond this, we find that Khrushchev was hardly a frustrated consumer advocate. If anything, he comes across—through most of his years in power—as a leader who sought to prove that consumer satisfaction and agricultural performance could be sharply improved without massive infusions of funds from the military and heavy-industrial sectors.

Khrushchev also followed the post-Stalin consensus in seeking to rationalize public administration by deconcentrating the super-centralized bureaucracy inherited from Stalin. His image as a decentralizer derives largely from his abolition of the ministerial

[1] For the characterization of Khrushchev as "great reformer," see Stephen Cohen, "Foreword," in Roy Medvedev and Zhores Medvedev, *Khrushchev: The Years in Power*, paperback edn (New York: Norton, 1979), p. viii. Some years ago I read a scholarly analysis that referred to Khrushchev as the "Tsar Liberator" of the peasantry; unfortunately, I have been unable to trace the source.

[2] See Schwartz, "Decisionmaking, administrative decentralization, and feedback mechanisms," fns 19 and 23 for examples of Western specialists' tendencies to characterize Khrushchev's administrative reforms as decentralization.

[3] Ploss, *Conflict and Decision-Making*; Linden, *Khrushchev and the Soviet Leadership*.

[4] Ploss, *Conflict and Decision-Making*, p. 280, and Linden, *Khrushchev and the Soviet Leadership*, pp. 18–21.

structure in 1957 in favor of regional economic councils. However far-reaching this move might have become had it fulfilled its potential, part of the reason it did not do so was that Khrushchev's perspectives on public administration were those of a deconcentrator, not those of a decentralizer. Until circumstances forced him to rethink his assumptions during his last two years in power, he was wedded to the claim that political intervention in managerial affairs, and a high-pressure administrative order, were prerequisites for managerial initiative and administrative efficiency. Simultaneously with his efforts to reduce detailed ministerial direction of managerial behavior, he increased the level of mass and local party intervention, and imposed wildly ambitious plan targets from above through the Central Committee Secretariat.

The literature on Brezhnev is less extensive than that on Khrushchev, but the most prevalent image in that literature is of a conservative elitist, who reversed Khrushchev's egalitarian reformism. To most observers, Brezhnev led a conservative reaction against de-Stalinization, against Khrushchev's attacks on Soviet officialdom, and against Khrushchev's campaigns for social homogeneity. In his administrative policies, Brezhnev is often characterized as a re-centralizer, who restored the ministerial structure and advocated centralist solutions to the problems of administrative efficiency. In his budgetary priorities, Brezhnev is often dubbed a conservative by those who stress his association with a massive military buildup, his opposition to heavy investment in light industry, and his repudiation of Khrushchev's "consumerite" promises to the masses.[5]

Indeed, Brezhnev *was* a conservative in many of these respects; but that is not the end of the story. It is not that these characterizations are incorrect, as far as they go; they simply do not go far enough. For they obscure or neglect aspects of policy in each of these issue-areas in which Brezhnev stood further from the Stalinist pole than did Khrushchev. With respect to political participation, Brezhnev was anti-populist on matters of fundamental political authority relationships, but he also advocated a reduction of dogma in technical, social, economic, and scientific fields, regularization of input into the policy process of advice from specialists, and the creation of a less pressured and more predictable environment for the politically conformist. As for administrative policy, Brezhnev certainly rejected the advice of decentralizers, but he also advocated deconcentrating the

[5] On these points, see Dornberg, *Brezhnev*; Robert Conquest, *Russia after Khrushchev* (New York: Praeger, 1965); Frederick C. Barghoorn, *Politics USSR*, 2nd edn (Boston, Mass.: Little, Brown, 1972), pp. 236–9; Richard Lowenthal, "The Soviet Union in the post-revolutionary era: an overview," in Alexander Dallin and Thomas B. Larson (eds), *Soviet Politics since Khrushchev* (Englewood Cliffs, NJ: Prentice-Hall, 1968).

administrative structure, reducing the level of pressure on managers, and reducing the scope of *arbitrary* political intervention in managerial affairs.

In the realm of investment priorities, Brezhnev did indeed sponsor a military buildup, but he also advocated massive investment in agriculture, to be paid for at the expense of growth rates in the heavy-industrial sector. And with respect to incentive policy, Brezhnev went much further than Khrushchev in his endorsement of material incentives (relative to moral exhortation, social pressure, and political coercion) as inducements to labor discipline. Thus, Brezhnev was more elitist than Khrushchev in some respects, less so in others.

By distinguishing among issue-areas, we can also explain differences among those who evaluate Khrushchev's and Brezhnev's contributions in positive and negative terms. Those who criticize Khrushchev for being a "hare-brained schemer" focus solely upon his approaches to economic and administrative problems.[6] Those who praise Khrushchev as a "great reformer" focus on his participatory innovations.[7] Similarly, those who criticize Brezhnev as a "dull clerk," lacking in "imagination," are primarily offended by his conservative approach to public criticism of the regime.[8] Those who praise Brezhnev for his skills as a politician are primarily impressed by his concern for economic and administrative stability, and for reducing dogmatic controls over depoliticized specialist input.[9]

Most Western scholars are inclined to evaluate Khrushchev's contributions more positively than Brezhnev's. This circumstance stems from the fact that most Western scholars admire Khrushchev's willingness to confront the entrenched power of Soviet officialdom, place highest value on participatory concerns, measure progress relative to the hopes inspired by Khrushchev, and see changes in the current terms of political participation in the USSR as necessary for significant improvements in economic performance. From this standpoint, the characterization and evaluation of Soviet leaders' contributions is not based on their behavior in individual issue-areas, treated separately, but is rather based on the leader's conception of the relationship among issue-areas and sectors in the Soviet system. Hence, Khrushchev could be viewed as a great reformer because of his claim that restructuring political and social relationships was a prerequisite for

[6] "Hare-brained scheme" was the standard Soviet press criticism of Khrushchev after his dismissal; see also Jerry Hough, "A hare-brained scheme in retrospect," *Problems of Communism* (July–August 1965).

[7] See note 1, above.

[8] Zbigniew Brzezinski, "The Soviet system: transformation or degeneration?" *Problems of Communism* (January–February 1966).

[9] Paul Cocks, "Science policy and Soviet development strategy," in Alexander Dallin (ed.), *The Twenty-Fifth Congress of the CPSU* (Stanford, Calif.: Hoover Institution Press, 1977).

achieving gains in productivity that no amount of budgetary redistribution could otherwise attain. And Brezhnev could be viewed as a conservative because he rejected this Khrushchevian contention, and instead threw money at problems. If one accepts the values and premises that underpin this evaluation, it is an entirely appropriate one that does not do violence to the historical record presented in this book.

Having described, characterized, and evaluated differences between Khrushchev's and Brezhnev's authority-building strategies, one is still left with the task of explaining their choice of such different strategies. One causal factor of great importance was surely the climate of opinion within the political establishment during the period of political succession. After Stalin, a widespread (though far from unanimous) yearning existed for both restoring a sense of physical security and restoring a sense of dynamism, to "get the country moving again."[10] Khrushchev sensed this yearning, shared it, played upon it, and worked to shape its policy expression. In contrast, after Khrushchev, officials of the party and state yearned primarily for a period of tranquility that would restore their material privileges, their job security, and their autonomy from both unregulated mass criticism and arbitrary, personalistic leadership.[11] Brezhnev sensed, shared, and responded to this yearning.

A second causal factor was the state of knowledge about their own system that Soviet leaders possessed during the periods of political succession and ascendancy. The unworkability of Khrushchev's program of the late 1950s was probably not widely understood in the Soviet political elite at the time. By the mid-1960s, however, Soviet leaders came to understand that Khrushchev was incorrect in predicting that his brand of populism would foster a sharp increase in labor productivity and economic performance. In addition, they had learned that campaigns for social transformation were impeding economic performance, and that the utopian goal of enforced collectivism was actually in conflict with the economic goal of stimulating worker and peasant initiative. Then, too, Soviet officials and leaders could rationalize the practicability of approaches to economic organization that fell short of decentralization. For the Khrushchev experience had taught many of them, not the necessity of genuine administrative decentralization, but rather the unworkability of excessively high-pressure

---

[10] This mood is discussed in Medvedev and Medvedev, *Khrushchev*; the notion of Khrushchev trying to "get the country moving again" is from Brzezinski, "The Soviet system."

[11] For striking evidence of this mood, see the speeches of republican party first secretaries at the March 1965 Plenum on agriculture: *Plenum tsentral'nogo komiteta Kommunisticheskoi Partii Sovetskogo Soiuza, 24–26 marta 1965 g.: Stenograficheskii otchet* (Moscow: Politizdat, 1965).

approaches to public administration. They had reevaluated the benefits to be obtained from increasing pressure on administrators, and had arrived at a more complex appreciation of the dilemmas facing the local official in a high-pressure, command economy. This allowed many of them to rationalize the rejection of decentralization in favor of a period of experimentation with efforts to improve the command economy by reducing the level of pressure, rationalizing jurisdictions and information flows within the bureaucracy, and allowing for a period of administrative stability.[12]

A third causal factor was the personality of the Party leader. Biographers of Khrushchev have frequently overstated the role of his personality in determining his policy choices, but it would also be misleading to underestimate that role.[13] Those biographies have demonstrated that Khrushchev, well before 1953, possessed a number of orientations and beliefs that helped to shape his response to the climate of opinion after Stalin: (1) a propensity for risk-taking; (2) impatience for results; (3) a belief in, and preference for, leadership that gets out among the people and does not issue directives from afar; and (4) relatedly, a strong distrust of bureaucrats, and a strong distaste for bureaucratic centralism (perhaps shaped by his frustrating experiences with the central bureaucracy when he was on the front during World War II, and when he was Party leader in the Ukraine after the war).[14] There were other traits, of course, but these would appear to be the ones that distinguished his orientations from his associates in the leadership at the time (Malenkov, Kaganovich, and Bulganin) and from his heirs (Brezhnev, Kosygin, and Suslov). These traits, moreover, either conditioned or determined his efforts to restructure authority relationships as the core of his program, for, as we have seen, his associates at the time did not endorse such a program.

It is much more difficult to weigh the relative role of personality in Brezhnev's policy choices. His consensus-building approach to leadership did not require a frontal assault on major interests, and

---

[12] See Richard Judy's outstanding study of the differences between computerizers and decentralizers in the Soviet economics establishment: "The economists," in H. Gordon Skilling and Franklyn Griffiths (eds), *Interest Groups in Soviet Politics* (Princeton, NJ: Princeton University Press, 1971).

[13] For biographies of Khrushchev, see: Crankshaw, *Khrushchev: A Career*; Medvedev and Medvedev, *Khrushchev*; Victor Alexandrov, *Khrushchev of the Ukraine* (New York: Philosophical Library, 1957); Lazar Pistrak, *The Grand Tactician* (New York: Praeger, 1961); Frankland, *Khrushchev*; George Paloczi-Horvath, *Khrushchev: The Road to Power* (London: Secker & Warburg, 1960). Of these biographies, that by Crankshaw centers most fully on personality.

[14] For suggestive evidence of this linkage, see Khrushchev, *Khrushchev Remembers*, Vol .1, pp. 76, 112; and Vol. 2, pp. 115–16,

did not require him to shape and redirect the prevailing climate of opinion, or state of knowledge, nearly to the extent that Khrushchev did. From the little we know of his personality and preconceived orientations, he did not share the Khrushchevian traits noted above. Hence, his personality was well suited to his authority-building strategy. But whether his personality was the main cause of his choice of that strategy is unclear. Brezhnev's wartime experiences may have conditioned his embracing nationalistic themes as partial substitutes for utopian themes, but any pragmatic Party leader after Khrushchev might have made such a choice. In any case, it seems safe to conclude that personality was a more influential cause of Khrushchev's embracing a confrontational authority-building strategy than it was a major cause of Brezhnev's embracing a consensual strategy.

Cycles, Stages, and Similarities: The Man and the System

With the kinds of evidence at hand (both in this book and elsewhere), it may not be possible to make confident assertions about the relative role of personality versus politics as determinants of policy choices by Soviet Party leaders. For example, did Brezhnev fail to purge Soviet administrative leaders because he was not so inclined, or because he did not think he could get away with it? We do not know. But one way to approach the question of how much "the system" (structures, processes, and the orientations of one's political support groups) shapes the choices of the Party leader is to compare the Khrushchev and Brezhnev administrations in search of similarities. For if we agree that the personalities of Khrushchev and Brezhnev were very different, and we find them nonetheless engaging in very similar patterns of behavior, then we may be justified in arguing that factors in the environment of policy-making, not personality itself, were decisive in determining the behavior pattern. In any given case, personality may have been reinforcing of the choice, but we cannot confidently claim it to have been decisive. Searching for similarities should not obscure the basic differences about which we have been talking up to this point; rather, it is a supplementary exercise.

In an important recent study, Professor Valerie Bunce has also examined cycles in the evolution of communist regimes.[15] Piecing together a time series of Soviet investment data for various consumer sectors during the Khrushchev and Brezhnev eras, Professor Bunce found that these sectors are "pumped" with funds during the years of political succession. After the succession has been decided, she

[15] Valerie Bunce, *Do New Leaders Make a Difference?: Executive Succession and Public Policy under Capitalism and Socialism* (Princeton, NJ: Princeton University Press, 1981).

discerns a significant reduction in priority for consumer-oriented sectors. This decline continues, according to her data, throughout the remainder of the administration. Turning to the evolution of Khrushchev's and Brezhnev's agricultural programs, Bunce argues that the distinctive character of those programs (beyond investment totals) was shaped and implemented during the stage of political succession (1953–4 and 1965 plenary sessions of the Central Committee). Subsequently, policy innovation declined markedly, and the Party leaders concentrated primarily on defending earlier gains and making marginal adjustments. Hence, Bunce concludes that policy-making in the USSR is neither uniformly incremental nor uniformly innovative. Rather, it is highly innovative during periods of political succession and relatively noninnovative thereafter, until the next succession period.

How does Bunce explain this pattern? Although she acknowledges that personality, ideology, and situational factors play a role in the determination of some choices, she does not consider these forces to be decisive determinants of the pattern uncovered in her study. Her proposed explanation is that, during the early years of an administration, the uncertainties of power struggle give the leadership a collective interest in buying off the masses through budgetary reallocation, and simultaneously give the Party leader a strong incentive to seize upon a consumer-oriented issue as "his own." Both the collective and the personal interest in the consumer sectors, according to Bunce, suffer a relative decline after the succession struggle has been decided. At that point, previously deprived, established interests line up at the budgetary trough to demand once again their fair shares.

Bunce's evidence and argumentation are compelling, all the more so because she documents similar cycles in other socialist states and in nonsocialist states (the USA and Great Britain). Moreover, some of the findings of my book lend strong support to Bunce's conclusions. Bunce's findings about funds actually invested during the stage of political succession square with my documentation of a "proconsumer" consensus in the leadership at this stage—that is, "proconsumer" relative to what was achieved before the death or dismissal of the previous leader. Moreover, we have also found that the Party leader seizes on the agricultural issue, and shapes it, in ways that allow him to "ride" the issue during the succession struggle. Finally, in contrast to the frequent claim that Party leaders first discredit, and then adopt, the program of their rivals,[16] I, like Bunce,

[16] For examples: Linden, *Khrushchev and the Soviet Leadership*, p. 30; Conquest, *Power and Policy*, p. 27; Darrell Hammer, *USSR: The Politics of Oligarchy* (Hinsdale, Ill.: Dryden Press, 1974), p. 306; Dornberg, *Brezhnev*, p. 254; Zbigniew Brzezinski and Samuel Huntington, *Political Power: USA/USSR* (New York: Viking Press, 1963), pp 193, 267.

have found that the character of the General Secretary's policy program is largely defined by him in the first years of his administration.

But there are differences in the basic methodology adopted by Bunce and me for studying Soviet politics. I study multiple budgetary issues, not just the consumer-oriented. I examine both budgetary and nonbudgetary issues, the trade-offs among them, and the packages put together by leaders at different points in time. And I examine elite conflict and strategies in these realms, rather than concentrating primarily on results (that is, policy outcomes).

The consequence of our different focuses is that my findings force me to revise some of the arguments advanced by Bunce. First, periods of political succession led not only to pumping of the consumer sector, but also to pumping of the defense sector. And the General Secretary also seized upon, and "rode" that issue during the succession struggle. This combination of budgetary positions is the key to his authority-building strategy on budgetary issues. It represents his distinctive synthesis of post-Stalin and traditional values.

Second, innovation in nonbudgetary policy does not follow the same progression as in budgetary policy. Nor does the correlation between stage of administration and degree of innovation hold true as between the Khrushchev and Brezhnev administrations on issues of administrative reform and political participation. For example, in both of these issue-areas, we find during the Khrushchev administration a steady increase over time in the level of innovativeness of policy, but a steady decrease over time during the Brezhnev administration.

Third, even within the issue-areas she examines, Bunce's overarching conceptual apparatus may be too blunt. To call Brezhnev's agricultural policies after 1968 "noninnovative" or "incremental" may be correct, if by that it is meant that he stayed within the premises of his program of 1965—that is, that he continued to throw money at the problem, resisting calls for decentralization. But the concepts obscure the fact that Brezhnev pushed through a series of agricultural policy changes during the 1970s that had significant opportunity costs in a tight budgetary situation: 35 billion rubles committed in principle to rapid development of the Non-Black-Earth Zone in 1974; rapid development of agro-industrial complexes (launched in December 1973); a program for the resettlement of hundreds of thousands of peasants living in "dying" villages (mid-1970s); and the commitment of huge sums of hard currency to grain importation (since 1972). Bunce's case study ignores these changes; but in doing so loses us the opportunity to understand the relationship between stage of administration and the authority needs of the Party leader. For these grandiose projects (along with others, in other policy realms) were pumped during the third stage of Brezhnev's administration, not the first.

Indeed, that brings us to the fourth, and final, distinction between Professor Bunce's conceptualization and my own. By examining policy advocacy (and, in Chapters 7 and 15, policies adopted), I have been sensitized to the existence of at least three, not two, stages in each administration. Bunce's methodology and conceptualization ignore the innovative, but compromise, reform packages that both Khrushchev and Brezhnev advanced during the second stage of their administrations. That those programs were not fully implemented was in part due to climatic conditions (dust-bowl conditions in the Virgin Lands in 1960; the drought of 1972), which led to retraction of previously promised investments in light industry. Bunce's indicators pick up on results, not promises or policies. Yet the promises that the Party leader chose to make (or felt the need to make) may be the more important indicators of the political pressures to which he is subject.[17]

What conclusions would I draw from reflecting upon the patterns of behavior engaged in by Khrushchev and Brezhnev? A number of observations emerge from looking at the similarities between stages of evolution in the Khrushchev and Brezhnev administrations. First, programs that rely heavily on party activism, political intervention, and pressure are the constant winners in post-Stalin politics. During the stage of political succession, Khrushchev and Brezhnev helped to outflank Malenkov and Kosygin by accusing them of excessively sacrificing such values. Thus, Georgi Malenkov advocated a program for expanded investment in light industry, conversion of selected heavy-industrial and defense plants to the production of consumer goods, long-term investment in the intensive development of agriculture, cuts in the defense budget to help pay for these programs, and restraints on party activism in order to improve administrative efficiency. In contrast, Nikita Khrushchev developed a program that was far less redistributive of traditional military–heavy-industrial interests and values, more inclined to assign a central role to party activism, and more inclined to seek political reforms, rather than administrative reforms (of a technocratic or decentralist sort) in order to improve the performance of the system. Thus, Khrushchev proposed a low-cost, short-term approach to solving the agricultural problem (the Virgin Lands Program), an expensive program for modernization and expansion of the defense forces (with particular emphasis on nuclear rocketry), cuts in the proposed budget for light industry, increased party activism and intervention as a means of stimulating administrative and labor initiative, and a populist approach to political participation.

Differences between Brezhnev and Kosygin after Khrushchev's

---

[17] Despite my criticisms and caveats, I consider the book by Professor Bunce to be a major accomplishment, and an important contribution to comparative analysis.

ouster were neither as large nor as stark as those between Khrushchev and Malenkov, but in certain respects they were analogous. Like Malenkov, Kosygin championed the cause of light industry in the battle for investments, and advanced a program for administrative reform that challenged the principle of party interventionism for the sake of economic efficiency. In defense policy, Kosygin formally endorsed the post-1965 rise in the military budget, but simultaneously urged heavy pressure on the military–industrial complex to produce consumer goods above-plan. In contrast, Leonid Brezhnev, like Khrushchev in the mid-1950s, identified himself with an alliance of heavy industry and agriculture (at the expense of light industry), seized upon a poor harvest (1965) to greatly expand the scope of his agricultural program by bringing new expanses of land under cultivation (the land reclamation program of May 1966), and insisted upon a costly program for expansion and modernization of the armed forces. Brezhnev's lyric endorsement of patriotic themes, coupled with his strong and frequent repetition of the need for increases in the defense budget, suggest that he was determined (as Khrushchev had been) to "ride" the issue for personal political gain. Moreover, Brezhnev (like Khrushchev) placed much greater emphasis than Kosygin on party activism and interventionism in his approach to public administration and worker mobilization. And Brezhnev (like Khrushchev) appealed to optimistic sentiments within the political elite about the ability of party activism to stimulate the initiative required to get the economy on its feet. Thus, Kosygin paralleled Malenkov in his greater willingness to challenge traditional values for the sake of administrative efficiency and consumer satisfaction, while Brezhnev paralleled Khrushchev in his more assertive defense of those traditional values and political mobilizational themes.

When Khrushchev and Brezhnev came forth with comprehensive programs during their stage of ascendancy, those programs—though sharply different in content—rested heavily on the principles of party activism and pressure. Thus, Khrushchev's program for the "full-scale construction of communism" called for a "storming" mentality in heavy-industrial enterprises. It intensified pressure on workers and peasants in order to increase discipline, productivity, collectivism, reinvestment of profits (in the rural sector), and political participation in national affairs. It also called for sharply expanded party and mass intervention in managerial affairs. Similarly, Brezhnev's program of 1971 rejected the hopes of those who had earlier looked forward to imminent decentralization of the economy. Like Khrushchev, Brezhnev instead offered a major deconcentration of public administration (production associations), combined with increased party and mass intervention as a means of spurring technological innovation. Like Khrushchev, Brezhnev intensified pressure on workers and peasants in order to increase discipline, productivity, reinvestment, and participation.

After the frustration of their programs, both Khrushchev and Brezhnev tried to recoup lost authority by sponsoring grandiose new projects that would require an intensification of party activism. Thus, Khrushchev called for a "second stage" in the development of the Virgin Lands, more extensive cultivation of corn, and, ultimately, forced development of the chemicals industry. Brezhnev advocated rapid development of the Non-Black-Earth Zone of the RSFSR, accelerated construction of the Baikal–Amur railway, more rapid exploitation of Siberian mineral resources and, ultimately, forced extraction of natural gas in Western Siberia. In addition, both leaders took to the countryside and turned up the pressure on local party officials for a quick win in the struggle for grain and/or cotton. Reliance on party-mobilizational approaches to problem-solving is not the exclusive tendency at each stage of the evolution of the Party leader's program, but it appears to be the dominant tendency.

My second observation is that the Party leader's program is usually accompanied by highly ambitious goals and targets that strain available resources and typically foster unbalanced planning. Khrushchev's various programs are, of course, famous for their ambitiousness. But Brezhnev's programs were also highly ambitious. His comprehensive program of 1971 assumed optimal environmental and climatic conditions and benign, if not benevolent, international conditions. His post-1972 programs for agro-industrial integration, development of the Non-Black-Earth Zone, Siberian development, and accelerated construction of the Baikal–Amur railway were certain to create bottlenecks and fall short of their stated targets. And his post-1977 energy program, including the wildly ambitious pipeline construction program of 1981, are bound to create major bottlenecks elsewhere in the economy. Indeed, they are reminiscent of Khrushchev's chemicals program of 1963. Thus, optimism may have been a personality trait of Khrushchev's, but personality alone cannot explain the persistent reappearance of ambitious, grandiose projects and programs.[18]

My third observation is that heavy reliance on political mobilization has, since 1959, been incapable of generating the economic efficiency, administrative effectiveness, or authentic initiative that have been part of the goal structure of Soviet politics since Stalin. Both Khrushchev and Brezhnev struggled to improve consumer satisfaction and the effectiveness of political mobilization, but both men, during the

---

[18] Energy targets for the Eleventh Five-Year Plan were scaled down somewhat before the final guidelines for the Plan were published in late 1981 (*Pravda*, 18 November 1981). Nonetheless, they remain extremely ambitious.

second half of their years in power, effectively conceded that they had fallen far short of their goals.

My fourth observation is that, in constant competition with the mobilizational impulse that favors elitist, conservative approaches to problem-solving, there has been a persistent reform impulse that is willing to sacrifice certain traditional values for the sake of improving the economic and political situations. Let me elaborate this point.

There are many definitions of reformism in the literature on Soviet politics. Minimalist definitions equate reformism with any policy change, of whatever magnitude, in a direction that attempts to improve economic efficiency or political responsiveness.[19] Maximalist definitions of the term equate it with a commitment to market socialism and political democracy.[20] I use the term differently, for these definitions do not strike me as very useful. The minimalist definition trivializes the concept by applying it to almost all change in a "positive" direction. The maximalist definition demands so much change that it leaves us without a conceptual apparatus for understanding differences between and within the Khrushchev and Brezhnev administrations.

As I use the term, reformist policies are those which significantly challenge the core traditional values of the Stalin era in the pursuit of post-Stalin goals. Conservative policies pursue post-Stalin goals with minimal damage to core traditional values. Abandonment of post-Stalin goals in deference to traditional values is best dubbed "reactionary," whereas abandonment of traditional values in pursuit of post-Stalin goals (the maximalist definition of reformism) is best dubbed "radicalism." We are then left with a continuum of degrees of reformism, depending upon the extent to which traditional values are being sacrificed.

Thus, at some point, each of the protagonists of this book— Malenkov, Khrushchev, Kosygin, and Brezhnev—advanced reformist programs of one kind or another. Khrushchev's programs of 1959 and 1961 were considerably more reformist than the others—perhaps "radical reformism" would be the proper label—for they called for a restructuring of political authority relationships between the bureaucratic establishment and the masses. In contrast, the programs advanced by Malenkov during 1953–5, and Kosygin in 1965–8 (and again in 1976), might be called "moderate reformism." For each of

[19] For example, Donald R. Kelley, "The Communist Party," in Donald R. Kelley (ed.), *Soviet Politics in the Brezhnev Era* (New York: Praeger, 1980), pp 28–30.

[20] For example, George R. Feiwel, "Economic performance and reforms in the Soviet Union," in ibid., pp. 80, 101. For varied approaches to the definition of significant change, see Cohen, "The friends and foes of change," *Slavic Review* (June 1979) and the comments on the article in ibid., by T. H. Rigby, Frederick Barghoorn, and S. Frederick Starr.

them was relatively conservative about mass political participation, but called for significant budgetary redistributions at the expense of defense and heavy industry, and administrative reforms that would restructure authority relationships within the establishment. Finally, Brezhnev's program of 1971 might be called "tepid reformism." It proposed: to increase investment in light industry; to pressure heavy-industrial and defense enterprises to produce more consumer goods above-plan; to struggle against local party resistance to the establishment of production associations according to criteria of economic efficiency (rather than political jurisdiction); to threaten certain social values for the sake of increasing labor productivity (by expanding material differentiation and releasing redundant labor); and to expand the budgetary pie by searching abroad for credits and capital. This went further than Brezhnev had ever gone before in public in challenging traditional values for the sake of economic progress, though it did not go as far as Malenkov and Kosygin had gone.

My fifth observation takes us back to the first. While the conservative impulse has been in constant competition with the reformist, conservative impulses have apparently been much the stronger. For, over the course of the last twenty years, we can observe the continuing attenuation of the reform impulse's impact on policy, and the continuing strengthening of the conservative impulse's impact on policy. Reformism in domestic policy has gone from "radical" to "moderate" to "tepid" to "virtually submerged" in the last two decades.

My sixth observation relates to conceptualization of the Brezhnev era. Some Western scholars after Khrushchev's dismissal argued that the Soviet system had become *immobiliste,* and that the leadership was no longer capable of sustaining a reform impulse.[21] Our findings suggest rather the more complex image of a political system which, for whatever reasons, continues to generate the urge for reform (not just policy changes), while simultaneously restricting its scope and obstructing its implementation. The impulse to reevaluate policies is, of course, nearly a universal in organizations and political systems. But the reform impulse is found much more frequently in political cultures shaped by a progressive ideological tradition (that is, a tradition that does not extol "muddling through" as a positive value), or in situations in which there is a contradiction between the newly defined goals of the leadership (here, the post-Stalin consensus) and the existing political, economic, and administrative structure. The Soviet system fits into these categories.

My seventh observation has to do with the relationship between authority and power in Soviet politics. That relationship is clearly

---

[21] Brzezinski, "The Soviet system"; also, Jerome Gilison, "New factors of stability in Soviet collective leadership," *World Politics* (July 1967).

a complex one. It is premature to conclude that one's effectiveness as a problem-solver is as important as patronage allocation in determining one's ability to stay in power. Brezhnev's longevity in office would seem to belie such assertions. It is also premature to argue that policy effectiveness is a necessary condition for the Party leader to survive the stage of political succession. One cannot gather conclusive evidence to support the claim that "socialist successions . . . force elites to be successful in their pet projects or be purged from office."[22] It is true that, in the 1950s, students of Soviet policy exaggerated the importance of patronage, and neglected the role of authority-building in Soviet politics. But it only compounds the error to argue that the reverse is closer to the truth. What we can conclude from this study, however, is that Soviet Party leaders behave as if authority-building is a very important matter indeed. Those leaders appear to operate within a political context that forces them continuously to legitimize their power by demonstrating their effectiveness. Many changes in policy advocacy by the General Secretary are inexplicable in terms of concrete threats to his right to remain in office. They can better be understood as products of his authority-building strategy.

My final observation has to do with conceptualization of the political role played by the Party leader. It has become standard in much literature to refer to Brezhnev as a "political broker" or mediator, presiding over an oligarchy or "incremental polity." As one scholar has argued: "oligarchical rule has necessarily made the need for unanimity more meaningful politically; it has forced the General Secretary to become more of a 'broker' and less of an 'initiator' . . ."[23] In contrast, the emphasis in studies of Khrushchev's leadership is on his role as initiator, and the idiosyncratic features of his leadership.

Such general characterizations are useful starting points; indeed, I have distinguished between Khrushchev's "confrontational," and Brezhnev's "consensual," authority-building strategies, which conveys much the same distinction. But the danger is that analysis will stop at that point, obscuring the fact that each leader's authority-building strategy evolved over time. In the stage of political succession, both Khrushchev and Brezhnev sought to project themselves as leaders uniquely suited to coming up with programs for alleviating the food crisis while protecting the political elite against programs that would frontally challenge party-mobilizational and military values. Thus, during this stage, they sought to build their authority by combining the roles of "initiator" and "protector." During the stage of ascend-

---

[22] Bunce, *Do New Leaders Make a Difference?*, p. 240.

[23] Ross, "Coalition maintenance in the Soviet Union," p. 261; "incremental polity" is Ross's term.

ancy, the role of protector diminishes, and the General Secretary seeks to build his authority by combining the roles of initiator and broker, seeking to reconcile maintenance of his policy priorities with compromises associated with other tendencies. In the third stage, there is no clear pattern. Khrushchev abandoned the broker role (as well as the protector), while Brezhnev reemphasized the protector role in domestic policy and the initiator–broker roles in foreign policy. In sum, changes in both policy and politics are the rule, rather than the exception, in post-Stalin Soviet politics. It is wise, therefore, to avoid over-arching concepts that so much emphasize continuity within administrations as to obscure this fact.

Explaining the Patterns

How might we explain the patterns just noted? Specifically: (1) What accounts for the persistence and strength of the mobilizational and conservative tendencies in Soviet policy? (2) What accounts for the persistence of highly ambitious programs? (3) What accounts for the persistence of the reform impulse? and (4) What accounts for the failure of the reform impulse in practice? We have already seen that personality goes far to explain Khrushchev's choice of a program based on radical reform. But to explain the similarities, we must go beyond personality; we must refer instead to the impact of political constituencies, political processes, political culture, and circumstantial factors. In so doing, we enter the realm of speculation, for we have not drawn evidence to document all these factors. But it will be informed speculation, as the patterns of policy advocacy documented in this book are highly suggestive.

The strength and persistence of conservatism in Soviet policy is easily explained as a product of the institutional and political legacy of Stalinism. The party apparatus may be a heterogeneous organization,[24] but officials of that apparatus share status concerns, political interests, and a sense of institutional identity that are bolstered by policies that rely heavily on party activism, intervention, and mobilization for their realization. Moreover, officials of the central party apparatus, central planners, high-level officials of the ministerial system, and officials of the military–industrial complex share an interest in maintaining a highly centralized political, economic, and administrative order. Finally, it may be an exaggeration to say that "the Soviet Union does not have a military–industrial complex; the

---

[24] As argued and documented in Jerry Hough, "The party apparatchiki," in Skilling and Griffiths, (eds), *Interest Groups in Soviet Politics*.

Soviet Union *is* a military–industrial complex,"[25] but the statement contains more than a kernel of truth. That is, it points to the fact that, at the uppermost levels of the system, civilian and military leaders share values and perspectives associated with high military budgets and "law and order" approaches to domestic policy. There may be other factors that reinforce this conservative institutional structure and identity (for example, conservatism ingrained in the mass culture),[26] but these institutional factors are probably sufficient to explain the persistence and strength of mobilizational and conservative policy orientations since Stalin.

Why do Party leaders typically come forth with highly ambitious programs? On this score as well, political constituencies and political culture are important, though political process (to be defined below) also explains a great deal. The interventionist prerogatives of party officials are more easily legitimized in an atmosphere of "storming," just as the atmosphere of economic campaigns justifies intensified party activism and political mobilization.[27] Then, too, one of the functions performed by party officials is to get things done and break through bottlenecks, so that ambitious planning creates the uncertainties that elevate the political importance of party officials. Ambitious campaigns also shorten time-horizons and focus resources on narrow goals, which raises the status of party officials charged with concentrating local resources on priority tasks.

This political pattern is reinforced by Soviet political culture in general. Leninism, Stalinism, Khrushchevism, and Brezhnevism all had in common a *Zeitgeist* of optimism, based on the premise that party activism could accomplish great things on short order. The ascendancy of the Party leader has always been accompanied by ambitious programs that promise to make a "great leap forward." In Khrushchev's case this meant "the full-scale construction of communism"; in Brezhnev's case it meant "combining the fruits of the scientific-technological revolution with the advantages of socialism" and "saturating the market with consumer goods." Thus, it would appear that the Party leader is surrounded by political expectations that urge him to be continuously creative, to stay out in front and sponsor new projects and new ideas. He is expected to supply ambitious leadership—both for reasons of constituents' political interest, and because of the ethos created and sustained by the political

25 "It is only partly in jest that one says 'the United States may *have* a military industrial complex, but the Soviet Union *is* a military industrial complex' " (Seweryn Bialer, "Soviet political elite and internal developments in the USSR," in William Griffith (ed.), *The Soviet Empire: Expansion and Detente* [Lexington, Mass.: Lexington Books, 1976], p. 37).
26 As argued in Cohen, "The friends and foes of change."
27 As noted in Paltiel, "DeStalinization and DeMaoization."

culture. Indeed, it would probably be politically costly for a Soviet leader to acquire the image of an immobilist, who ignores problems rather than attacking them (by one means or another).

Political constituencies and political culture, however, only get us part of the way toward an explanation. Khrushchev and Brezhnev came forth with ambitious programs at each stage of their administrations, but, depending upon the stage, those programs were ambitious in very different ways. The stage of administration appears to have an independent impact on the way in which ambitious programs are put together, for the political process (that is, the way in which political constituencies interact and bargain) undoubtedly varies by stage.

During the stage of political succession, the leadership is divided over questions of power and policy, but for that very reason (as Professor Bunce has argued) has a collective interest in appeasing the masses through budgetary reallocations. This is reflected in the pumping of funds into consumer-oriented sectors (wages included) at the start of each administration. Within this context, however, the political process is also marked by a high level of political opportunism, with rival leaders advancing competing programs. The Party leader is tempted to discredit his rival by demonstrating that only his program can markedly advance the interests of national security and consumer satisfaction without sacrificing traditional values. The result of such competition, however, is that the Party leader advances highly ambitious programs in the sectors with which he is most closely identified (defense and agriculture) at a time when the regime consensus calls for pumping funds into a large number of consumer-oriented sectors. In part, this results in policy zig-zags; but in part, it leads to very tight budgeting.

During the stage of ascendancy, when the power struggle has been provisionally decided and the fear of the masses has lessened, established interests seek to make up for earlier deprivations caused by pumping of the consumer sectors, and line up at the budgetary trough to grab their fair shares.[28] Moreover, the atmosphere of political opportunism and artificial polarization within the leadership no longer needs to be sustained, and is replaced by a political context in which the Party leader is expected to come forth with a comprehensive program at the Party Congress. Thus, there are three competing aspects to the political process during this stage: (1) role expansion by the Party leader, such that he has greater power to initiate policy in issue-areas previously dominated by others in the Politburo; (2) a heightened expectation that he will take the lead in forging a comprehensive program for progress in most realms; and

[28] As argued in Bunce, *Do New Leaders Make a Difference?*

(3) a rise in the overall level of group demands within the political establishment.[29]

This is hypothesis, of course, but it is consistent with the patterns of evidence adduced in this study. It is perfectly consistent with our observation that the General Secretary appears to combine the roles of initiator and broker in forging a comprehensive program during the stage of ascendancy. Moreover, it goes far to explain the content of those programs. It would explain the fact that his program reincorporates certain budgetary or structural changes that he had earlier denounced. It would explain the fact that his expanded program attempts to appease previously deprived interests, that it is based on a search for new sources of capital (at home and abroad), and that it opts for structural reforms as a means of increasing productivity (given the tight budgetary situation). Moreover, if the strain on resources caused by the rise in group demands makes it more difficult to maintain the previous rate of increase in consumer satisfaction, then it makes sense to attempt (as both Khrushchev and Brezhnev did) to stimulate labor initiative and productivity by altering the structure of material incentives, increasing social and political pressure on the undisciplined and unproductive workers, and making public promises about the imminence of abundance that could serve (hopefully) as an intangible material incentive to produce. All of these strategies were features of Khrushchev's and Brezhnev's programs, and both Party leaders additionally struck deals with the representatives of military and heavy-industrial interests to exceed their plans for the sake of the consumer—in Khrushchev's case, by channeling above-plan fulfillments to light industry and agriculture, in Brezhnev's case, by producing consumer goods above-plan in enterprises belonging to the military–industrial complex. Thus, features of the political

---

[29] Bunce (ibid.) argues that the General Secretary's power over policy declines after the political succession has been decided. She bases this hypothesis on two types of evidence: (1) demonstration that pro-consumer expenditures decline after the succession; and (2) deduction from studies of presidential leadership in the West, where the honeymoon period immediately after election is typically marked by the greatest opportunities for policy innovation. In contrast, I would argue a very different case. After the political succession, the General Secretary *expands his role* into new policy realms, and forges a comprehensive program that bears his stamp. Along these dimensions, he appears to have greater power after the political succession than during it, even though he may face a tighter political situation on budgetary policy during the stage of ascendancy. Furthermore, it may be misleading to argue deductively from the case of presidential systems to the Soviet case. There is no analogue in presidential systems to the Soviet phenomenon of collective leadership giving way to a "first among equals" political boss. If there exists a Soviet "honeymoon period," I am more inclined to see it *following* the succession struggle, corresponding to the short period after the General Secretary has forged a comprehensive program.

process during the stage of ascendancy contributed to highly ambitious planning.

After the almost predictable frustration of the ambitious, comprehensive program, the political process changes once again. It is now marked by: (1) the need to forge an alternative program; (2) high uncertainty within the political establishment as to what policies might simultaneously appease the masses and protect the interests of the most powerful institutional forces; (3) lack of the pro-consumer consensus associated with political succession periods; and (4) an authority crisis, in which the General Secretary feels the need to recoup his image as an effective problem-solver and to reinforce his political base. This is the kind of political environment in which almost anything can happen, and in which the personality of the leader may be decisive—and that explains why Khrushchev and Brezhnev went off in such different directions. But there was more than just personality involved, for the nature of their authority crises differed. Khrushchev had promised so very much, and had identified himself as leader so closely with the success of his policies, that he responded like a man in panic when his policies failed. Brezhnev had promised less, and had sought to diffuse responsibility for policy-making (to a greater extent than Khrushchev, anyway), so that he was less out-on-a-limb when his policies faltered.[30] Yet both men appear to have felt the need for a quick win, and both turned up the pressure toward that end, thereby reinforcing ambitious campaignism. Moreover, both launched ambitious, grandiose projects of immense proportions, in hopes of either securing a quick win or creating an atmosphere of national mobilization in which the establishment would defer to their leadership.

There is, in this stage, a parallel with the stage of political succession. In both cases, the General Secretary is attempting to build his authority under conditions of duress: power struggle in the first case, authority "leakage" in the second. In both cases, his response or strategy is to emphasize highly ambitious campaignism at the expense of interests he had selectively accommodated (or would selectively accommodate) during the stage of ascendancy.

If conservative tendencies and highly ambitious campaignism find support in the dominant political constituencies, political culture, and

[30] Archie Brown ("The power of the General Secretary," pp. 151–2) makes the following observation: "A head of executive can lead from the front or lead from the middle. Nikita Khrushchev . . . led from the front— took vital policy decisions and bypassed his colleagues when he deemed it necessary. Leonid Brezhnev . . . leads from the middle. If you follow the first course, you can wield more power while you are in office, but your tenure of office is likely to be shorter, for when things go wrong . . . it will be too late to seek the security of collective responsibility."

political processes, then how are we to explain the persistence of the reform impulse in Soviet politics? Why is that impulse not suppressed? Or why does it not disappear? The answer, I believe, is that conservative political constituencies are cross-pressured, in the following ways. First, since the disgrace of Molotov, there has emerged a far-reaching consensus within the Soviet political elite that neither a return to Stalinism nor a breakthrough toward Yugoslav levels of market socialism or political democracy is necessary, desirable, or feasible. Yet having committed themselves to the post-Stalin goals of increasing consumer satisfaction and expanding political participation, the elite has had to face the fact that traditional structures and priorities are limited in their ability to service these goals.[31] Hence, the urge for reform can be legitimized as a regrettable necessity if bleaker alternatives are to be avoided.

Conservative political constituencies are cross-pressured in other ways as well. Many of them must fear popular responses to continued food shortages. Many of them are technological zealots who have learned through bitter experience the deficiencies of the system as constituted. Many of them are influenced by an ideological tradition that legitimizes their "leading role" by demanding periodic demonstrations of progress in the direction of a more abundant society. Many officials in the military–industrial complex have come to realize that improvements in the standard of living are a prerequisite for making labor incentives effective as spurs to productivity. Finally, perennial budgetary strain makes Soviet leaders susceptible to appeals for administrative reforms that would substitute for budgetary redistribution.

All of these factors have been in evidence throughout most of the post-Stalin era, though in different forms, to different degrees, and with different concrete consequences. They created a structure of political interests and expectations tentatively supportive of reform efforts. However, those who had such interests, and held such expectations, were not willing at the time to go as far as Malenkov and Kosygin were portrayed as wanting to go, or as far as Khrushchev went after 1960. They would tolerate reform efforts in the service of post-Stalin goals, but they demanded simultaneous affirmation that such reformism would not threaten the leading role of the party, the primacy of political-mobilizational approaches to public administration, and the budgetary prerogatives of the military–industrial complex.

This pattern would also go far to explain the continual failure of the reformist impulse. Malenkov and Kosygin advocated coupling structural reform and budgetary reform with a reduction of pressure and political intervention—and their programs never proved to be politically acceptable. Reforms sponsored by the Party leader, in contrast, were coupled with an increase in pressure and political intervention as spurs to managerial and worker initiative. The effect of such a combination, however, was typically to nullify the impact of whatever structural reforms were being advocated. Heightened pressure reinforced taut planning, which made impossible the creation of economic slack and reserves required to make administrative reforms effective in practice.[32] Similarly, intensified pressure inhibited the managerial propensity to engage in regular technological innovation, and was of little help in raising labor productivity.[33]

In addition to politics and political culture, one circumstantial factor played a large role in the continual failure of reformism: the precarious agricultural situation. Crop failures exacerbate the food situation, reduce the incentive effect of material rewards, cause slowdowns in light industry due to shortfalls in deliveries of fibers, drain funds from other sectors by demanding large infusions of funds into agriculture, and demand large expenditures of hard currency on world markets to import grain. Crop failures in 1959–60, and again in 1963, scuttled Khrushchev's economic programs. Crop failures in 1972 and 1975 did the same to Brezhnev. By proposing highly ambitious programs that took a high-pressure, centralized approach to agricultural production and delivery, and given the erratic climatic conditions that regularly plague Soviet grain-producing regions, both Khrushchev and Brezhnev were tempting fate. And fate was cruel.

The International Context

This study has not focused on Soviet foreign policy, and has brought the international context into the discussion only insofar as matters of foreign trade had an impact on budgetary policy, or when the general state of Soviet–US relations appeared to have an impact on domestic policy. Hence, any conclusions we might draw about the underlying causes of similarities and differences between the Khrushchev and Brezhnev eras must be tentative ones. The importance of the international context as a determinant of the fact, direction, or magnitude of changes in Soviet domestic policies may be decisive, contributory, or nil. To what extent have international conditions had an impact on the strength of either the reformist or the conserva-

[31] For this argument, see Thane Gustafson, *Reform in Soviet Politics* (New York: Cambridge University Press, 1981), chs 1, 10, 11.

[32] On this point, see Seweryn Bialer, "The Soviet Political Elite and Internal Developments in the USSR," in Griffith (ed.), *The Soviet Empire*, p. 49.

[33] See Joseph Berliner, *The Innovation Decision in Soviet Industry* (Cambridge, Mass.: MIT, 1978).

tive forces in Soviet policy? This study was not designed to address that question, so we cannot say. For we have not explored the relationship between change in Soviet domestic policy and change in the international environment. Nor have we explored the ways in which Soviet leaders' perceptions of the international situation conditioned their notions about what was feasible and desirable in domestic policy.

Yet, there are several reasons for believing that the international context may well have contributed to both the timing and the content of changes in domestic policy. For one thing, both Khrushchev's and Brezhnev's reformist programs of 1959 and 1971 linked economic and military détente abroad with structural and budgetary reform at home. This accounts for the striking similarities in the two men's foreign-policy behavior in those years. Both Party leaders made significant collaborative offerings to the USA in their Party Congress speeches, and followed them up with major personal initiatives to further the causes of arms control, reduced tension, and expanded trade.[34]

Second, there were numerous similarities in the international situation preceding these collaborative offerings (that is, in 1958 and 1970) that distinguished it from the international context of the stage of political succession.[35] This forces us to temper conclusions that domestic factors alone led Soviet Party leaders to search abroad for new sources of capital. Changes in the international environment may well have created perceived opportunities making such a search feasible in the eyes of Soviet leaders.

Third, our examination of the standard of comparison by which Soviet leaders measure their economic progress has revealed the very great importance they place on competition with Western capitalist countries. This raises the possibility that Soviet propensity for launching ambitious programs, based on budgetary and structural reform, has been conditioned by their current standing in the "race with capitalism," rather than solely by domestic pressures and impulses.[36]

A fourth reason to study the international context is circumstantial, but compelling. It relates to the periodization of changes in domestic policy programs and domestic power relations under Khrushchev and

---

[34] For further discussion, see George Breslauer, "Political succession and the Soviet policy agenda," *Problems of Communism* (May–June 1980), p. 42. I should note that, in this article, I referred to two stages of the political succession. In the present book, however, the stage of ascendancy corresponds to the second stage of political succession in the article.

[35] For a catalogue of these similarities, see ibid., pp. 47–8.

[36] This argument has been made in Joseph Berliner, "Some international aspects of Soviet technological progress," *South Atlantic Quarterly* (Summer 1973); it has been further discussed in Bruce Parrott, "Politics and economics in the USSR," *Problems of Communism* (May–June 1977), pp. 55–6.

Brezhnev. It is instructive to consider the rough turning-points that have informed the organization of this book: 1957, 1960–1, 1965, 1968–9, 1973, 1976–7. It is striking to note how closely these turning-points correspond to US presidential election years and/or inauguration years, and how closely the resultant stages correspond to the US electoral cycle. It would be absurd to make too much of this correlation; but it would also be unwise to ignore it. For it raises the possibility that attempts to influence US presidential elections, or reactions to foreign-policy changes by presidents during their honeymoon periods, may have a major impact on the timing and content of Soviet domestic policy changes.

Part Five
Bibliography of Works Cited

Bibliography of Works Cited

Adams, Arthur E., "Educated specialists and change in Soviet agriculture," *Agricultural History* (January 1966).
Adams, Jan S., *Citizen Inspectors in the Soviet Union* (New York: Praeger, 1977).
Aizikovich, A. S., "Vazhnaia sotsiologicheskaia problema," *Voprosy filosofii*, no. 11 (1965).
Alexandrov, Victor, *Khrushchev of the Ukraine* (New York: Philosophical Library, 1957).
Anonymous, "Agrarian-industrial integration in the Soviet Union," *Radio Liberty Research Bulletin*, RL 351/76 (New York: Radio Liberty, 14 July, 1976).
Anonymous, "Financial aid for the construction of private homes in rural areas," *Radio Liberty Research Bulletin*, RL 124/77 (New York: Radio Liberty, 25 May, 1977).
Anonymous, "Further aid to private farms," *Radio Liberty Research Bulletin*, RL 125/77 (New York: Radio Liberty, 25 May, 1977).
Anonymous, "Interes," *Bol'shaia sovetskaia entsiklopediia*, Vol. 18 (Moscow: Gosizdat, 1953).
Azrael, Jeremy, "Varieties of de-Stalinization," in Chalmers Johnson (ed.), *Change in Communist Systems* (Stanford, Calif.: Stanford University Press, 1970).
Barghoorn, Frederick C., *Politics USSR*, 2nd edn. (Boston, Mass.: Little, Brown, 1972).
Barnard, Chester, *The Functions of the Executive* (Cambridge, Mass.: Harvard University Press, 1945).
Becker, Abraham, *Soviet Military Outlays since 1955* (Santa Monica, Calif.: RAND Corporation, 1964).
Berliner, Joseph, *The Innovation Decision in Soviet Industry* (Cambridge, Mass.: MIT, 1978).
Berliner, Joseph, "Prospects for technological progress," in *Soviet Economy in a New Perspective*, compiled by US Congress, Joint Economic Committee (Washington, DC: US Government Printing Office, 1976).
Berliner, Joseph, "Some international aspects of Soviet technological progress," *South Atlantic Quarterly* (Summer 1973).
Bialer, Seweryn, "The Soviet political elite and internal developments in the USSR," in William Griffith (ed.), *The Soviet Empire: Expansion and Detente* (Lexington, Mass.: Lexington Books, 1976).
Bloomfield, Lincoln P., Clemens, Walter C., Jr, and Griffiths, Franklyn, *Khrushchev and the Arms Race* (Cambridge Mass.: MIT, 1966).
Bond, Daniel L., and Levine, Herbert S., "The 11th Five-Year Plan, 1981–1985," in Seweryn Bialer and Thane Gustafson (eds), *Russia at the Crossroads: The 26th Congress of the CPSU* (London: Allen & Unwin, 1982).

Breslauer, George, "Dilemmas of leadership in the Soviet Union since Stalin 1953–1976," (unpublished, 1978).

Breslauer, George, *Five Images of the Soviet Future* (Berkeley, Calif.: University of California, Institute of International Studies, 1978).

Breslauer, George, "Khrushchev reconsidered," *Problems of Communism* (September–October 1976).

Breslauer, George, "Political succession and the Soviet policy agenda," *Problems of Communism* (May–June 1980).

Beslauer, George, "Research note," *Soviet Studies* (July 1981).

Breslauer, George, "The Twenty-Fifth Party Congress: Domestic Issues," in Alexander Dallin (ed.), *The Twenty-Fifth Congress of the CPSU* (Stanford, Calif.: Hoover Institution Press, 1977).

Brezhnev, L. I., *Leninskim kursom,* 7 vols (Moscow, Politizdat, 1970–9).

Brezhnev, L. I., *Ob osnovnykh voprosakh ekonomicheskoi politiki KPSS na sovremennom etape,* 2 vols (Moscow: Politizdat, 1975).

Brezhnev, L. I., *Ob osnovnykh voprosakh ekonomicheskoi politiki KPSS na sovremennom etape: rechi i doklady,* 2 vols, expanded edn (Moscow: Politizdat, 1979).

Brinkley, George, "Khrushchev remembered: on the theory of Soviet statehood," *Soviet Studies* (January 1973).

Brown, Archie, "The power of the General Secretary," in T. H. Rigby, Archie Brown, and Peter Reddaway (eds), *Authority, Power and Policy in the USSR* (London: Macmillan, 1980).

Brown, Archie, and Kaser, Michael (eds), *The Soviet Union since the Fall of Khrushchev* (New York: The Free Press, 1975).

Brzezinski, Zbigniew, "The Soviet system: transformation or degeneration?" *Problems of Communism* (January–February 1966).

Brzezinski, Zbigniew, and Huntington, Samuel, *Political Power: USA/USSR* (New York: Viking Press, 1963).

Bunce, Valerie, *Do New Leaders Make a Difference?: Executive Succession and Public Policy under Capitalism and Socialism* (Princeton, N.J.: Princeton University Press, 1981).

Bundesinstitut für ostwissenschaftliche und internationale Studien, *The Soviet Union 1976–1977: Volume 4* (New York: Holmes & Meier, 1979).

Burns, James MacGregor, *Leadership* (New York: Harper & Row, 1978).

Bush, Keith, "Major decree on private plots and livestock holdings," *Radio Liberty Research Bulletin,* RL 38/81 (New York: Radio Liberty, 26 January, 1981).

Bush, Keith, "Resource allocation policy: capital investment," in *Soviet Economic Prospects for the Seventies,* compiled by US Congress, Joint Economic Committee (Washington, DC: US Government Printing Office, 1973).

Bush, Keith, *Soviet Agriculture: Ten Years under New Management* (New York: Radio Liberty Research Paper, 21 August, 1974).

Bush, Keith, "Soviet capital investment since Khrushchev: a note," *Soviet Studies* (July 1972).

Caldwell, Lawrence T., *Soviet Attitudes to SALT*, Adelphi Papers no. 75 (London: Institute of Strategic Studies, 1971).

Chapman, Janet, *Wage Variation in Soviet Industry: The Impact of the 1956–1960 Wage Reform* (Santa Monica, Calif.: RAND Corporation, 1970).

Cocks, Paul, "Controlling communist bureaucracy," (unpublished, 1975).

Cocks, Paul, "Rethinking the organizational weapon: the Soviet system in a systems age," *World Politics* (January 1980).

Cocks, Paul, "Science policy and Soviet development strategy," in Alexander Dallin (ed.), *The Twenty-Fifth Congress of the CPSU* (Stanford, Calif.: Hoover Institution Press, 1977).

Cohen, Stephen F., "Foreword," in Roy Medvedev and Zhores Medvedev (eds), *Khrushchev: The Years in Power*, paperback edn (New York: Norton, 1979).

Cohen, Stephen F., "The friends and foes of change: reformism and conservatism in the Soviet Union," *Slavic Review* (June 1979).

Conolly, Violet, "The territorial-production complex in Siberia and the Far East," *Radio Liberty Research Bulletin*, RL 339/76 (New York: Radio Liberty, 6 July, 1976).

Conquest, Robert, *Power and Policy in the USSR* (New York: Harper & Row, 1961).

Conquest, Robert, *Russia after Khrushchev* (New York: Praeger, 1965).

Conyngham, William J., *Industrial Management in the Soviet Union* (Stanford, Calif.: Hoover Institution Press, 1973).

Crankshaw, Edward, *Khrushchev: A Career* (New York: Viking Press, 1966).

Current Digest of the Soviet Press (CDSP) (weekly).

Dallin, Alexander, and Larson, Thomas B. (eds.), *Soviet Politics since Khrushchev* (Englewood Cliffs, NJ: Prentice-Hall, 1968).

Daniels, Robert, "Stalin's rise to dictatorship," in Alexander Dallin and Alan F. Westin (eds), *Politics in the Soviet Union: Seven Cases* (New York: Harcourt, Brace & World, 1966).

Deuvel, Christian, "An unprecedented Plenum of the CPSU Central Committee," *Radio Liberty Research Bulletin*, RL 145/73 (New York: Radio Liberty, 3 May, 1973).

Diamond, Douglas B., "Soviet agricultural plans for 1981–1985," in Seweryn Bialer and Thane Gustafson (eds), *Russia at the Crossroads: The 26th Congress of the CPSU* (London: Allen & Unwin, 1982).

Dinerstein, H. S., *War and the Soviet Union*, rev. edn (New York: Praeger, 1962).

Dornberg, John, *Brezhnev: The Masks of Power* (New York: Basic Books, 1974).

Dunmore, Timothy, "Local party organs in industrial administration: the case of the *ob"edinenie* reform," *Soviet Studies* (April 1980).

XXIII s"ezd Kommunisticheskoi Partii Sovetskogo Soiuza, 29 marta–8 aprelia 1966 g.: Stenograficheskii otchet, 2 vols (Moscow: Politizdat, 1966).

XXIV s"ezd Kommunisticheskoi Partii Sovetskogo Soiuza, 30 marta–9 aprelia 1971 g.: Stenograficheskii otchet, 2 vols (Moscow, Politizdat, 1971).

XXV s"ezd Kommunisticheskoi Partii Sovetskogo Soiuza, 24 fevralia–5 marta 1976 g.: Stenograficheskii otchet, 3 vols (Moscow: Politizdat, 1976).

Etzioni, Amitai, *The Active Society* (New York: The Free Press, 1968).

Fainsod, Merle, *How Russia Is Ruled,* 2nd edn (Cambridge, Mass.: Harvard University Press, 1963).

Fainsod, Merle, "Khrushchevism," in Milorad M. Drachkovitch (ed.), *Marxism in the Modern World* (Stanford, Calif.: Stanford University Press, 1965).

Feiwel, George R., "Economic performance and reforms in the Soviet Union," in Donald R. Kelley (ed.), *Soviet Politics in the Brezhnev Era"* (New York: Praeger, 1980).

Foreign Broadcast Information Service, USSR (daily).

Frankland, Mark, *Khrushchev* (New York: Stein & Day, 1967).

Friedgut, Theodore, *Political Participation in the USSR* (Princeton, NJ.: Princeton University Press, 1979).

Gilison, Jerome, "New factors of stability in Soviet collective leadership," *World Politics* (July 1967).

Glezerman, G. E., *Polnoe sootvetstvie proizvodstvennykh otnosheniy i proizvoditel'nykh sil v sotsialisticheskom obshchestve* (Moscow: Gosizdat, 1951).

Glezerman, G. E., "Sotsial'naia struktura sotsialisticheskogo obshchestva," *Kommunist,* vol. 13 (1968).

Gorlin, Alice, "Industrial reorganization: the associations," *Soviet Economy in a New Perspective,* compiled by US Congress, Joint Economic Committee (Washington, DC: US Government Printing Office, 1976).

Gorlin, Alice, "Socialist corporations: the wave of the future in the USSR?" in Morris Bornstein and Daniel Fusfeld (eds), *The Soviet Economy: A Book of Readings,* 4th edn (Homewood, Ill.: Irwin, 1974).

Green, Donald, "Capital formation in the USSR: an econometric investigation of bureaucratic intervention in the process of capital construction," *Review of Economics and Statistics* (February 1978).

Greenberg, Linda Lubrano, "Soviet science policy and the scientific establishment," *Survey* (Autumn 1971).

Grossman, Gregory, "The Brezhnev era: an economy at middle age," *Problems of Communism* (March–April 1976).

Grossman, Gregory, "From the Eighth to the Ninth Five-Year Plan," in Norton T. Dodge (ed.), *Analysis of the USSR's 24th Party Congress and 9th Five-Year Plan* (Mechanicsville, Md.: Cremona Foundation, 1971).

Grossman, Gregory, "Notes for a theory of the command economy," *Soviet Studies* (October 1963).

Grossman, Gregory, "Soviet growth: routine, inertia, and pressure," *American Economic Review* (May 1960).

Gruliow, Leo (ed.), *Current Soviet Policies: The Documentary Record of the Nineteenth Communist Party Congress and the Reorganization after Stalin's Death* (New York: Praeger, 1953).

Gruliow, Leo (ed.), *Current Soviet Policies II: The Documentary*

Record of the 20th Communist Party Congress and its Aftermath (New York: Praeger, 1957).

Gruliow, Leo (ed.), *Current Soviet Policies III: The Documentary Record of the Extraordinary 21st Congress of the Communist Party of the Soviet Union* (New York: Columbia University Press, 1960).

Gruliow, Leo, and Saikowski, Charlotte (eds), *Current Soviet Policies IV: The Documentary Record of the 22nd Party Congress of the Communist Party of the Soviet Union* (New York: Columbia University Press, 1962).

Gruliow, Leo, et al. (eds), *Current Soviet Policies V: The Documentary Record of the 23rd Congress of the Communist Party of the Soviet Union* (Columbus, Ohio: American Association for the Advancement of Slavic Studies, 1973).

Gruliow, Leo, et al. (eds), *Current Soviet Policies VI: The Documentary Record of the 24th Congress of the Communist Party of the Soviet Union* (Columbus, Ohio: American Association for the Advancement of Slavic Studies, 1973).

Gruliow, Leo, et al. (eds), *Current Soviet Policies VII: The Documentary Record of the 25th Congress of the Communist Party of the Soviet Union* (Columbus, Ohio: American Association for the Advancement of Slavic Studies, 1976).

Gustafson, Thane, *Reform in Soviet Politics* (New York: Cambridge University Press, 1981).

Gustafson, Thane, "Soviet energy policy: from big coal to big gas," in Seweryn Bialer and Thane Gustafson (eds), *Russia at the Crossroads: The 25th Congress of the CPSU* (London: Allen & Unwin, 1982).

Hahn, Werner, *The Politics of Soviet Agriculture, 1960–1970* (Baltimore, Md.: Johns Hopkins University Press, 1972).

Hammer, Darrell, *USSR: The Politics of Oligarchy* (Hinsdale, Ill.: Dryden Press, 1974).

Hodnett, Grey, "The pattern of leadership politics," in Seweryn Bialer (ed.), *The Domestic Context of Soviet Foreign Policy* (Boulder, Colo.: Westview Press, 1980).

Hodnett, Grey, "Succession contingencies in the Soviet Union," *Problems of Communism* (March–April 1975).

Holzman, Franklyn, *Financial Checks on Soviet Defense Expenditures* (Lexington, Mass.: Lexington Books, 1975).

Horelick, Arnold, and Rush, Myron, *Strategic Power and Soviet Foreign Policy* (Chicago: University of Chicago Press, 1966).

Hough, Jerry, "A hare-brained scheme in retrospect," *Problems of Communism* (July–August 1965).

Hough, Jerry, "The Brezhnev era: the man and the system," *Problems of Communism* (March–April 1976).

Hough, Jerry, "Enter N. S. Khrushchev," *Problems of Communism* (July–August 1964).

Hough, Jerry, "The party apparatchiki," in H. Gordon Skilling and Franklyn Griffiths (eds), *Interest Groups in Soviet Politics* (Princeton, NJ: Princeton University Press, 1971).

Hough, Jerry, *Soviet Leadership in Transition* (Washington DC: Brookings Institution, 1980).

Hough, Jerry, *The Soviet Prefects* (Cambridge, Mass.: Harvard University Press, 1968).

Hough, Jerry, *The Soviet Union and Social Science Theory* (Cambridge, Mass.: Harvard University Press, 1977).

Hough, Jerry, and Fainsod, Merle, *How the Soviet Union Is Governed* (Cambridge, Mass.: Harvard University Press, 1979).

Joravsky, David, *The Lysenko Affair* (Cambridge, Mass.: Harvard University Press, 1970).

Jowitt, Kenneth, "An organizational approach to the study of political culture in Marxist–Leninist Systems," *American Political Science Review* (September 1974).

Jowitt, Kenneth, "Inclusion and mobilization in European Leninist regimes," *World Politics* (October 1975).

Jowitt, Kenneth, "National, state and civic development in Marxist–Leninist regimes," unpublished paper presented to the American Political Science Association, San Francisco, September 1975.

Jowitt, Kenneth, *Revolutionary Breakthroughs and National Development* (Berkeley, Calif.: University of California Press, 1971).

Judy, Richard, "The economists," in H. Gordon Skilling and Franklyn Griffiths (eds), *Interest Groups in Soviet Politics* (Princeton, NJ: Princeton University Press, 1971).

Juviler, Peter, *Revolutionary Law and Order* (New York: The Free Press, 1976).

Kanet, Roger, "The rise and fall of the 'All-People's State', recent changes in the Soviet theory of the state," *Soviet Studies* (July 1968).

Katsenelinboigen, Aron, *Soviet Economic Thought and Political Power in the USSR* (New York: Pergamon, 1980).

Katz, Abraham, *The Politics of Economic Reform in the Soviet Union* (London: Pall Mall Press, 1973).

Kelley, Donald R., "The Communist Party," in Donald R. Kelley (ed.), *Soviet Politics in the Brezhnev Era* (New York: Praeger, 1980).

Kerst, Kenneth, "CPSU history re-revised," *Problems of Communism* (May–June 1977).

Khrushchev, Nikita, *Khrushchev Remembers*, Vol. 1, translated and edited by Strobe Talbott (Boston, Mass.: Little, Brown, 1970).

Khrushchev, Nikita, *Khrushchev Remembers: The Last Testament*, Vol. 2, translated and edited by Strobe Talbott (Boston, Mass.: Little, Brown, 1974).

Khrushchev, N. S., *Stroitel'stvo kommunizma v SSSR i razvitie sel'skogo khoziaistva*, 8 vols (Moscow: Gospolitizdat, 1962–4).

Kirby, E. Stuart, "The Soviet Far East and Eastern Siberia," *The Far East and Australasia, 1975–1976* (yearbook) (London: Europa Publications, 1975).

Kirsch, Leonard, *Soviet Wages: Changes in Structure and Administration since 1956* (Cambridge, Mass.: MIT, 1972).

Kniazev, B. V., *et al.*, "O prirode interesa kak sotsial'nogo iavleniia," *Vestnik MGU (Seriia Filosofii)*, no. 4 (1968).

Kommunist (Moscow, 18 issues per year).

Kosygin, A. N., *A. N. Kosygin: izbrannye rechi i stat'i* (Moscow: Politizdat, 1974).

Kotok, V., and Farberov, N., "Konstitutsiia SSSR-razvivaiushchiisia osnovnoi zakon obshchestva i gosudarstva," *Sovetskoe gosudarstvo i pravo* (June 1973).

Lee, William, *The Estimation of Soviet Defense Expenditures for 1955–1975* (New York: Praeger, 1977).

Leonhard, Wolfgang, *The Kremlin since Stalin* (New York: Praeger, 1962).

Levi, Arrigo, "The evolution of the Soviet system," in Zbigniew Brzezinski (ed.), *Dilemmas of Change in Soviet Politics* (New York: Columbia University Press, 1969).

Levine, Herbert, "Pressure and planning in the soviet economy," in Henry Rosovsky (ed.), *Industrialization in Two Systems: Essays in Honor of Alexander Gerschenkron* (New York: Wiley, 1966).

Lindblom, Charles E., "The science of 'muddling through'," *Public Administration Review*, no. 19 (1959).

Linden, Carl, *Khrushchev and the Soviet Leadership 1957–1964* (Baltimore, Md.: Johns Hopkins University Press, 1966).

Lowenthal, Richard, "Development versus Utopia in communist policy," in Chalmers Johnson (ed.), *Change in Communist Systems* (Stanford, Calif.: Stanford University Press, 1970).

Lowenthal, Richard, "The Soviet Union in the post-revolutionary era: an overview," in Alexander Dallin and Thomas B. Larson (eds), *Soviet Politics since Khrushchev* (Englewood Cliffs, NJ: Prentice-Hall, 1968).

McAuley, Mary, *Labor Disputes in Soviet Russia 1957–1965* (Oxford: Clarendon Press, 1969).

McCauley, Martin, *Khrushchev and the Development of Soviet Agriculture* (London: Macmillan, 1976).

March, James G., and Simon, Herbert A., *Organizations* (New York: Wiley, 1958).

Medvedev, Roy, and Medvedev, Zhores, *Khrushchev: The Years in Power* (New York: Norton, 1977).

Medvedev, Zhores, *The Rise and Fall of T. D. Lysenko* (New York: Columbia University Press, 1969).

Meyer, Alfred G., "Authority in communist political systems," in Lewis J. Edinger (ed.), *Political Leadership in Industrial Societies* (New York: Wiley, 1967).

Mickiewicz, Ellen, "Policy applications of public opinion research in the USSR," *Public Opinion Quarterly* (Winter 1972–3).

Mickiewicz, Ellen, *Soviet Political Schools* (New Haven, Conn.: Yale University Press, 1969).

Miller, Robert F., "Continuity and change in the administration of Soviet agriculture since Stalin," in James R. Millar (ed.), *The Soviet Rural Community* (Urbana, Ill.: University of Illinois Press, 1971).

Miller, Robert F., "The politics of policy implementation in the USSR: Soviet policies on agricultural integration under Brezhnev," *Soviet Studies* (April 1980).

Mitchell, R. Judson, "The Soviet succession: who, and what, will follow Brezhnev?" *Orbis* (Spring 1979).

New York Times (daily).

Nicolaevsky, Boris, *Power and the Soviet Elite* (New York: Praeger, 1965).

Nimitz, Nancy, "Reform and technological innovation in the Eleventh Five-Year Plan," in Seweryn Bialer and Thane Gustafson (eds), *Russia at the Crossroads: The 26th Congress of the CPSU* (London: Allen & Unwin, 1982).

Nove, Alec, "Agriculture," in Archie Brown and Michael Kaser (eds), *The Soviet Union since the Fall of Khrushchev* (New York: The Free Press, 1975).

Nove, Alec, *An Economic History of the USSR* (London: Allen Lane, 1969).

Nove, Alec, "Economic policy and economic trends," in Alexander Dallin and Thomas Larson (eds), *Soviet Politics since' Khrushchev* (Englewood Cliffs, NJ: Prentice-Hall, 1968).

Nove, Alec, "Peasants and officials," in Jerzy F. Karcz (ed.), *Soviet and East European Agriculture* (Berkeley, Calif.: University of California Press, 1967).

Olgin, Constantin, *Socialist Competition under Brezhnev: An Interim Report* (New York: Radio Liberty Research Supplement, 16 May, 1975).

Osborn, Robert, *The Evolution of Soviet Politics* (Homewood, Ill.: Dorsey Press, 1974).

Paloczi-Horvath, George, *Khrushchev: The Road to Power* (London: Secker & Warburg, 1960).

Paltiel, Jeremy, "DeStalinization and DeMaoization," paper presented at the Annual Meeting of the Canadian Political Science Association, Université du Québec à Montréal, 2–4 June, 1980.

Parrott, Bruce, "Politics and economics in the USSR," *Problems of Communism* (May–June 1977).

Pistrak, Lazar, *The Grand Tactician* (New York: Praeger, 1961).

Planovoe khoziaistvo (Moscow monthly).

Plenum tsentral'nogo komiteta Kommunisticheskoi Partii Sovetskogo Soiuza, 22–25 dekabria 1959 g.: Stenograficheskii otchet (Moscow: Politizdat, 1960).

Plenum tsentral'nogo komiteta Kommunisticheskoi Partii Sovetskogo Soiuza, 24–26 marta 1965 g.: Stenograficheskii otchet (Moscow: Politizdat, 1965).

Ploss, Sidney, *Conflict and Decision-Making in Soviet Russia: A Case Study of Agricultural Policy, 1953–1963* (Princeton, NJ: Princeton University Press, 1965).

Ploss, Sidney (ed.), *The Soviet Political Process* (Waltham, Mass.: Ginn, 1970).

Pospielovsky, Dimitry, "The 'link system' in Soviet agriculture," *Soviet Studies* (April 1970).

Pravda (Moscow, daily).

Rabbot, Boris, "An open letter to Leonid Brezhnev," *New York Times Magazine Section* (6 November, 1977).

Rigby, T. H., "A conceptual approach to authority, power and policy in the Soviet Union," in T. H. Rigby, Archie Brown, and Peter

Reddaway (eds), *Authority, Power and Policy in the USSR* (New York: St Martin's Press, 1980).

Rigby, T. H., "The extent and limits of authority (a rejoinder)," *Problems of Communism* (September–October 1963).

Rigby, Thomas H., "How strong is the leader?" *Problems of Communism* (September–October 1962).

Rigby, T. H., and Miller R. F., *Political and Administrative Aspects of the Scientific and Technological Revolution in the USSR* (Canberra: Australian National University, 1976).

Rosefielde, Steven, *Underestimating the Soviet Military Threat* (New Brunswick, NJ: Transaction Press, 1981).

Ross, Dennis, "Coalition maintenance in the Soviet Union," *World Politics* (January 1980).

Rothberg, Abraham, *The Heirs of Stalin* (Ithaca, NY: Cornell University Press, 1972).

Ruble, Blair Aldridge, "Soviet trade unions: changing balances in their functions," (Ph.D. dissertation, University of Toronto, 1977).

Rush, Myron, *Political Succession in the USSR*, 2nd edn. (New York: Columbia University Press, 1968).

Rush, Myron, *The Rise of Khrushchev* (Washington, DC: Public Affairs Press, 1958).

Rush, Myron, "Underestimating Brezhnev's political strength," *Wall Street Journal* (20 August, 1981).

Ryavec, Karl, *Implementation of Soviet Economic Reforms* (New York: Praeger, 1976).

Schattschneider, E. E., *The Semi-Sovereign People* (New York: Holt, Rinehart & Winston, 1960).

Schroeder, Gertrude E., "Recent developments in Soviet planning and incentives," *Soviet Economic Prospects for the Seventies*, compiled by US Congress, Joint Economic Committee (Washington, DC: US Government Printing Office, 1973).

Schwartz, Donald V., "Decisionmaking, administrative decentralization, and feedback mechanisms: comparison of Soviet and Western models," *Studies in Comparative Communism* (Spring–Summer 1974).

Schwartz, Harry, *The Soviet Economy since Stalin* (Philadelphia, Pa.: Lippincott, 1965).

Seligman, Lester, "Leadership: political aspects," in David L. Sills (ed.), *International Encyclopedia of the Social Sciences*, Vol. 9 (New York: The Free Press, 1968).

Selznick, Philip, *Leadership in Administration* (New York: Harper & Row, 1957).

Service, R. J., "The road to the Twentieth Party Congress: an analysis of the events surrounding the Central Committee Plenum of July 1953," *Soviet Studies* (April 1981).

Sharlet, Robert, *The New Soviet Constitution of 1977: Analysis and Text* (Brunswick, Ohio: King's Court Communications, 1978).

Sheetz, Elizabeth C., "Stepped-up efforts to curb dissent in the USSR," *Radio Liberty Research Bulletin*, RL 164/77 (New York: Radio Liberty, 12 July, 1977).

Slusser, Robert M., *The Berlin Crisis of 1961* (Baltimore, Md: Johns Hopkins University Press, 1973).

Solomon, Peter, Jr, *Soviet Criminologists and Criminal Policy: Specialists in Policy-Making* (New York: Columbia University Press, 1978).

Solovyov, Vladimir, and Klepikova, Elena, "Inside the Kremlin," *Partisan Review*, vol. 48, no. 2 (1981).

Sovetskoe gosudarstvo i pravo (Moscow, monthly).

Spechler, Dina, "Permitted dissent in the decade after Stalin," in Paul Cocks, Robert Daniels, and Nancy Heer (eds), *The Dynamics of Soviet Politics* (Cambridge, Mass.: Harvard University Press, 1976).

Stepanian, Ts. A., and Semenov, V. S. (eds), *Klassy sotsial'nye sloi i gruppy v SSSR* (Moscow: Nauka, 1968).

Strauss, Erich, *Soviet Agriculture in Perspective* (New York: Praeger, 1969).

Suslov, M. A., *Izbrannoe: rechi i stat'i* (Moscow: Politizdat, 1972).

Suslov, M. A., *Na putiakh stroitel'stva kommunizma* (Moscow: Politizdat, 1977).

Swayze, Harold, *Political Control of Literature in the USSR, 1946–1959* (Cambridge, Mass.: Harvard University Press, 1962).

Tatu, Michel, *Power in the Kremlin: From Khrushchev to Kosygin* (New York: Viking Press, 1969).

Taubman, William, *Governing Soviet Cities* (New York: Praeger, 1973).

Tucker, Robert C., *Stalin as Revolutionary 1879–1929* (New York: Norton, 1973).

Ulam, Adam, *Expansion and Coexistence,* 2nd edn (New York: Praeger, 1974).

Ulam, Adam B., *A History of Soviet Russia* (New York: Praeger, 1976).

Unger, Aryeh, "Politinformator or agitator: a decision blocked," *Problems of Communism* (September–October 1970).

Unger, Aryeh, *The Totalitarian Party* (Cambridge: Cambridge University Press, 1974).

United States Central Intelligence Agency (CIA), *Estimated Soviet Defense Spending in Rubles, 1970–1975* (Washington, DC: CIA, May 1976).

United States Congress, Joint Economic Committee (comp.), *Soviet Economic Prospects for the Seventies* (Washington, DC: US Government Printing Office, 1973).

United States Congress, Joint Economic Committee (comp.), *Soviet Economy in a New Perspective* (Washington, DC: US Government Printing Office, 1976).

United States Congress, Joint Economic Committee (comp.), *Soviet Economy in a Time of Change,* 2 vols (Washington, DC: US Government Printing Office, 1979).

Vickers, Geoffrey, *The Art of Judgment* (London: Chapman & Hall, 1965).

Vishnevskii, S. S., "Interesy i upravlenie obshchestvennymi protsessami," in V. Afanas'ev (ed.), *Nauchnoe upravlenie obshchestvom,* 8 vols (Moscow: Mysl', 1967–74).

Volten, Peter M. E., *The Soviet "Peace Program" and its Implementa-

tion Towards the West (Amsterdam: Foundation for the Promotion of East–West Contacts, Free University, 1977).

Waedekin, Karl-Eugen, *The Private Sector in Soviet Agriculture* (Berkeley, Calif.: University of California Press, 1973).

Whitehouse, F. Douglas, and Converse, Ray, "Soviet industry: recent performance and future prospects," in *Soviet Economy in a Time of Change*, 2 vols, compiled by US Congress, Joint Economic Committee (Washington, DC: US Government Printing Office, 1979).

Wolfe, Thomas, *Soviet Strategy at the Crossroads* (Cambridge, Mass.: Harvard University Press, 1965).

Yanov, Alexander, *Detente after Brezhnev* (Berkeley, Calif.: University of California, Institute of International Studies, 1977).

Yanov, Alexander, *The Russian New Right* (Berkeley, Calif.: University of California, Institute of International Studies, 1978).

Yanov, Alexander, "Social contradictions of the countryside in the sixties," *International Journal of Sociology*. special issue (Summer/Fall 1976).

Yanowitch, Murray, and Fisher, Wesley A., (eds), *Social Stratification and Mobility in the USSR* (White Plains, NY: International Arts and Sciences Press, 1973).

Index

DATE DUE	
ill : 3/25/95	

GAYLORD   PRINTED IN U.S.A.